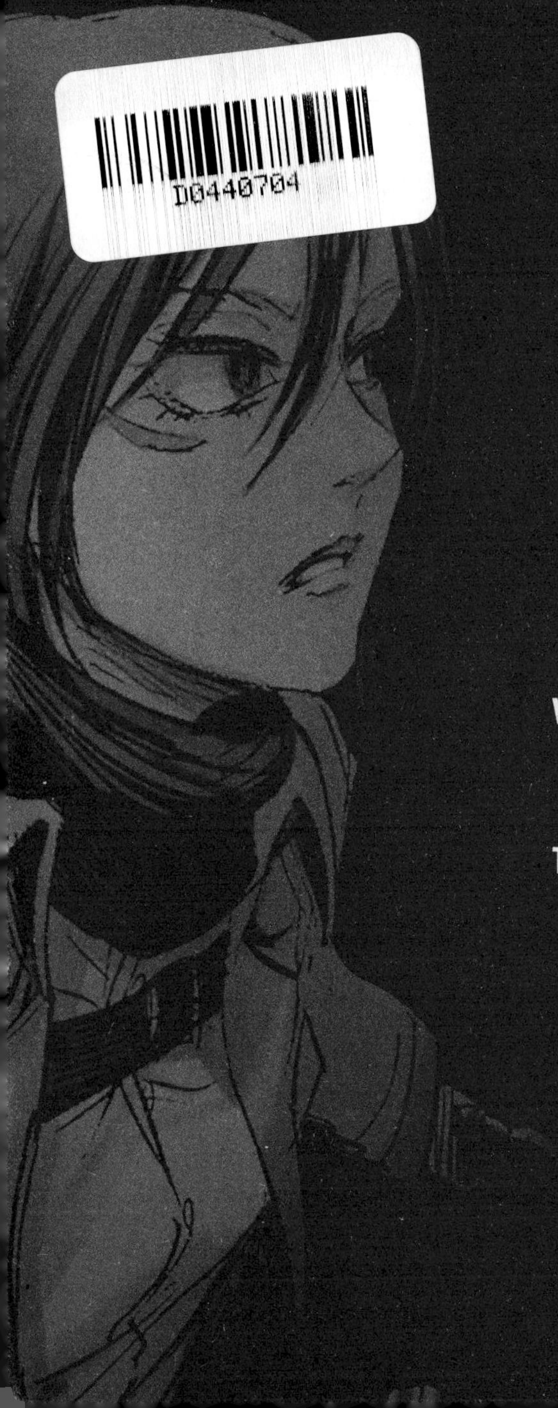

ATTACK ON TITAN

19

HAJIME ISAYAMA

"Attack on Titan" Character Introductions

104th Corps

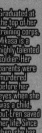

Graduated at the top of her training corps, Mikasa is a highly talented soldier. Her parents were murdered before her eyes when she was a child, but Eren saved her life. Since then, she has made it her mission to protect him.

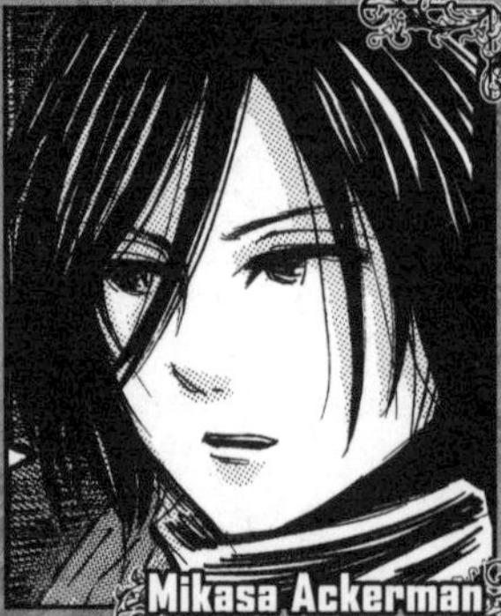
Mikasa Ackerman

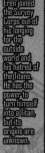

Eren joined the Survey Corps out of his longing for the outside world and his hatred of the Titans. He has the power to turn himself into a Titan, but its origins are unknown.

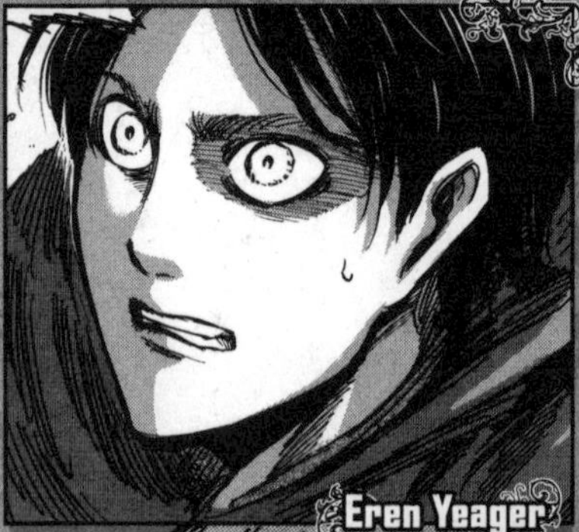
Eren Yeager

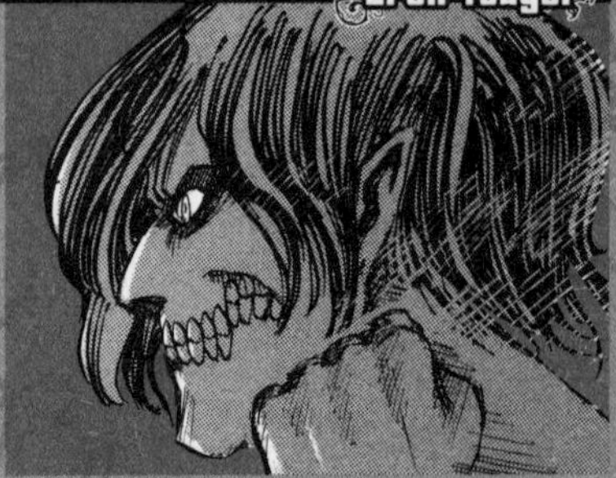

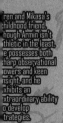

Eren and Mikasa's childhood friend. Though Armin isn't athletic in the least, he possesses both sharp observational powers and keen insight, and he exhibits an extraordinary ability to develop strategies.

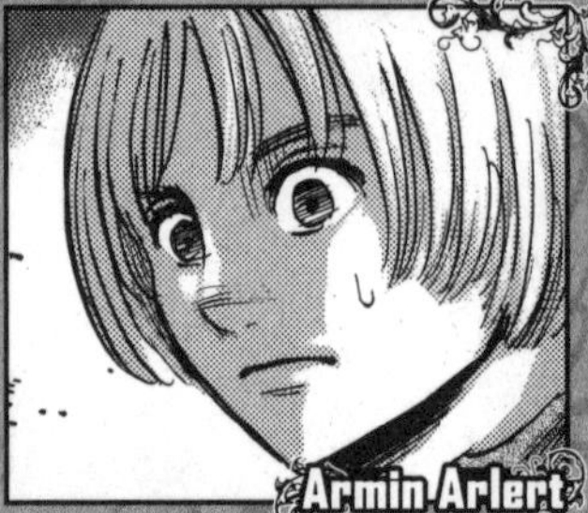
Armin Arlert

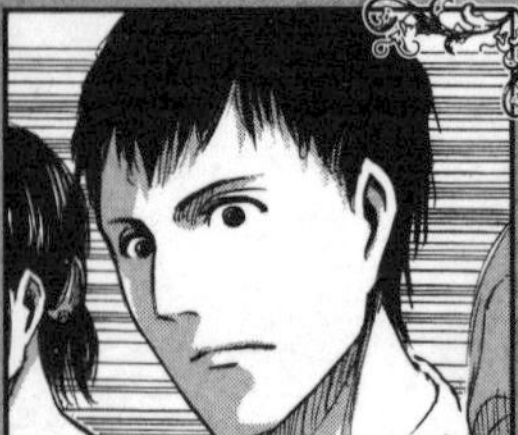
Bertolt Hoover

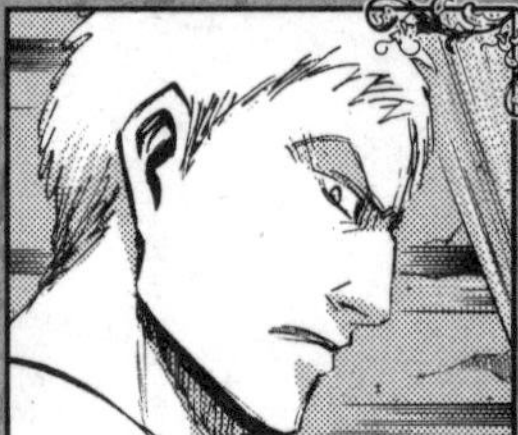
Reiner Braun

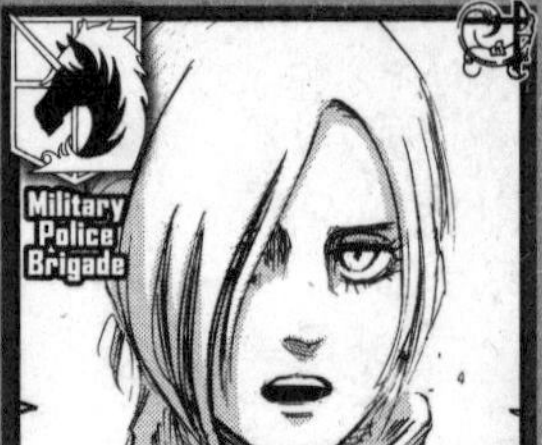
Military Police Brigade
Annie Leonhart

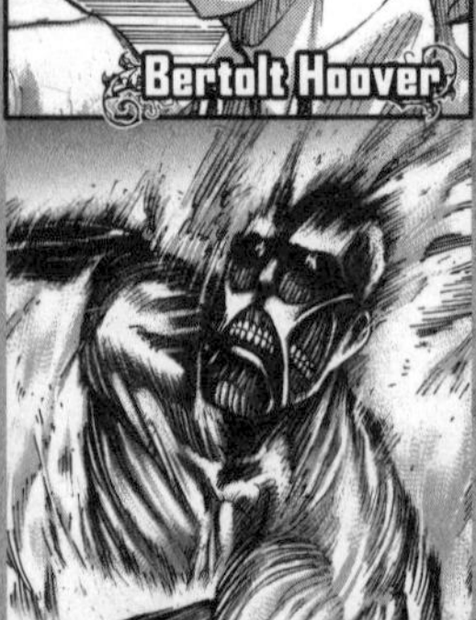
The Colossus Titan

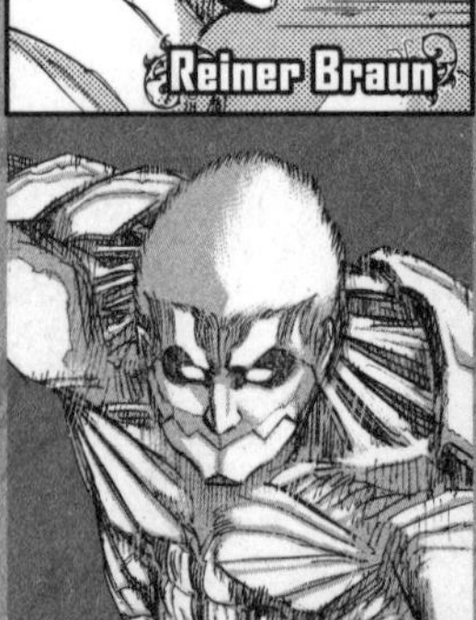
The Armored Titan

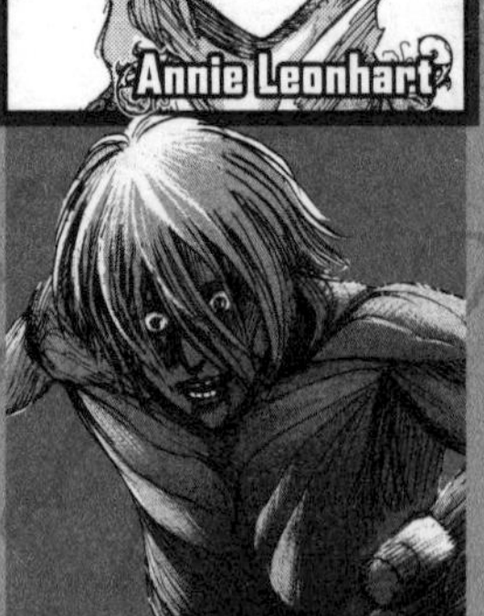
The Female Titan

Survey Corps

Soldiers who are prepared to sacrifice themselves as they brave the Titan territory outside the walls.

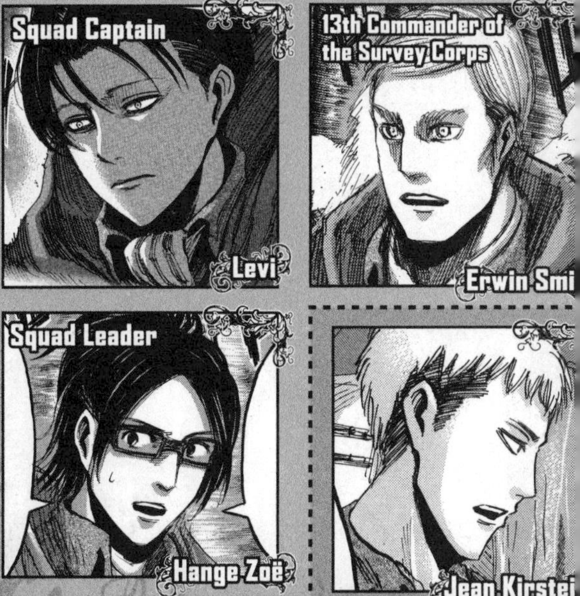
13th Commander of the Survey Corps
Erwin Smi
Squad Captain
Levi
Jean Kirstei
Squad Leader
Hange Zoë

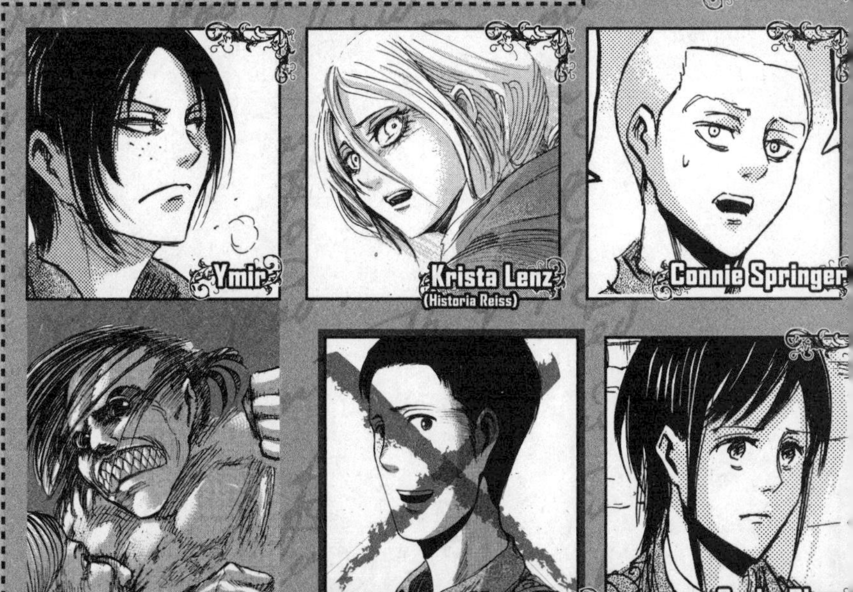
Connie Springer
Krista Lenz
(Historia Reiss)
Ymir
Sasha Blous
Marco Bott

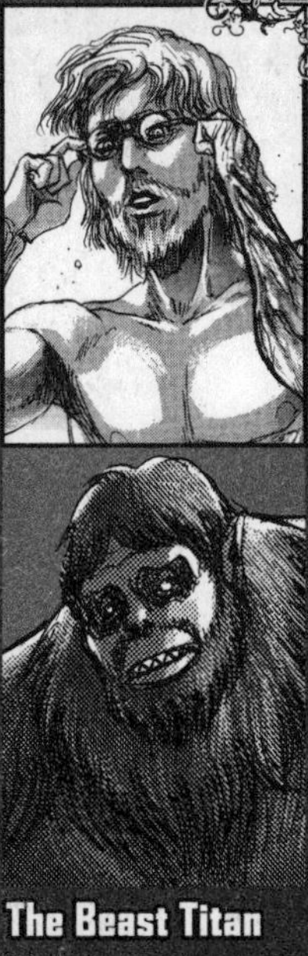
The Beast Titan

ATTACK on TITAN

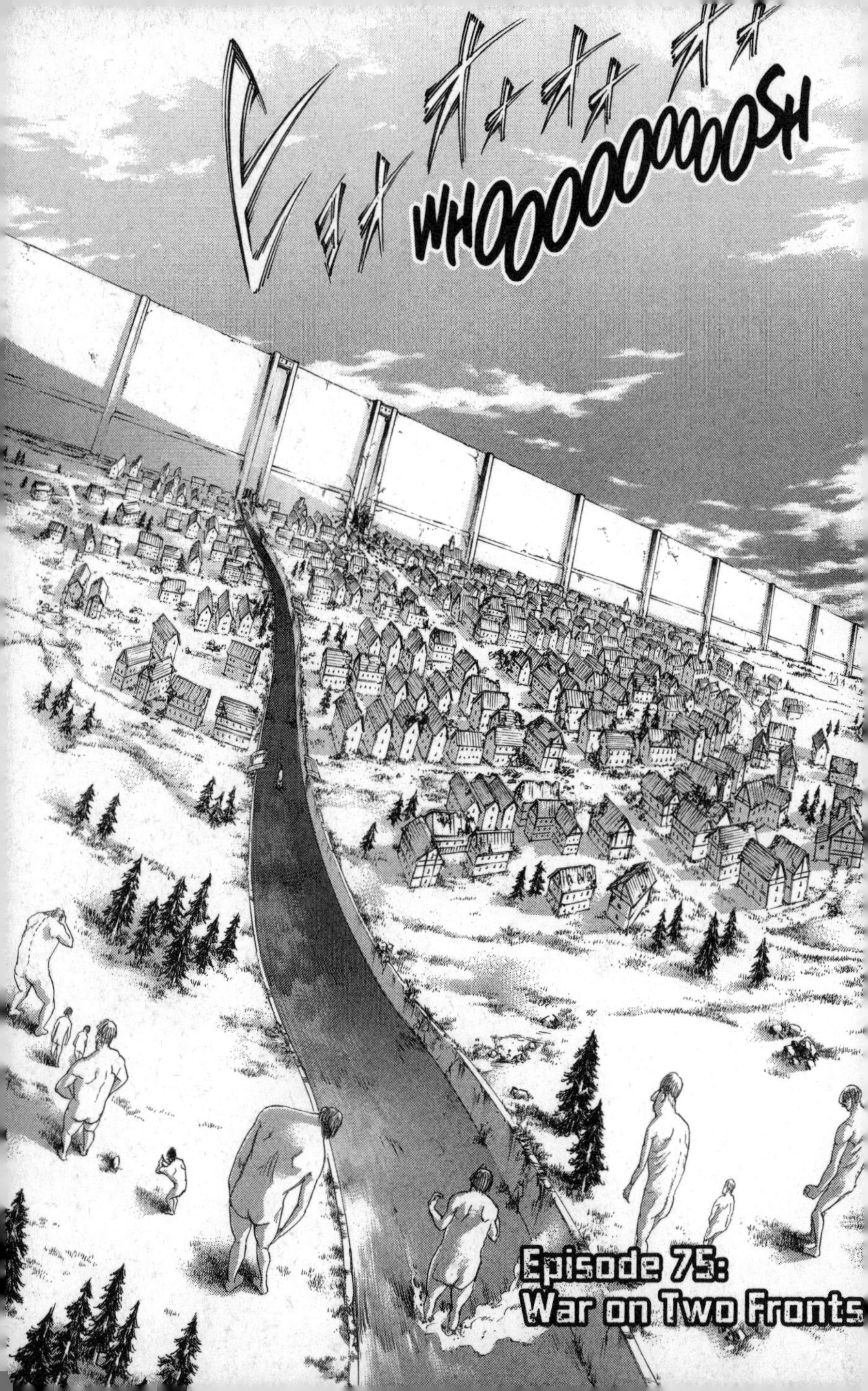
ヒョオオオオオオオオ
WHOOOOOOOOOSH
Episode 75:
War on Two Fronts

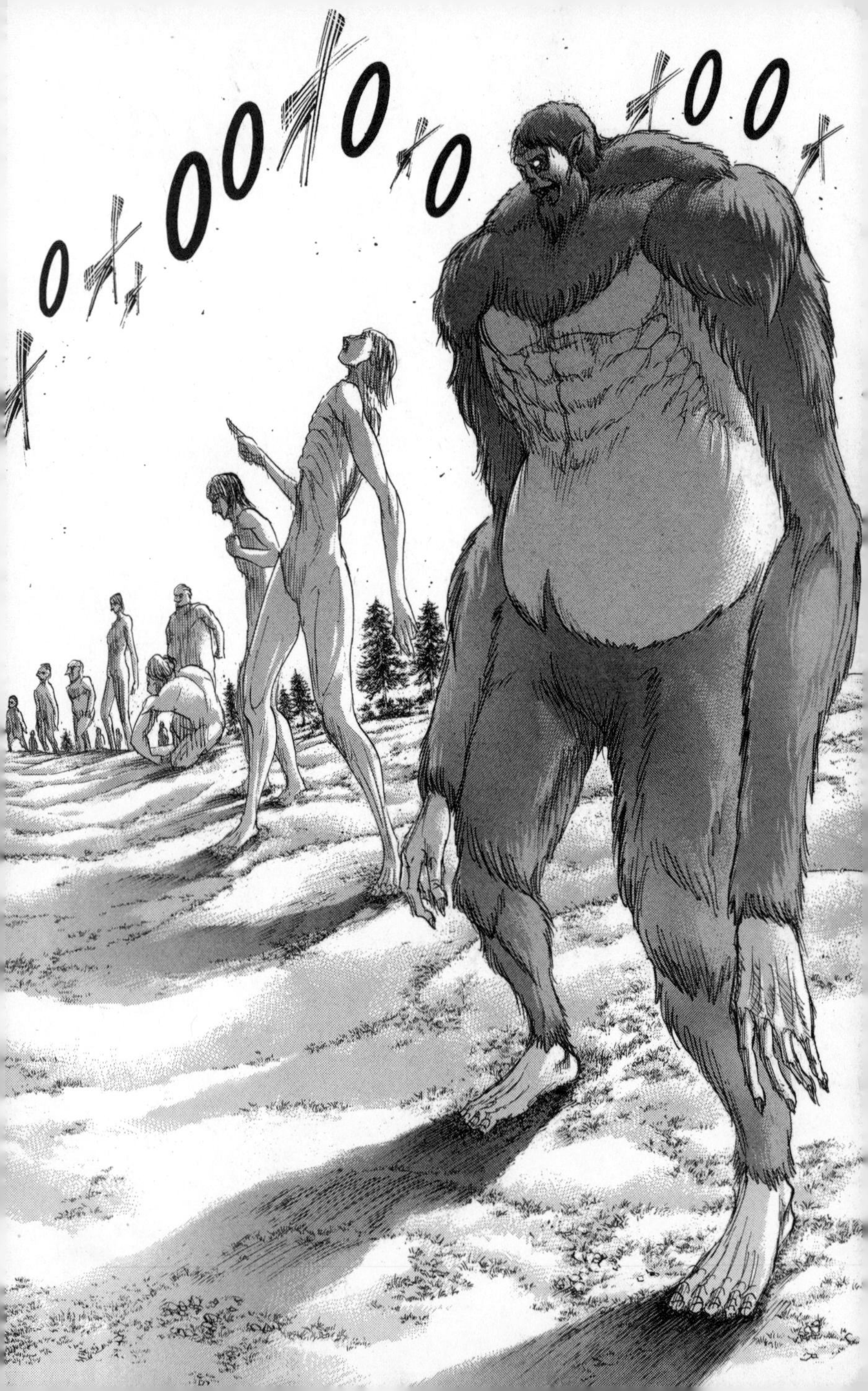

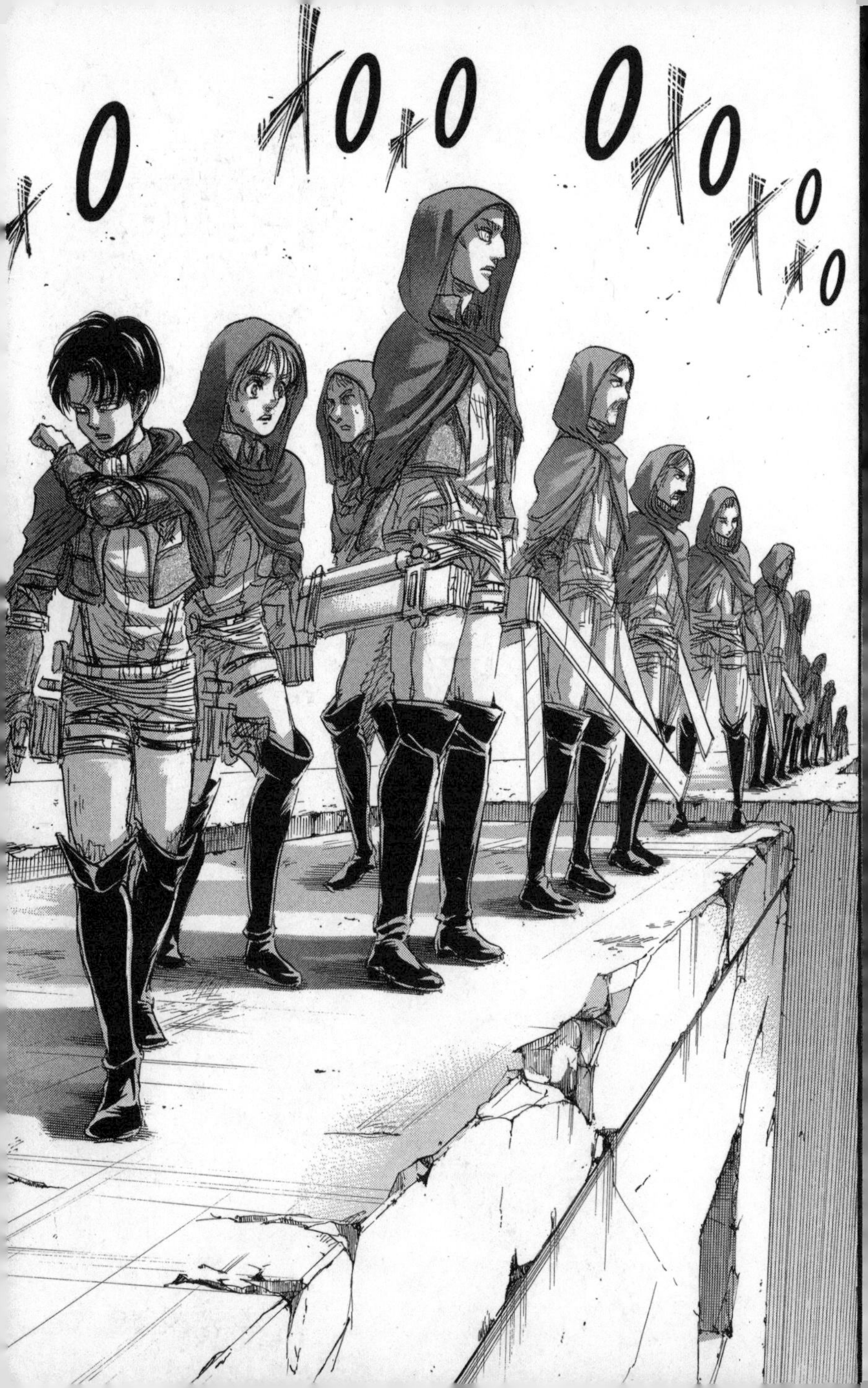
オO オO オO O オO オO オO

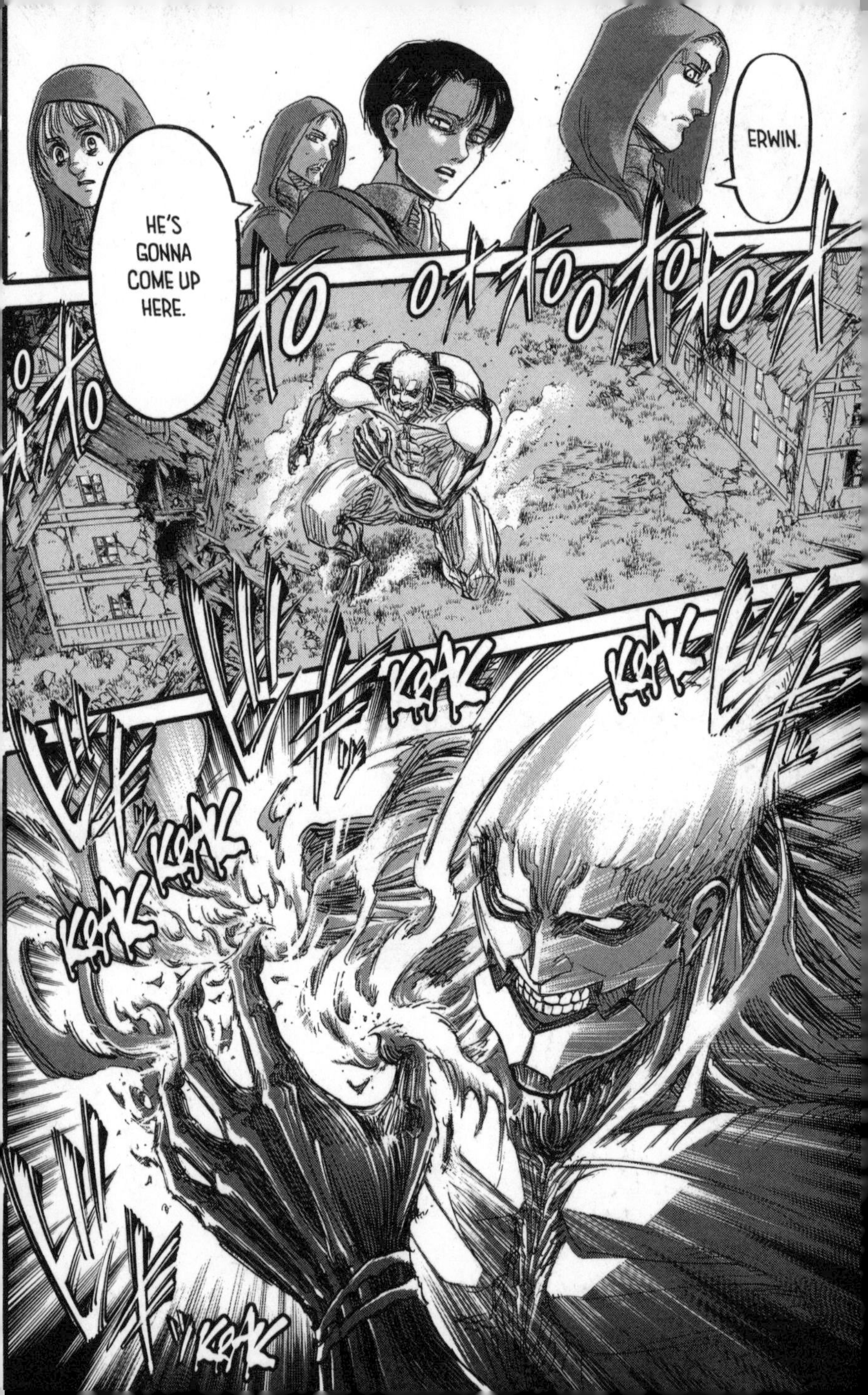
ERWIN.
HE'S GONNA COME UP HERE.
KRAK
KRAK
KRAK
KRAK
KRAK
KRAK

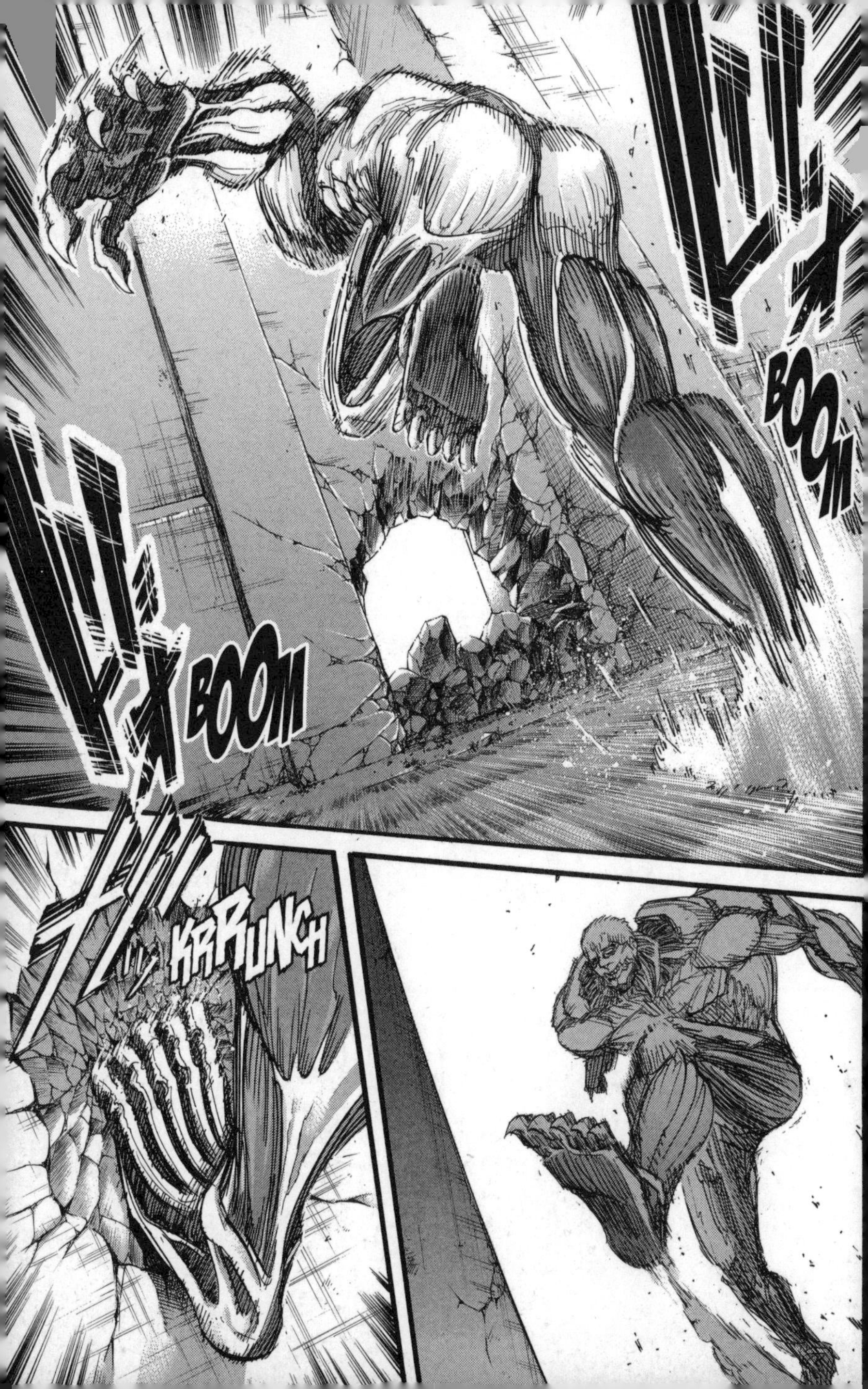
BOOM
BOOM
KRRUNCH

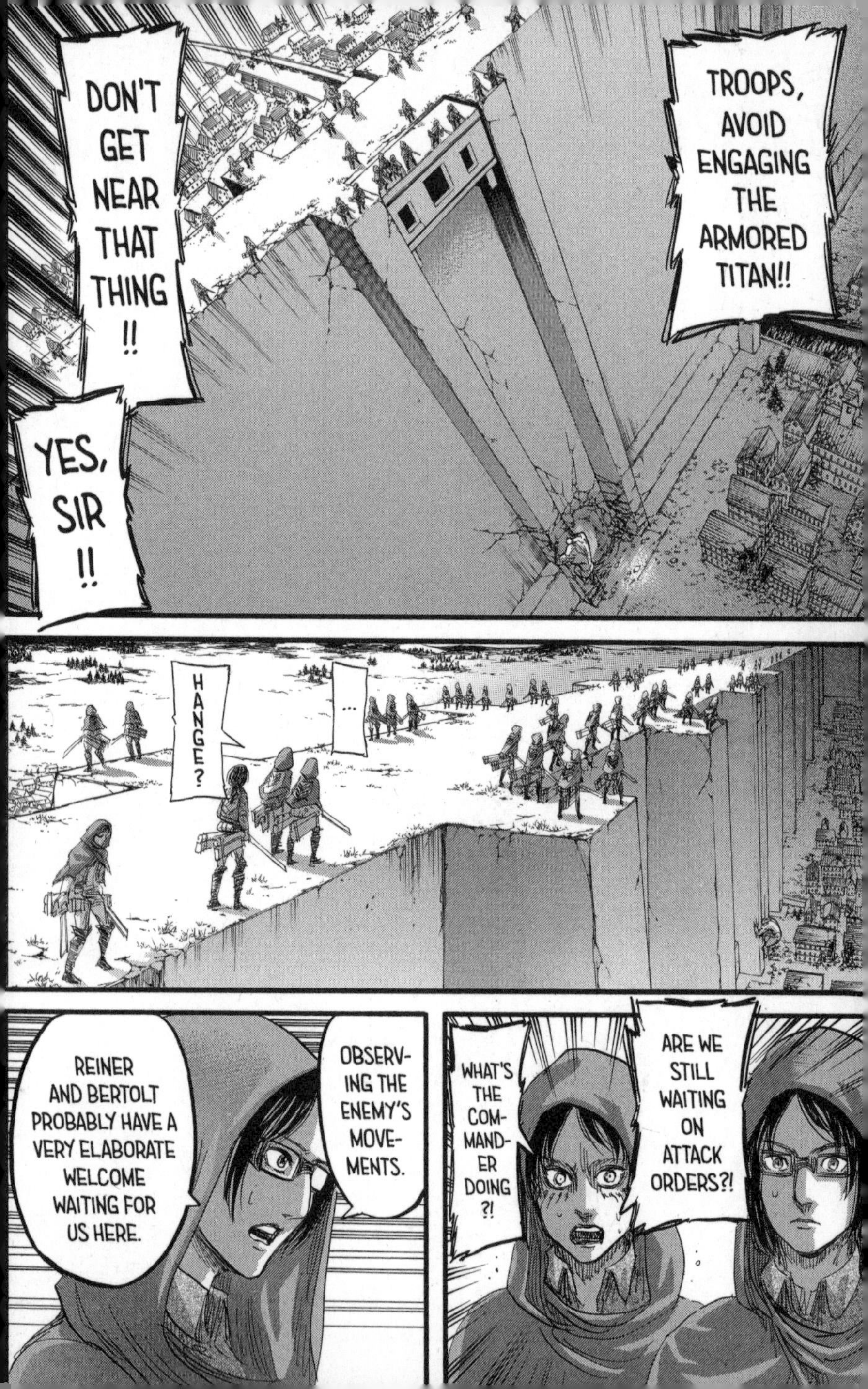
TROOPS, AVOID ENGAGING THE ARMORED TITAN!!
DON'T GET NEAR THAT THING!!
YES, SIR!!
...
HANGE?
ARE WE STILL WAITING ON ATTACK ORDERS?!
WHAT'S THE COMMANDER DOING?!
OBSERVING THE ENEMY'S MOVEMENTS.
REINER AND BERTOLT PROBABLY HAVE A VERY ELABORATE WELCOME WAITING FOR US HERE.

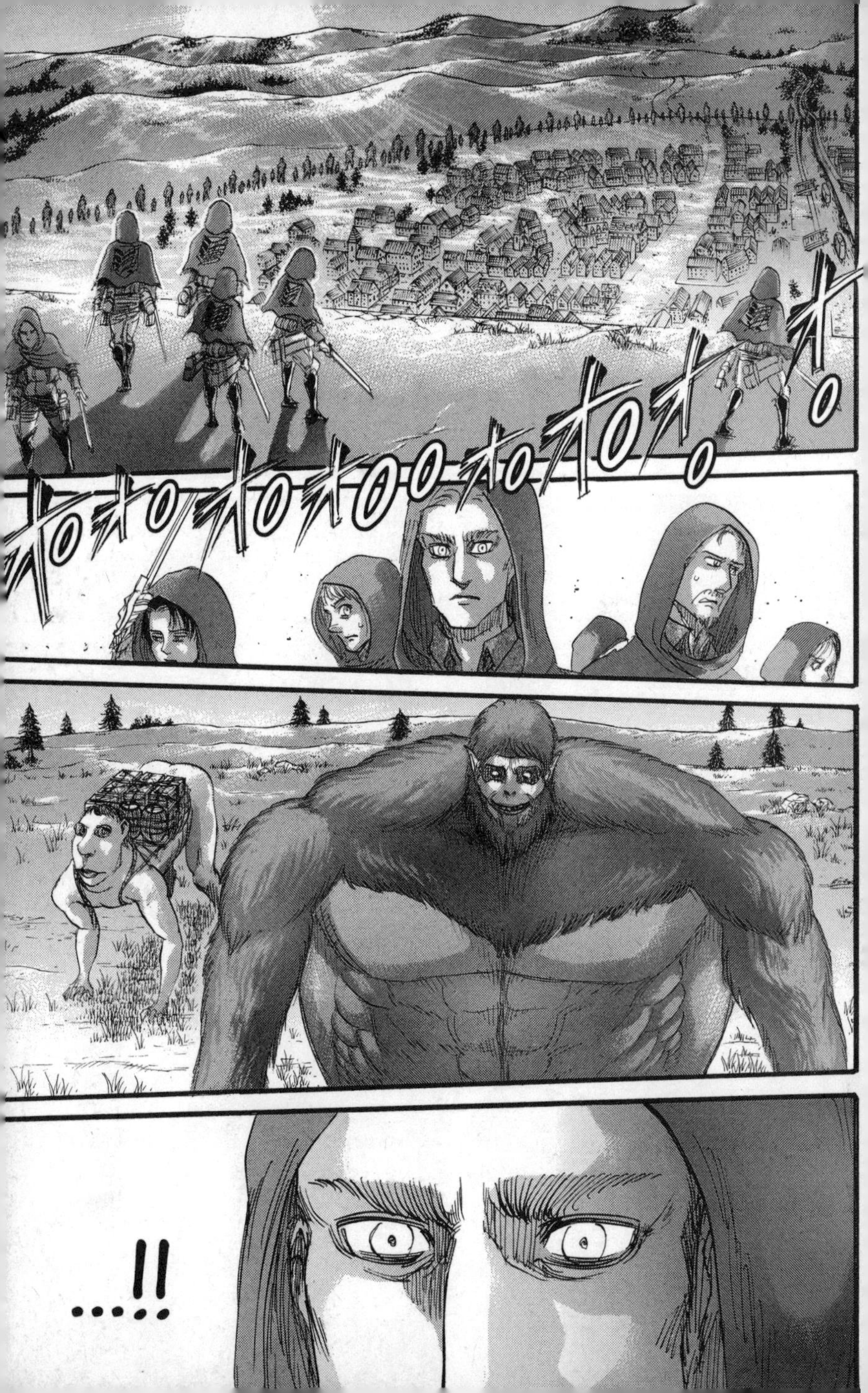
...!!

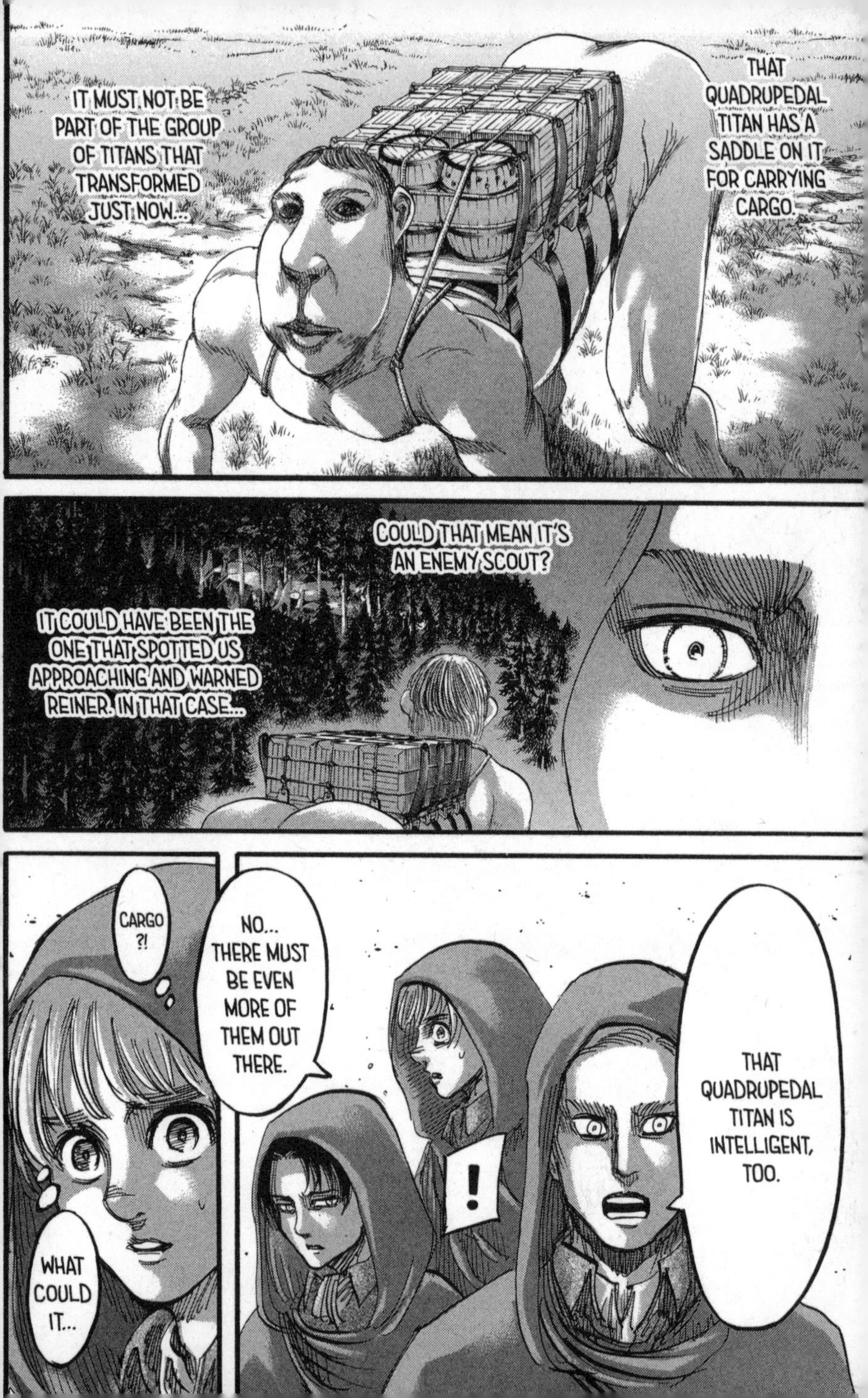
THAT QUADRUPEDAL TITAN HAS A SADDLE ON IT FOR CARRYING CARGO.
IT MUST NOT BE PART OF THE GROUP OF TITANS THAT TRANSFORMED JUST NOW...
COULD THAT MEAN IT'S AN ENEMY SCOUT?
IT COULD HAVE BEEN THE ONE THAT SPOTTED US APPROACHING AND WARNED REINER. IN THAT CASE...
THAT QUADRUPEDAL TITAN IS INTELLIGENT, TOO.
!
NO... THERE MUST BE EVEN MORE OF THEM OUT THERE.
CARGO ?!
WHAT COULD IT...

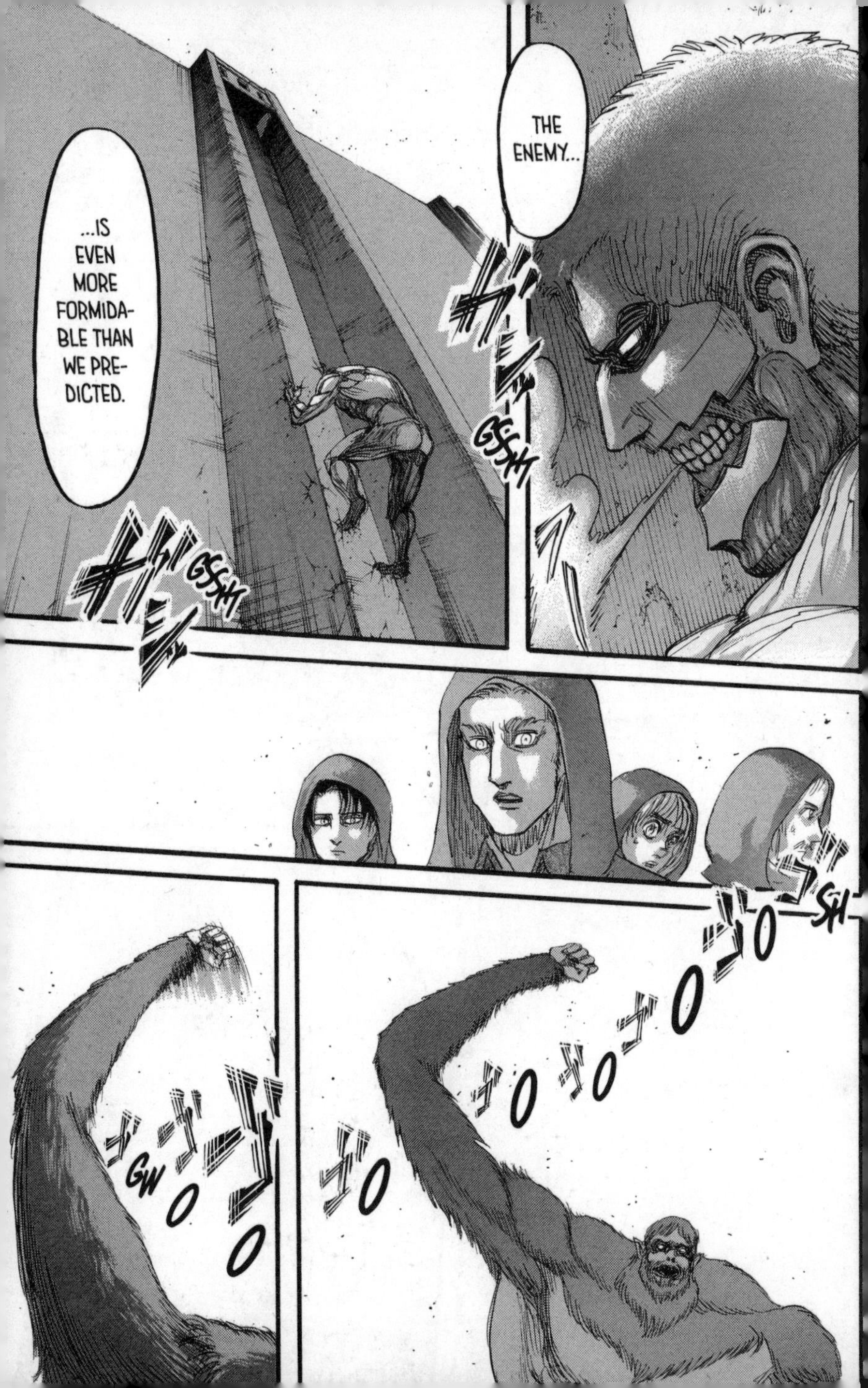
THE ENEMY...
GSSHH
...IS EVEN MORE FORMIDABLE THAN WE PREDICTED.
GSSHH
SH
O O O O O O
GW O O O

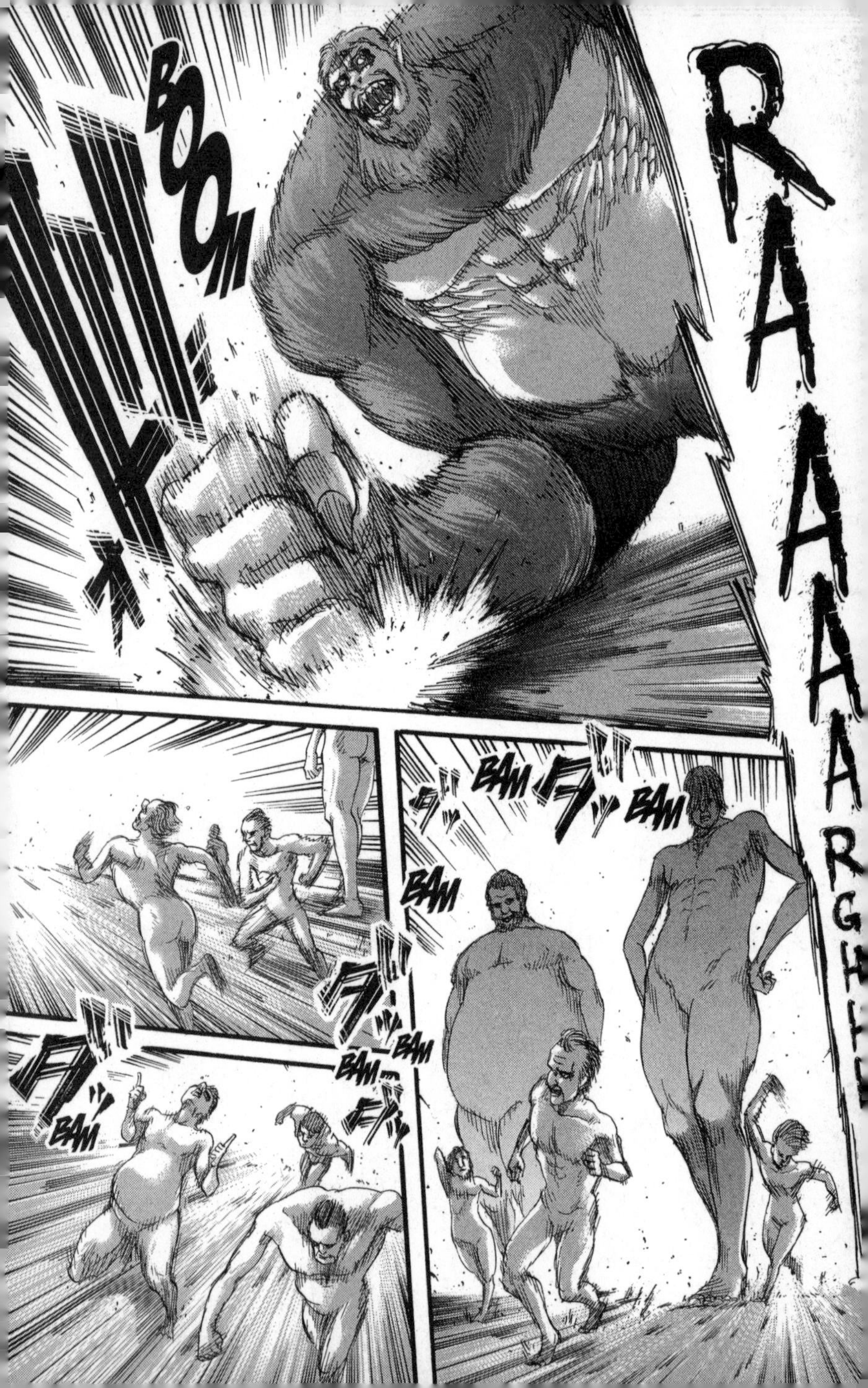
RAAAAARGHH
BOOOM
BAM
BAM
BAM
BAM
BAM
BAM

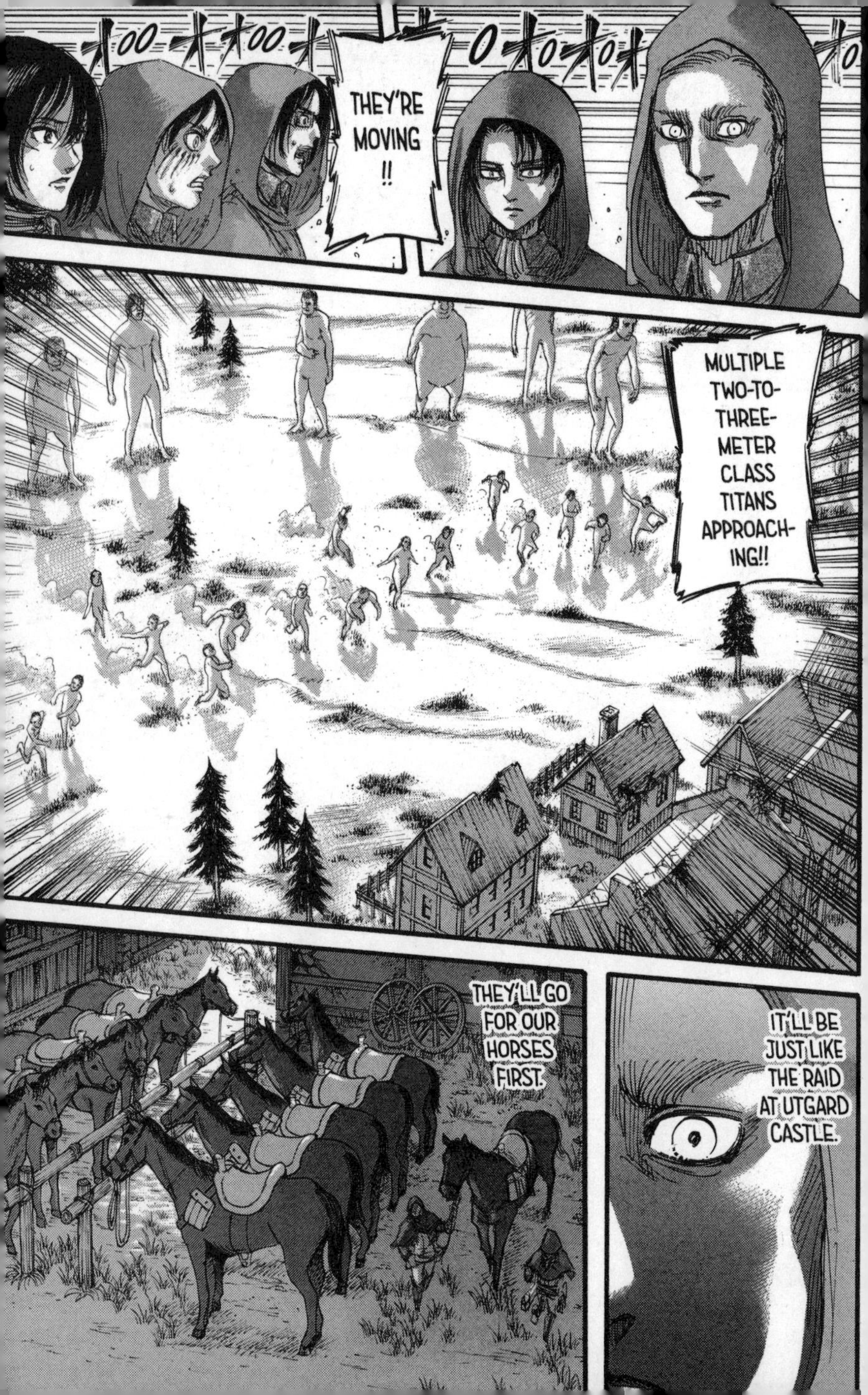
THEY'RE MOVING !!
MULTIPLE TWO-TO-THREE-METER CLASS TITANS APPROACHING!!
IT'LL BE JUST LIKE THE RAID AT UTGARD CASTLE.
THEY'LL GO FOR OUR HORSES FIRST.

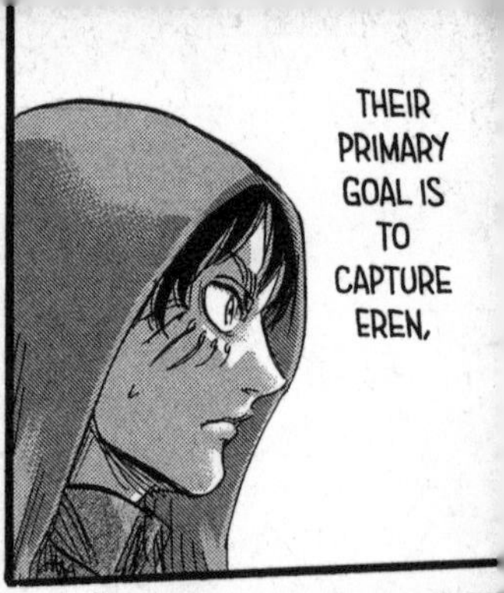
THEIR PRIMARY GOAL IS TO CAPTURE EREN,
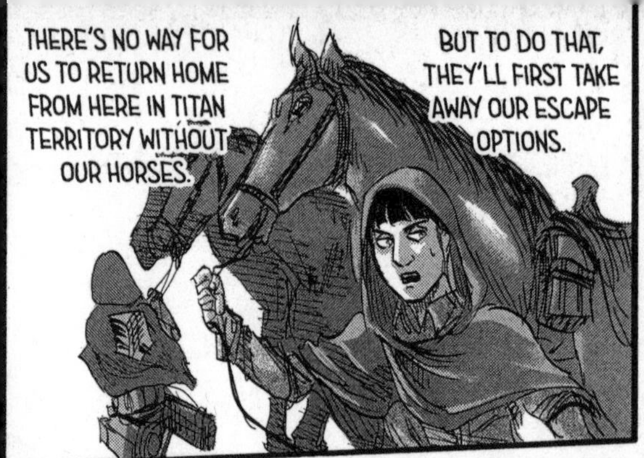
BUT TO DO THAT, THEY'LL FIRST TAKE AWAY OUR ESCAPE OPTIONS.
THERE'S NO WAY FOR US TO RETURN HOME FROM HERE IN TITAN TERRITORY WITHOUT OUR HORSES.
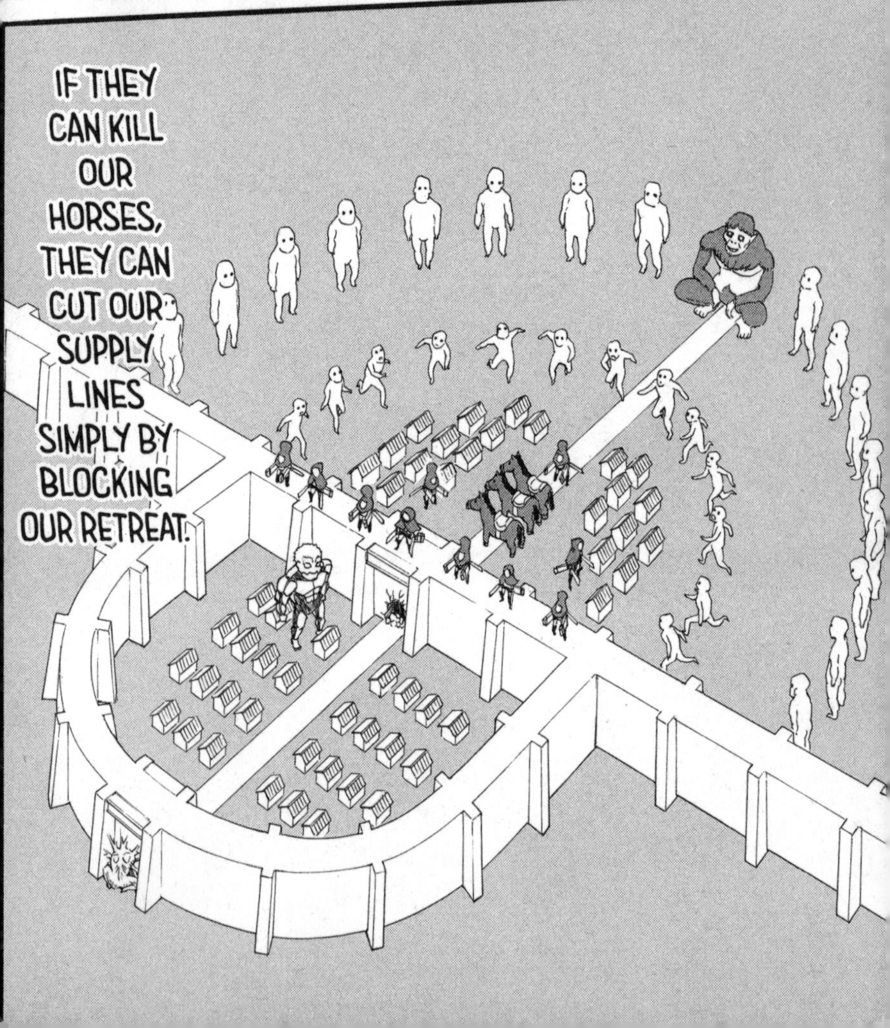
IF THEY CAN KILL OUR HORSES, THEY CAN CUT OUR SUPPLY LINES SIMPLY BY BLOCKING OUR RETREAT.

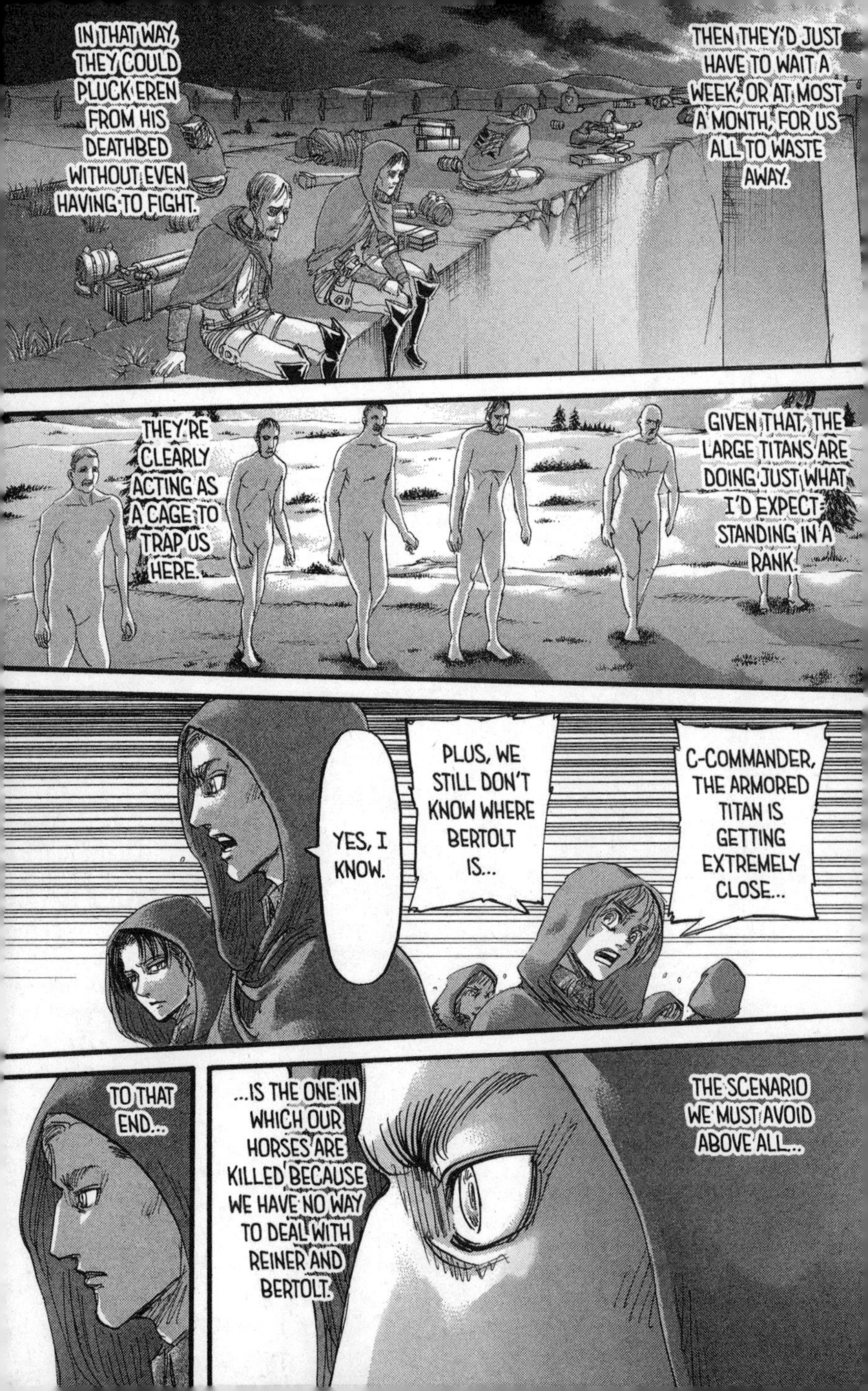
THEN THEY'D JUST HAVE TO WAIT A WEEK, OR AT MOST A MONTH, FOR US ALL TO WASTE AWAY.
IN THAT WAY, THEY COULD PLUCK EREN FROM HIS DEATHBED WITHOUT EVEN HAVING TO FIGHT.
GIVEN THAT, THE LARGE TITANS ARE DOING JUST WHAT I'D EXPECT STANDING IN A RANK.
THEY'RE CLEARLY ACTING AS A CAGE TO TRAP US HERE.
C-COMMANDER, THE ARMORED TITAN IS GETTING EXTREMELY CLOSE...
PLUS, WE STILL DON'T KNOW WHERE BERTOLT IS...
YES, I KNOW.
THE SCENARIO WE MUST AVOID ABOVE ALL...
...IS THE ONE IN WHICH OUR HORSES ARE KILLED BECAUSE WE HAVE NO WAY TO DEAL WITH REINER AND BERTOLT.
TO THAT END...

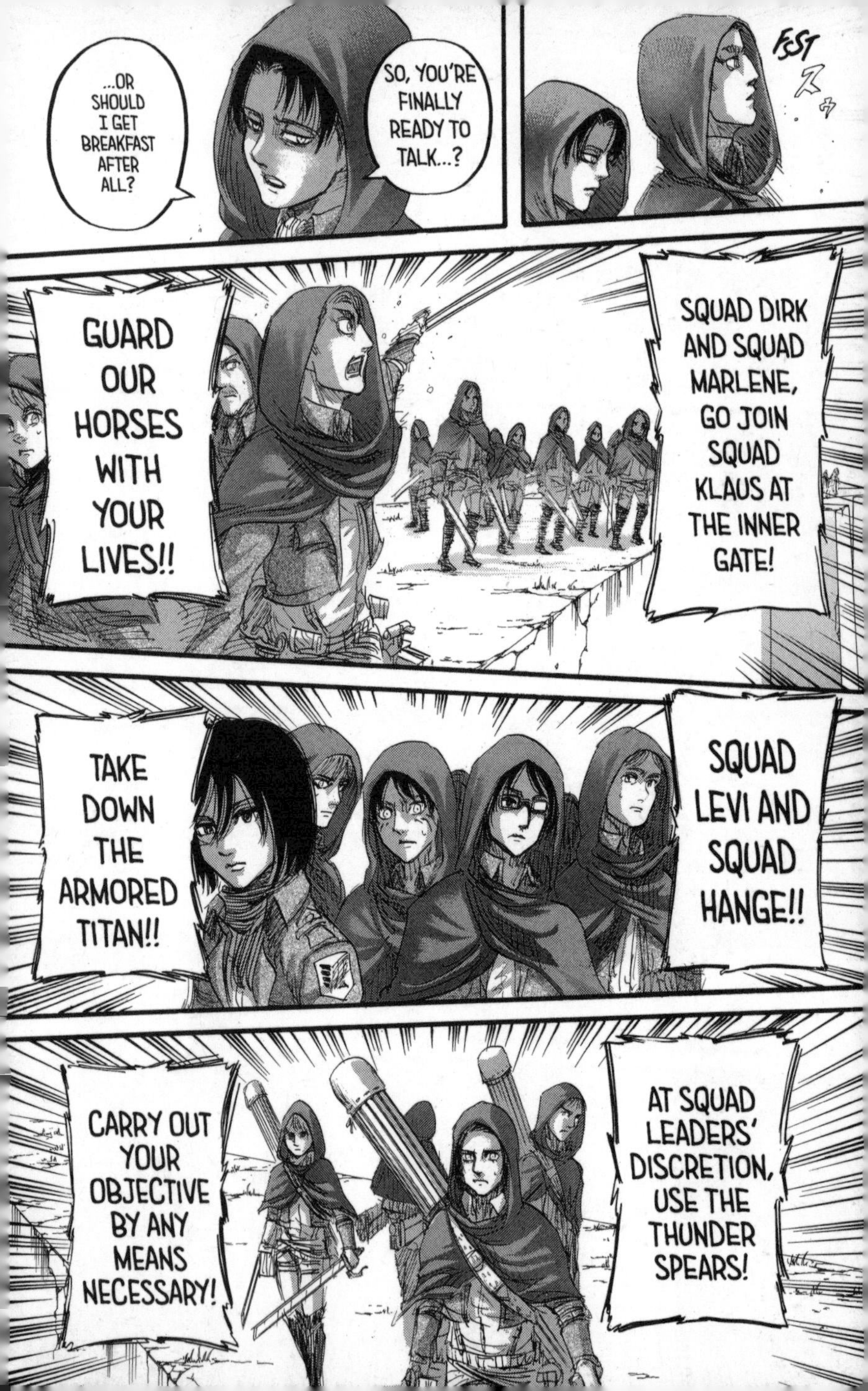
FST
SO, YOU'RE FINALLY READY TO TALK...?
...OR SHOULD I GET BREAKFAST AFTER ALL?
SQUAD DIRK AND SQUAD MARLENE, GO JOIN SQUAD KLAUS AT THE INNER GATE!
GUARD OUR HORSES WITH YOUR LIVES!!
SQUAD LEVI AND SQUAD HANGE!!
TAKE DOWN THE ARMORED TITAN!!
AT SQUAD LEADERS' DISCRETION, USE THE THUNDER SPEARS!
CARRY OUT YOUR OBJECTIVE BY ANY MEANS NECESSARY!

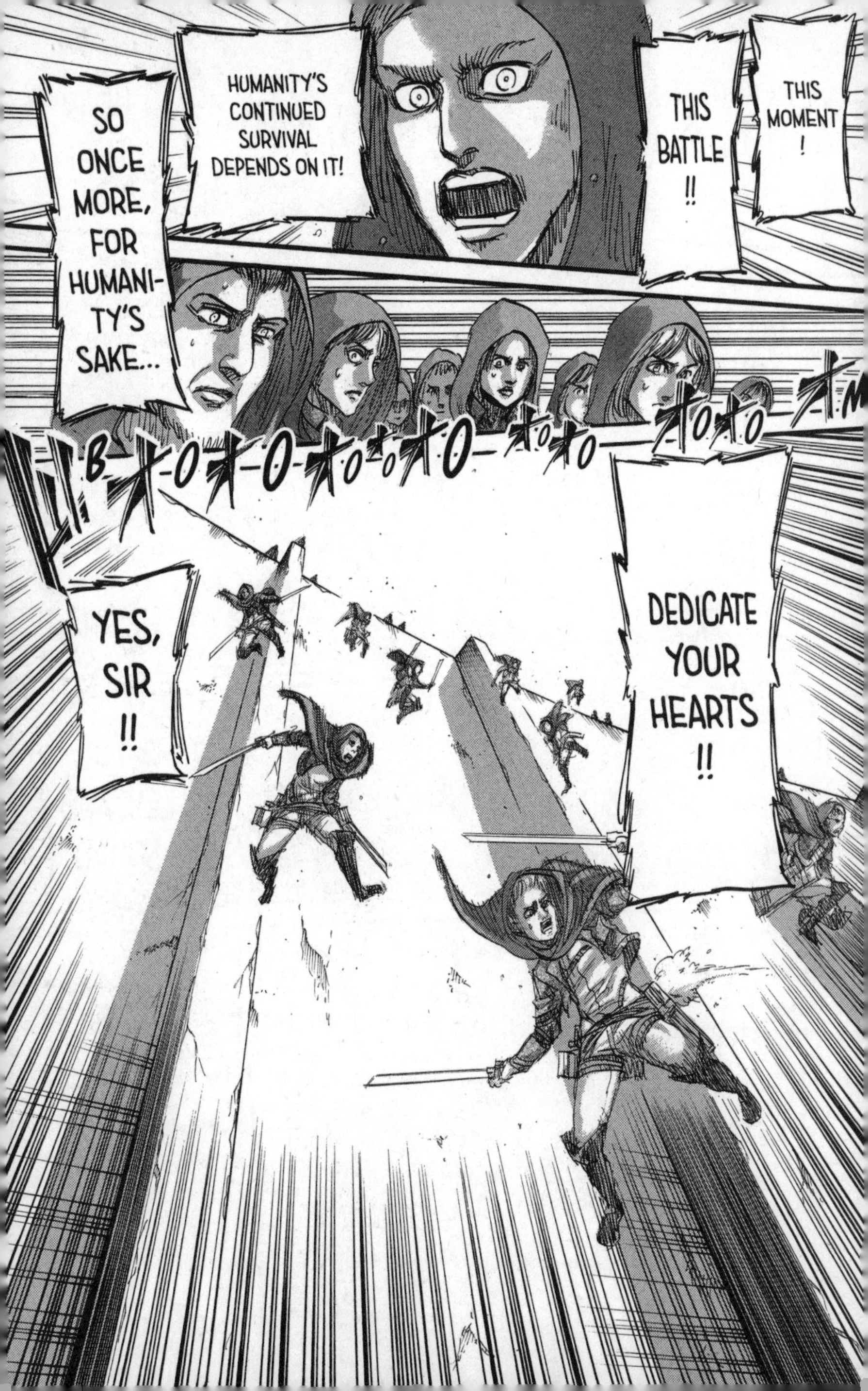
THIS MOMENT!
THIS BATTLE!!
HUMANITY'S CONTINUED SURVIVAL DEPENDS ON IT!
SO ONCE MORE, FOR HUMANITY'S SAKE...
DEDICATE YOUR HEARTS!!
YES, SIR!!

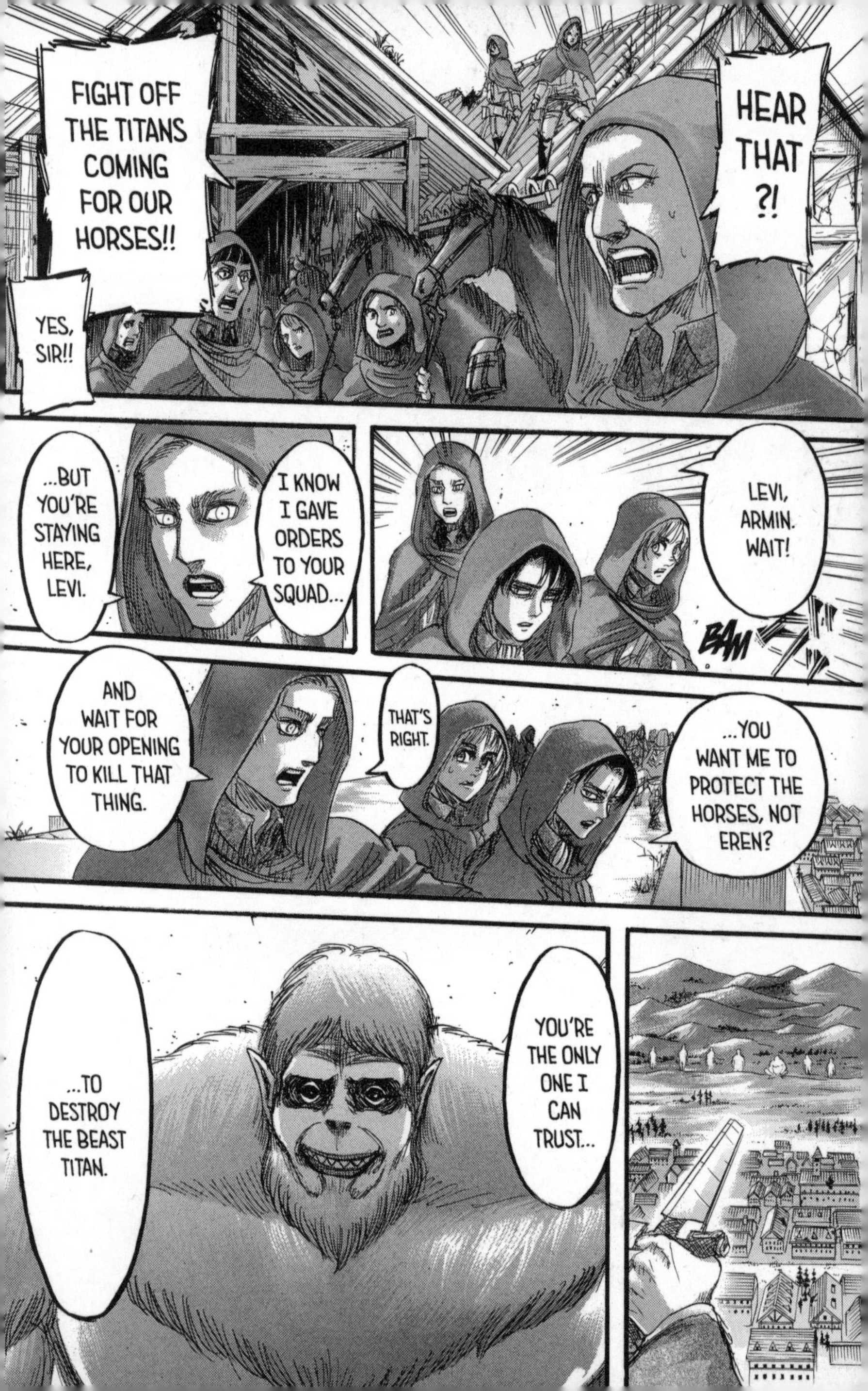
HEAR THAT?!
FIGHT OFF THE TITANS COMING FOR OUR HORSES!!
YES, SIR!!
LEVI, ARMIN. WAIT!
BAM
I KNOW I GAVE ORDERS TO YOUR SQUAD...
...BUT YOU'RE STAYING HERE, LEVI.
...YOU WANT ME TO PROTECT THE HORSES, NOT EREN?
THAT'S RIGHT.
AND WAIT FOR YOUR OPENING TO KILL THAT THING.
YOU'RE THE ONLY ONE I CAN TRUST...
...TO DESTROY THE BEAST TITAN.

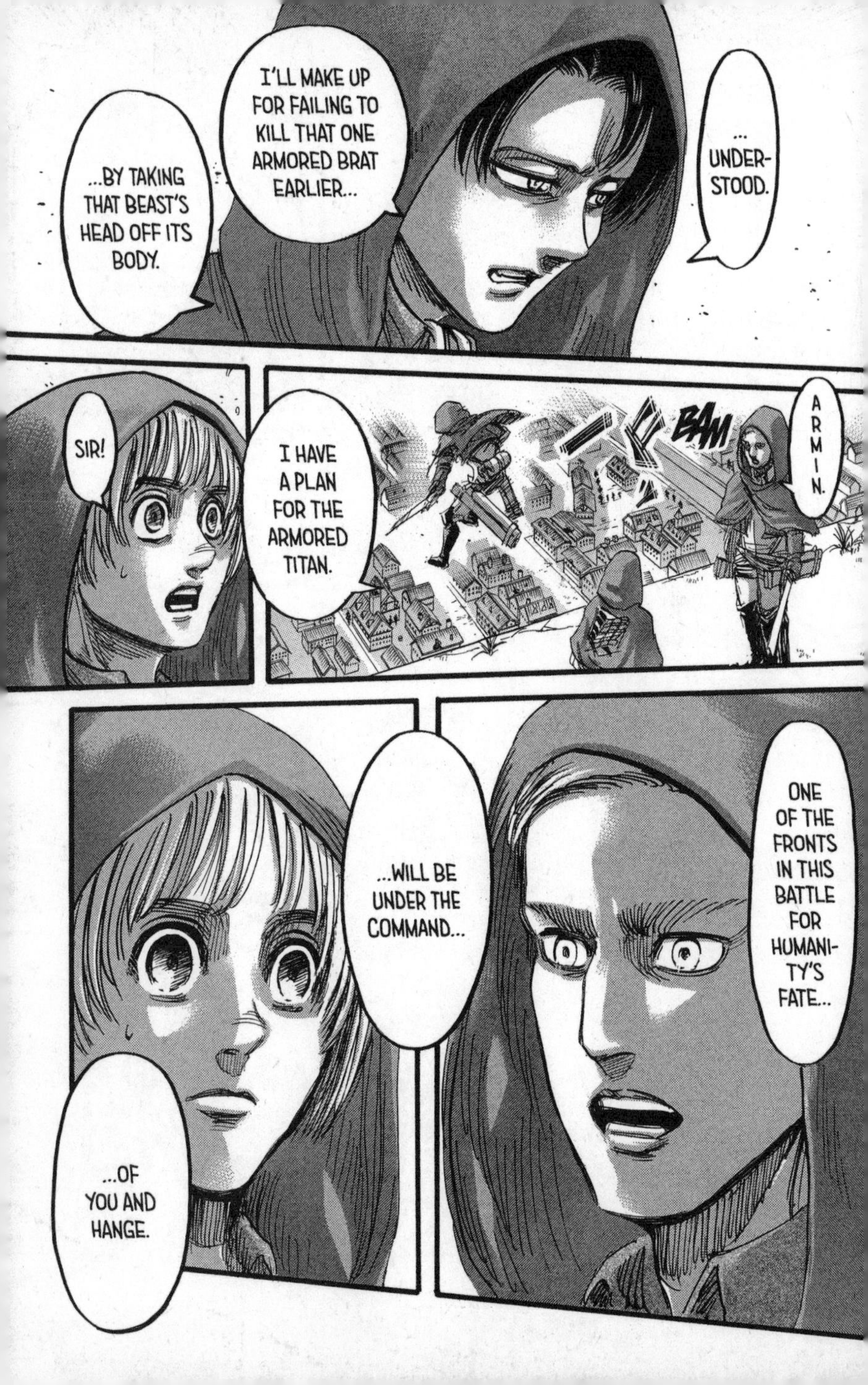
...UNDERSTOOD.
I'LL MAKE UP FOR FAILING TO KILL THAT ONE ARMORED BRAT EARLIER...
...BY TAKING THAT BEAST'S HEAD OFF ITS BODY.
ARMIN.
BAM
I HAVE A PLAN FOR THE ARMORED TITAN.
SIR!
ONE OF THE FRONTS IN THIS BATTLE FOR HUMANITY'S FATE...
...WILL BE UNDER THE COMMAND...
...OF YOU AND HANGE.

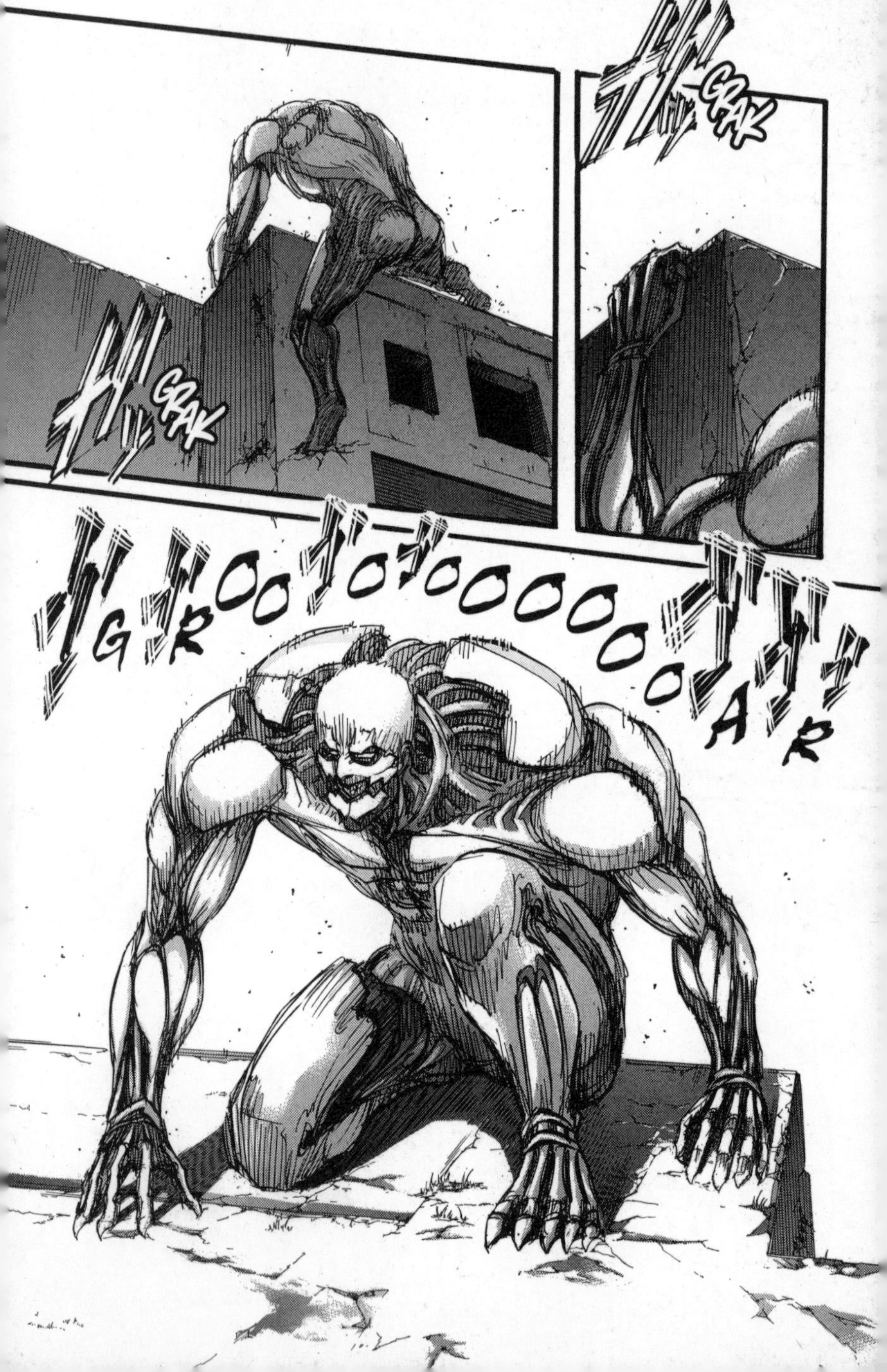
GRAK
GRAK
GROOOOOOOOOAR

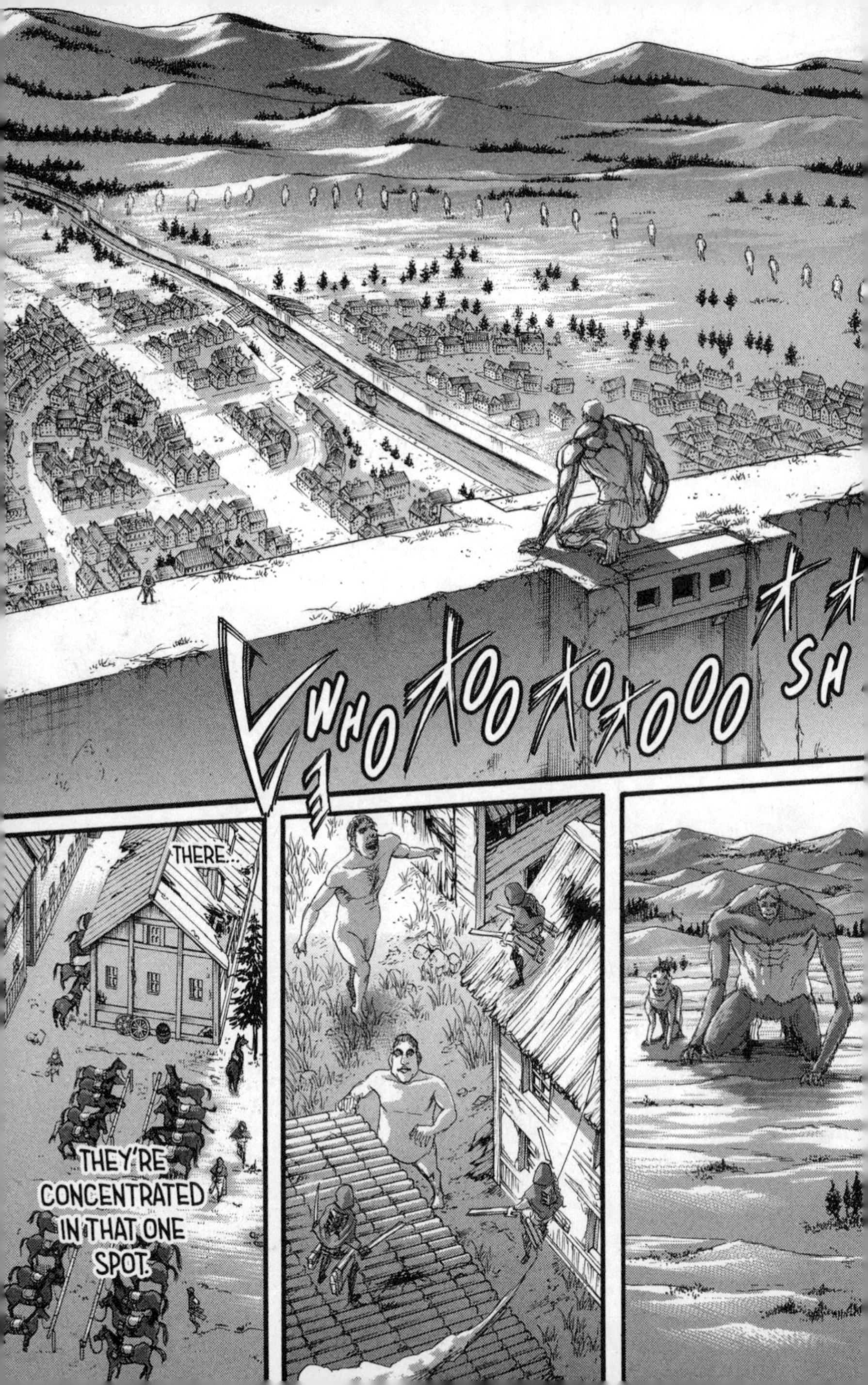
WHOOOOOOOOOSH
THERE...
THEY'RE CONCENTRATED IN THAT ONE SPOT.

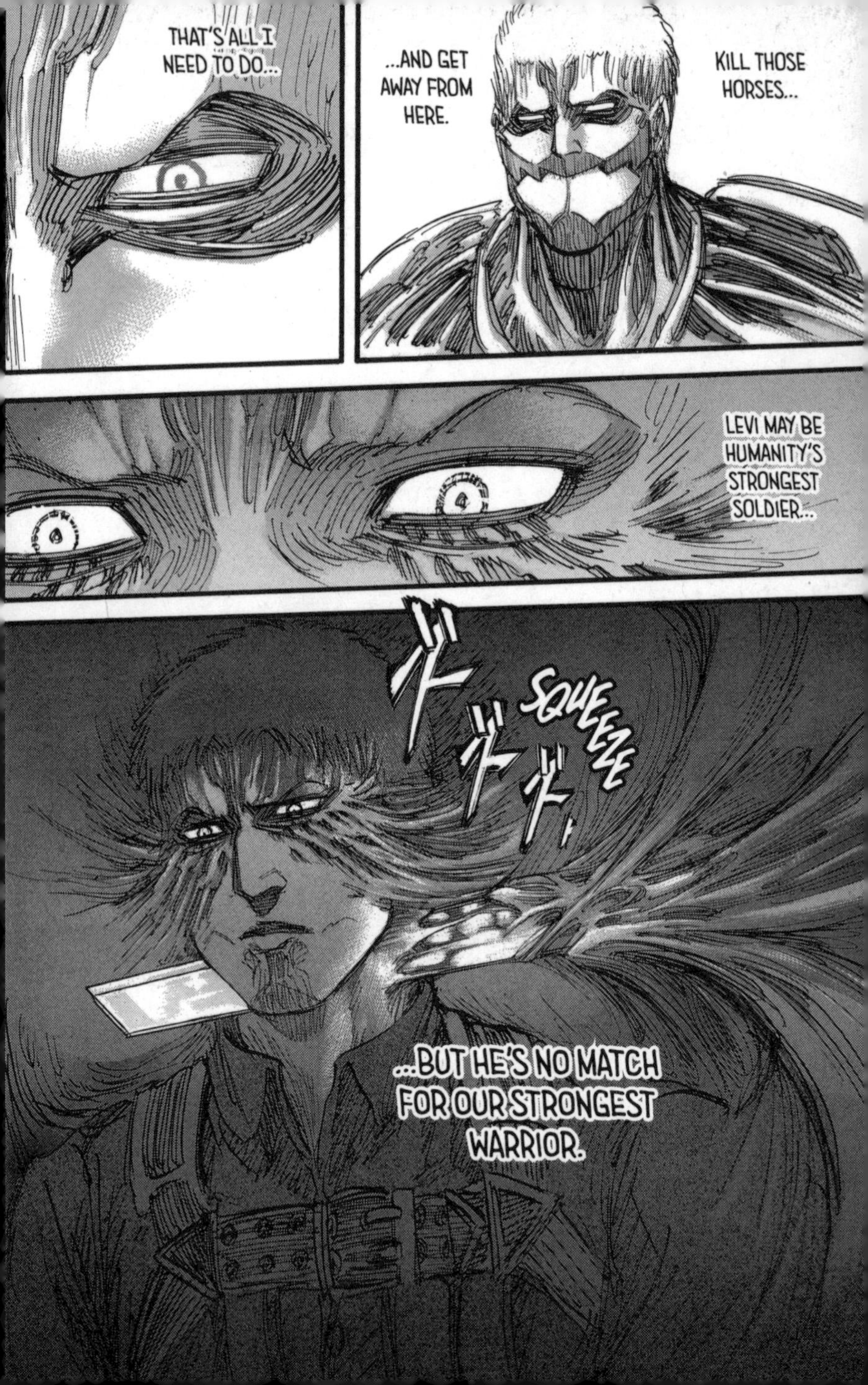
KILL THOSE HORSES...
...AND GET AWAY FROM HERE.
THAT'S ALL I NEED TO DO...
LEVI MAY BE HUMANITY'S STRONGEST SOLDIER...
SQUEEZE
...BUT HE'S NO MATCH FOR OUR STRONGEST WARRIOR.

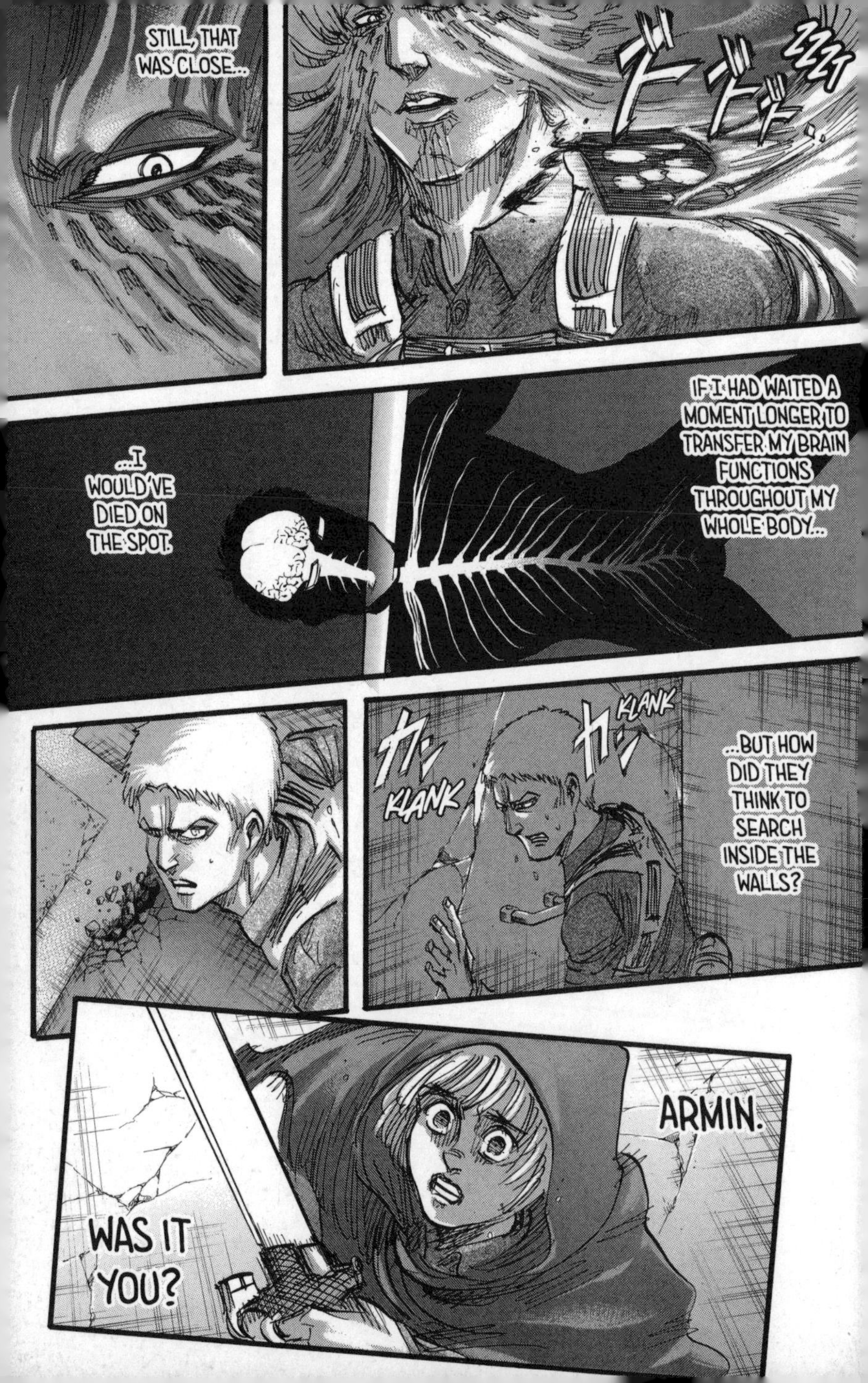
ZZZT
ドドド…
STILL, THAT WAS CLOSE...
IF I HAD WAITED A MOMENT LONGER TO TRANSFER MY BRAIN FUNCTIONS THROUGHOUT MY WHOLE BODY...
...I WOULD'VE DIED ON THE SPOT.
KLANK
カン
KLANK
カン
...BUT HOW DID THEY THINK TO SEARCH INSIDE THE WALLS?
ARMIN.
WAS IT YOU?

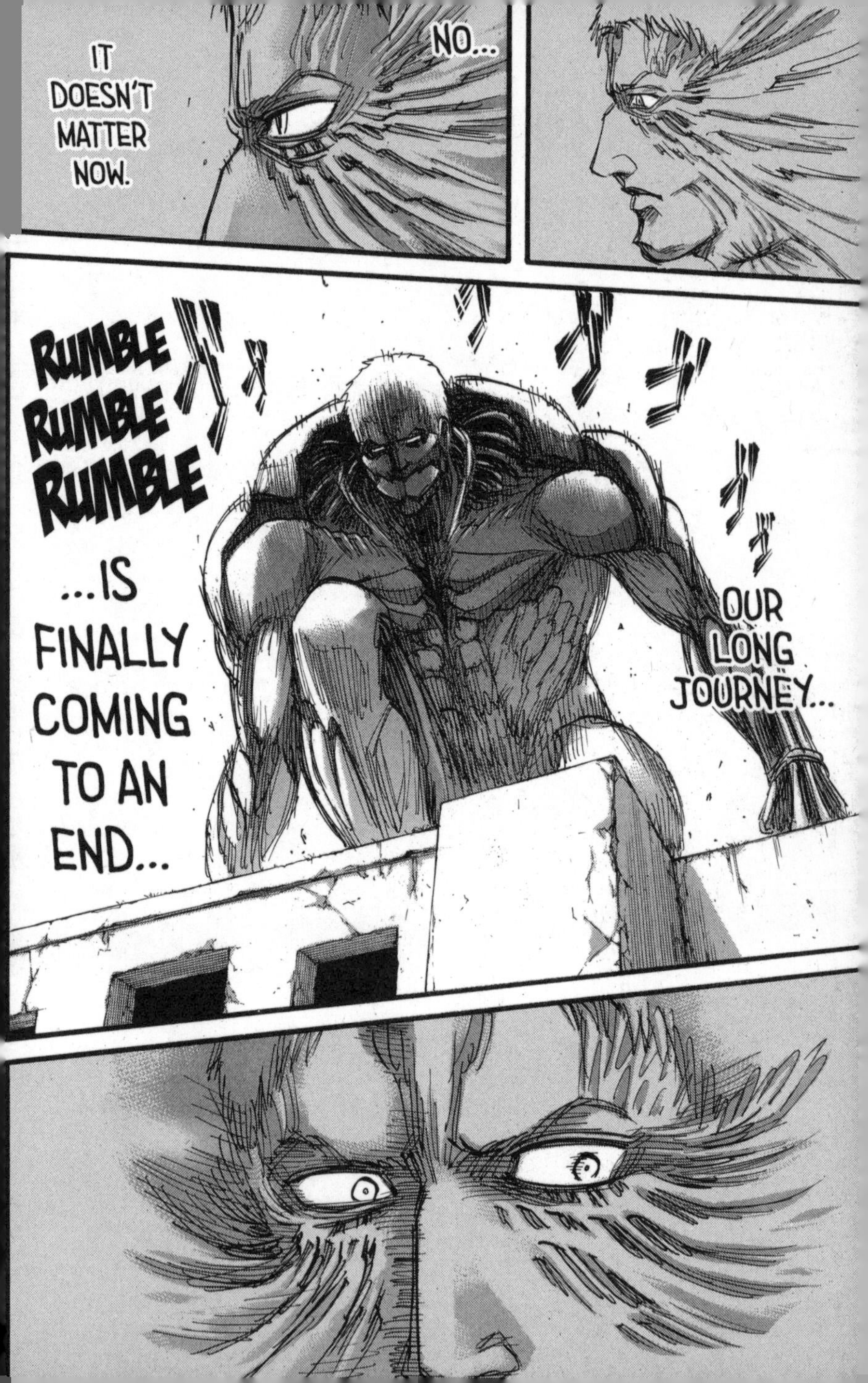
NO...
IT DOESN'T MATTER NOW.
RUMBLE RUMBLE RUMBLE
OUR LONG JOURNEY...
...IS FINALLY COMING TO AN END...

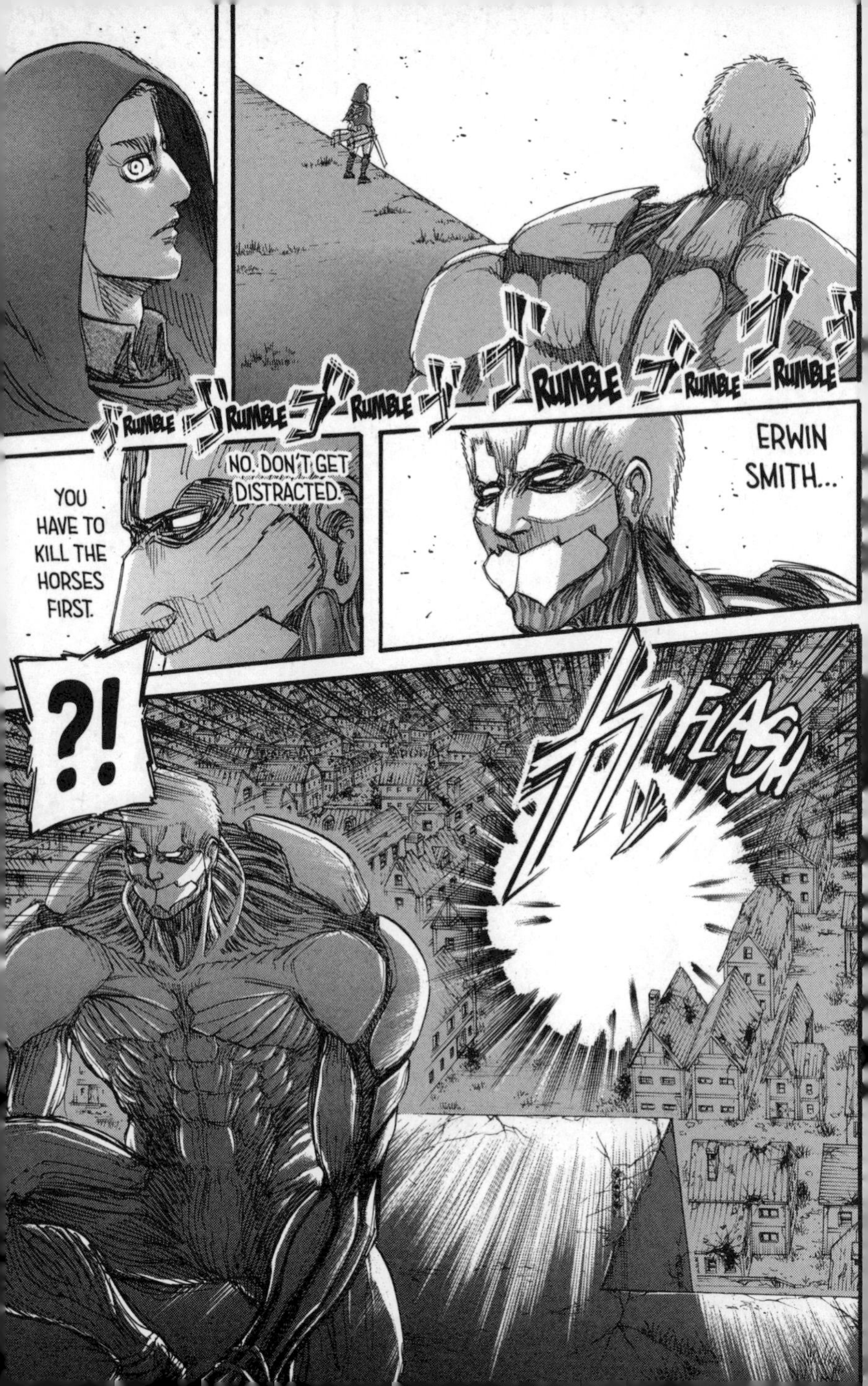
RUMBLE RUMBLE RUMBLE RUMBLE RUMBLE RUMBLE RUMBLE
ERWIN SMITH...
NO. DON'T GET DISTRACTED.
YOU HAVE TO KILL THE HORSES FIRST.
FLASH
?!

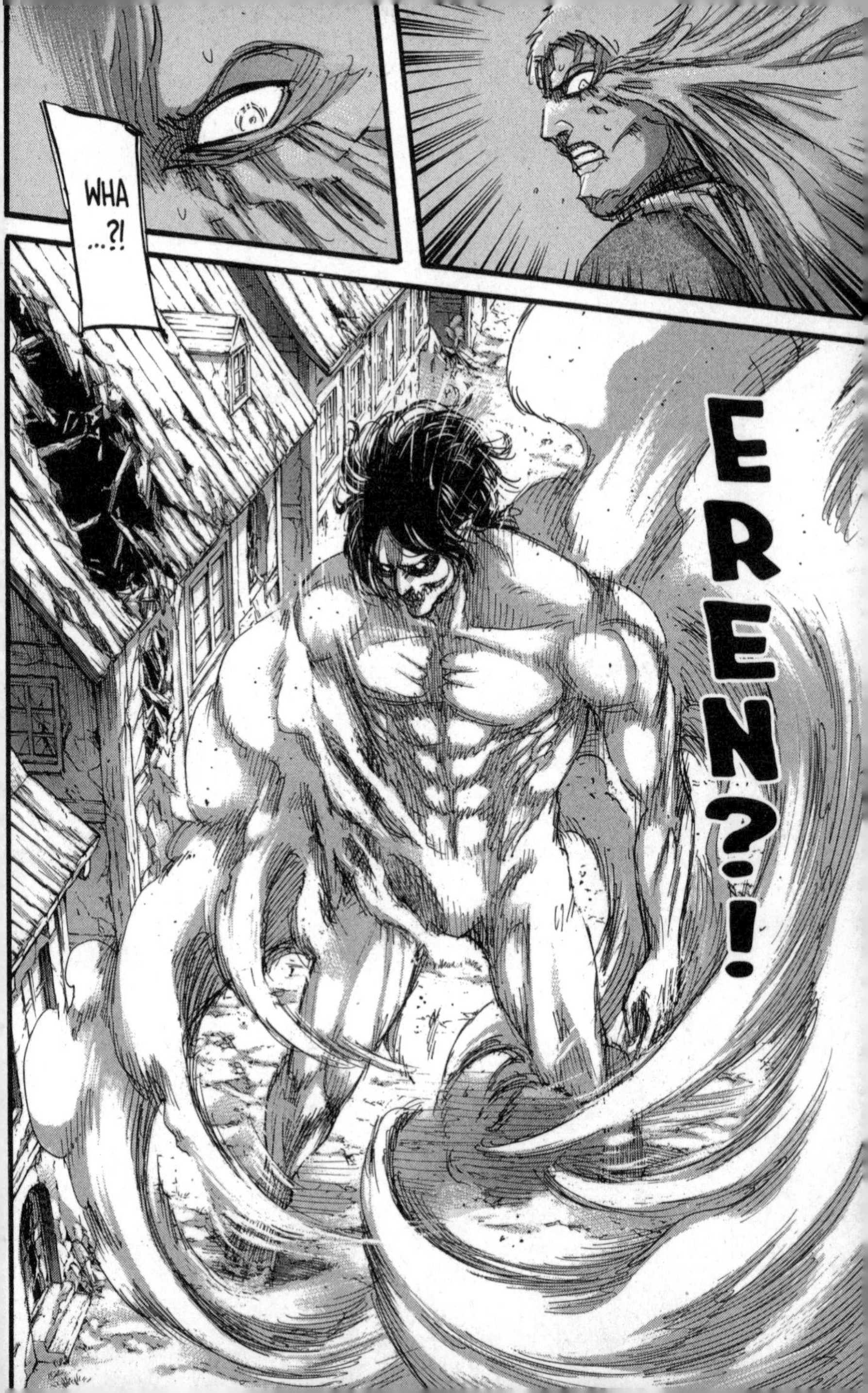
WHA ...?!
EREN?!

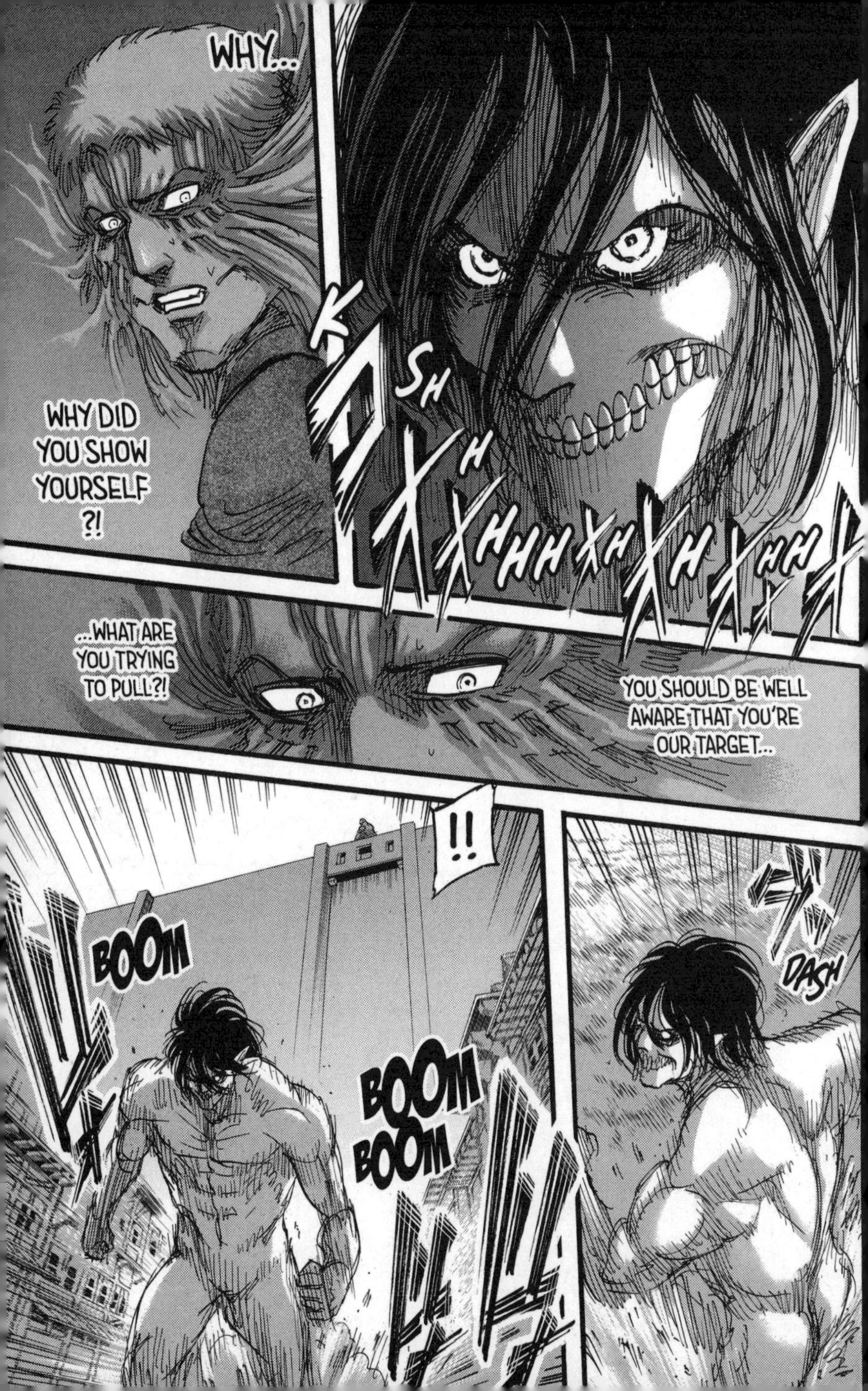
KSHH
WHY...
WHY DID YOU SHOW YOURSELF ?!
...WHAT ARE YOU TRYING TO PULL?!
YOU SHOULD BE WELL AWARE THAT YOU'RE OUR TARGET...
DASH
!!
BOOM
BOOM BOOM BOOM

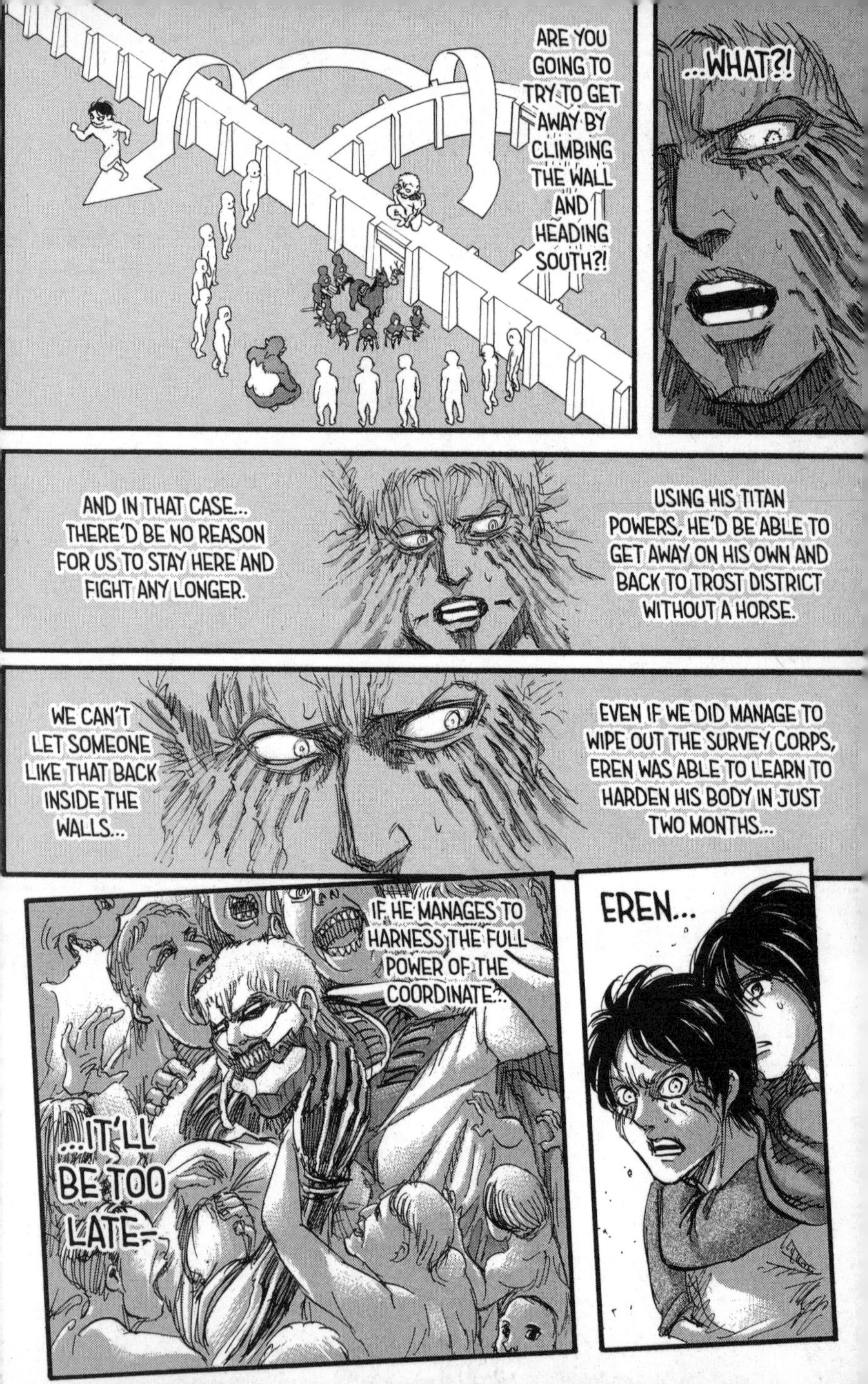
...WHAT?!
ARE YOU GOING TO TRY TO GET AWAY BY CLIMBING THE WALL AND HEADING SOUTH?!
USING HIS TITAN POWERS, HE'D BE ABLE TO GET AWAY ON HIS OWN AND BACK TO TROST DISTRICT WITHOUT A HORSE.
AND IN THAT CASE... THERE'D BE NO REASON FOR US TO STAY HERE AND FIGHT ANY LONGER.
EVEN IF WE DID MANAGE TO WIPE OUT THE SURVEY CORPS, EREN WAS ABLE TO LEARN TO HARDEN HIS BODY IN JUST TWO MONTHS...
WE CAN'T LET SOMEONE LIKE THAT BACK INSIDE THE WALLS...
EREN...
IF HE MANAGES TO HARNESS THE FULL POWER OF THE COORDINATE...
...IT'LL BE TOO LATE–

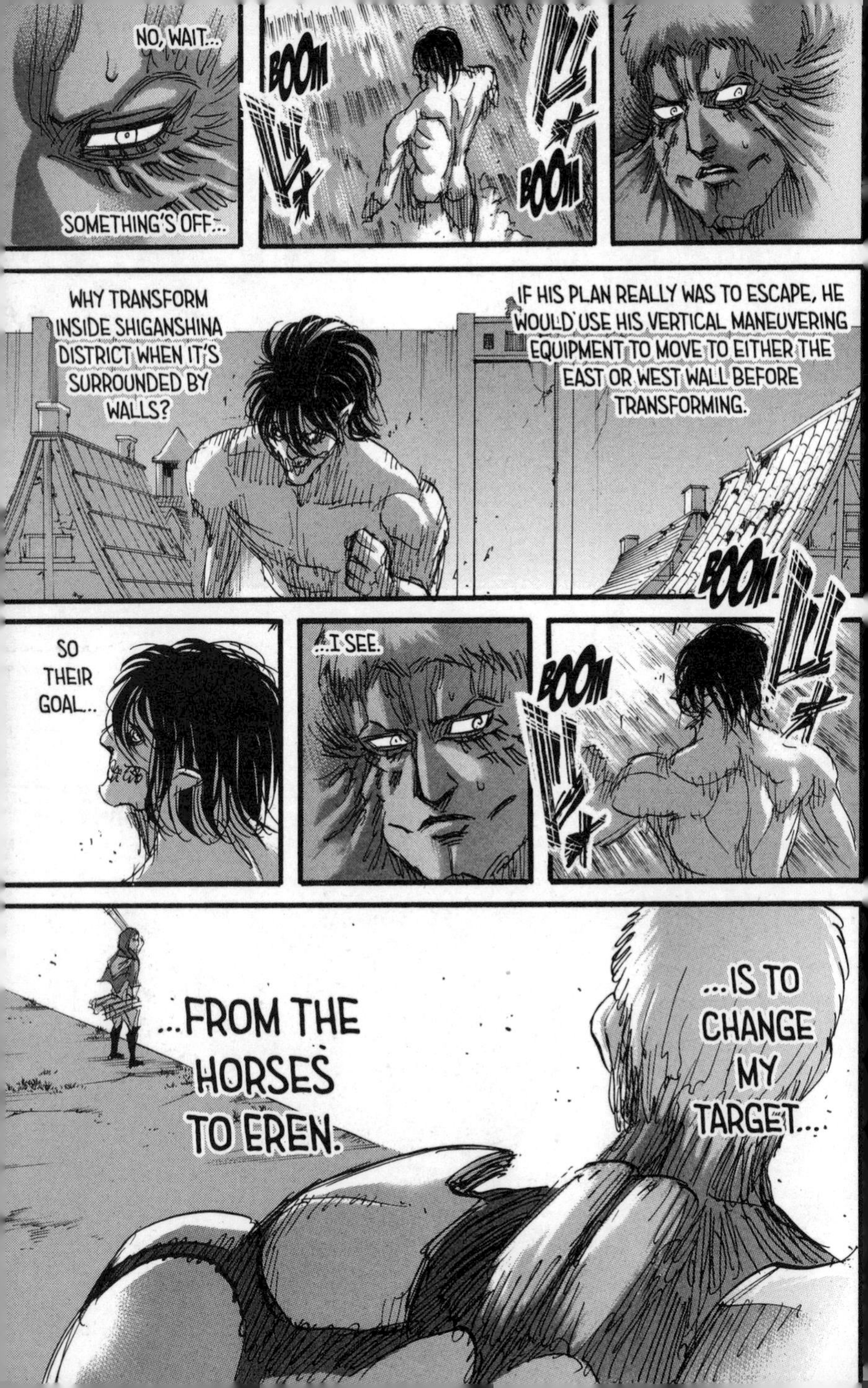
BOOM
BOOM
NO, WAIT...
SOMETHING'S OFF...
IF HIS PLAN REALLY WAS TO ESCAPE, HE WOULD USE HIS VERTICAL MANEUVERING EQUIPMENT TO MOVE TO EITHER THE EAST OR WEST WALL BEFORE TRANSFORMING.
WHY TRANSFORM INSIDE SHIGANSHINA DISTRICT WHEN IT'S SURROUNDED BY WALLS?
BOOM
BOOM
...I SEE.
SO THEIR GOAL...
...IS TO CHANGE MY TARGET...
...FROM THE HORSES TO EREN.

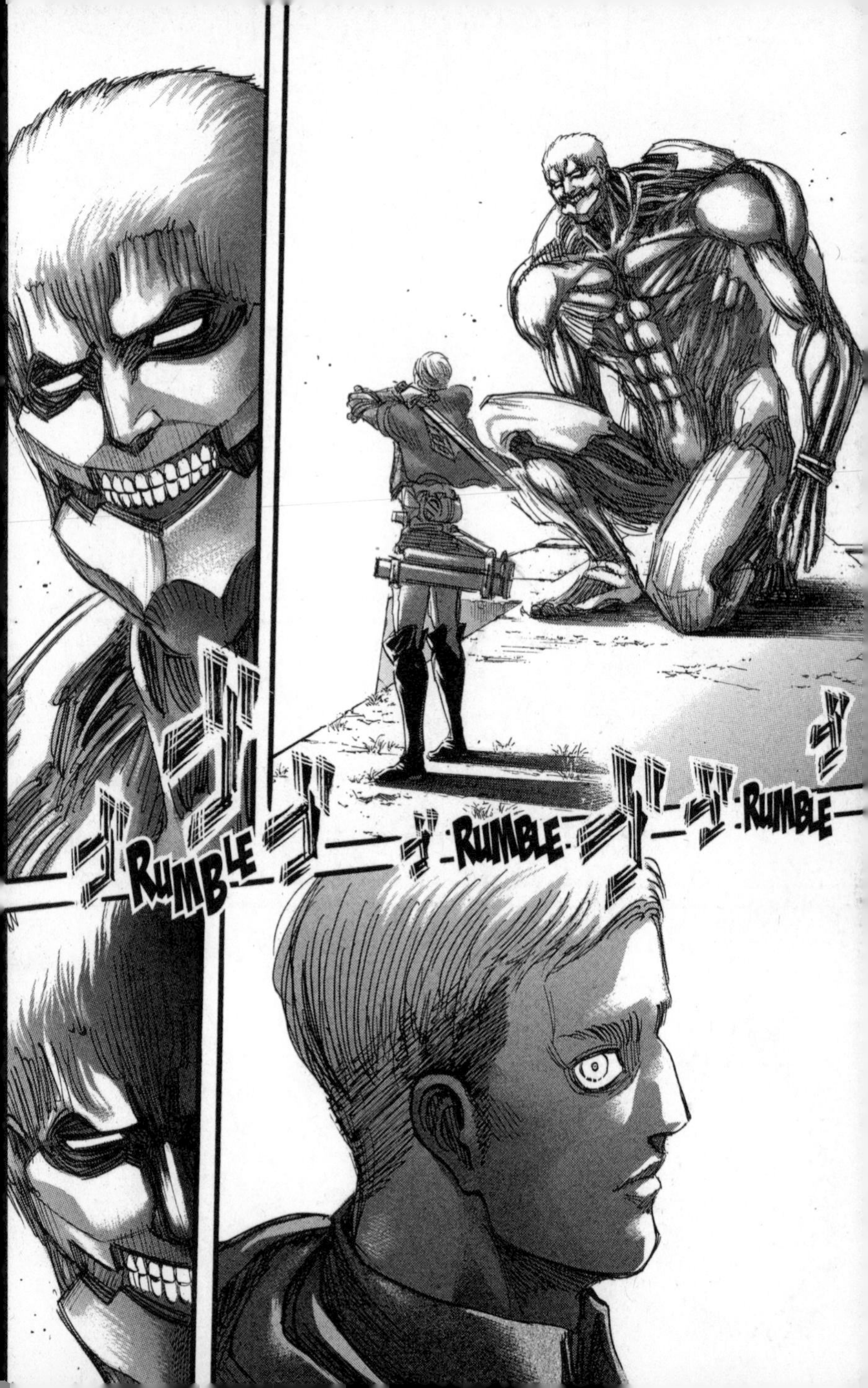
RUMBLE
RUMBLE
RUMBLE

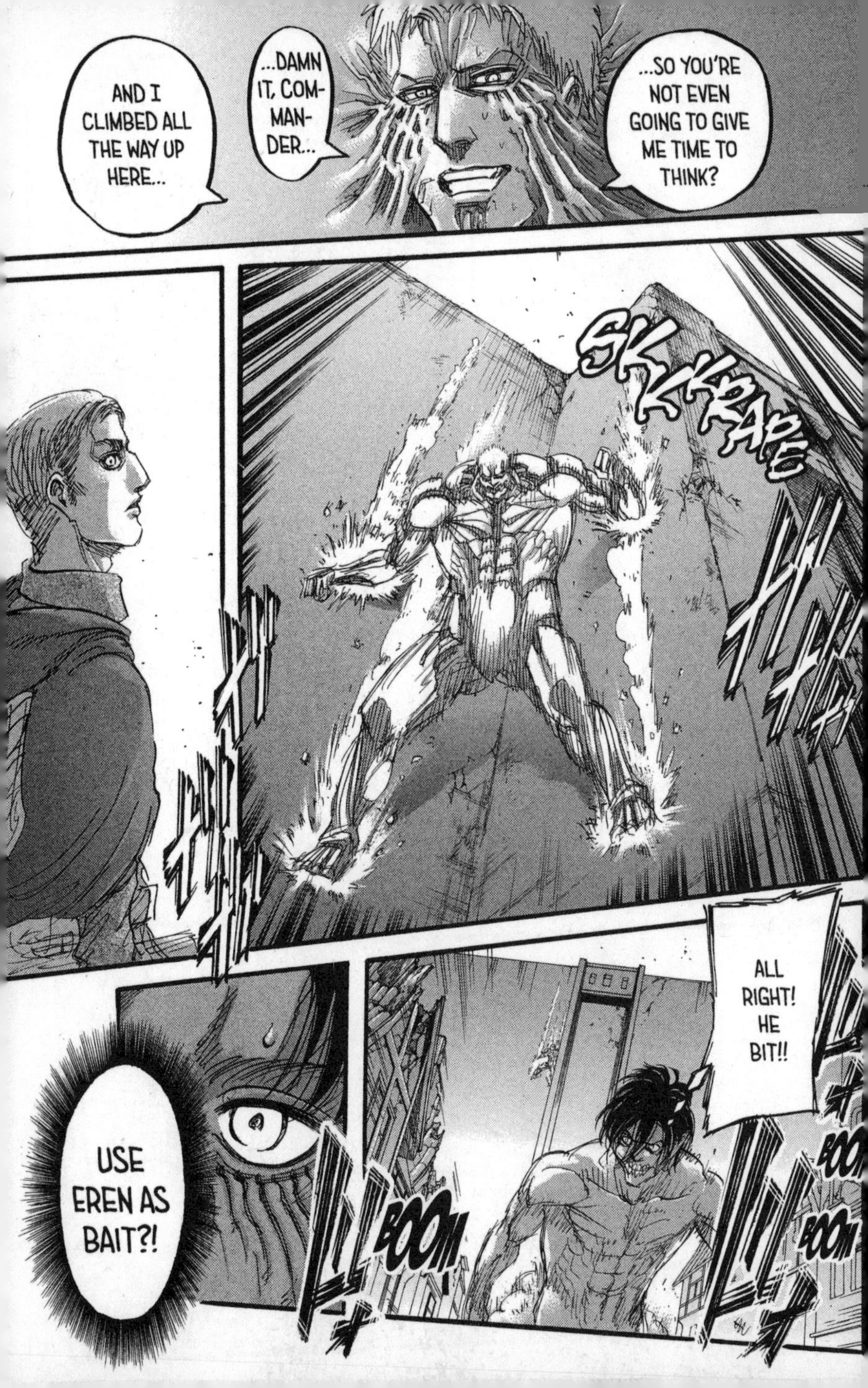
...SO YOU'RE NOT EVEN GOING TO GIVE ME TIME TO THINK?
...DAMN IT, COMMANDER...
AND I CLIMBED ALL THE WAY UP HERE...
SKKKRAPE
ALL RIGHT! HE BIT!!
BOOM
BOOM
BOOM
USE EREN AS BAIT?!

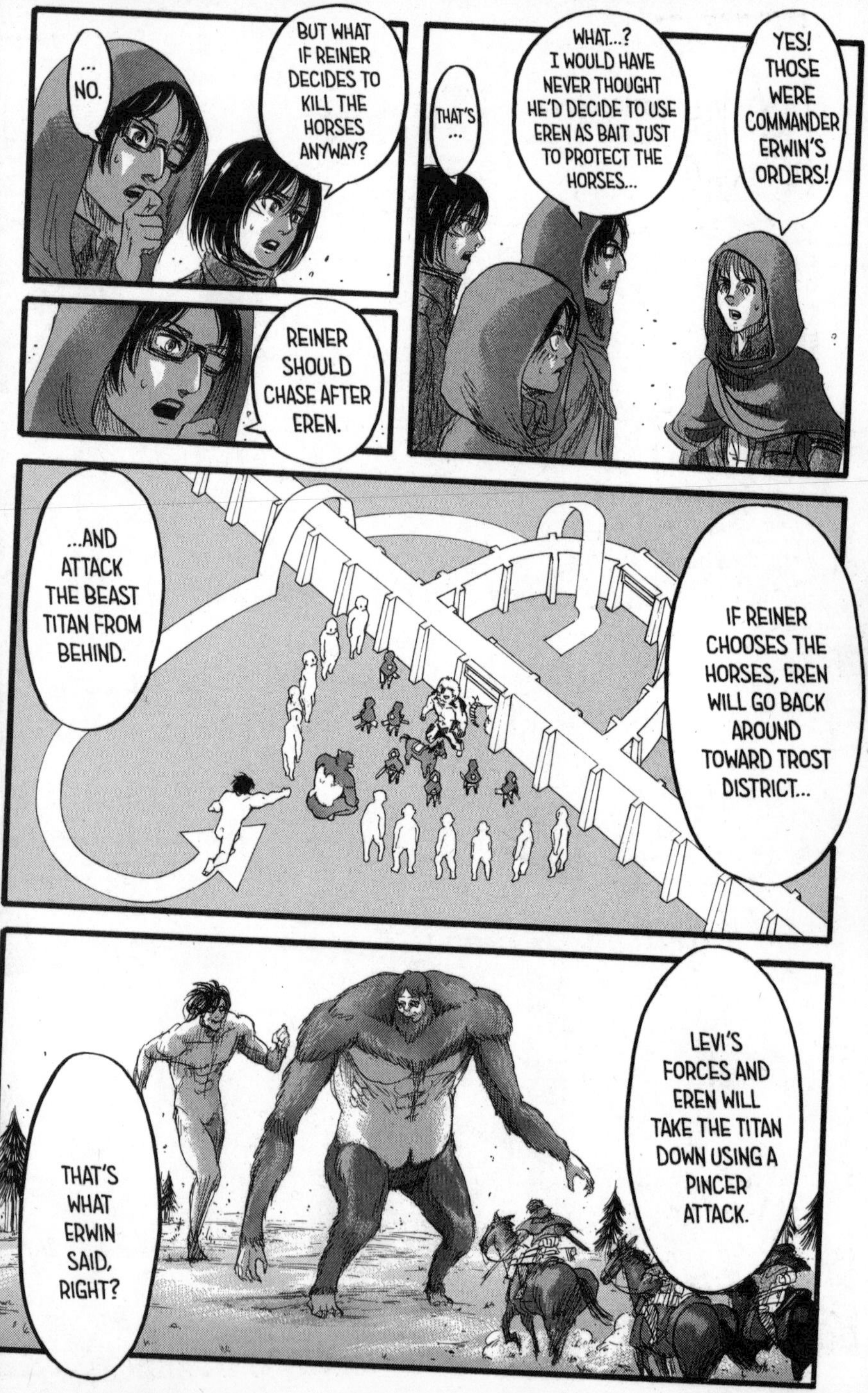
YES! THOSE WERE COMMANDER ERWIN'S ORDERS!
WHAT...? I WOULD HAVE NEVER THOUGHT HE'D DECIDE TO USE EREN AS BAIT JUST TO PROTECT THE HORSES...
THAT'S ...
BUT WHAT IF REINER DECIDES TO KILL THE HORSES ANYWAY?
... NO.
REINER SHOULD CHASE AFTER EREN.
IF REINER CHOOSES THE HORSES, EREN WILL GO BACK AROUND TOWARD TROST DISTRICT...
...AND ATTACK THE BEAST TITAN FROM BEHIND.
LEVI'S FORCES AND EREN WILL TAKE THE TITAN DOWN USING A PINCER ATTACK.
THAT'S WHAT ERWIN SAID, RIGHT?

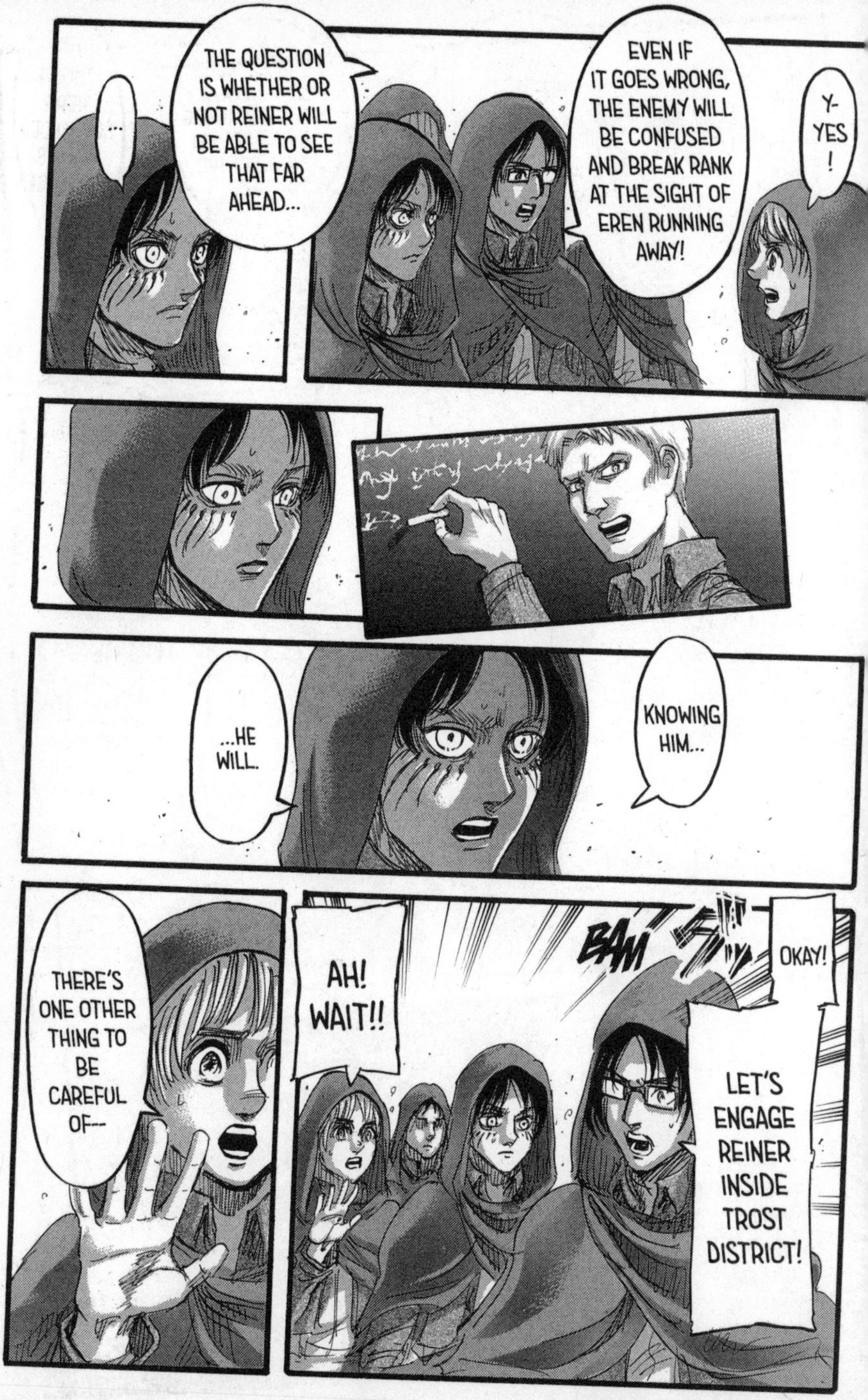
EVEN IF IT GOES WRONG, THE ENEMY WILL BE CONFUSED AND BREAK RANK AT THE SIGHT OF EREN RUNNING AWAY!
Y-YES!
THE QUESTION IS WHETHER OR NOT REINER WILL BE ABLE TO SEE THAT FAR AHEAD...
...
KNOWING HIM...
...HE WILL.
LET'S ENGAGE REINER INSIDE TROST DISTRICT!
OKAY!
BAM
AH! WAIT!!
THERE'S ONE OTHER THING TO BE CAREFUL OF--

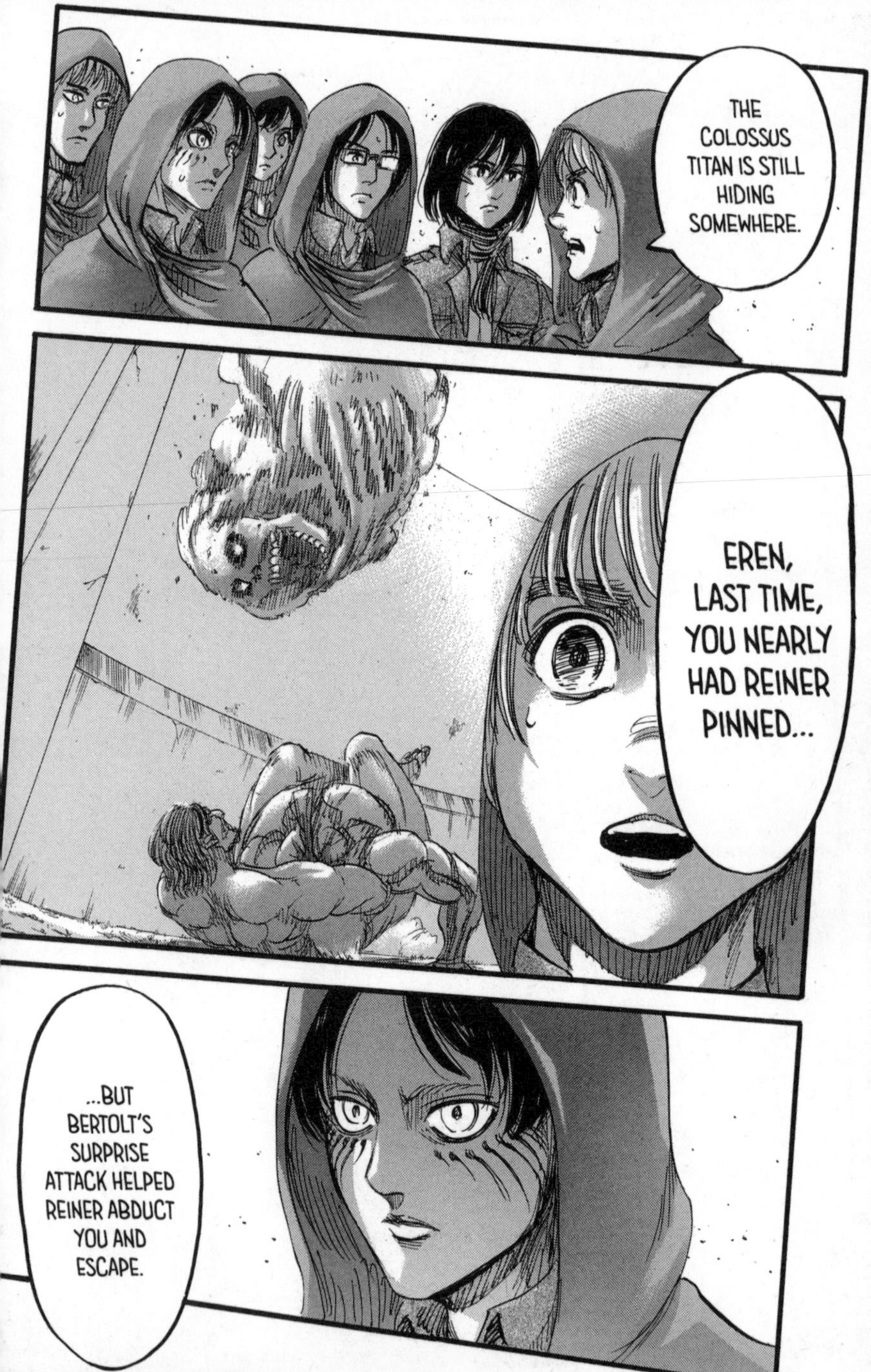
THE COLOSSUS TITAN IS STILL HIDING SOMEWHERE.
EREN, LAST TIME, YOU NEARLY HAD REINER PINNED...
...BUT BERTOLT'S SURPRISE ATTACK HELPED REINER ABDUCT YOU AND ESCAPE.

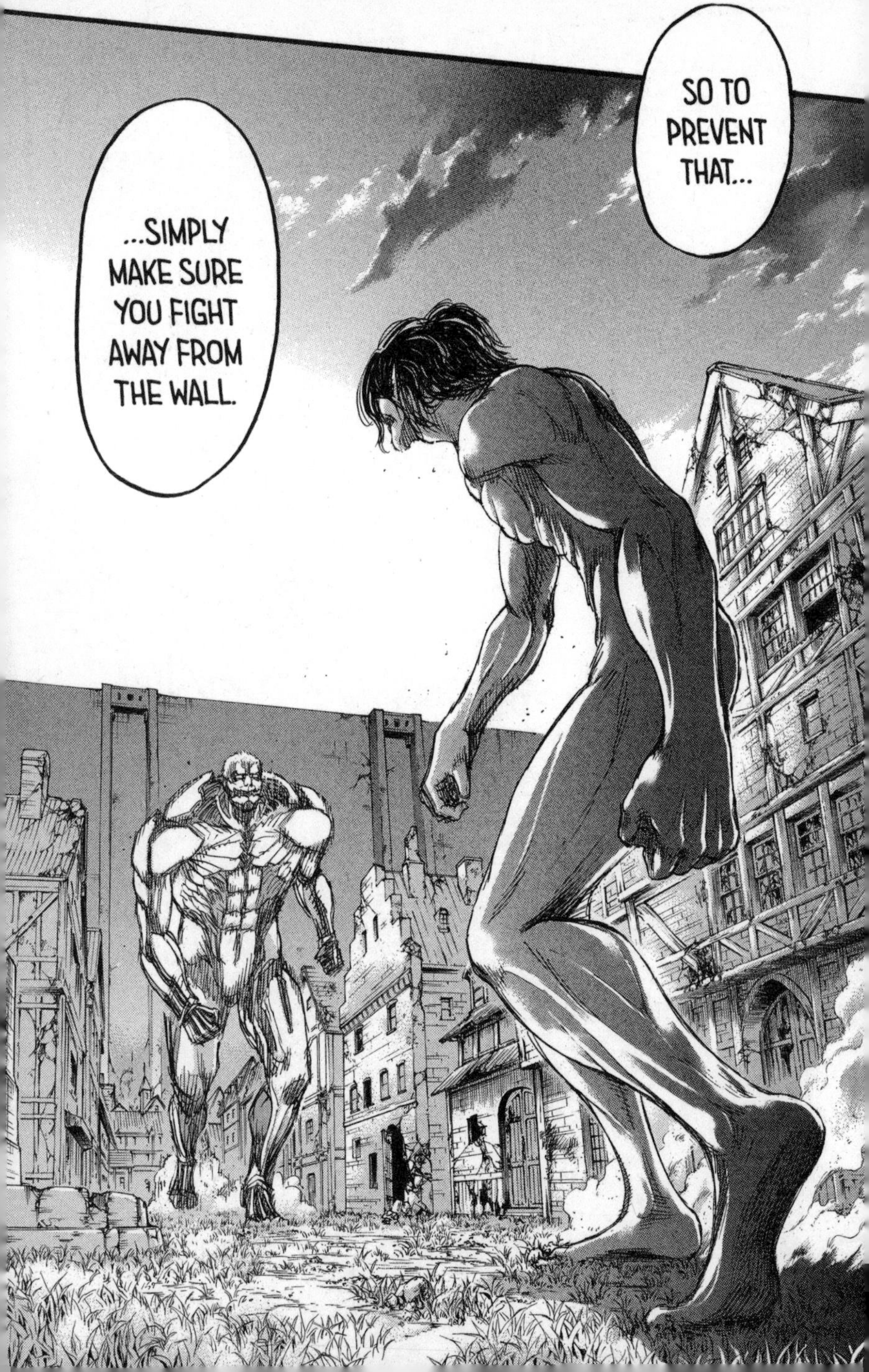
SO TO PREVENT THAT...
...SIMPLY MAKE SURE YOU FIGHT AWAY FROM THE WALL.

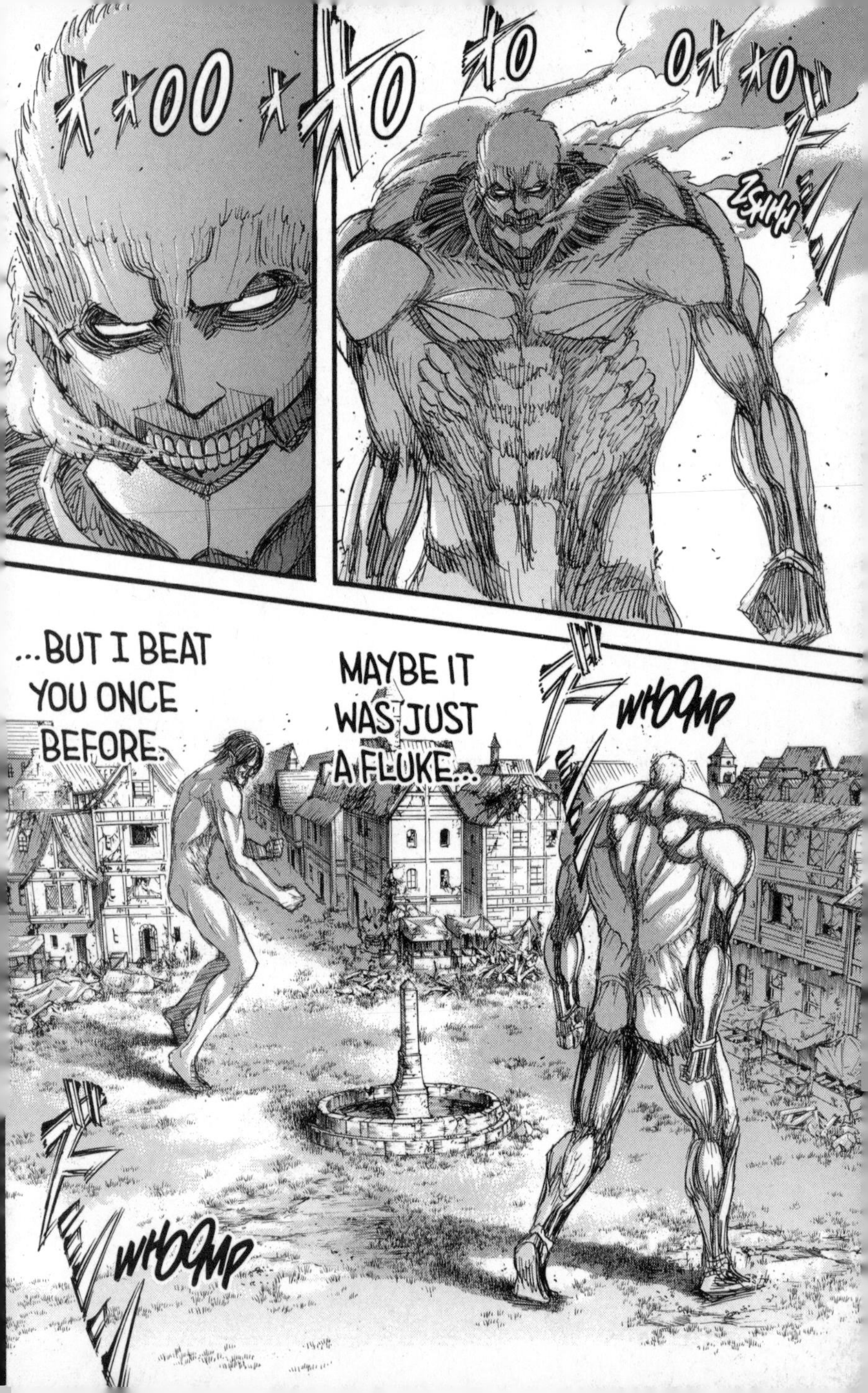
ZSHHH
MAYBE IT WAS JUST A FLUKE...
...BUT I BEAT YOU ONCE BEFORE.
WHOOMP
WHOOMP

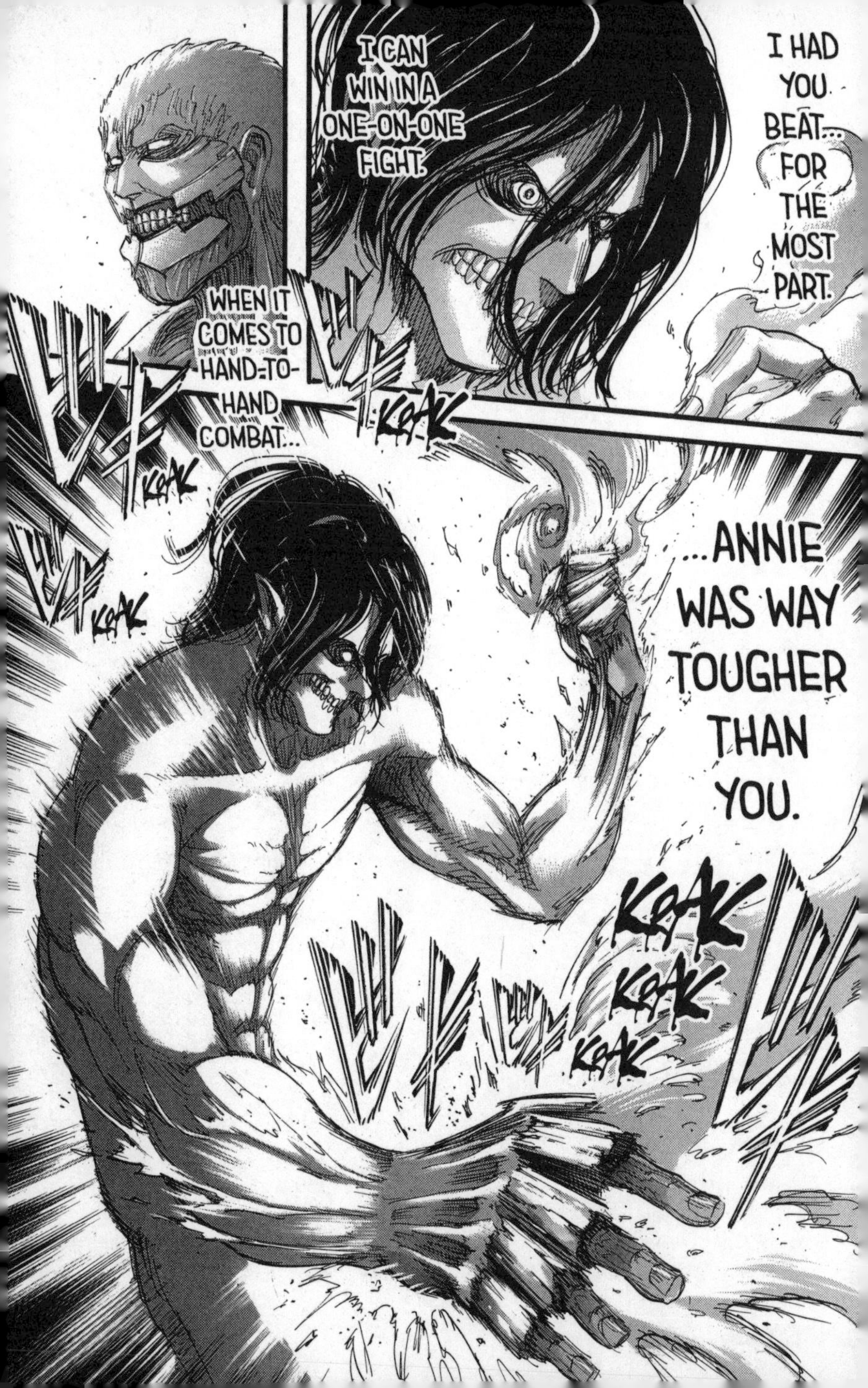
I HAD YOU BEAT... FOR THE MOST PART.
I CAN WIN IN A ONE-ON-ONE FIGHT.
KRAK
WHEN IT COMES TO HAND-TO-HAND COMBAT...
KRAK
KRAK
...ANNIE WAS WAY TOUGHER THAN YOU.
KRAK
KRAK
KRAK

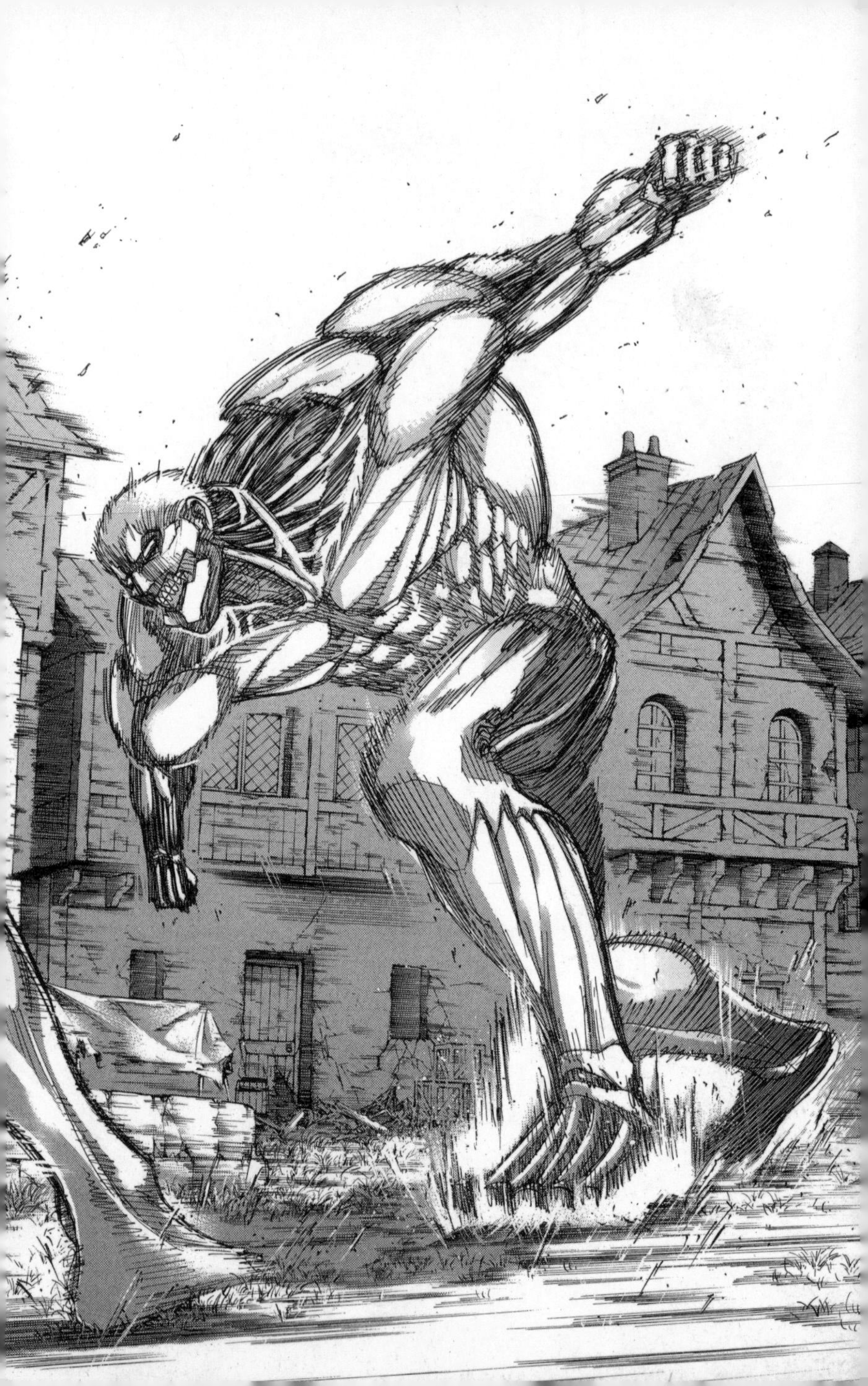

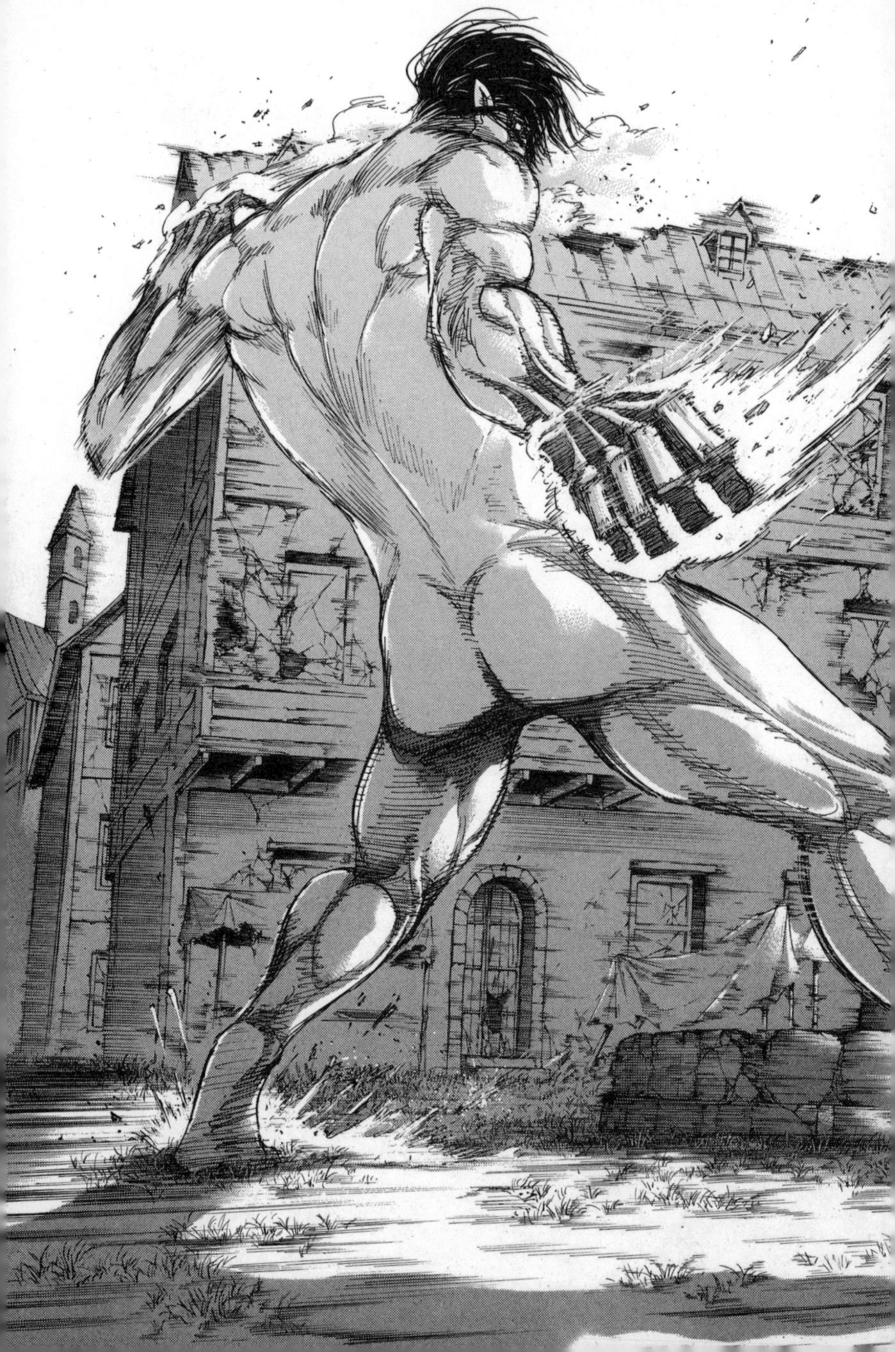

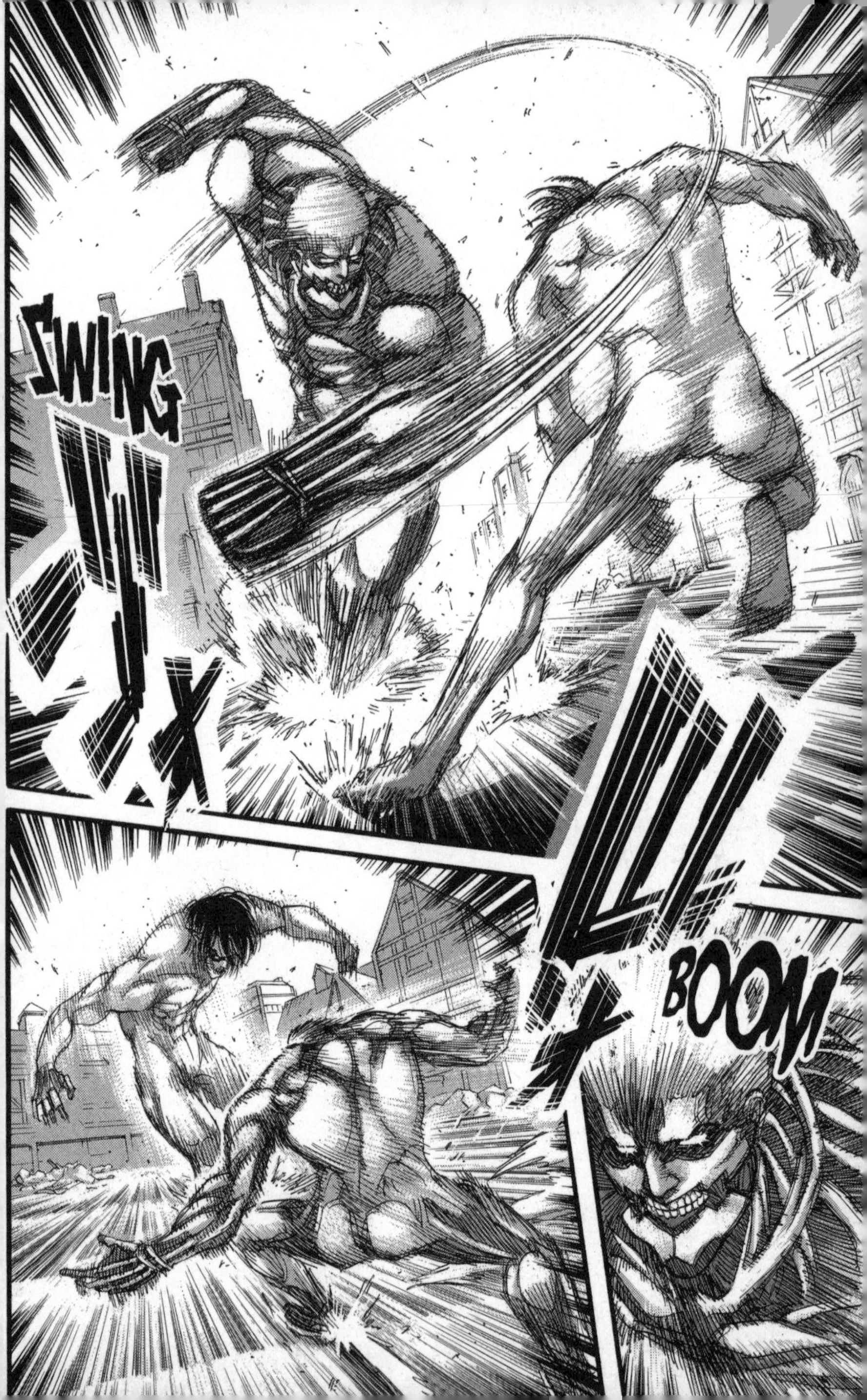
SWING
BOOM

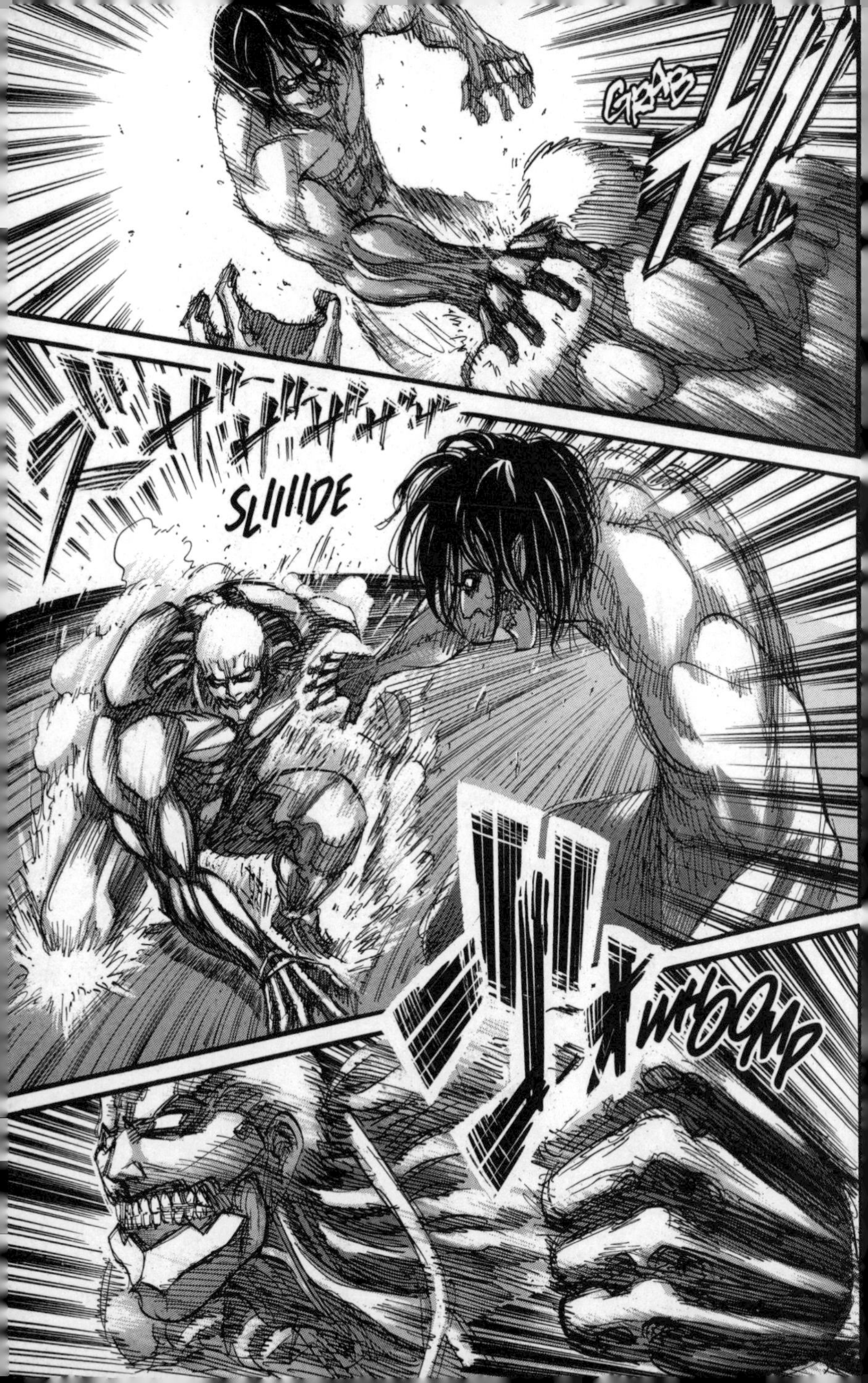
GRAB
SLIIIIDE

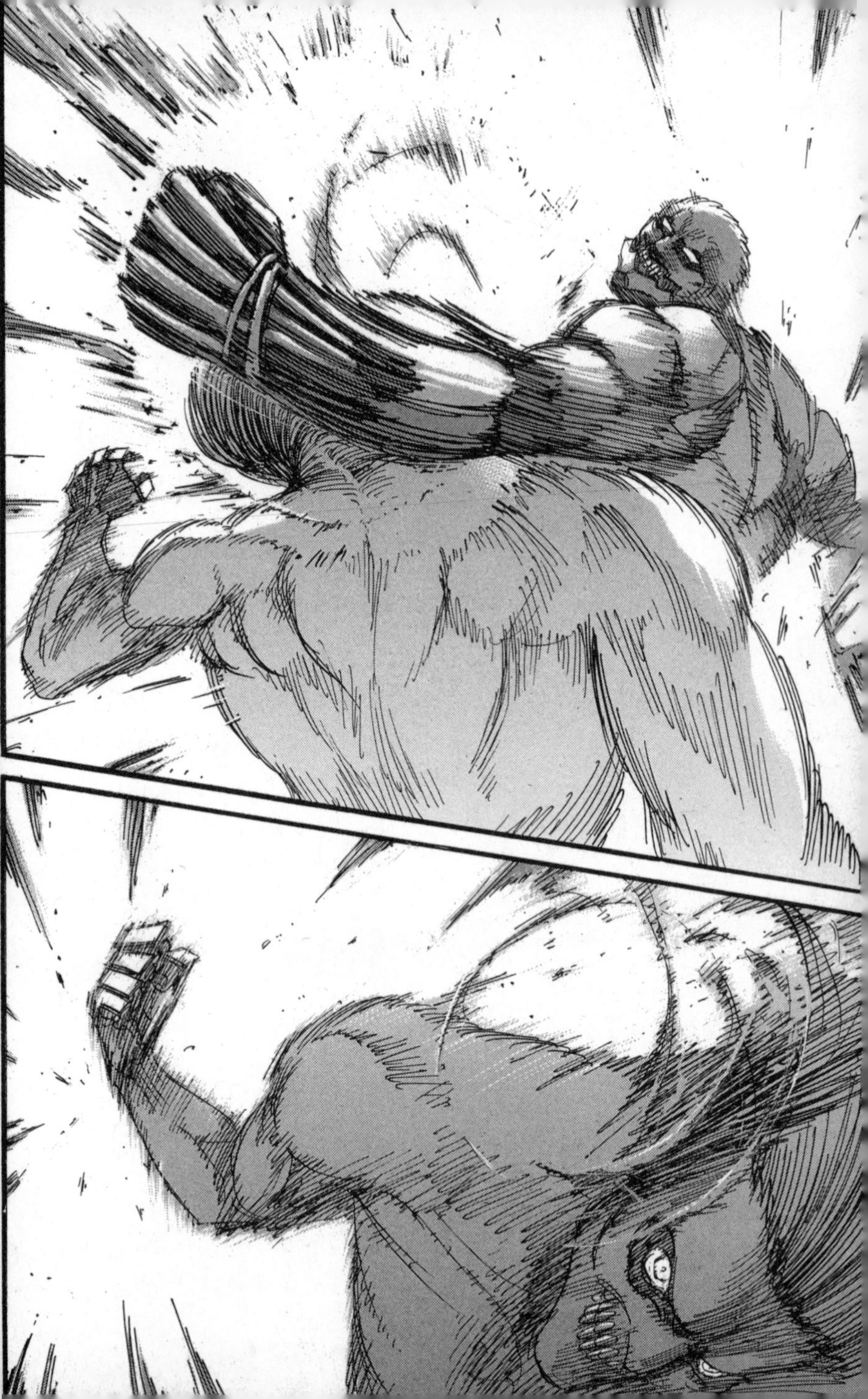

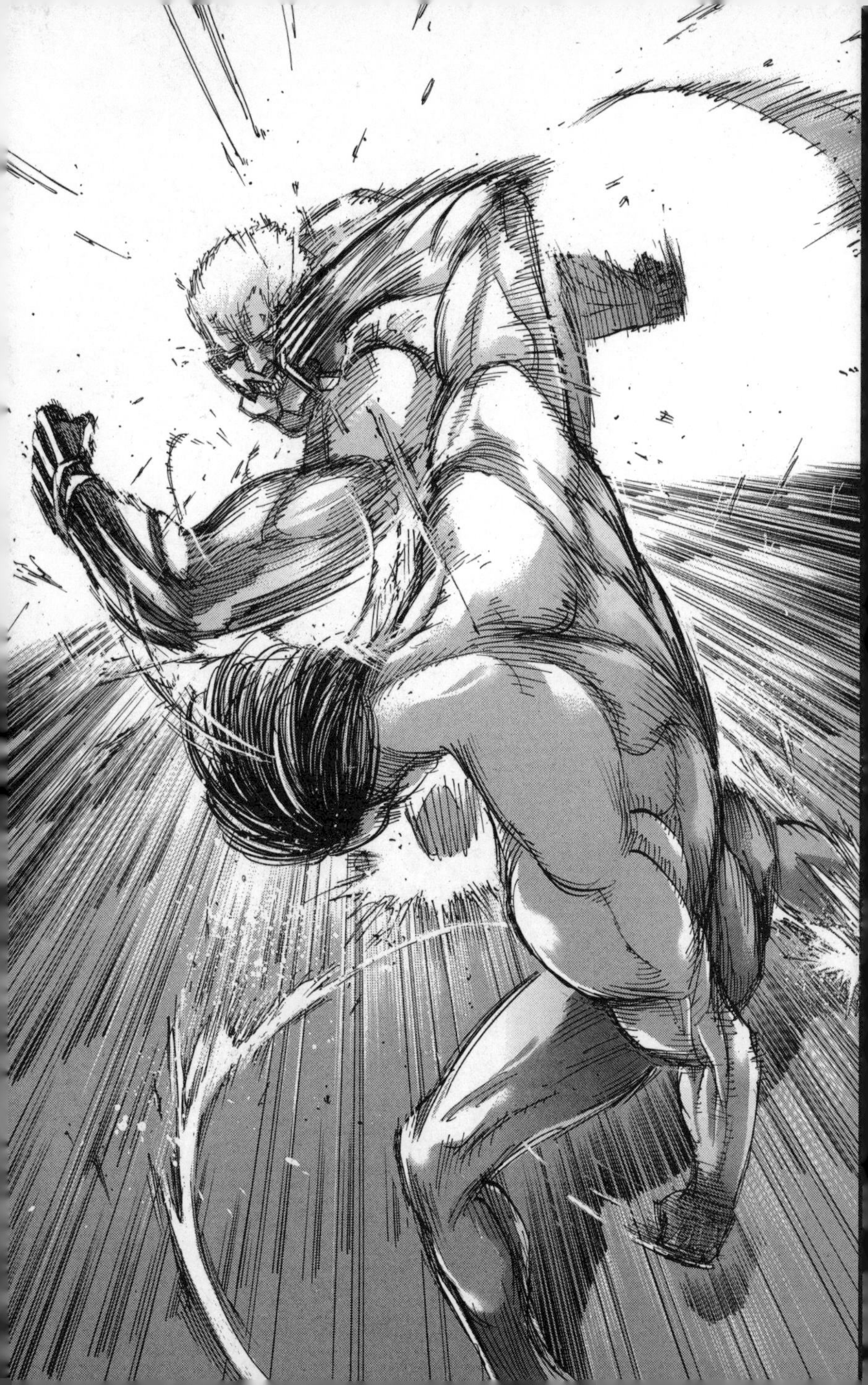

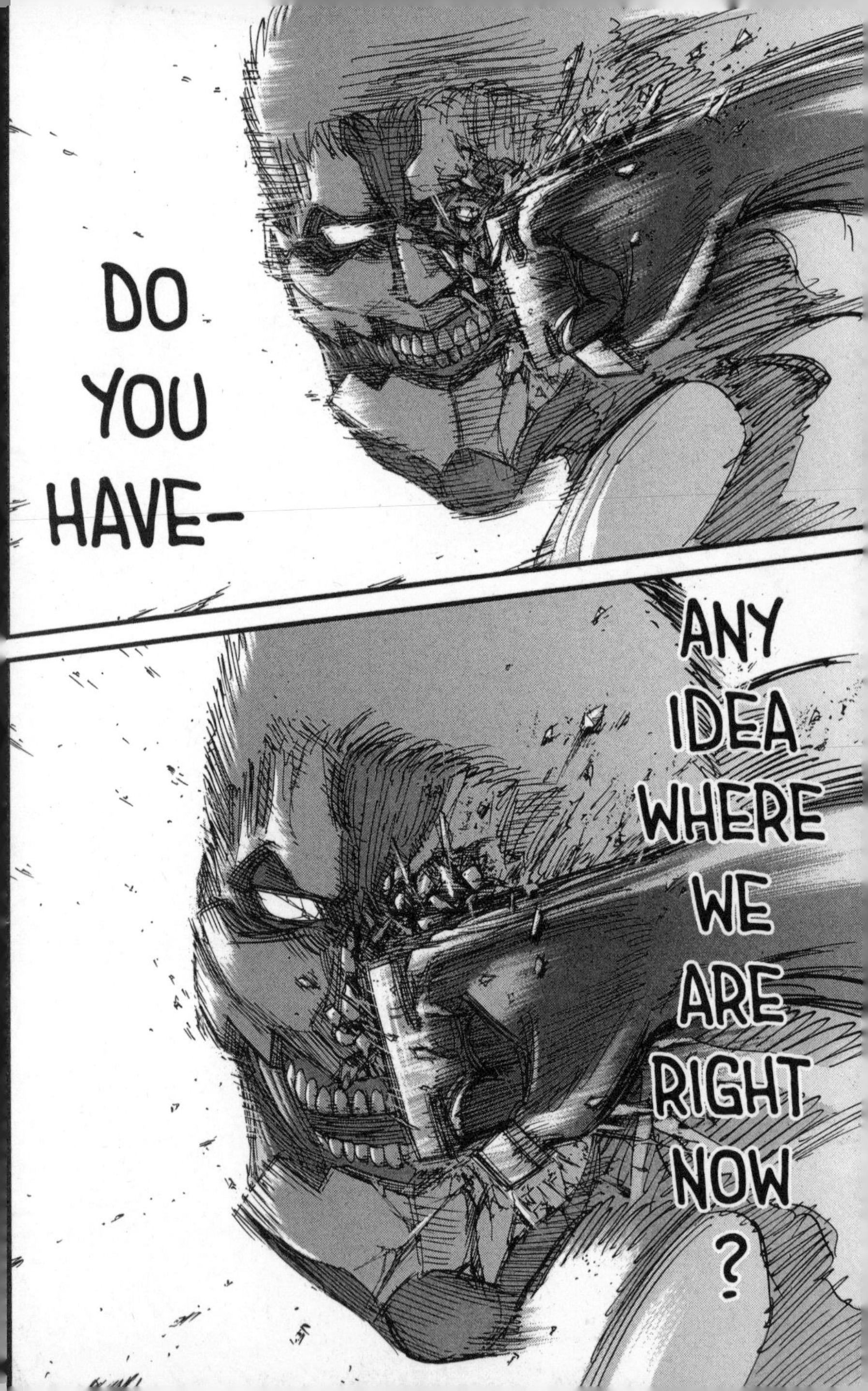
DO YOU HAVE-
ANY IDEA WHERE WE ARE RIGHT NOW?

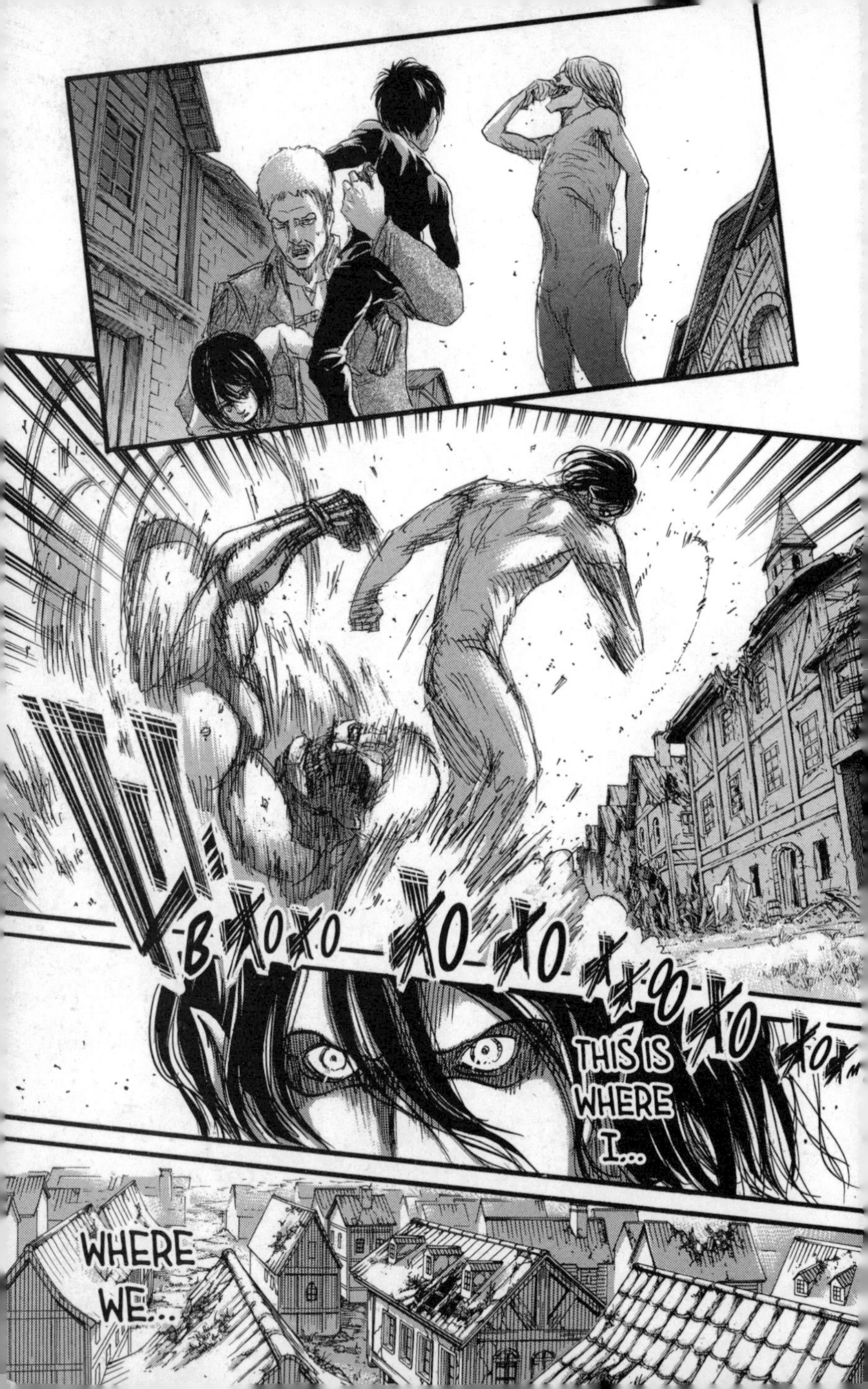
BOOO OO OO OOO OO OO
THIS IS WHERE I...
WHERE WE...

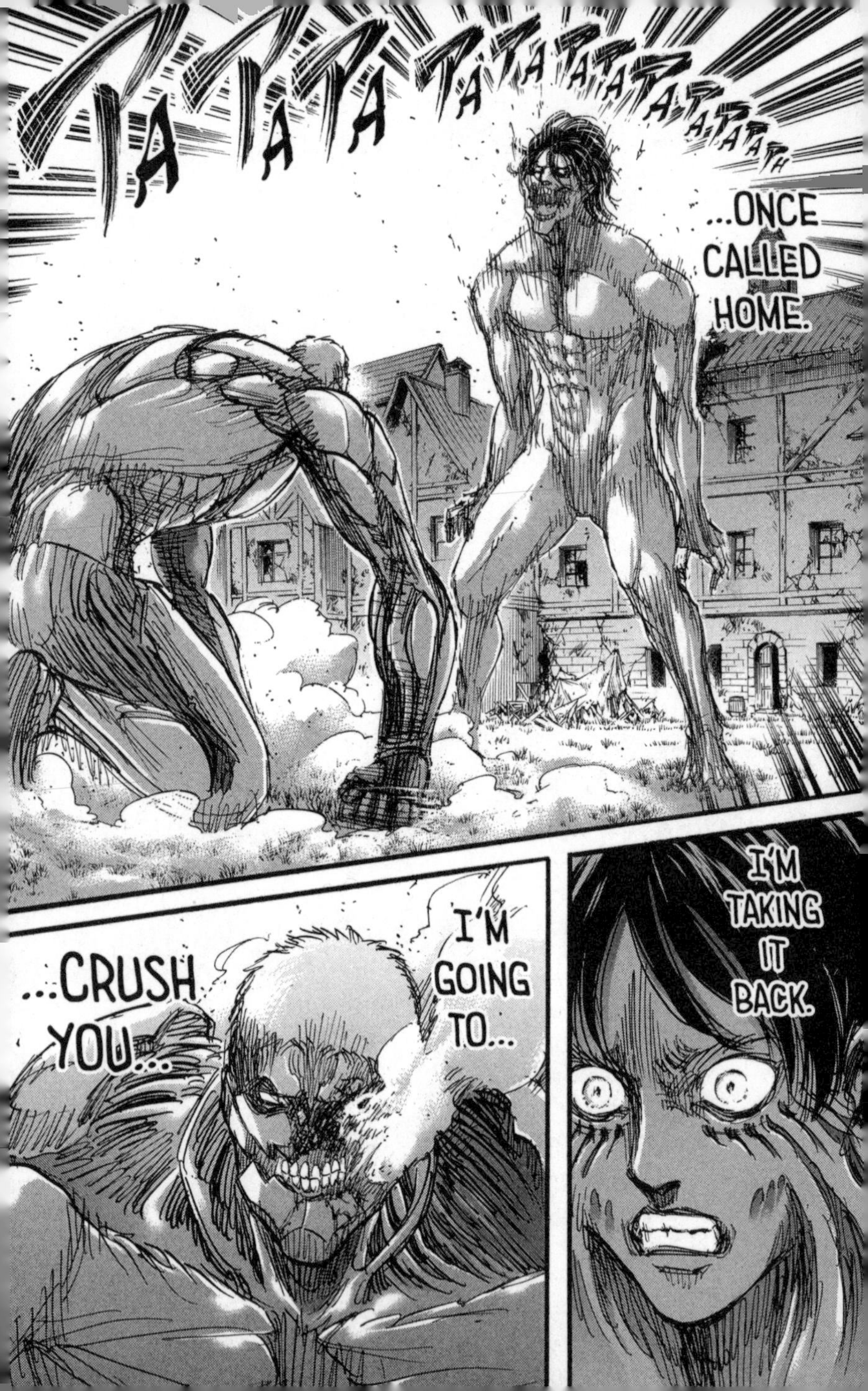
...ONCE CALLED HOME.
I'M TAKING IT BACK.
I'M GOING TO...
...CRUSH YOU...

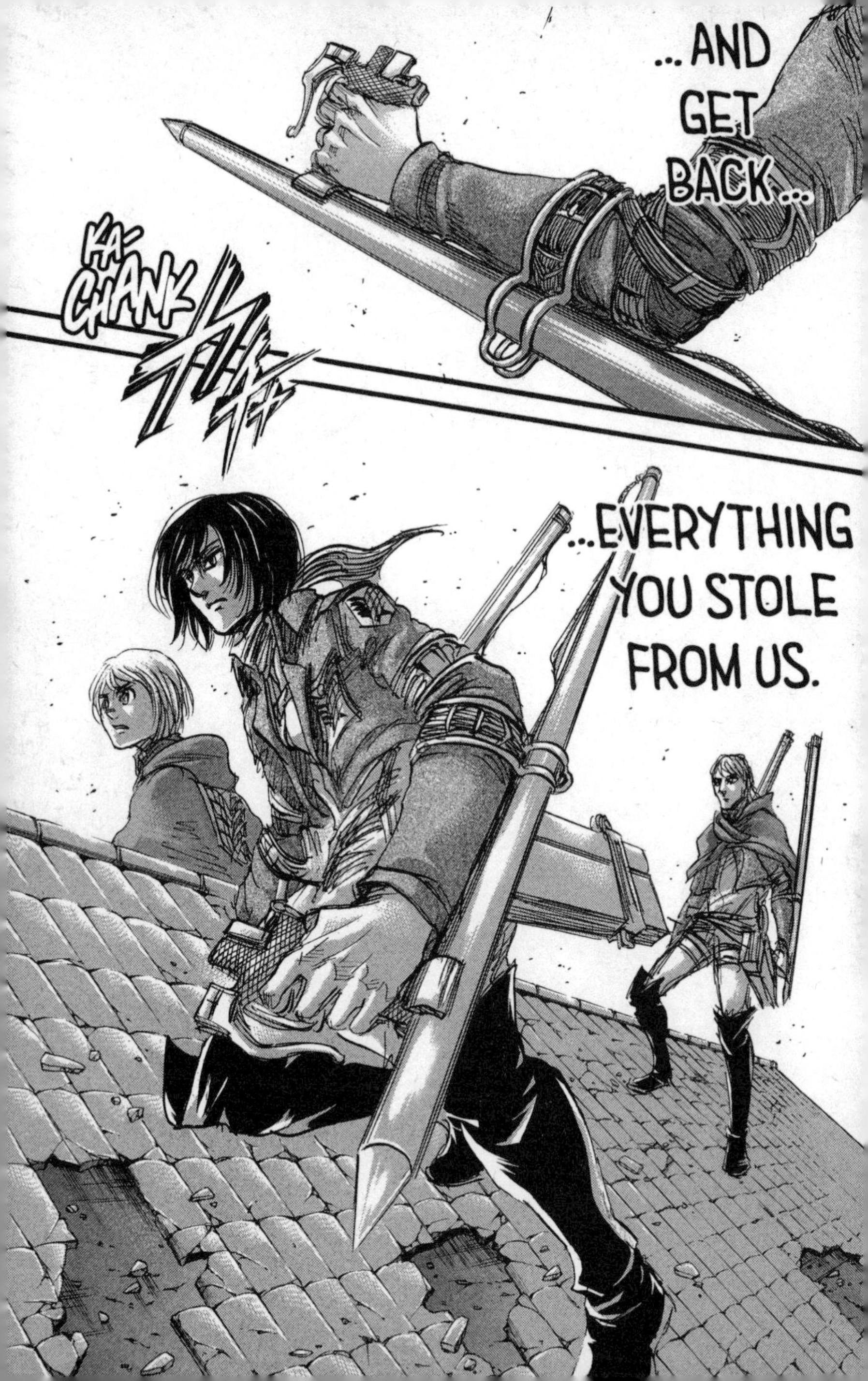
...AND GET BACK...
KA-CHANK
...EVERYTHING YOU STOLE FROM US.

ATTACK on TITAN

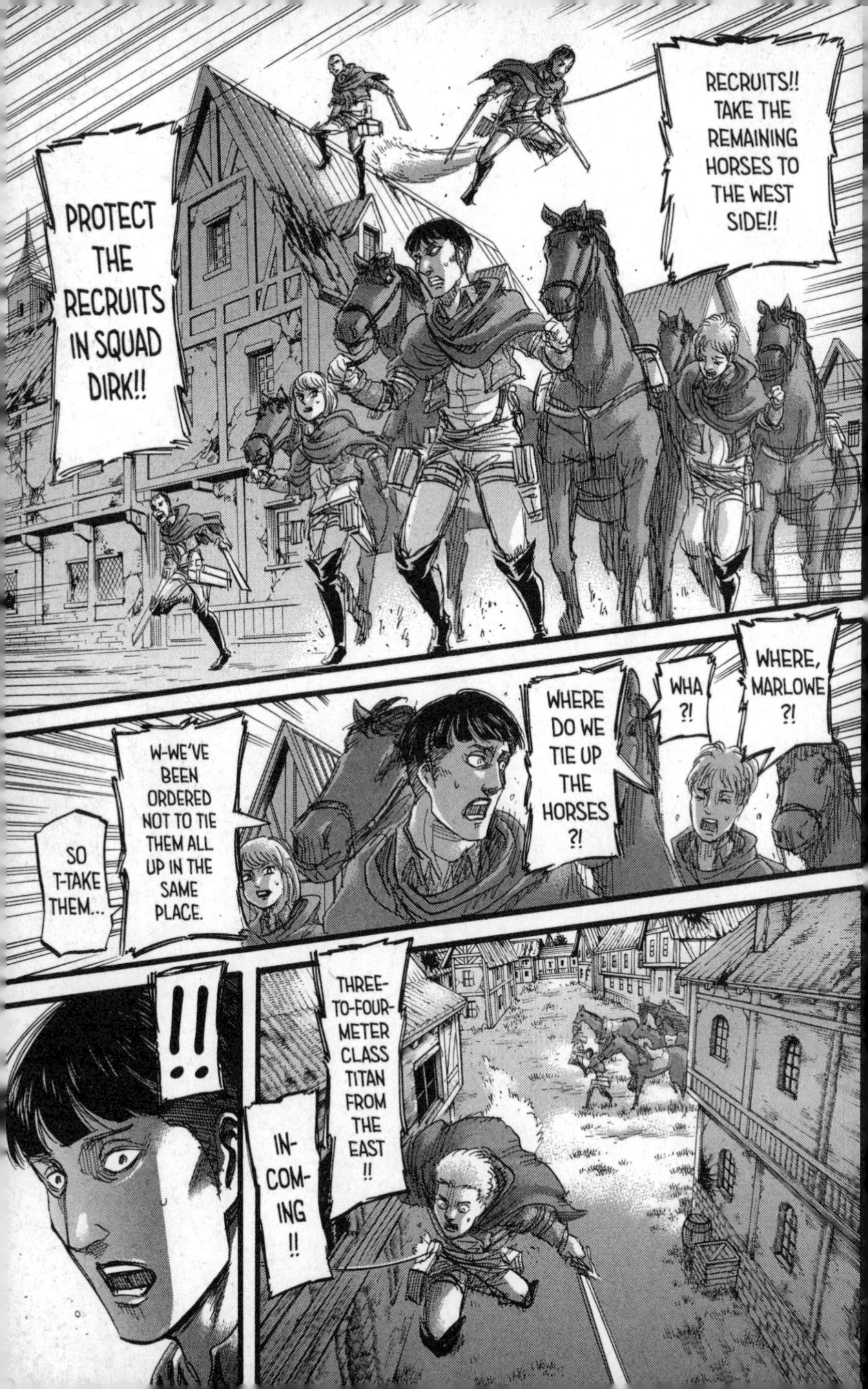
RECRUITS!! TAKE THE REMAINING HORSES TO THE WEST SIDE!!
PROTECT THE RECRUITS IN SQUAD DIRK!!
WHERE, MARLOWE?!
WHA?!
WHERE DO WE TIE UP THE HORSES?!
W-WE'VE BEEN ORDERED NOT TO TIE THEM ALL UP IN THE SAME PLACE.
SO T-TAKE THEM...
THREE-TO-FOUR-METER CLASS TITAN FROM THE EAST!!
IN-COMING!!
!!

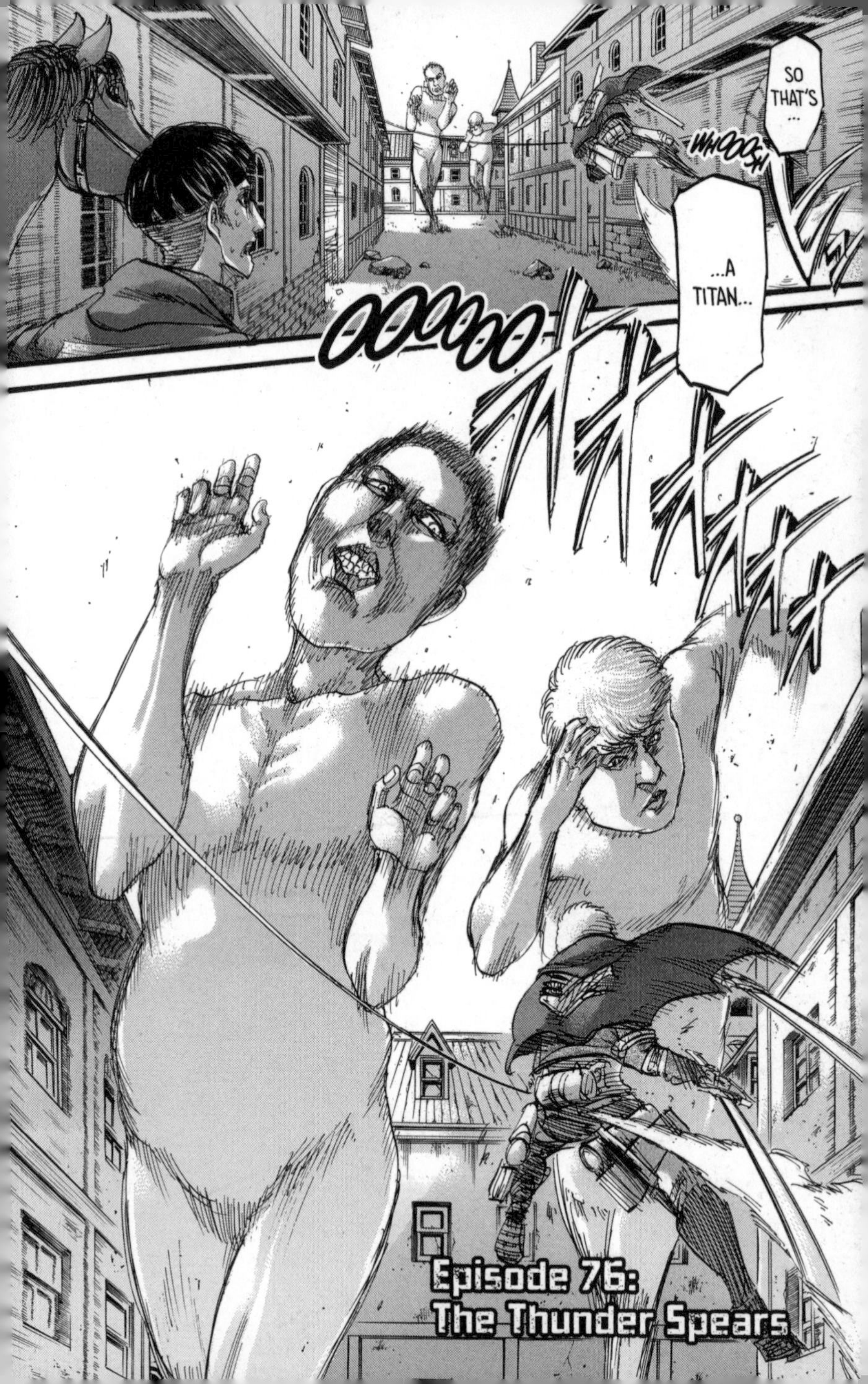
SO THAT'S ...
WHOOOSH
...A TITAN...
OOOOOOO
Episode 76: The Thunder Spears

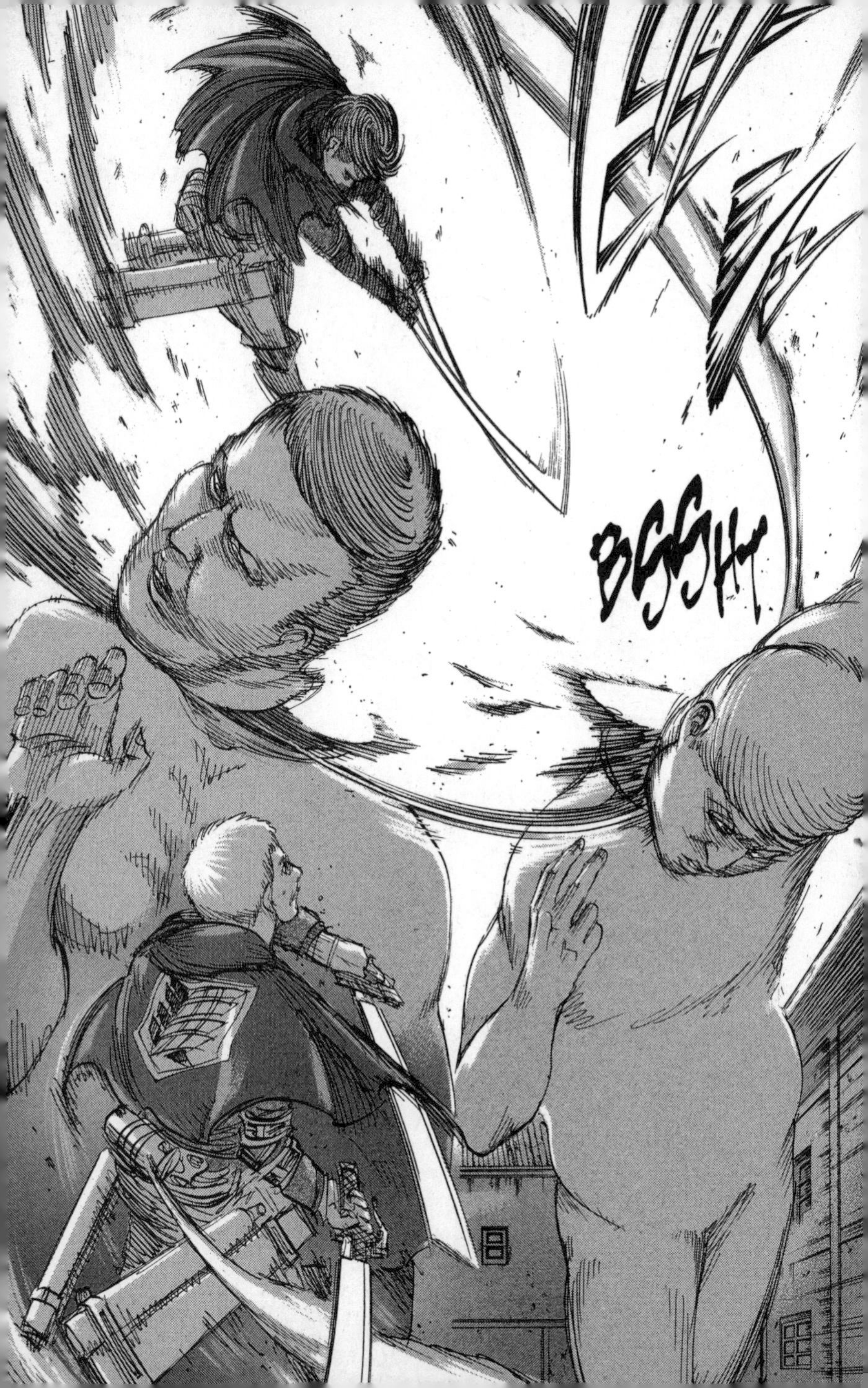

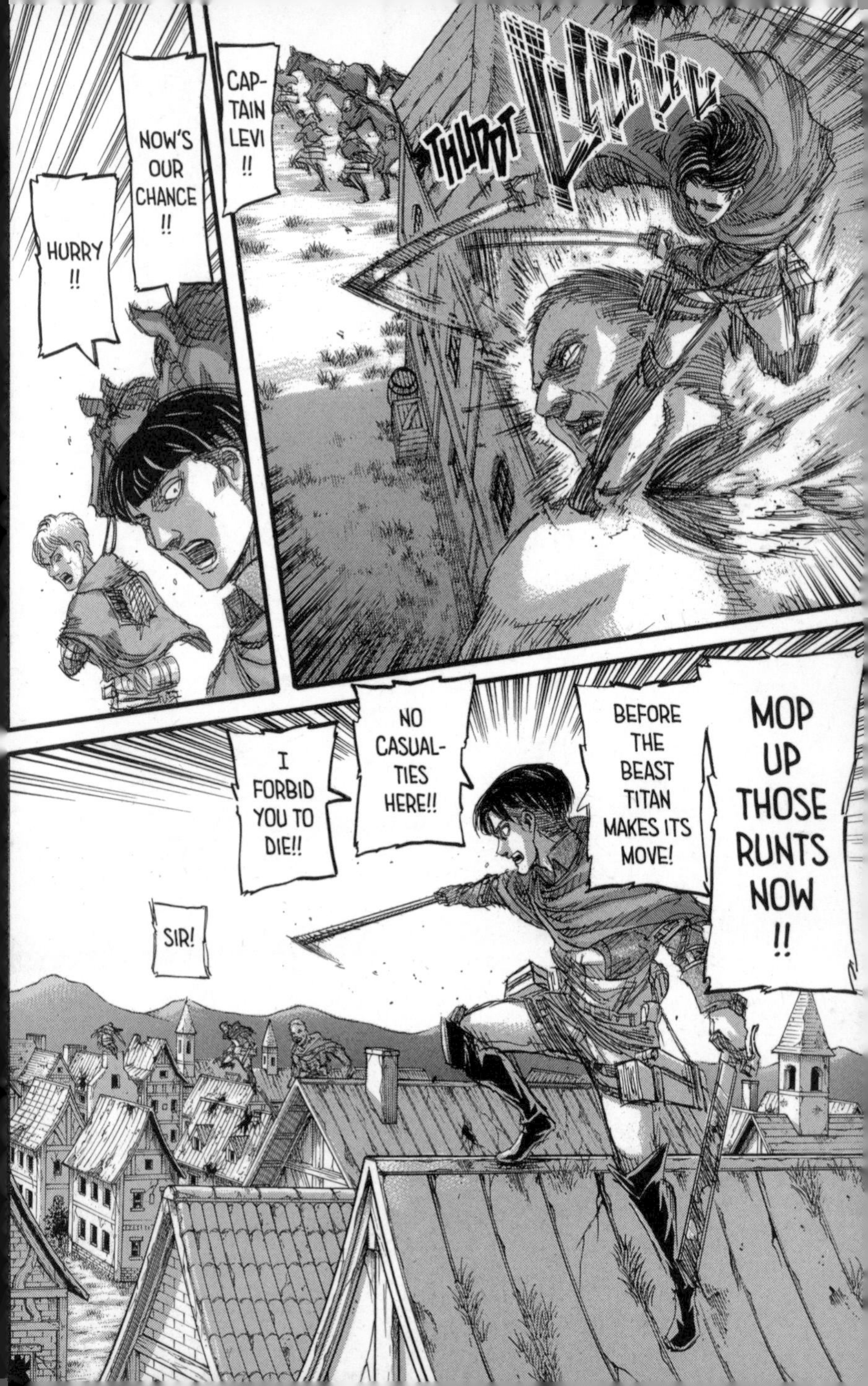
THUDDT
CAPTAIN LEVI!!
NOW'S OUR CHANCE!!
HURRY!!
MOP UP THOSE RUNTS NOW!!
BEFORE THE BEAST TITAN MAKES ITS MOVE!
NO CASUALTIES HERE!!
I FORBID YOU TO DIE!!
SIR!

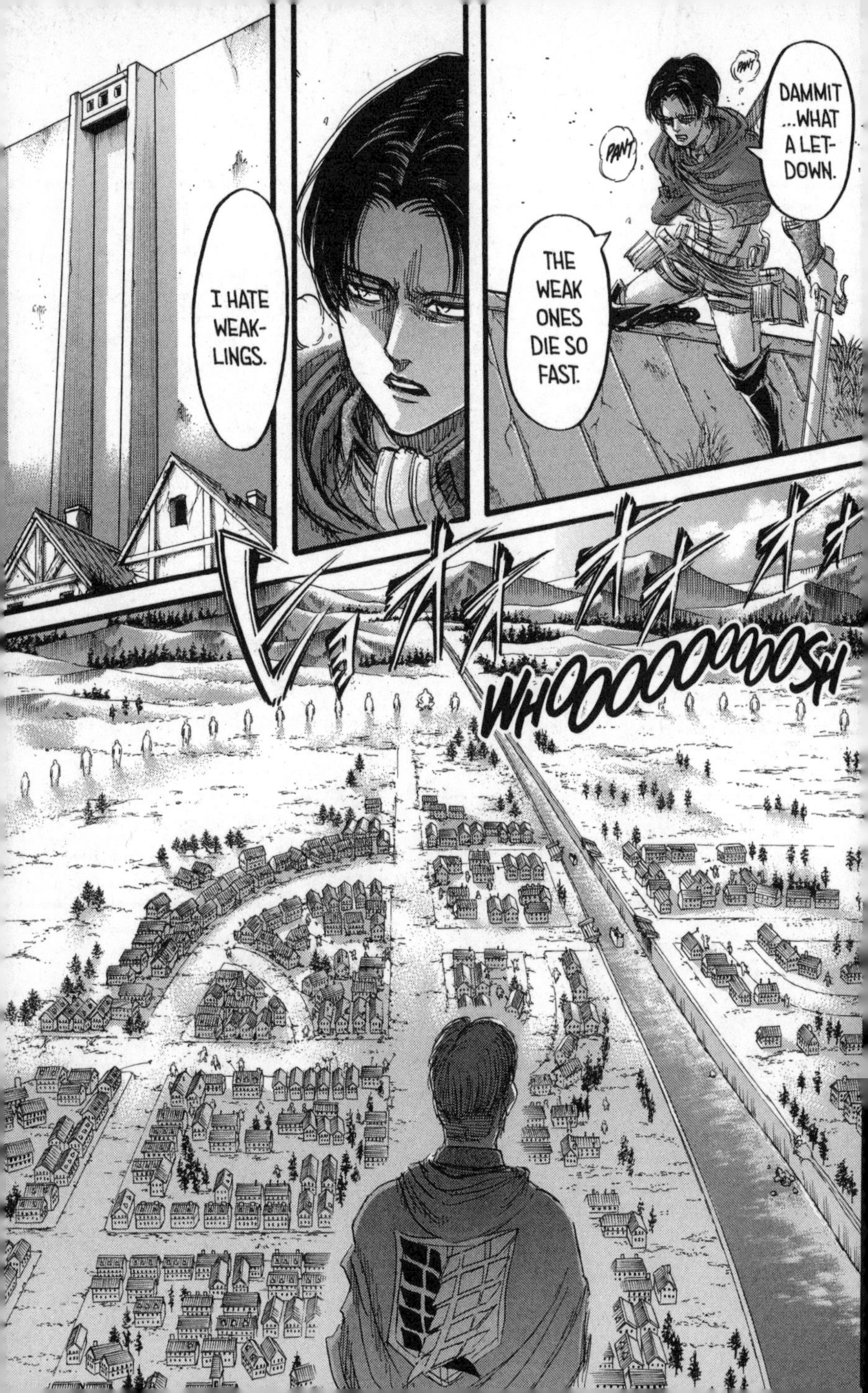
PANT
PANT
DAMMIT ...WHAT A LET-DOWN.
THE WEAK ONES DIE SO FAST.
I HATE WEAK-LINGS.
WHOOOOOOOOOSH

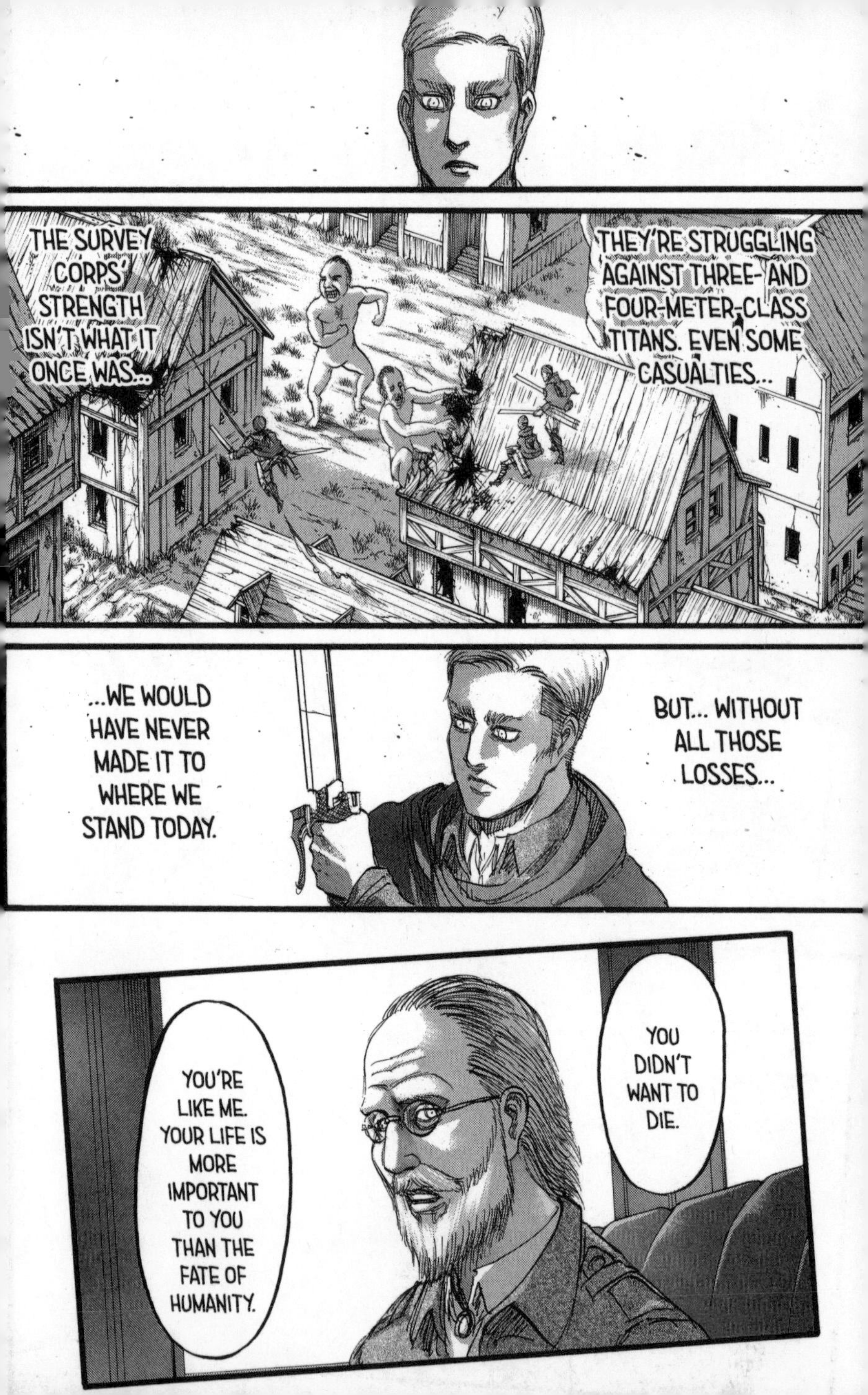
THEY'RE STRUGGLING AGAINST THREE- AND FOUR-METER-CLASS TITANS. EVEN SOME CASUALTIES...
THE SURVEY CORPS' STRENGTH ISN'T WHAT IT ONCE WAS...
BUT... WITHOUT ALL THOSE LOSSES...
...WE WOULD HAVE NEVER MADE IT TO WHERE WE STAND TODAY.
YOU DIDN'T WANT TO DIE.
YOU'RE LIKE ME. YOUR LIFE IS MORE IMPORTANT TO YOU THAN THE FATE OF HUMANITY.

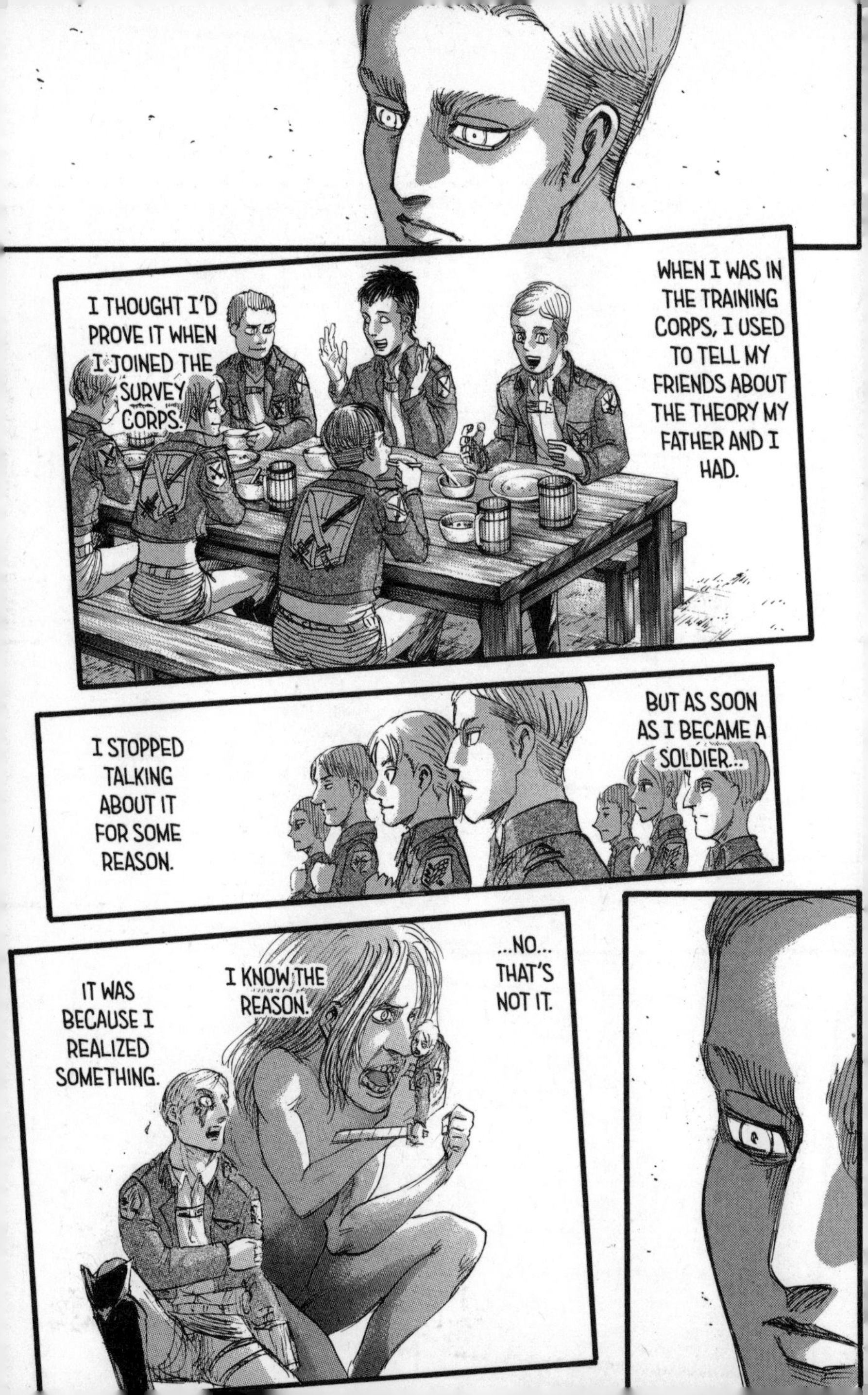
WHEN I WAS IN THE TRAINING CORPS, I USED TO TELL MY FRIENDS ABOUT THE THEORY MY FATHER AND I HAD.
I THOUGHT I'D PROVE IT WHEN I JOINED THE SURVEY CORPS.
BUT AS SOON AS I BECAME A SOLDIER...
I STOPPED TALKING ABOUT IT FOR SOME REASON.
...NO... THAT'S NOT IT.
I KNOW THE REASON.
IT WAS BECAUSE I REALIZED SOMETHING.

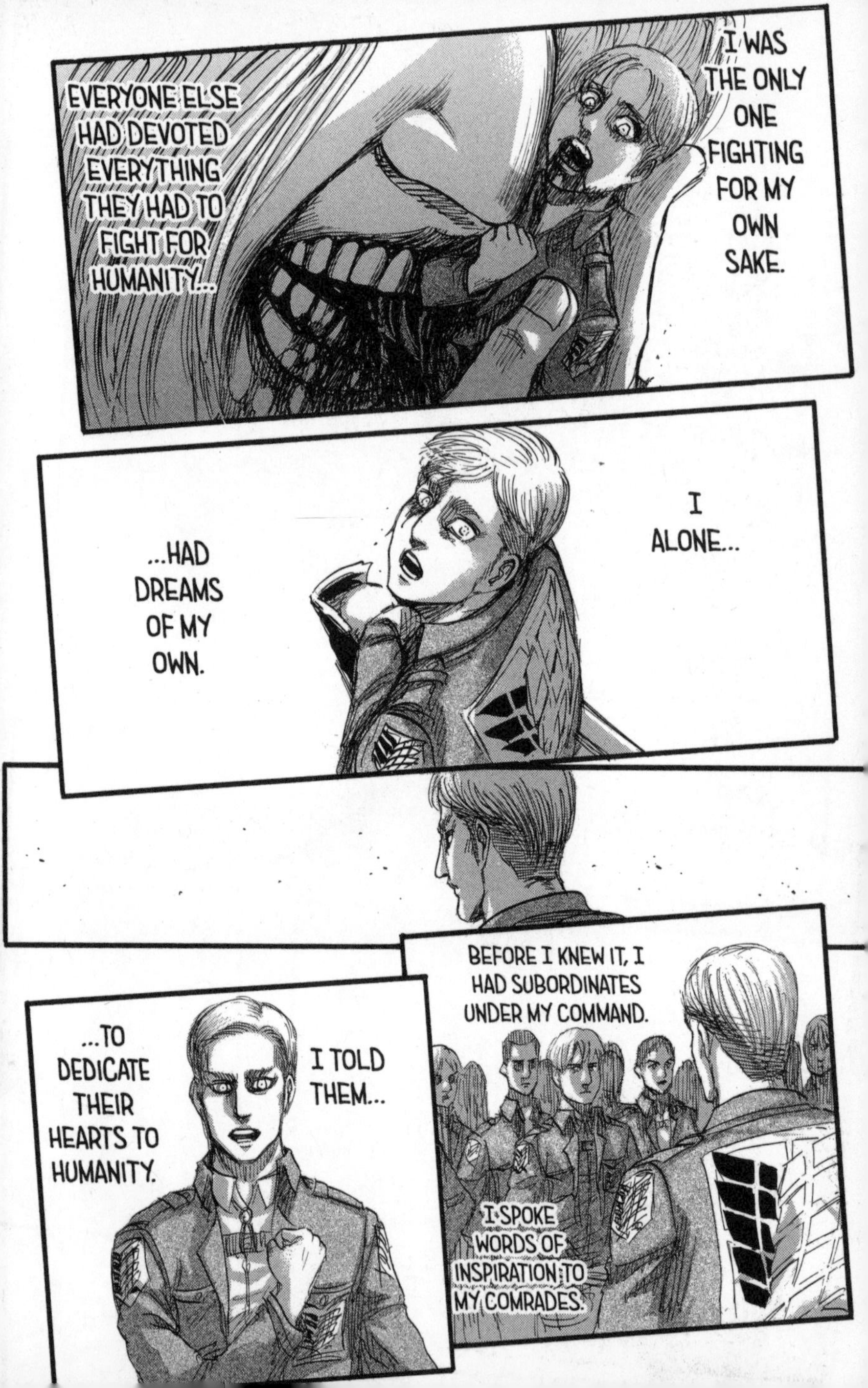
I WAS THE ONLY ONE FIGHTING FOR MY OWN SAKE.
EVERYONE ELSE HAD DEVOTED EVERYTHING THEY HAD TO FIGHT FOR HUMANITY...
I ALONE...
...HAD DREAMS OF MY OWN.
BEFORE I KNEW IT, I HAD SUBORDINATES UNDER MY COMMAND.
I SPOKE WORDS OF INSPIRATION TO MY COMRADES.
I TOLD THEM...
...TO DEDICATE THEIR HEARTS TO HUMANITY.

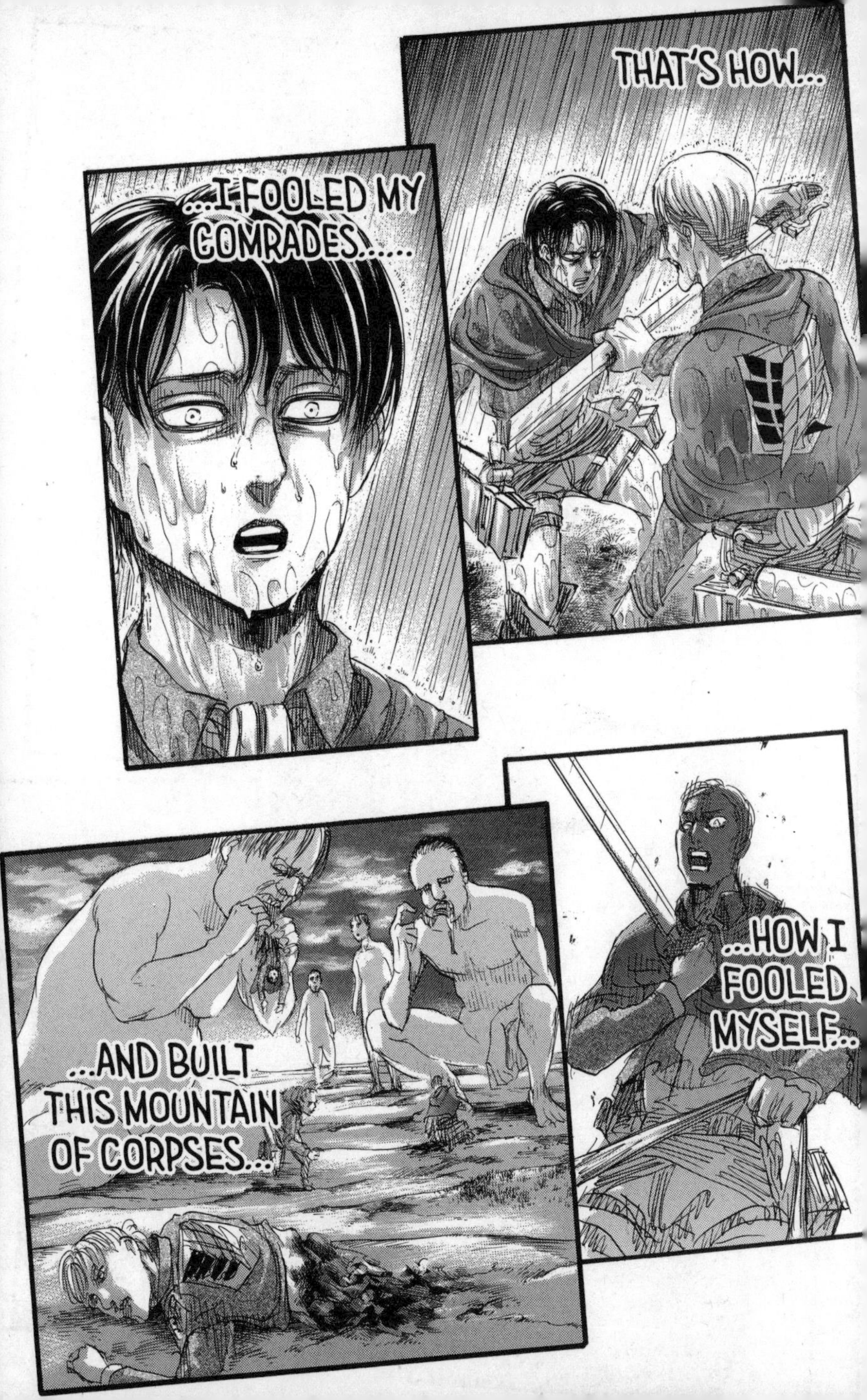
THAT'S HOW...
...I FOOLED MY COMRADES......
...HOW I FOOLED MYSELF...
...AND BUILT THIS MOUNTAIN OF CORPSES...

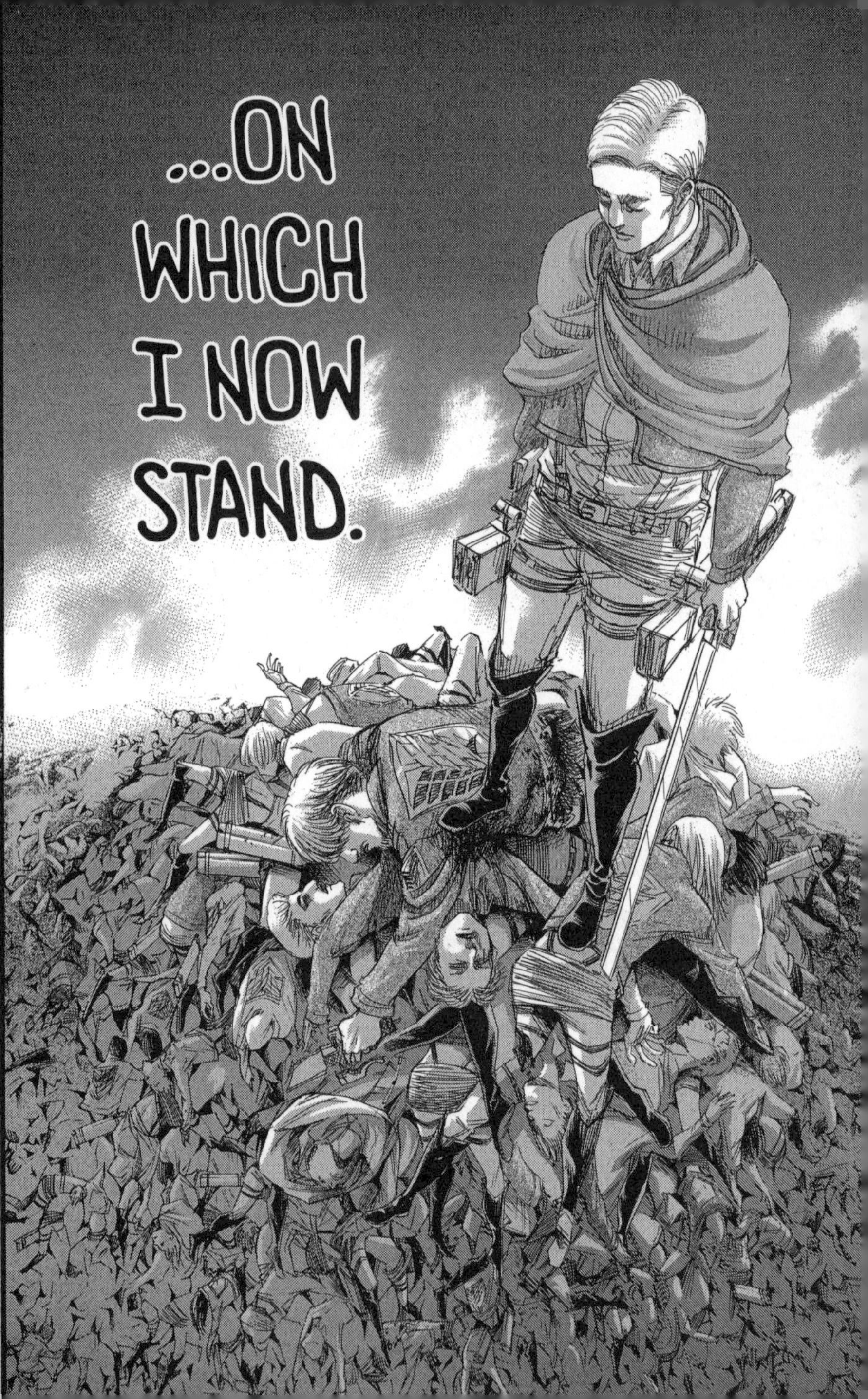
...ON WHICH I NOW STAND.

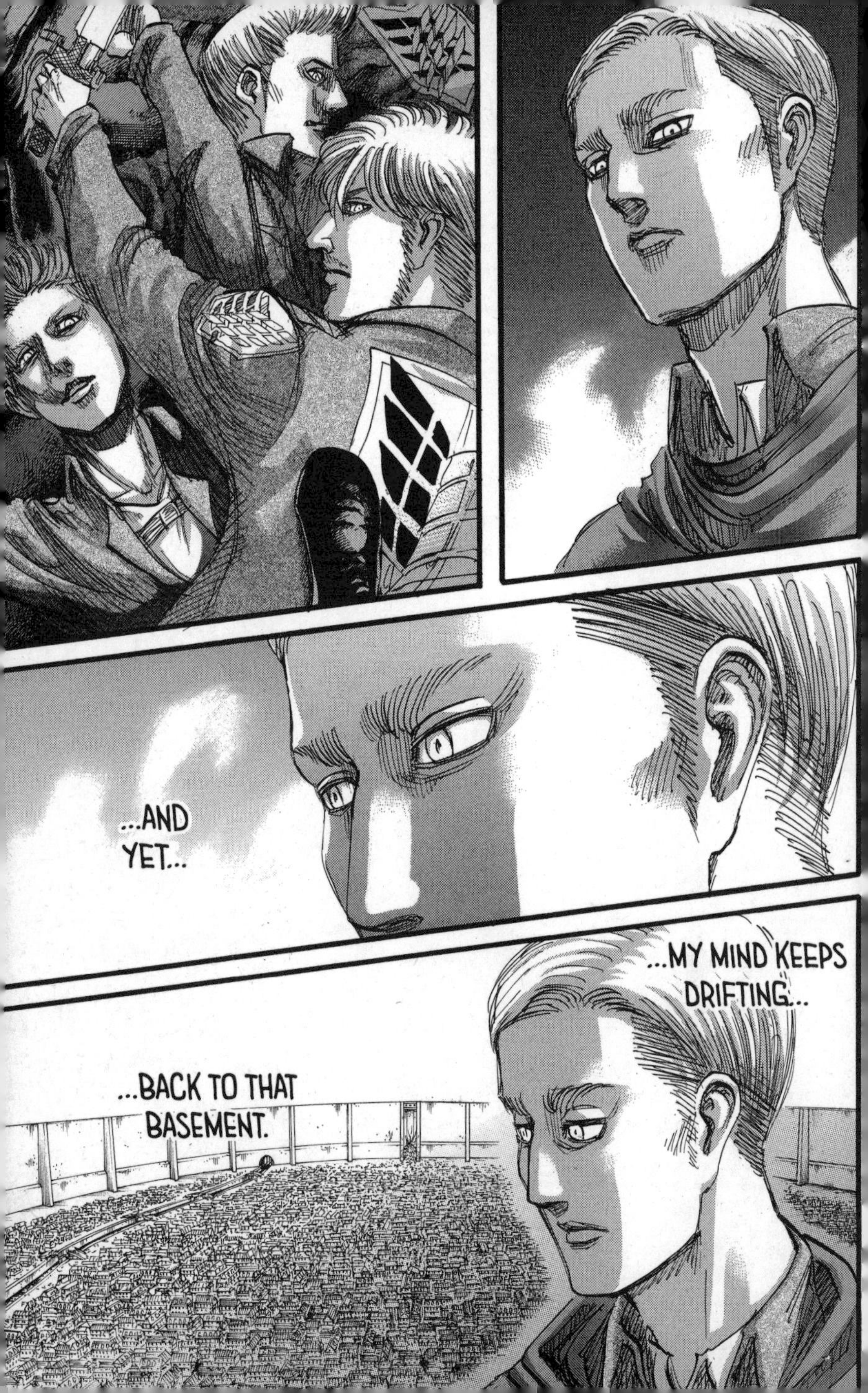
...AND YET...
...MY MIND KEEPS DRIFTING...
...BACK TO THAT BASEMENT.

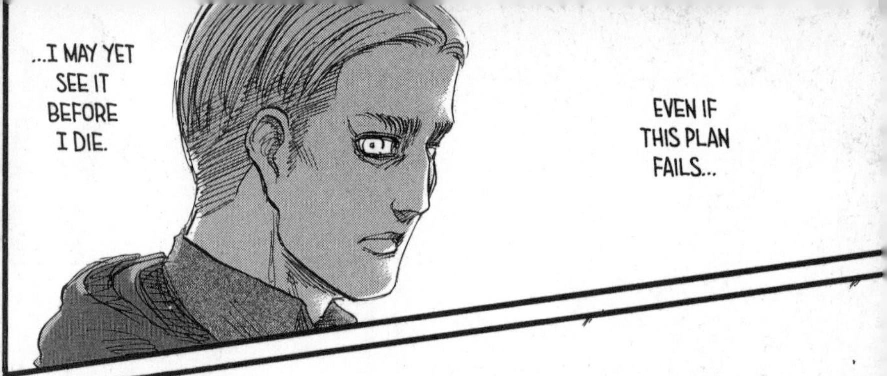
EVEN IF THIS PLAN FAILS...
...I MAY YET SEE IT BEFORE I DIE.

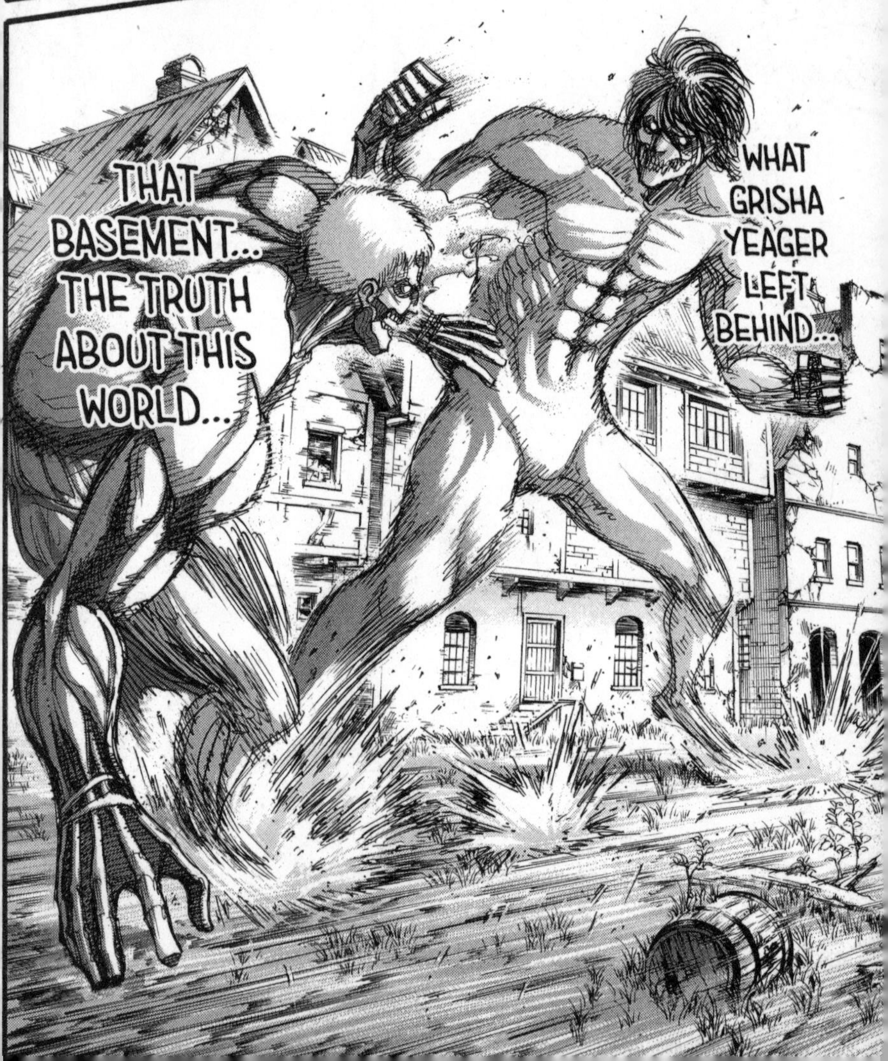
WHAT GRISHA YEAGER LEFT BEHIND...
THAT BASEMENT... THE TRUTH ABOUT THIS WORLD...

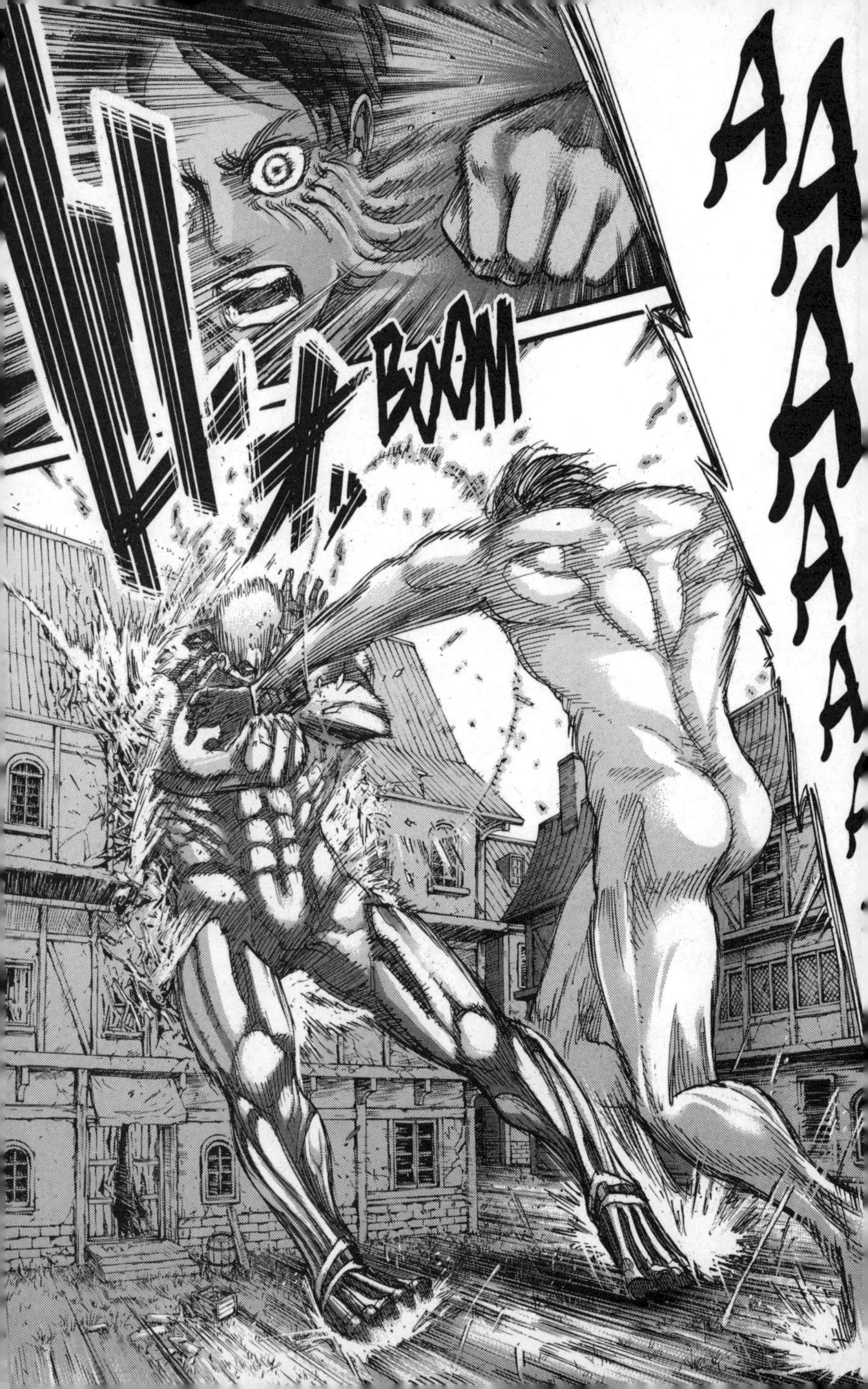
AAAAAAA
BOOM

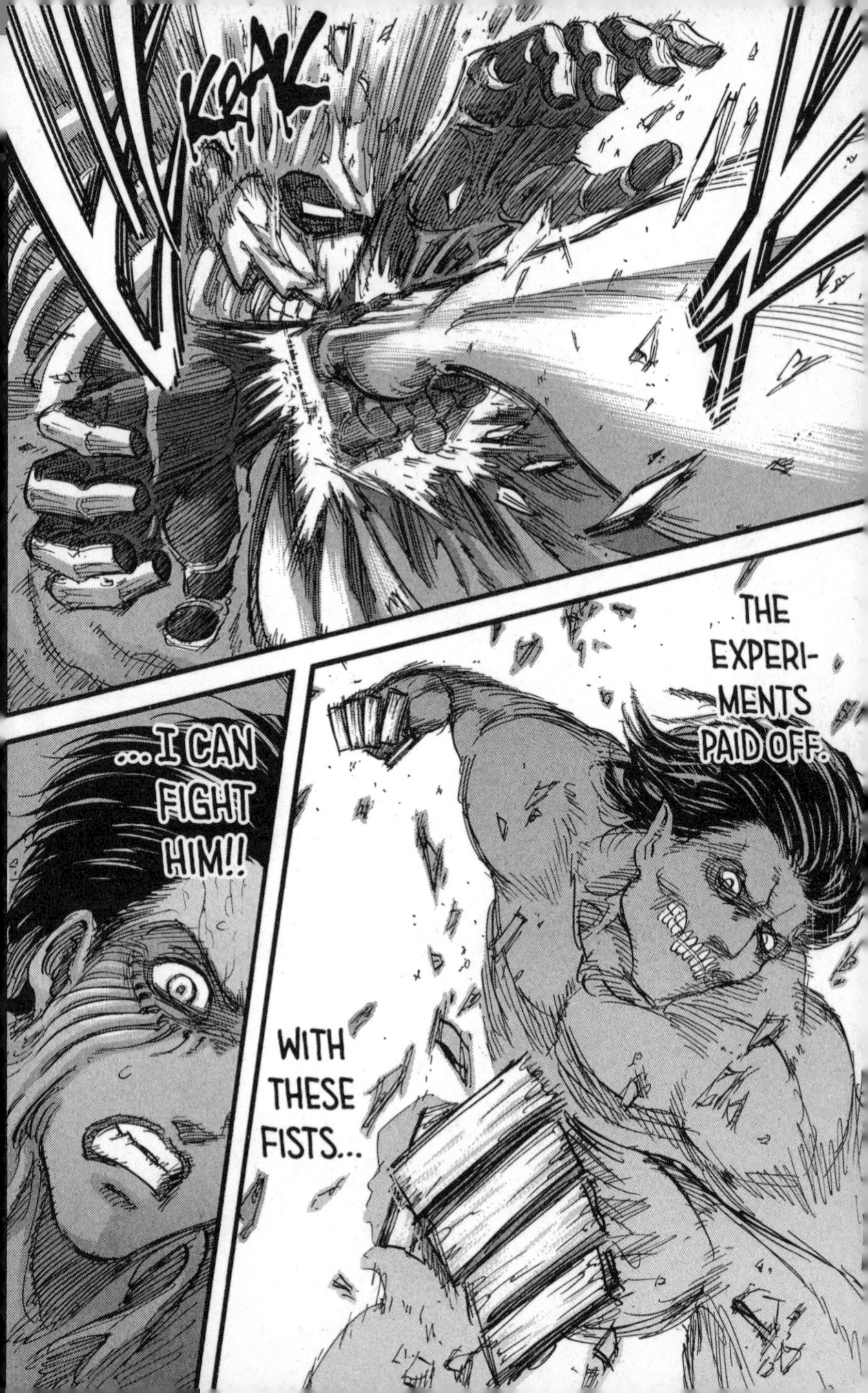
KRAK
THE EXPERI-MENTS PAID OFF.
WITH THESE FISTS...
...I CAN FIGHT HIM!!

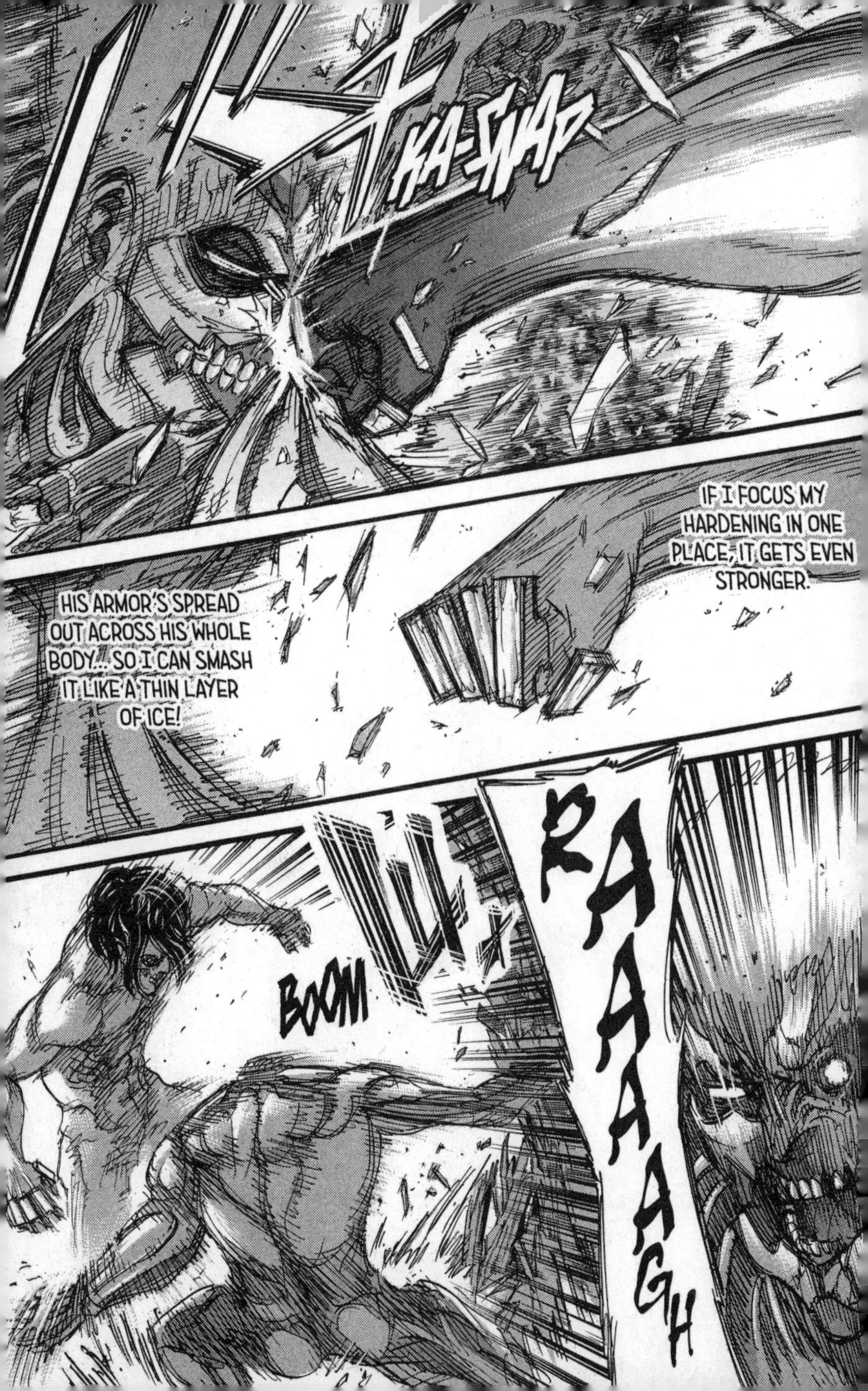
KA-SNAP
IF I FOCUS MY HARDENING IN ONE PLACE, IT GETS EVEN STRONGER.
HIS ARMOR'S SPREAD OUT ACROSS HIS WHOLE BODY... SO I CAN SMASH IT LIKE A THIN LAYER OF ICE!
RAAAAAGH
BOOM

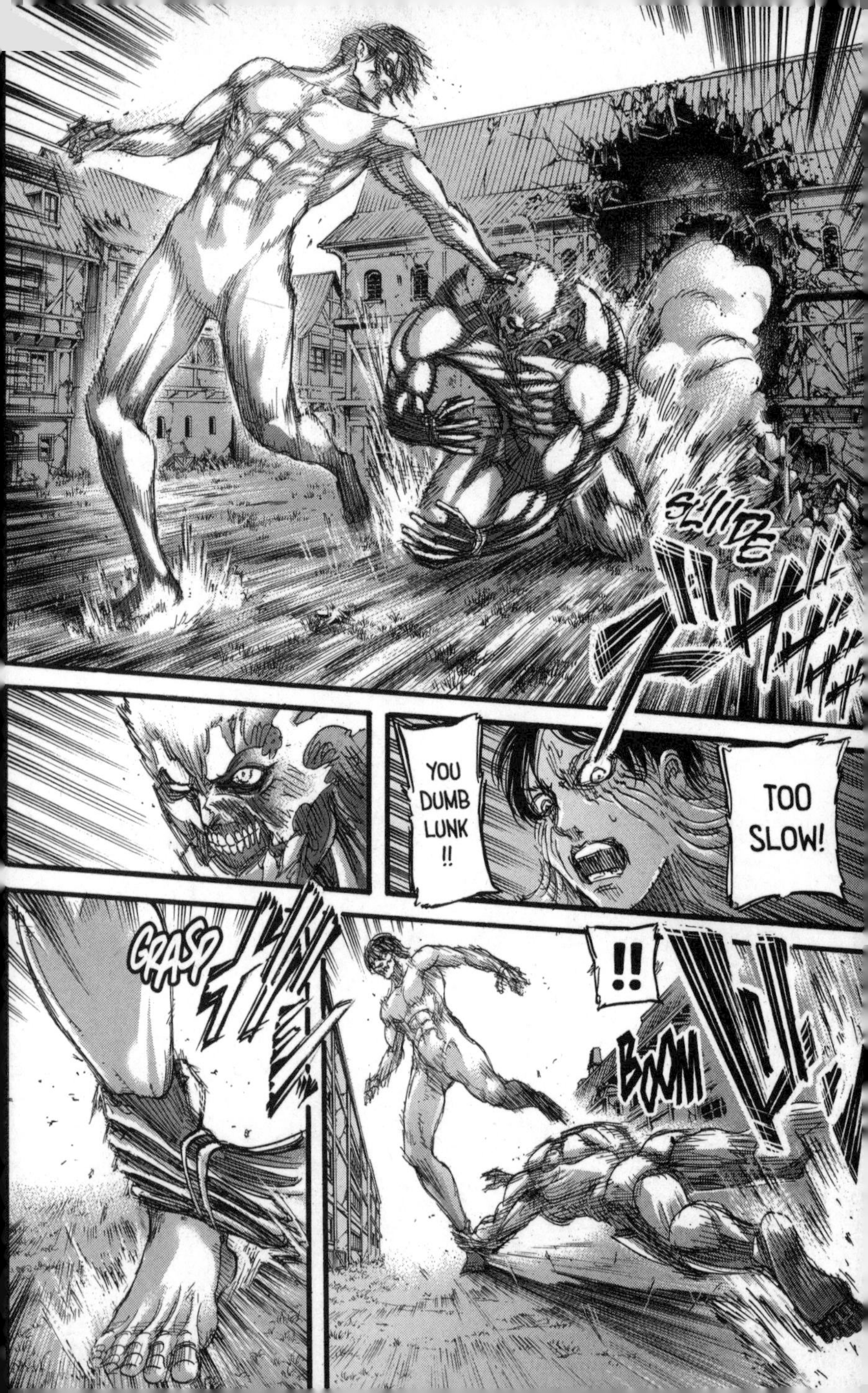
SLIIDE
TOO SLOW!
YOU DUMB LUNK !!
!!
BOOM
GRASP

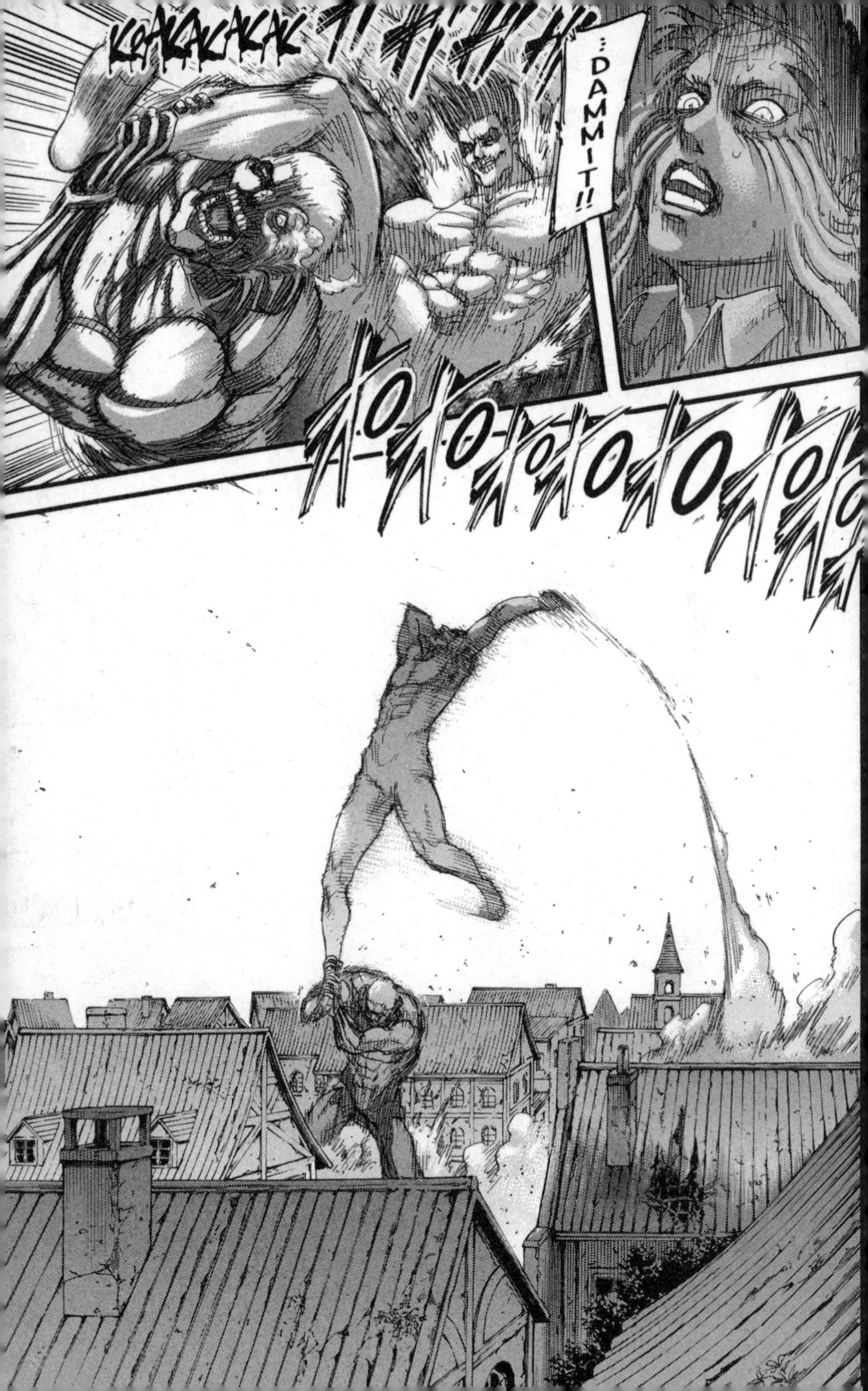
...DAMMIT!!
KRAKAKAKAK

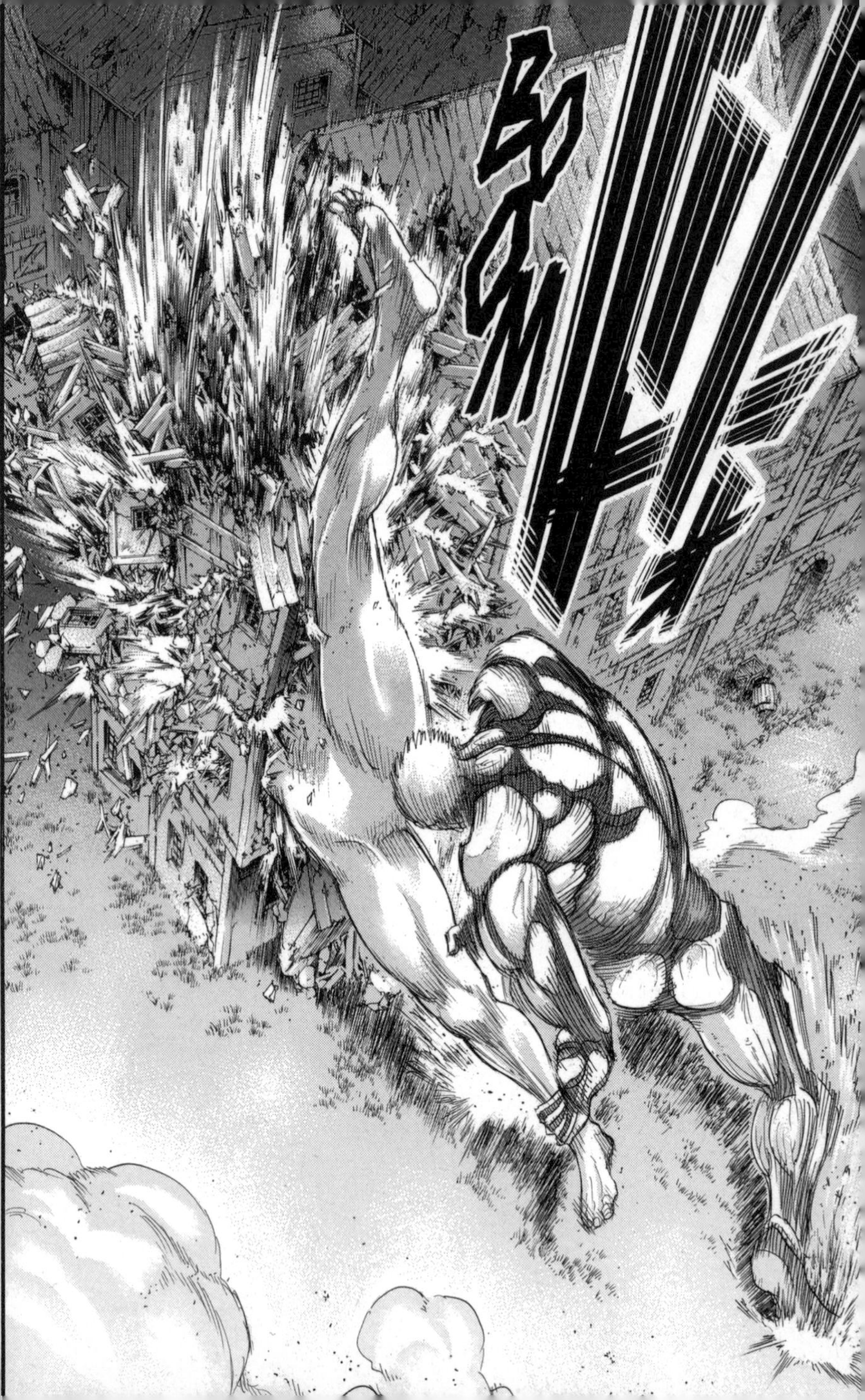

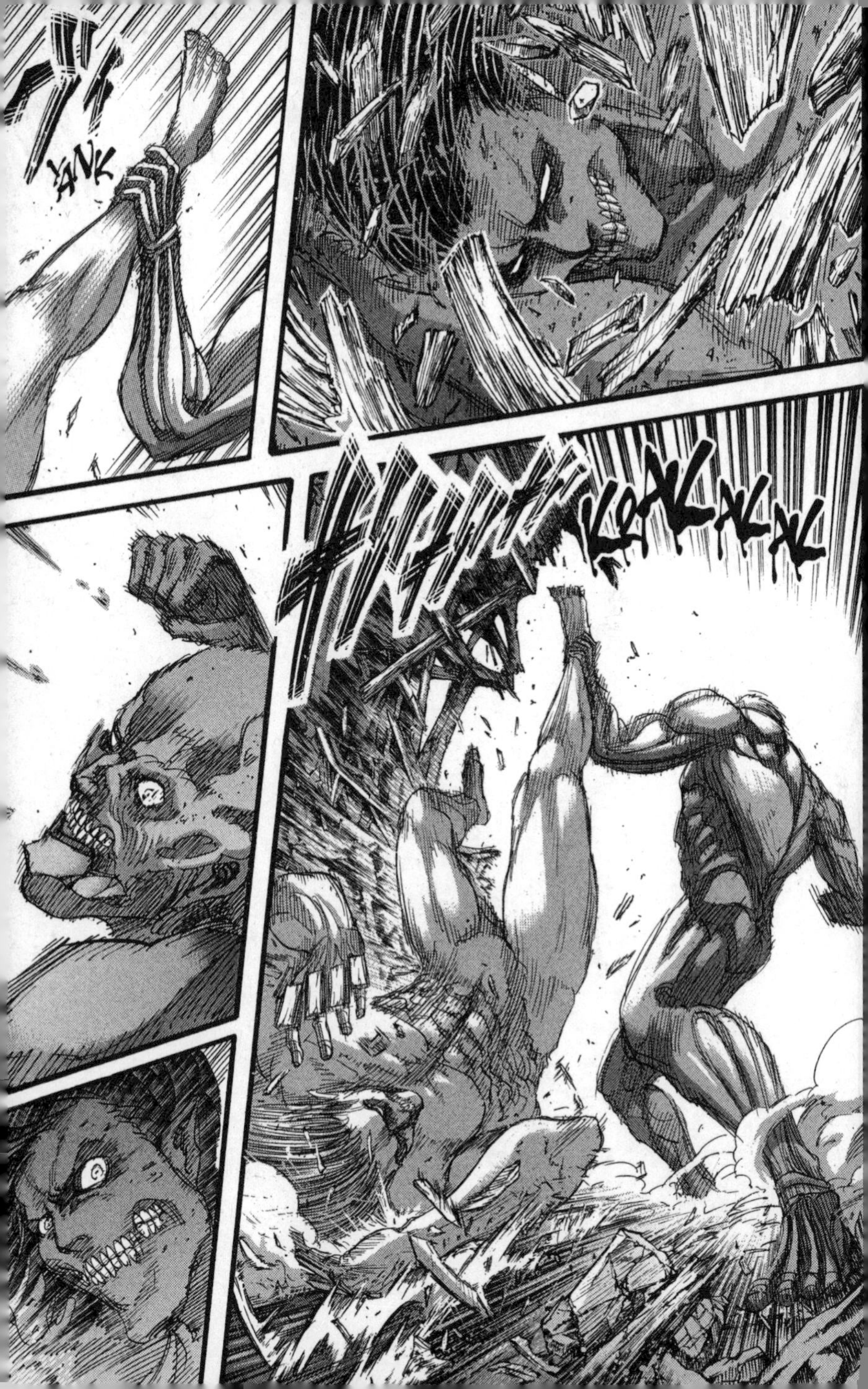
YANK
KRAKAKAK

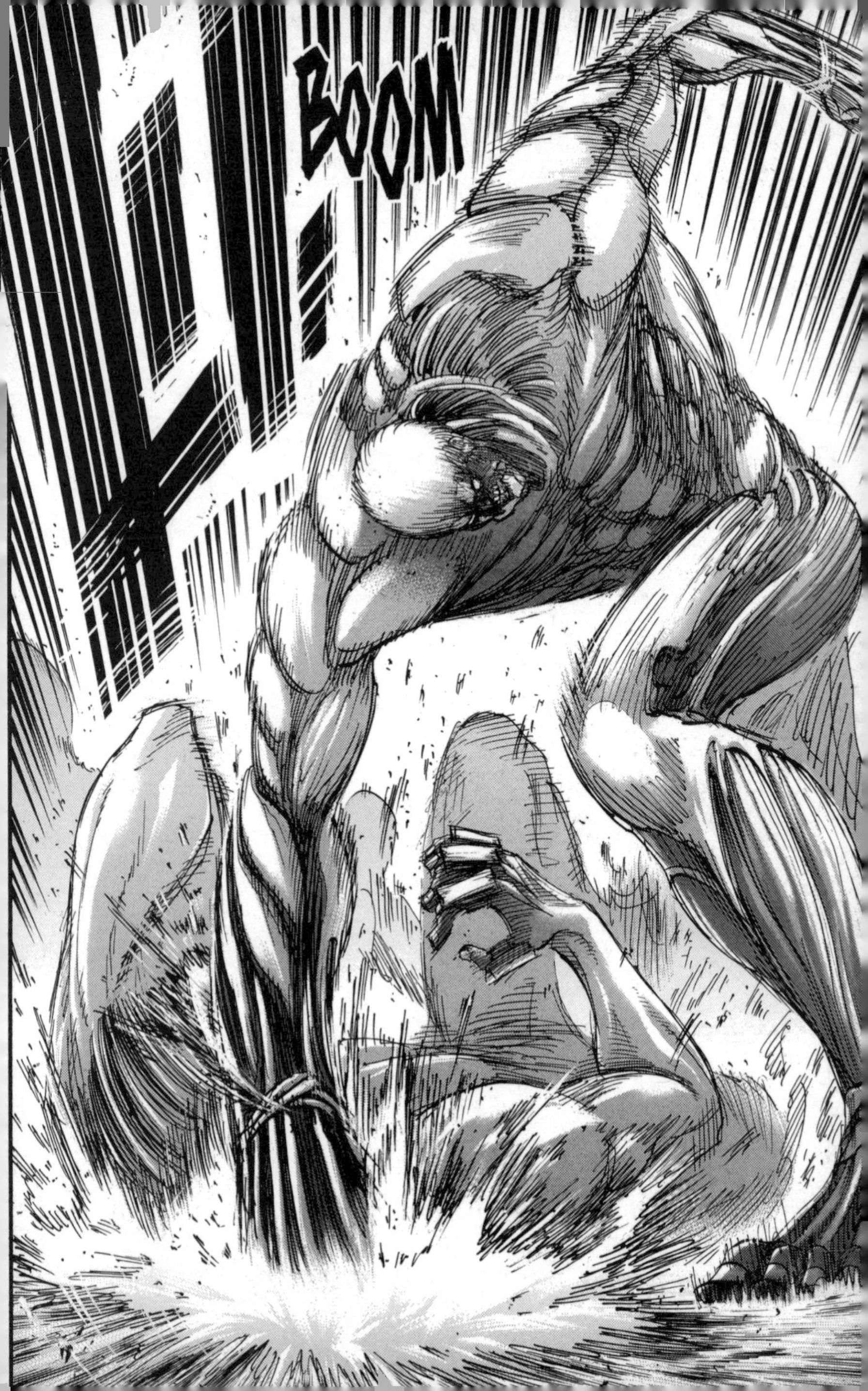
BOOM

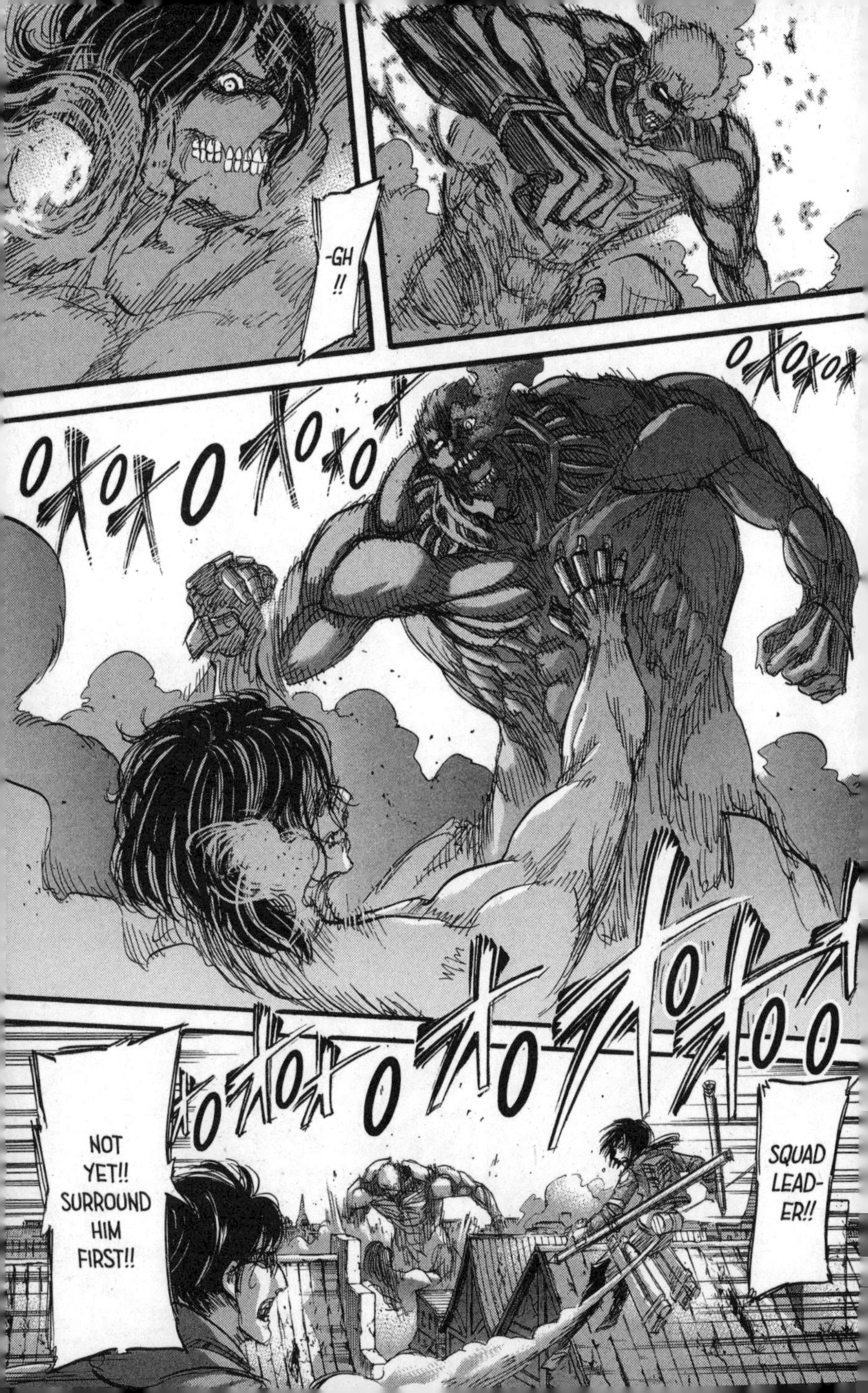

-GH !!
SQUAD LEAD-ER!!
NOT YET!! SURROUND HIM FIRST!!

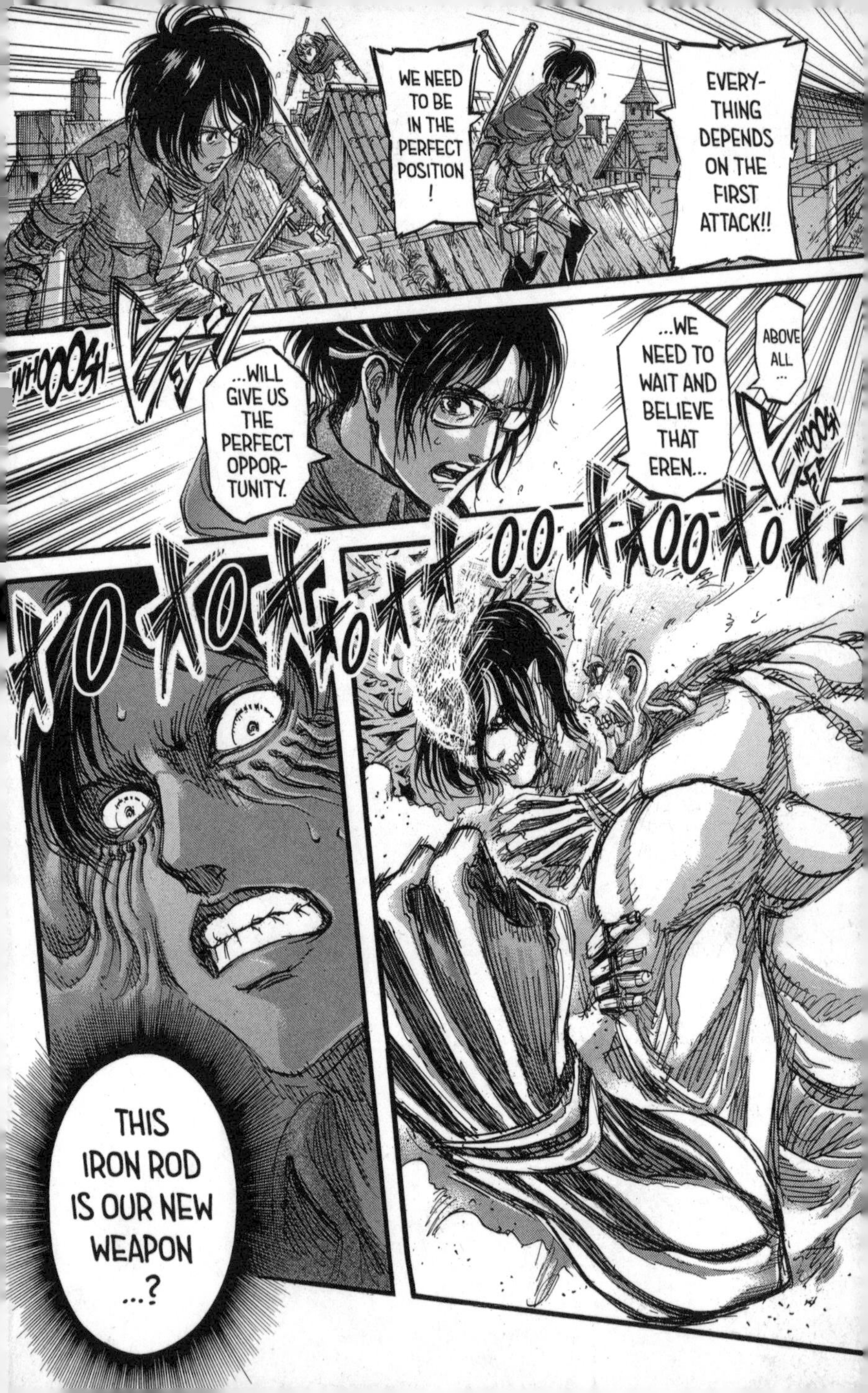
EVERY-THING DEPENDS ON THE FIRST ATTACK!!
WE NEED TO BE IN THE PERFECT POSITION!
WHOOOSH
ABOVE ALL...
...WE NEED TO WAIT AND BELIEVE THAT EREN...
...WILL GIVE US THE PERFECT OPPOR-TUNITY.
WHOOOSH
THIS IRON ROD IS OUR NEW WEAPON ...?

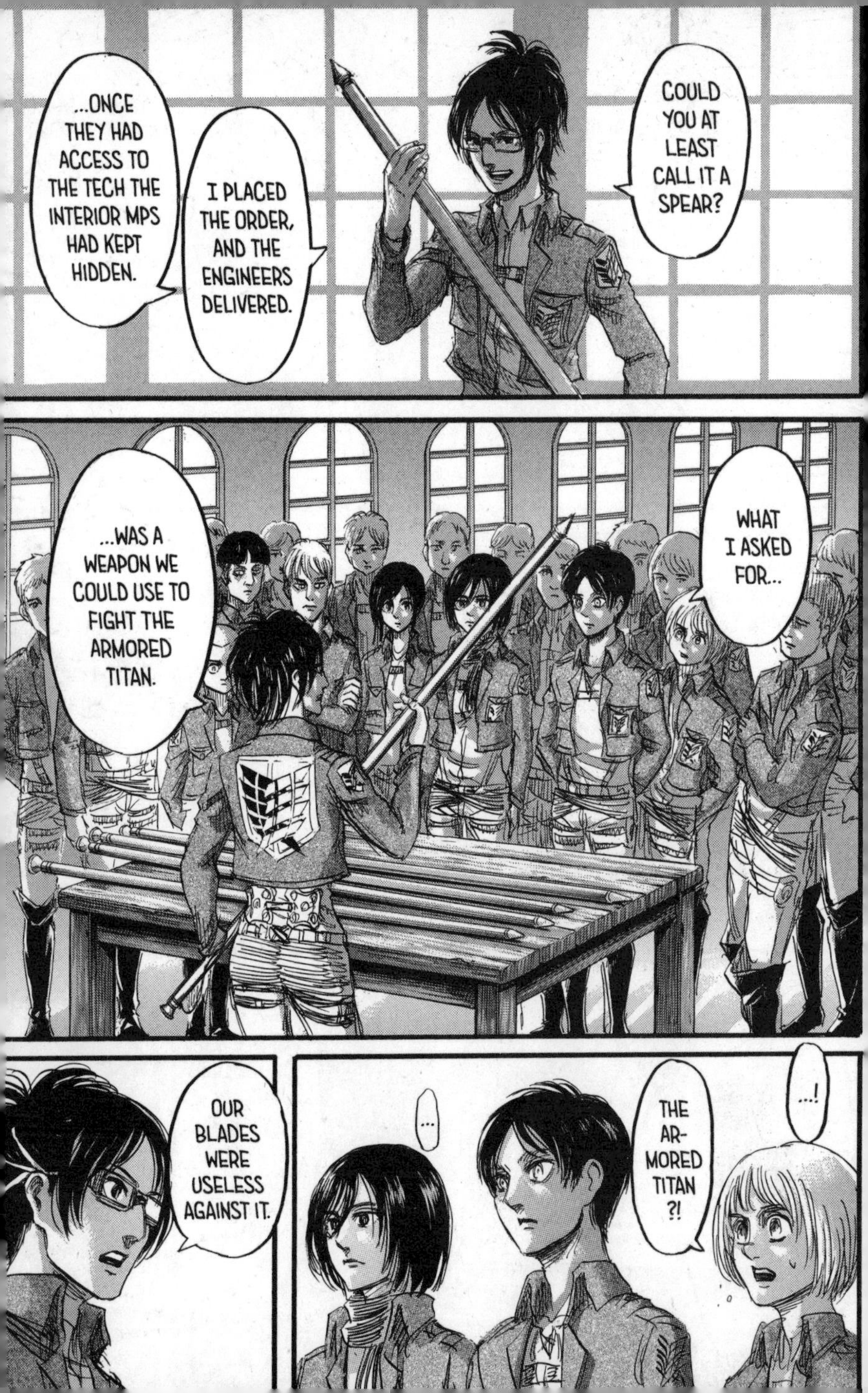
COULD YOU AT LEAST CALL IT A SPEAR?
I PLACED THE ORDER, AND THE ENGINEERS DELIVERED.
...ONCE THEY HAD ACCESS TO THE TECH THE INTERIOR MPS HAD KEPT HIDDEN.
WHAT I ASKED FOR...
...WAS A WEAPON WE COULD USE TO FIGHT THE ARMORED TITAN.
...!
THE AR-MORED TITAN?!
...
OUR BLADES WERE USELESS AGAINST IT.

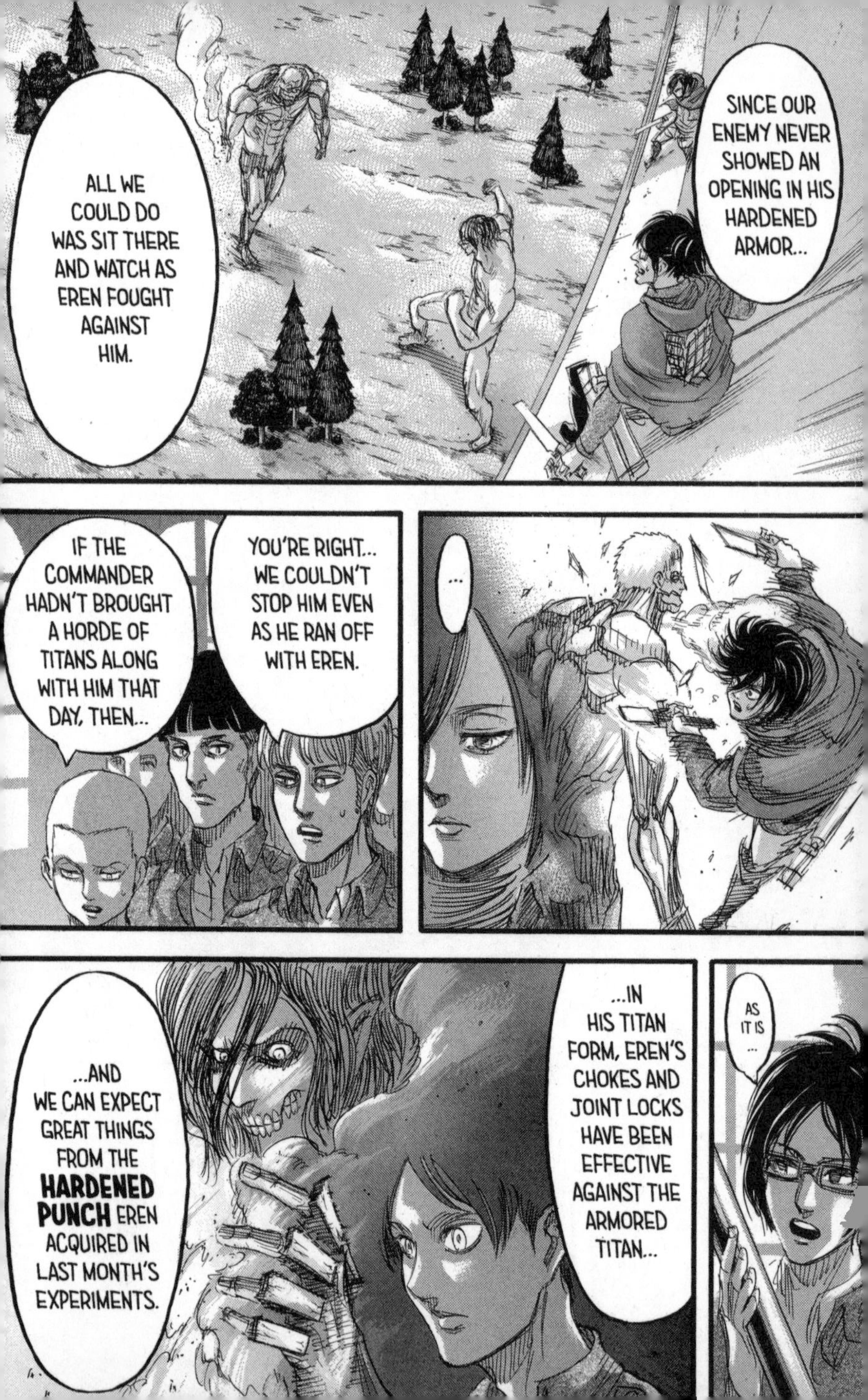
SINCE OUR ENEMY NEVER SHOWED AN OPENING IN HIS HARDENED ARMOR...
ALL WE COULD DO WAS SIT THERE AND WATCH AS EREN FOUGHT AGAINST HIM.
...
YOU'RE RIGHT... WE COULDN'T STOP HIM EVEN AS HE RAN OFF WITH EREN.
IF THE COMMANDER HADN'T BROUGHT A HORDE OF TITANS ALONG WITH HIM THAT DAY, THEN...
AS IT IS...
...IN HIS TITAN FORM, EREN'S CHOKES AND JOINT LOCKS HAVE BEEN EFFECTIVE AGAINST THE ARMORED TITAN...
...AND WE CAN EXPECT GREAT THINGS FROM THE **HARDENED PUNCH** EREN ACQUIRED IN LAST MONTH'S EXPERIMENTS.

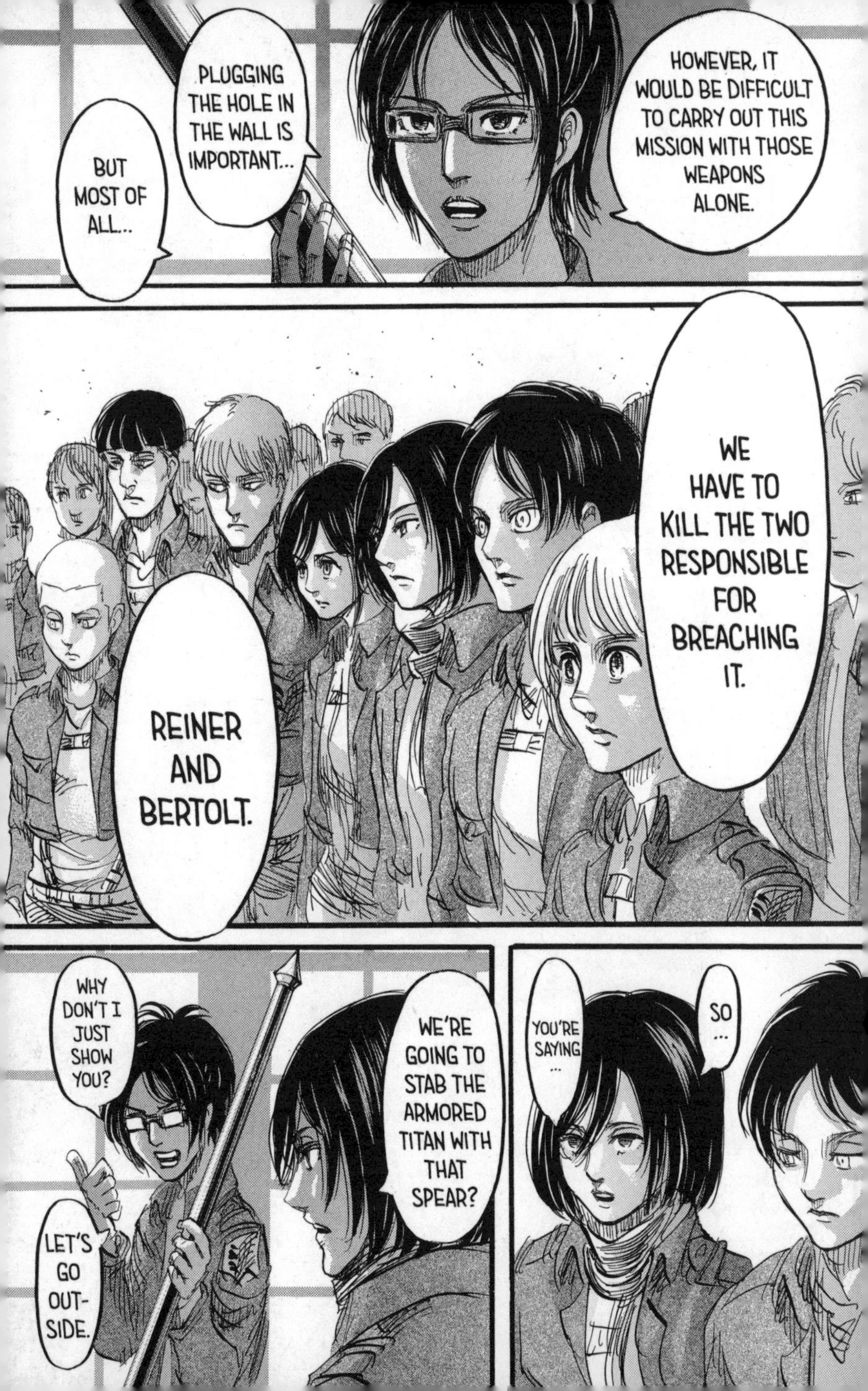
HOWEVER, IT WOULD BE DIFFICULT TO CARRY OUT THIS MISSION WITH THOSE WEAPONS ALONE.
PLUGGING THE HOLE IN THE WALL IS IMPORTANT...
BUT MOST OF ALL...
WE HAVE TO KILL THE TWO RESPONSIBLE FOR BREACHING IT.
REINER AND BERTOLT.
SO...
YOU'RE SAYING...
WE'RE GOING TO STAB THE ARMORED TITAN WITH THAT SPEAR?
WHY DON'T I JUST SHOW YOU?
LET'S GO OUT-SIDE.

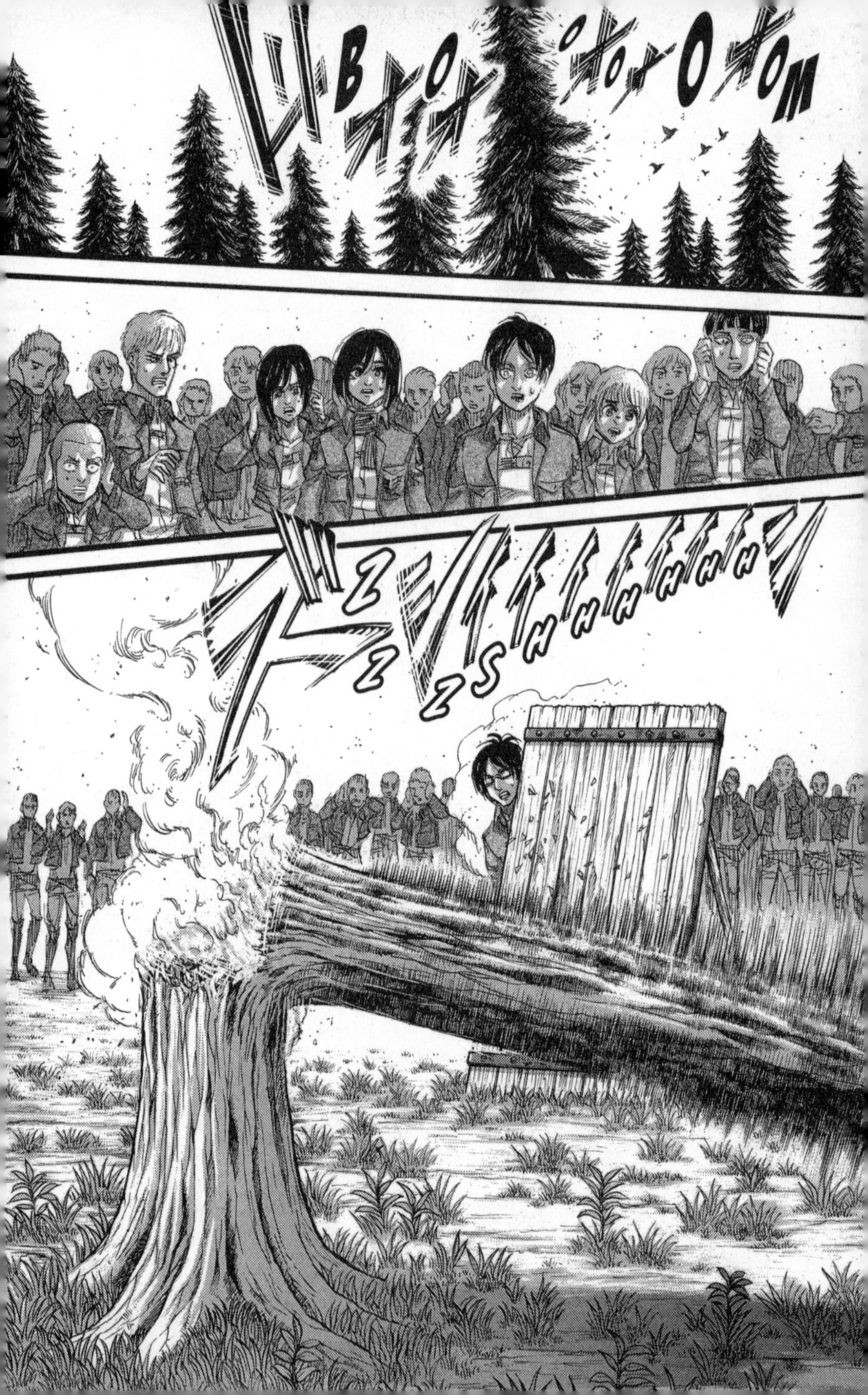
BOOOOOM
ZZZSHHHHHH

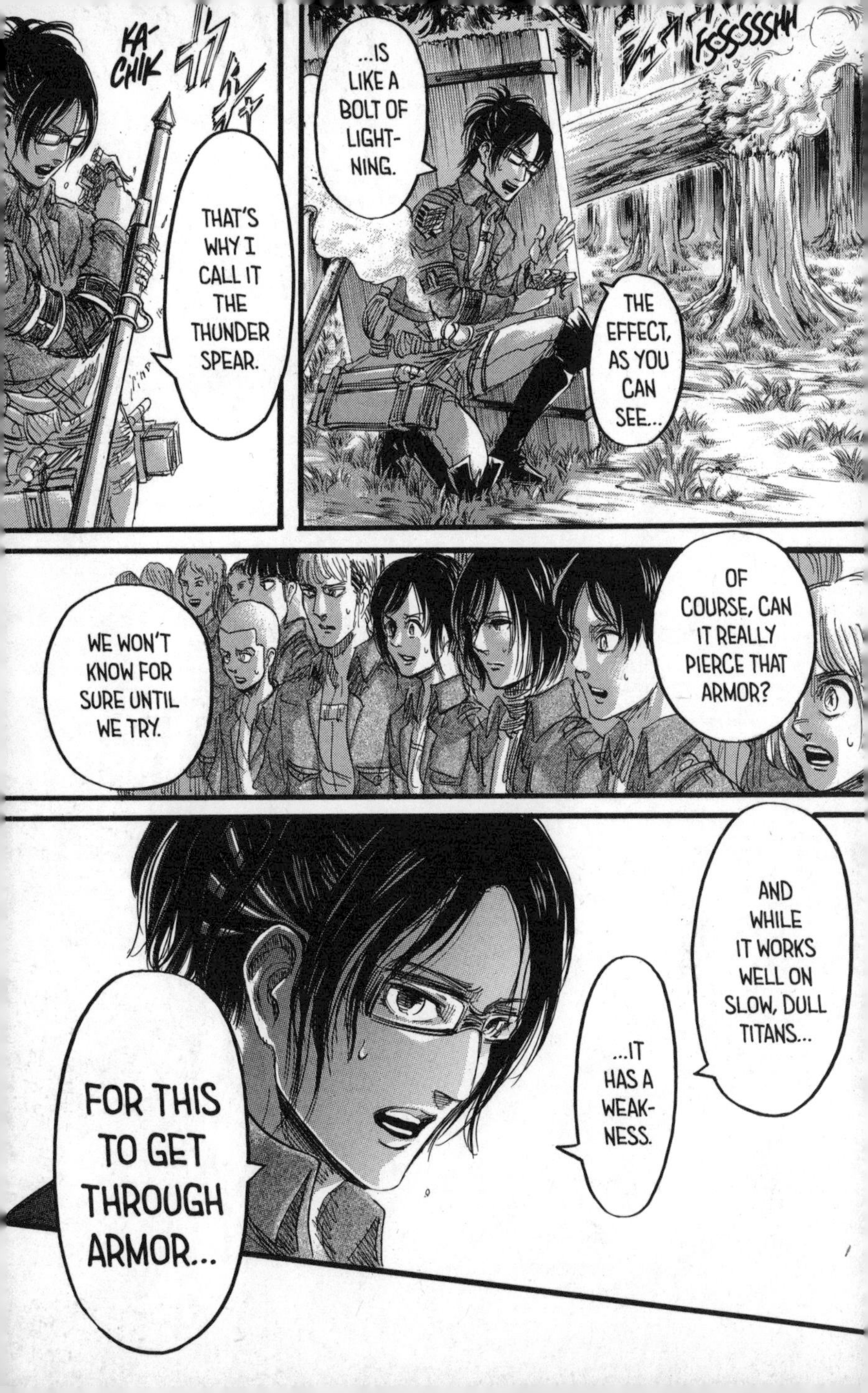

FSSSSSSHH
THE EFFECT, AS YOU CAN SEE...
...IS LIKE A BOLT OF LIGHT-NING.
KA-CHIK
THAT'S WHY I CALL IT THE THUNDER SPEAR.
OF COURSE, CAN IT REALLY PIERCE THAT ARMOR?
WE WON'T KNOW FOR SURE UNTIL WE TRY.
AND WHILE IT WORKS WELL ON SLOW, DULL TITANS...
...IT HAS A WEAKNESS.
FOR THIS TO GET THROUGH ARMOR...

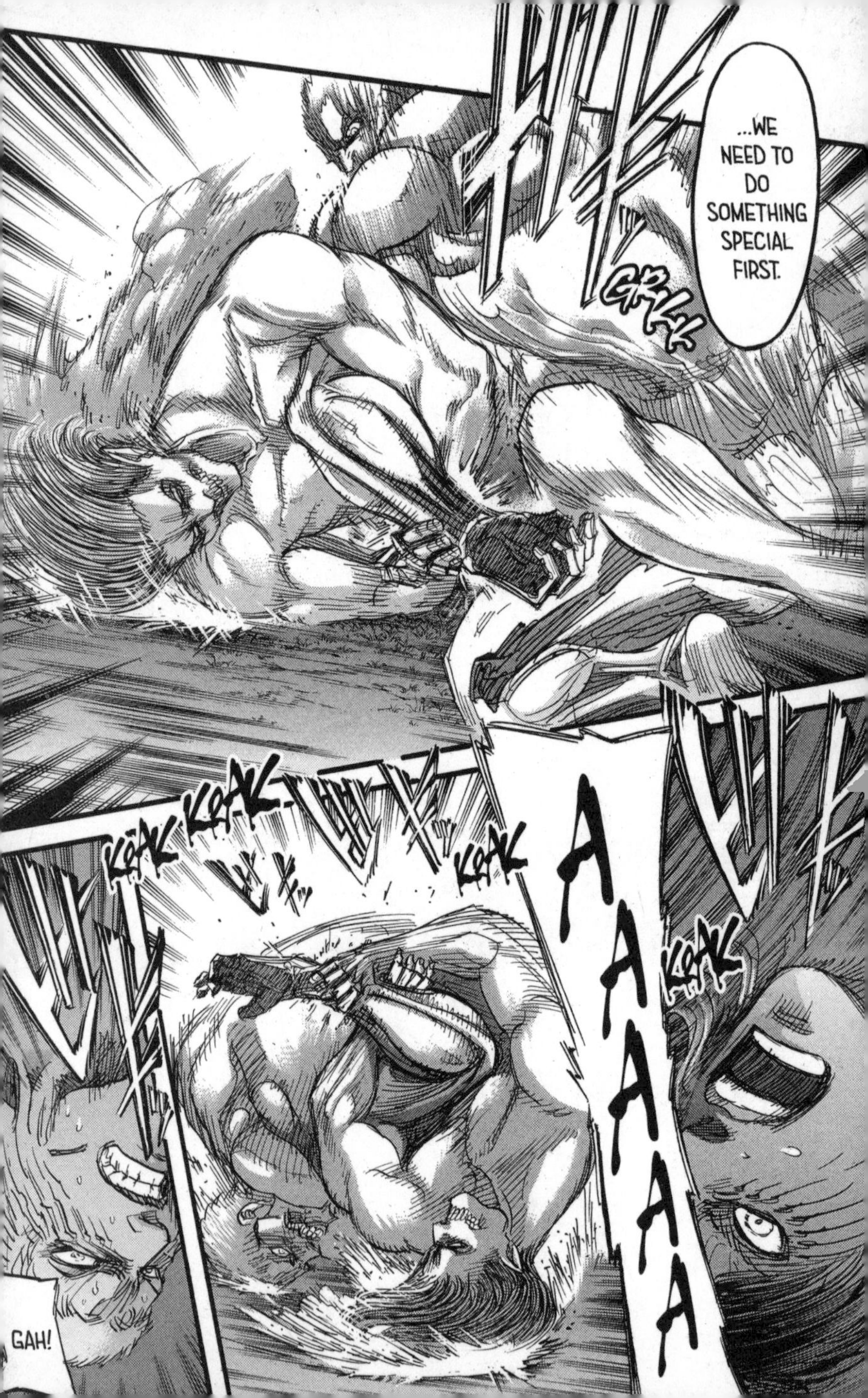
...WE NEED TO DO SOMETHING SPECIAL FIRST.
GAH!

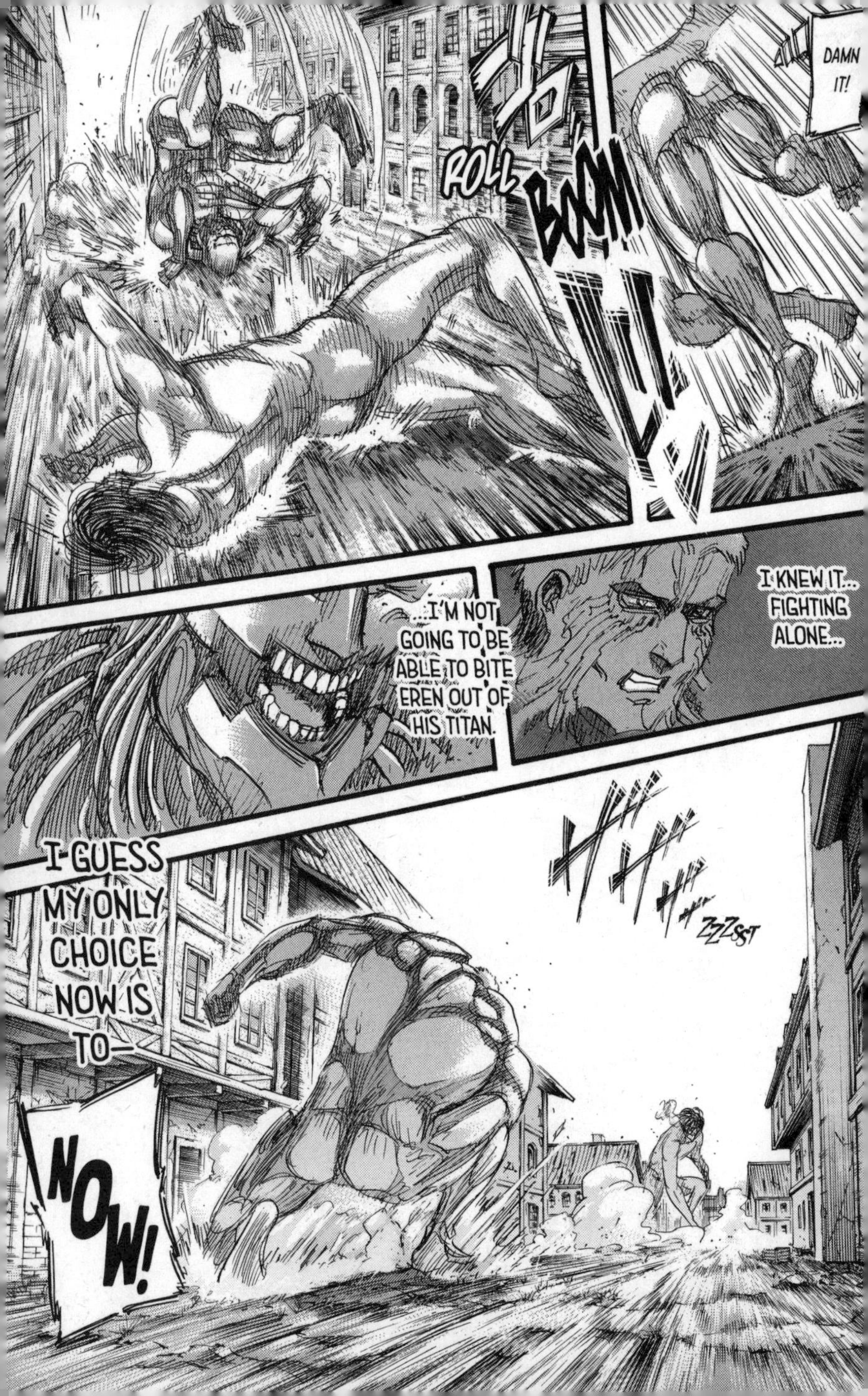
DAMN IT!
ROLL
BOOM
I KNEW IT... FIGHTING ALONE...
...I'M NOT GOING TO BE ABLE TO BITE EREN OUT OF HIS TITAN.
ZZZSST
I GUESS MY ONLY CHOICE NOW IS TO—
NOW!

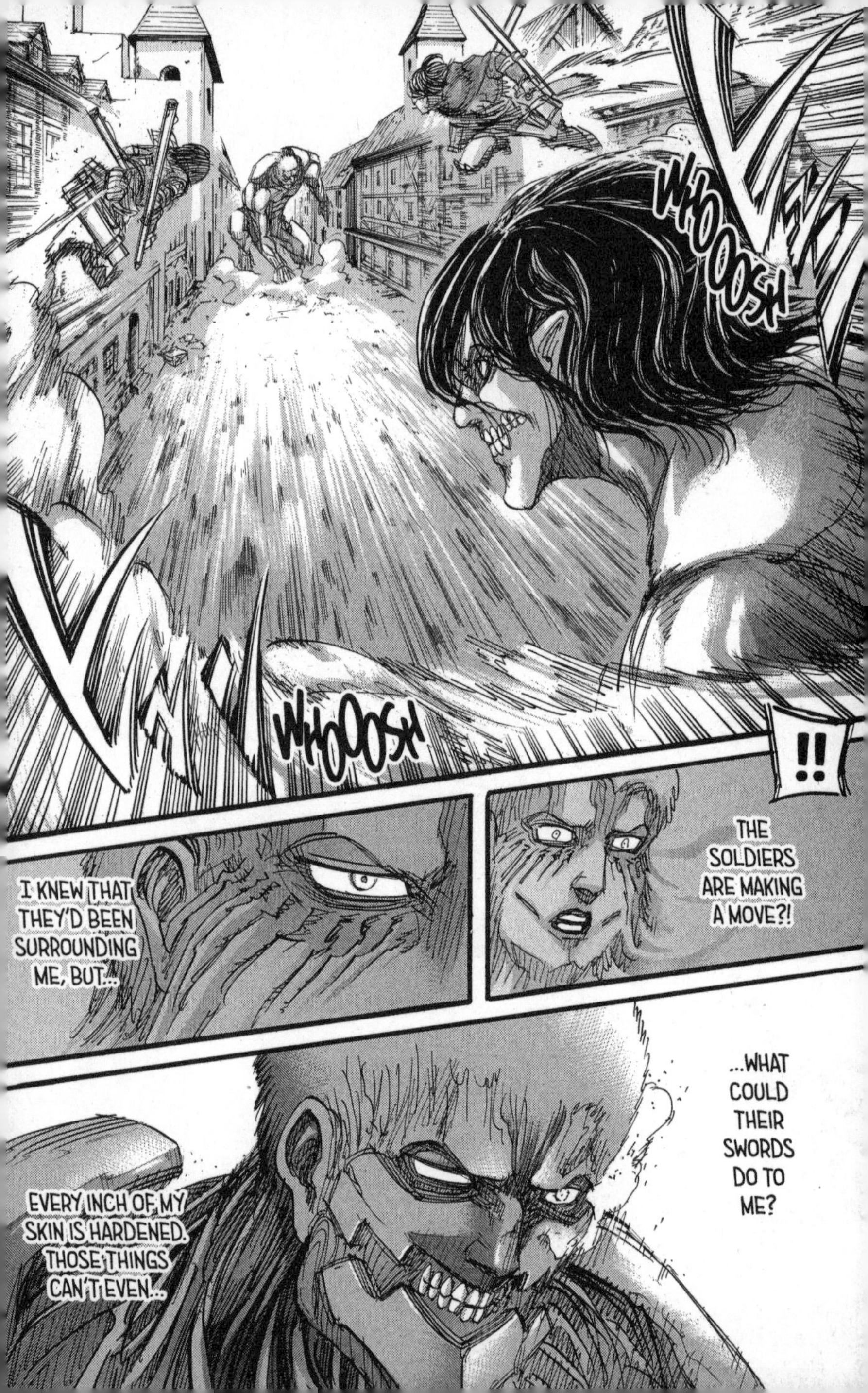
WHOOOSH
WHOOOSH
!!
THE SOLDIERS ARE MAKING A MOVE?!
I KNEW THAT THEY'D BEEN SURROUNDING ME, BUT...
...WHAT COULD THEIR SWORDS DO TO ME?
EVERY INCH OF MY SKIN IS HARDENED. THOSE THINGS CAN'T EVEN...

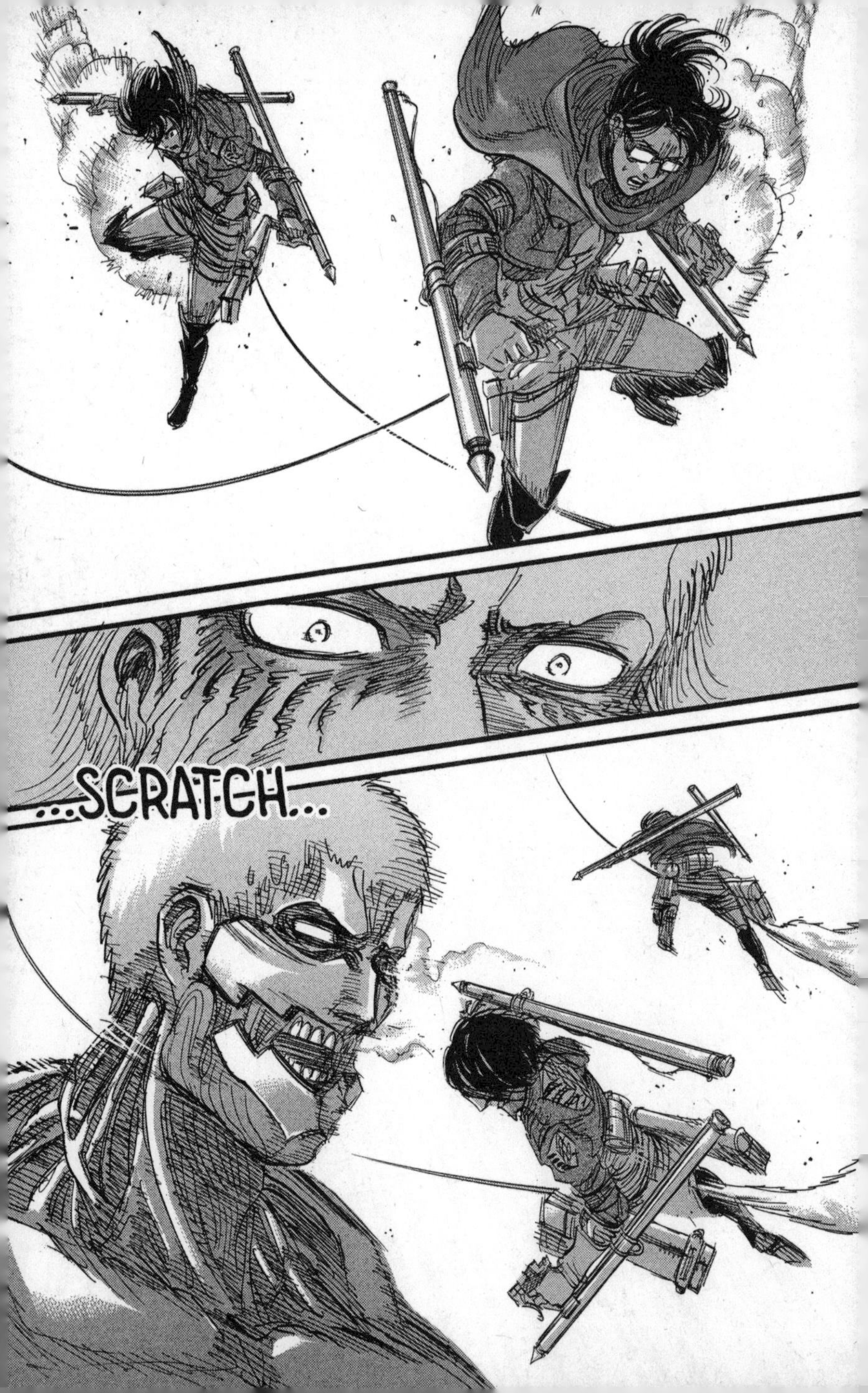
...SCRATCH...

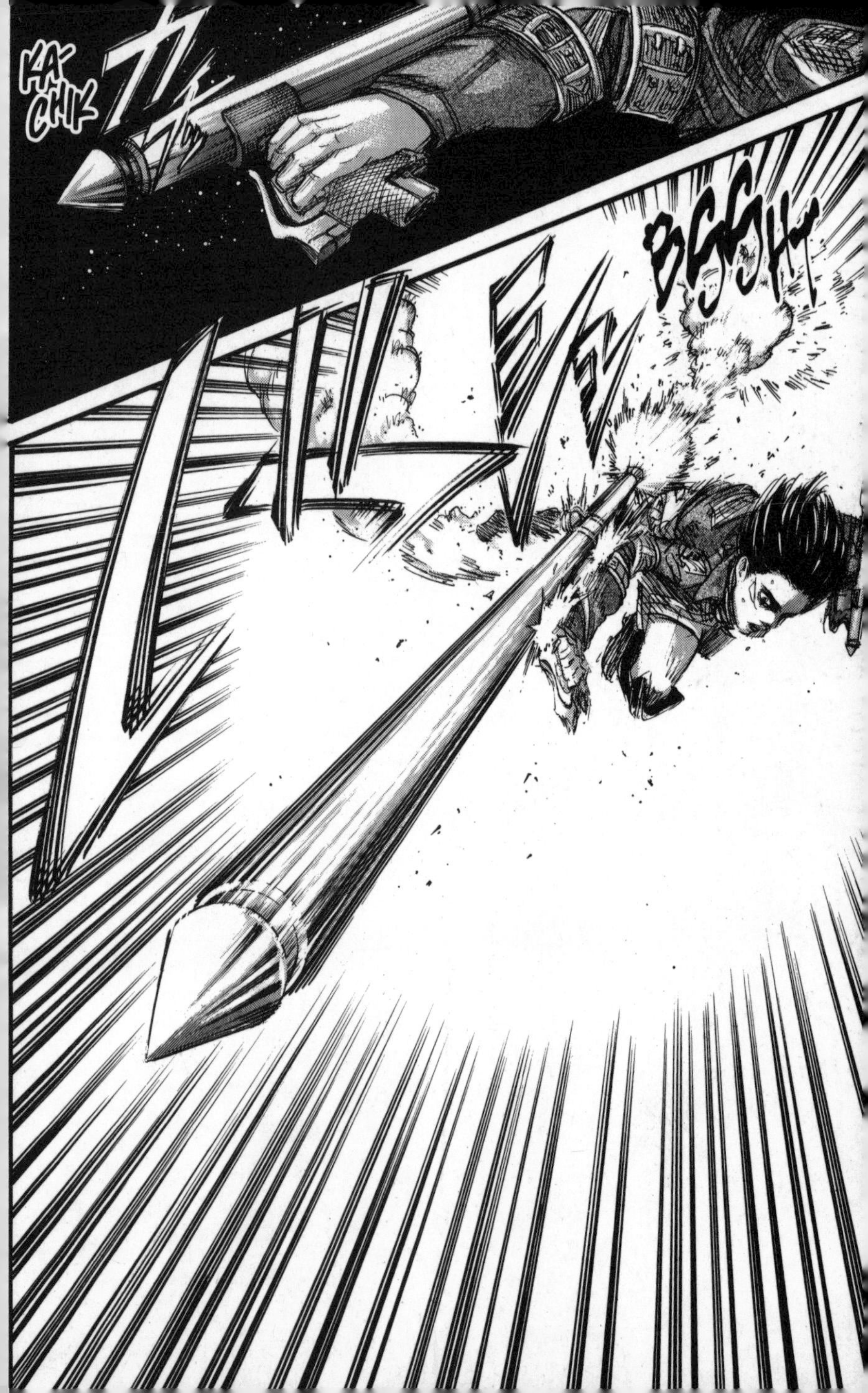
KA-CHIK
BGGSH

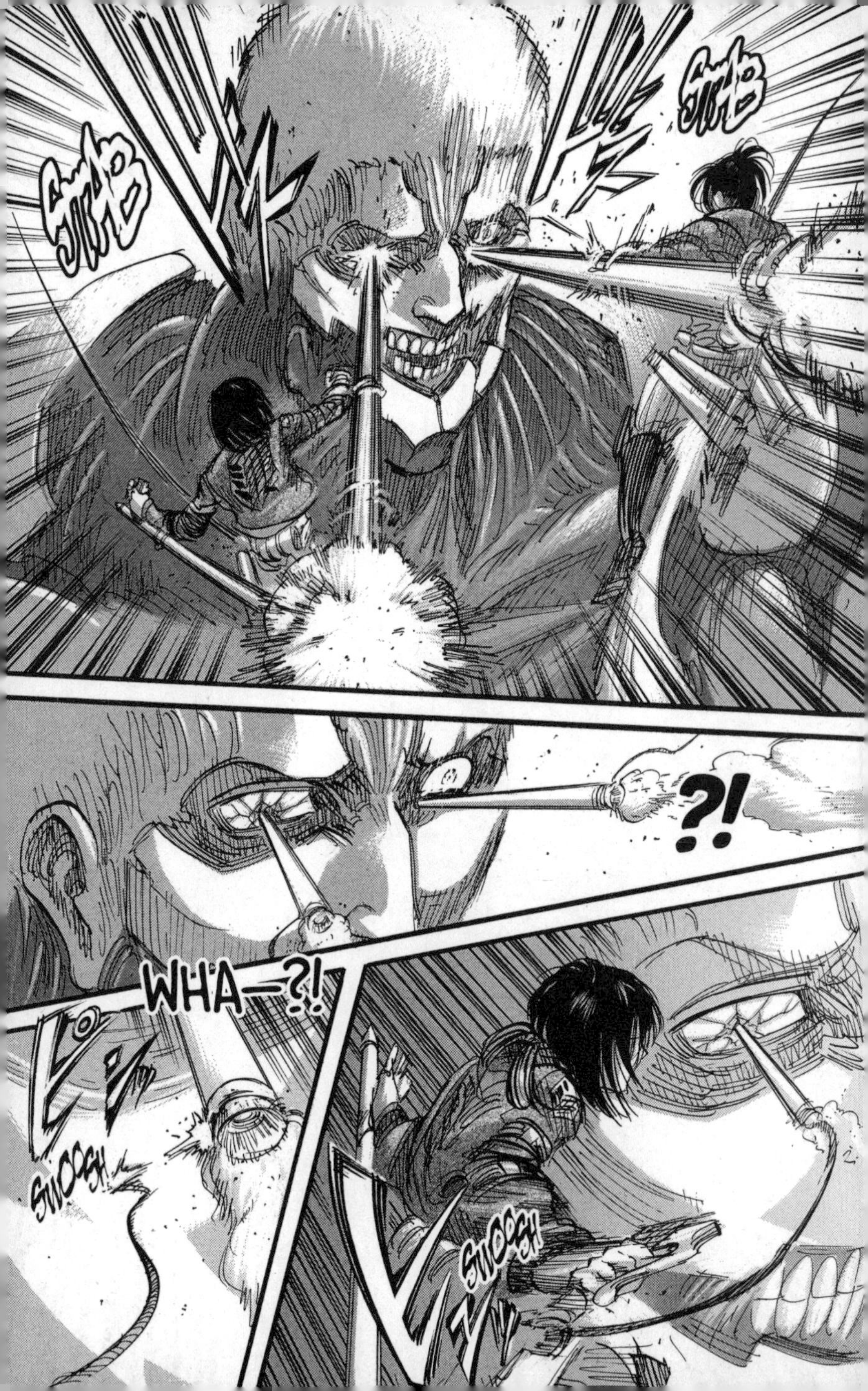
STAB
STAB
?!
SWOOSH
WHA—?!
SWOOSH!

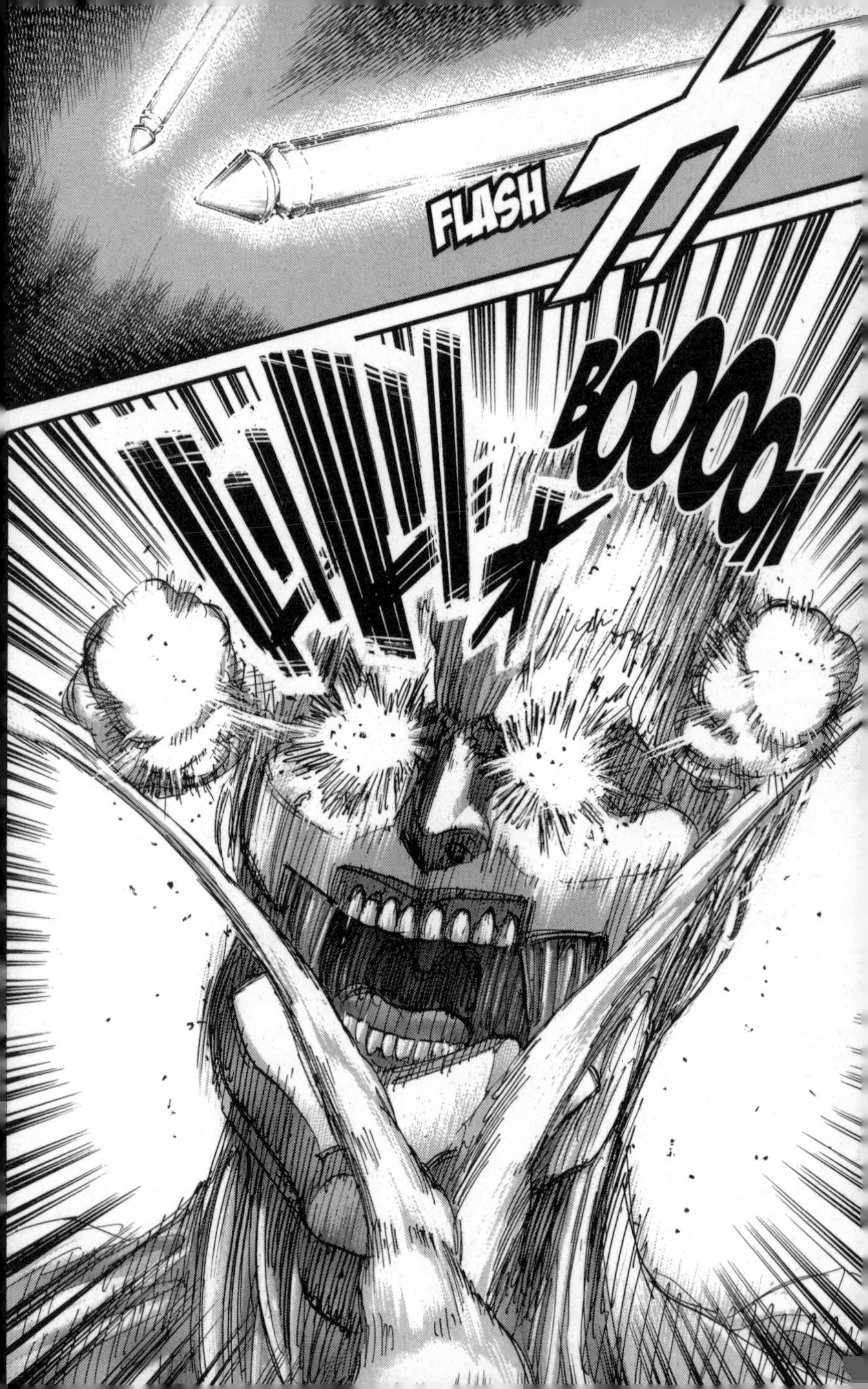
FLASH
BOOOOM

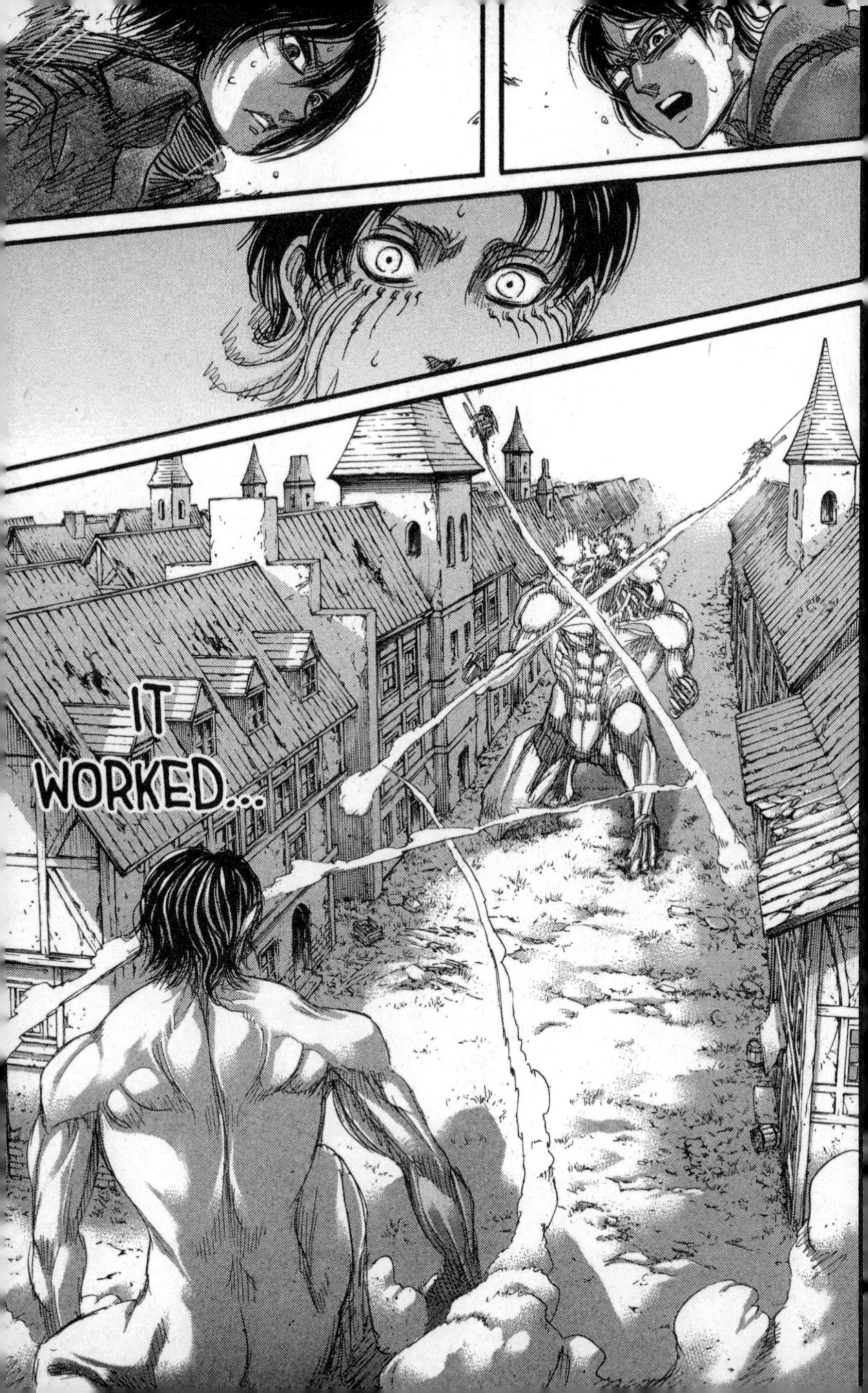
IT WORKED...

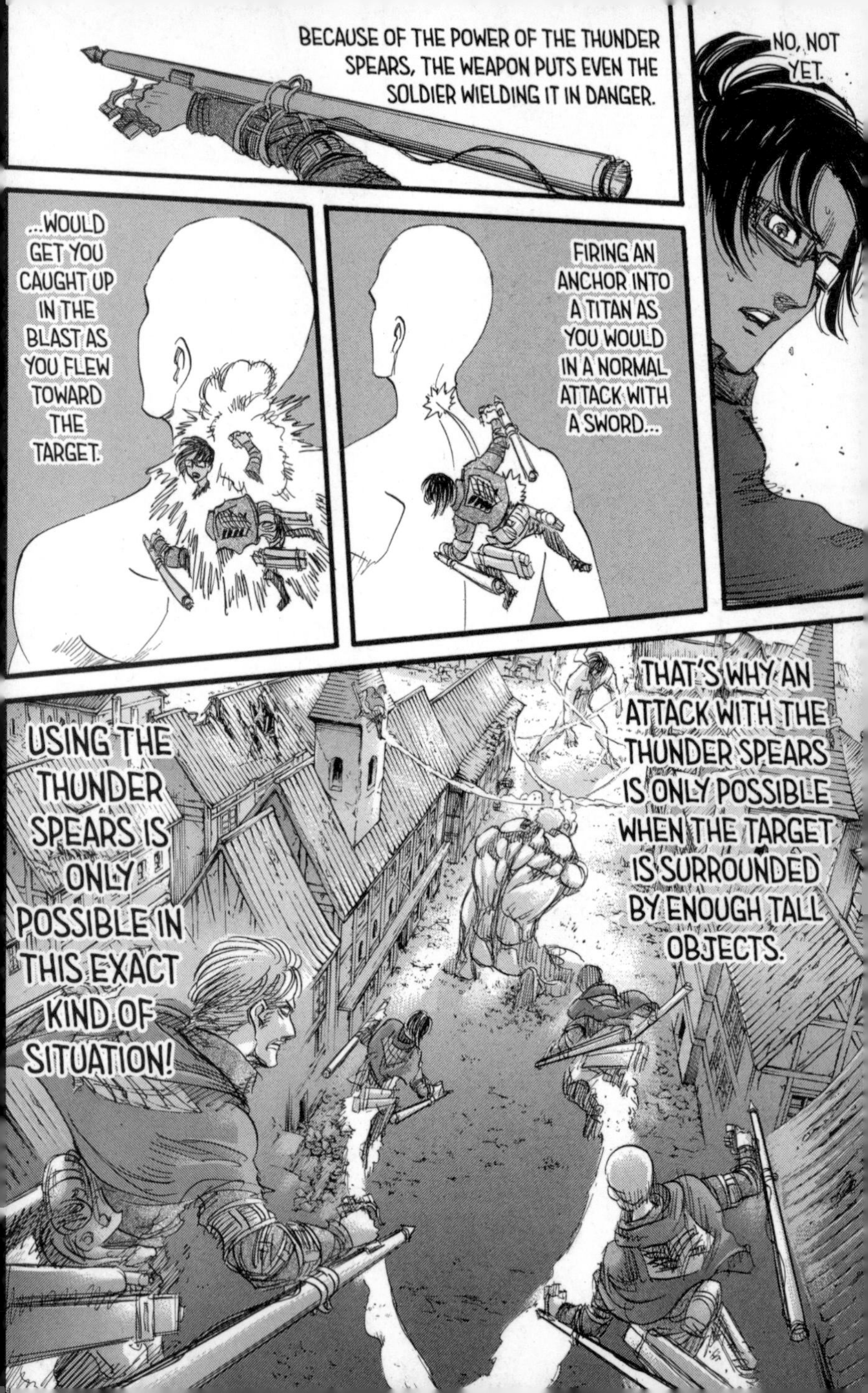
NO, NOT YET.
BECAUSE OF THE POWER OF THE THUNDER SPEARS, THE WEAPON PUTS EVEN THE SOLDIER WIELDING IT IN DANGER.
FIRING AN ANCHOR INTO A TITAN AS YOU WOULD IN A NORMAL ATTACK WITH A SWORD...
...WOULD GET YOU CAUGHT UP IN THE BLAST AS YOU FLEW TOWARD THE TARGET.
THAT'S WHY AN ATTACK WITH THE THUNDER SPEARS IS ONLY POSSIBLE WHEN THE TARGET IS SURROUNDED BY ENOUGH TALL OBJECTS.
USING THE THUNDER SPEARS IS ONLY POSSIBLE IN THIS EXACT KIND OF SITUATION!

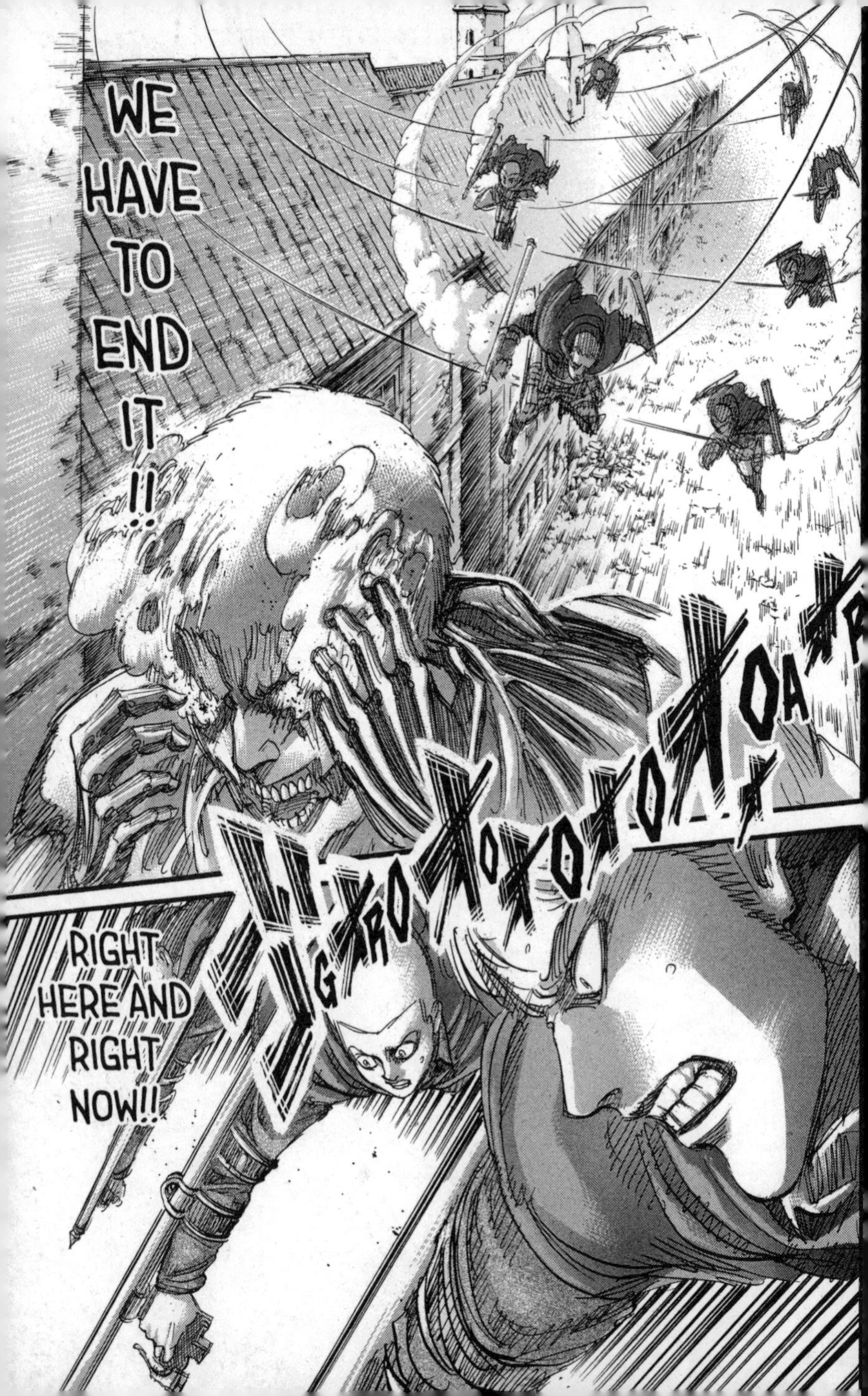
WE HAVE TO END IT!!
GROOOOOOAR
RIGHT HERE AND RIGHT NOW!!

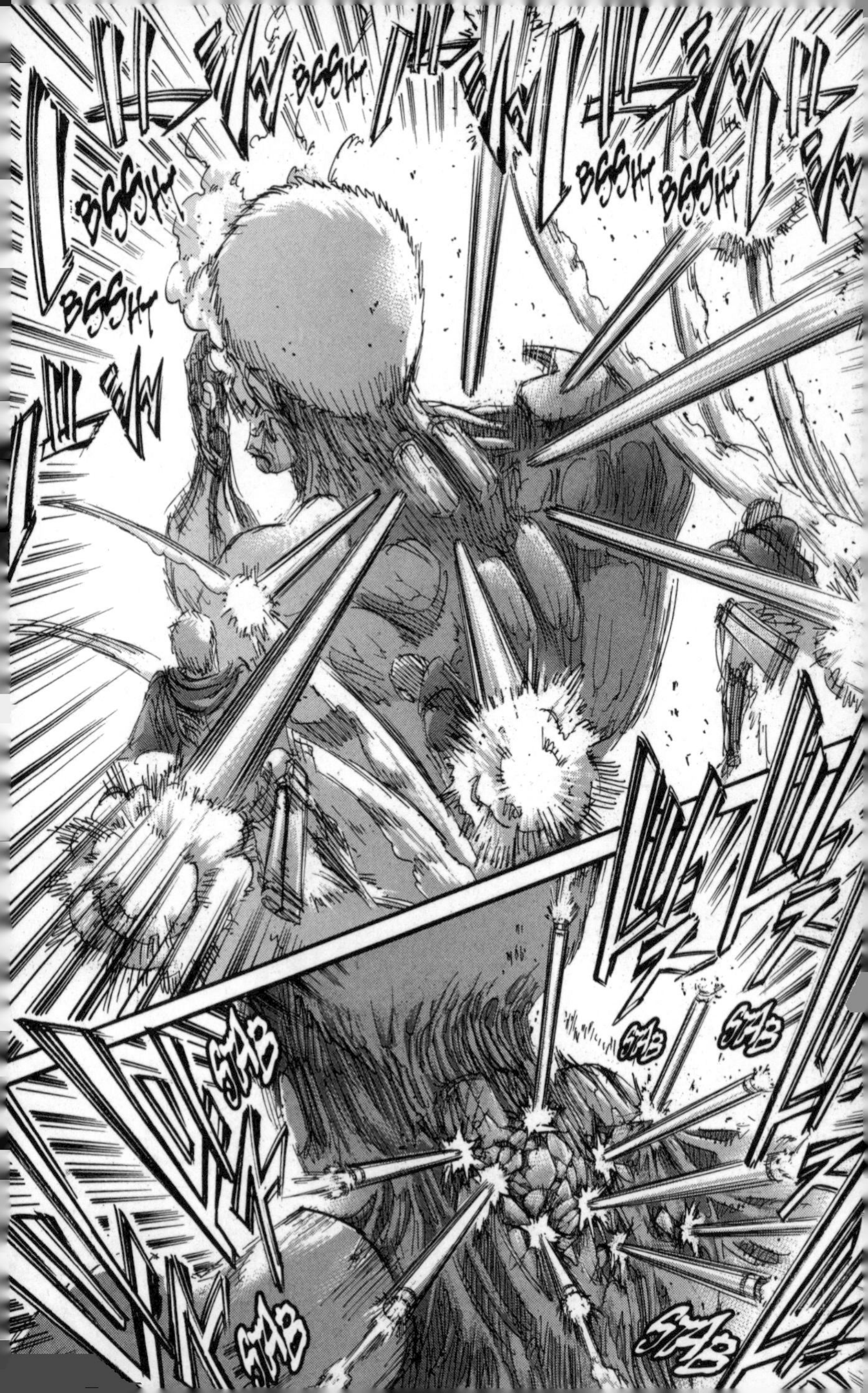
BSSHH
BSSHH
BSSHH
BSSHH
BSSHH
STAB
STAB
STAB
STAB
STAB

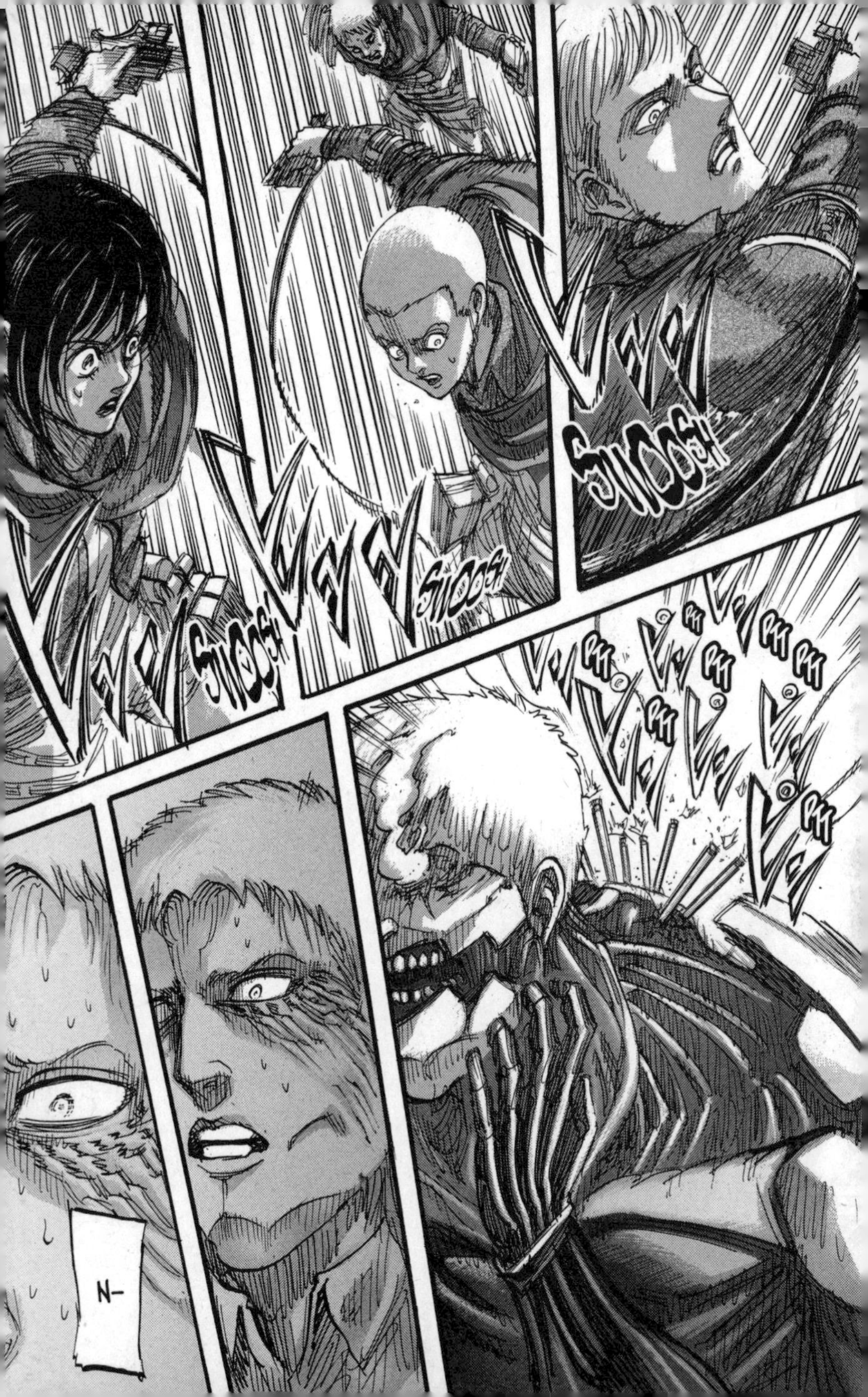
SHOOSH
SHOOSH
SHOOSH
PKK PKK PKK PKK PKK PKK PKK PKK PKK PKK
N-

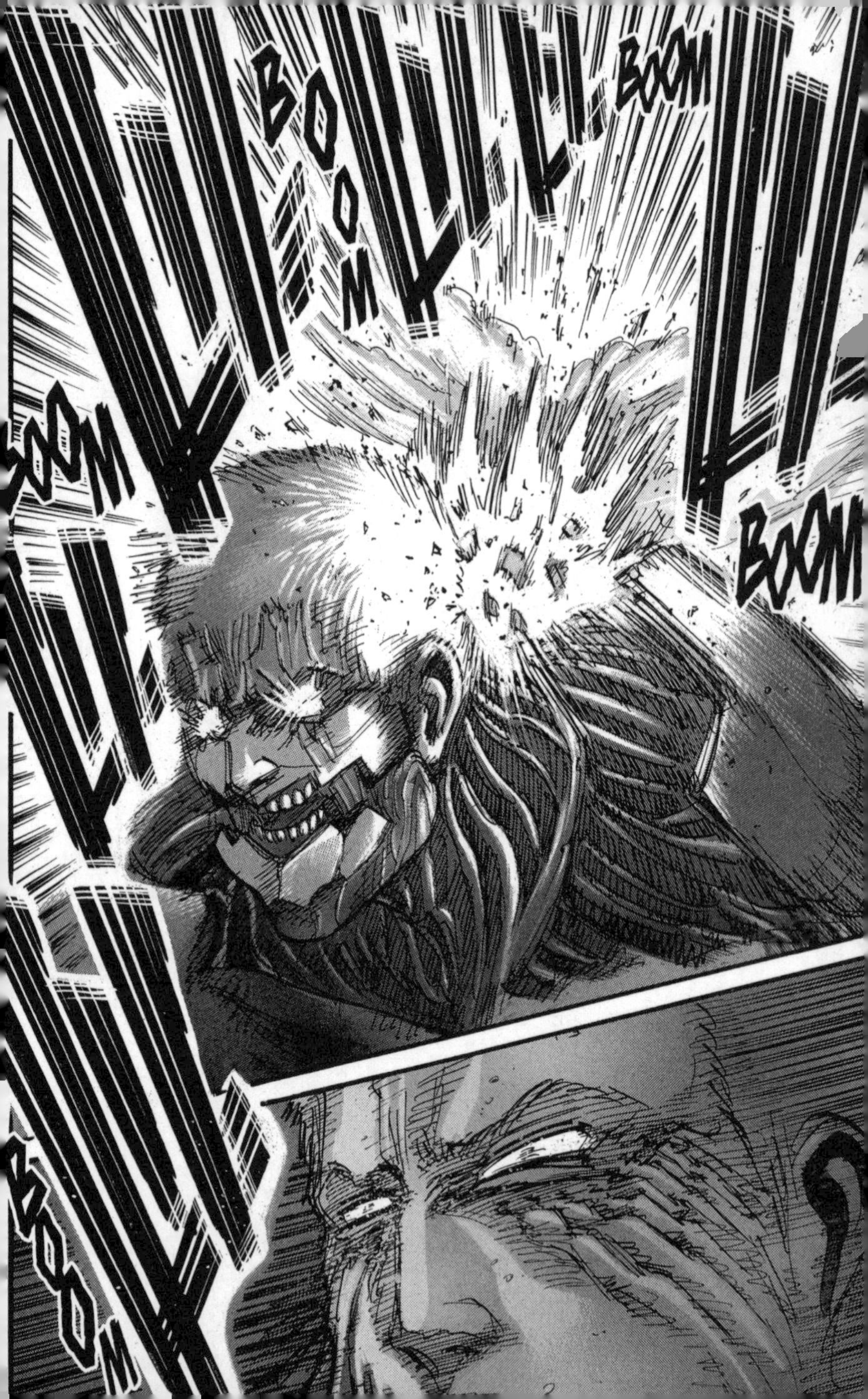
BOOM
BOOOM
BOOM
BOOM
BOOOOM

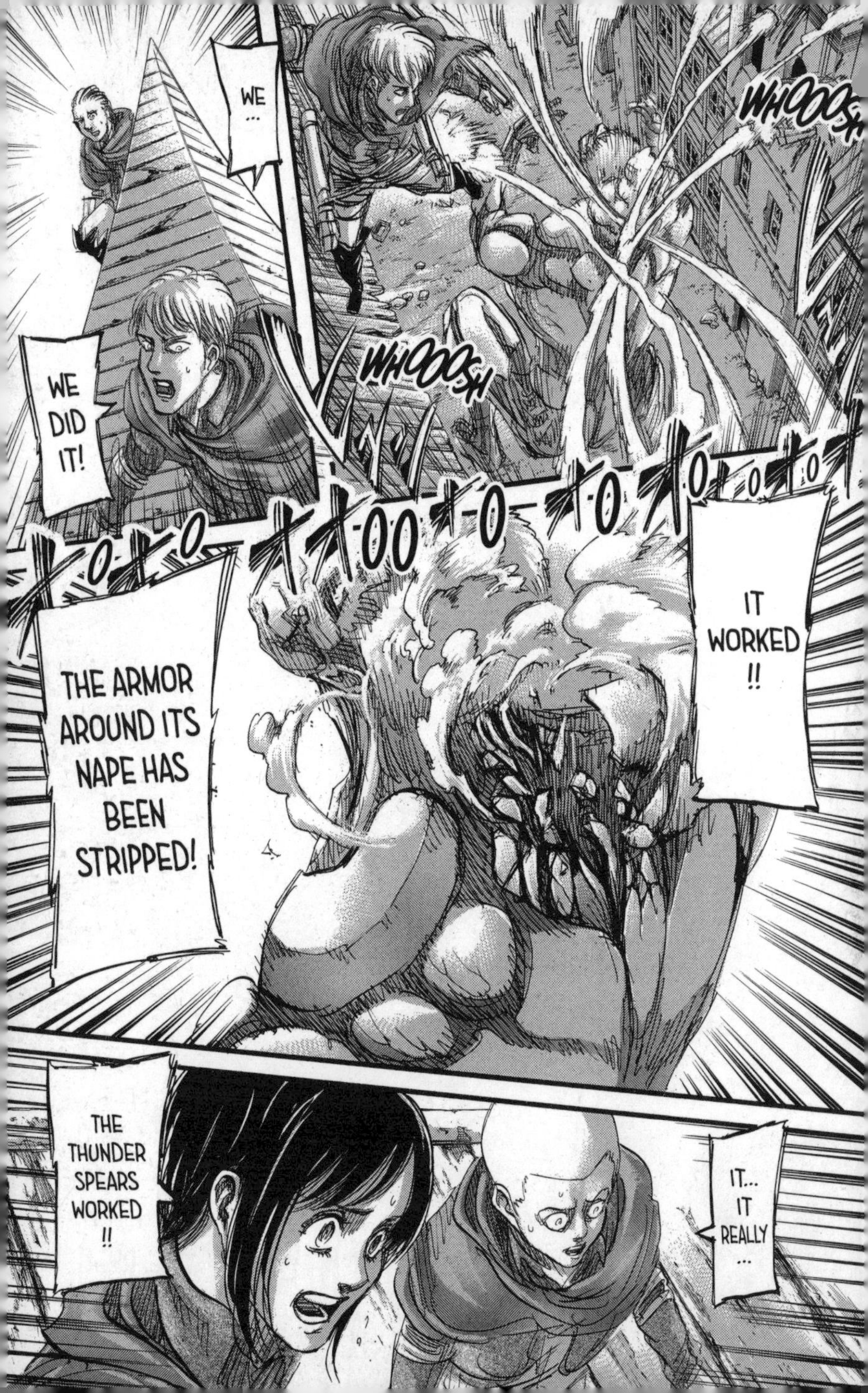
WHOOOSH
WE ...
WHOOOSH
WE DID IT!
IT WORKED !!
THE ARMOR AROUND ITS NAPE HAS BEEN STRIPPED!
IT... IT REALLY ...
THE THUNDER SPEARS WORKED !!

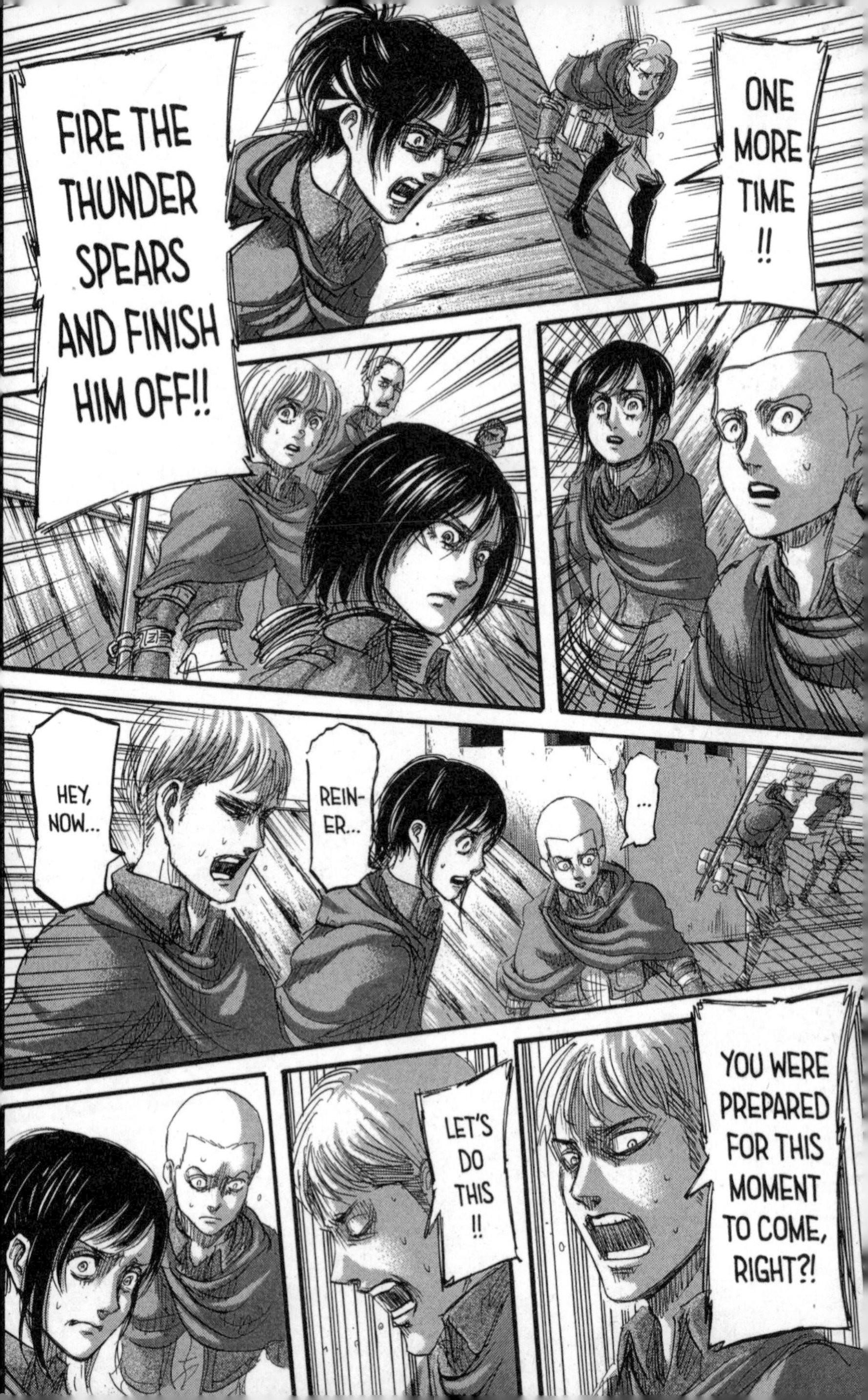
ONE MORE TIME !!
FIRE THE THUNDER SPEARS AND FINISH HIM OFF!!
...
REIN-ER...
HEY, NOW...
YOU WERE PREPARED FOR THIS MOMENT TO COME, RIGHT?!
LET'S DO THIS !!

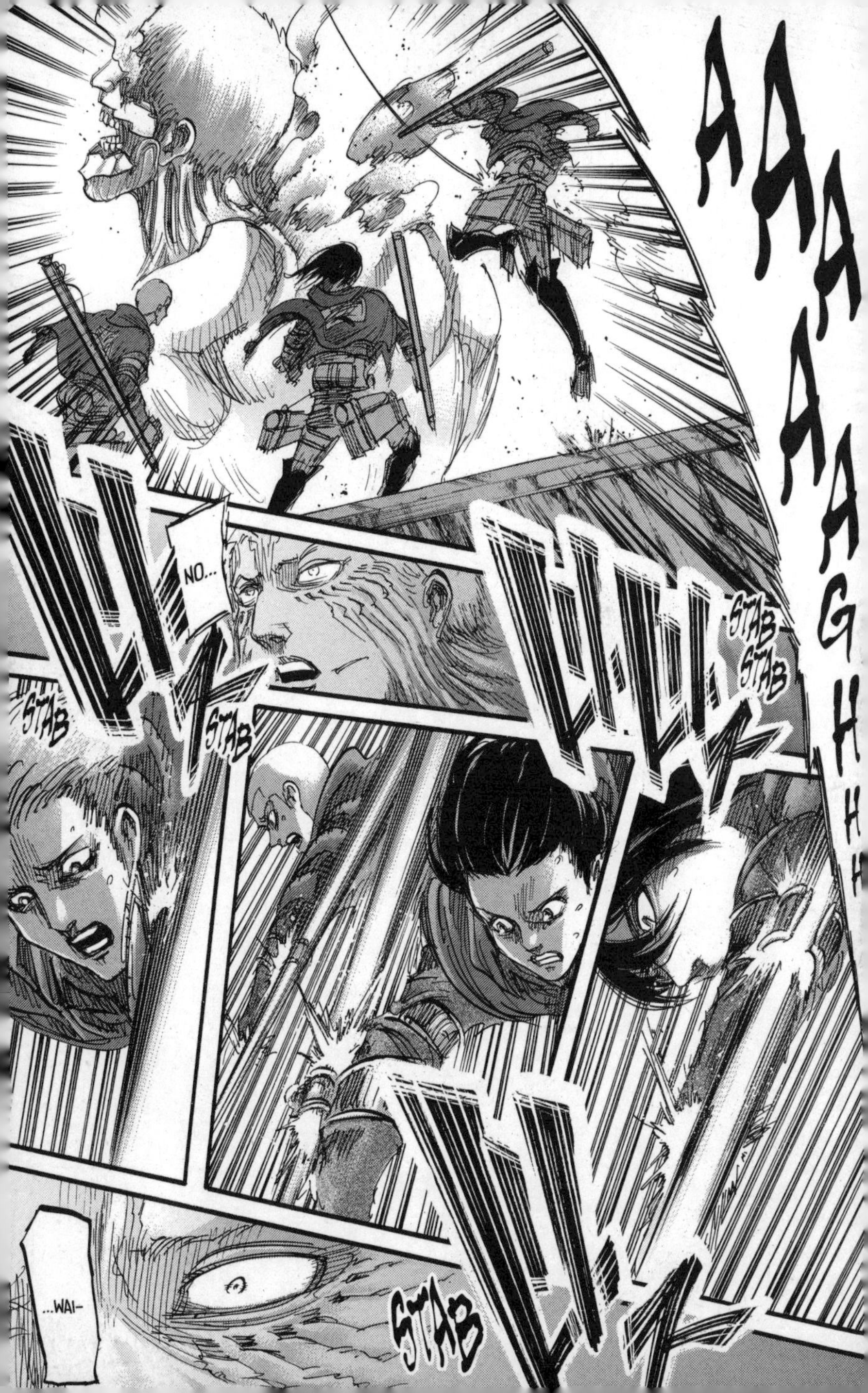
AAAAAAGHHHH
STAB STAB
NO...
STAB
STAB
STAB
...WAI-

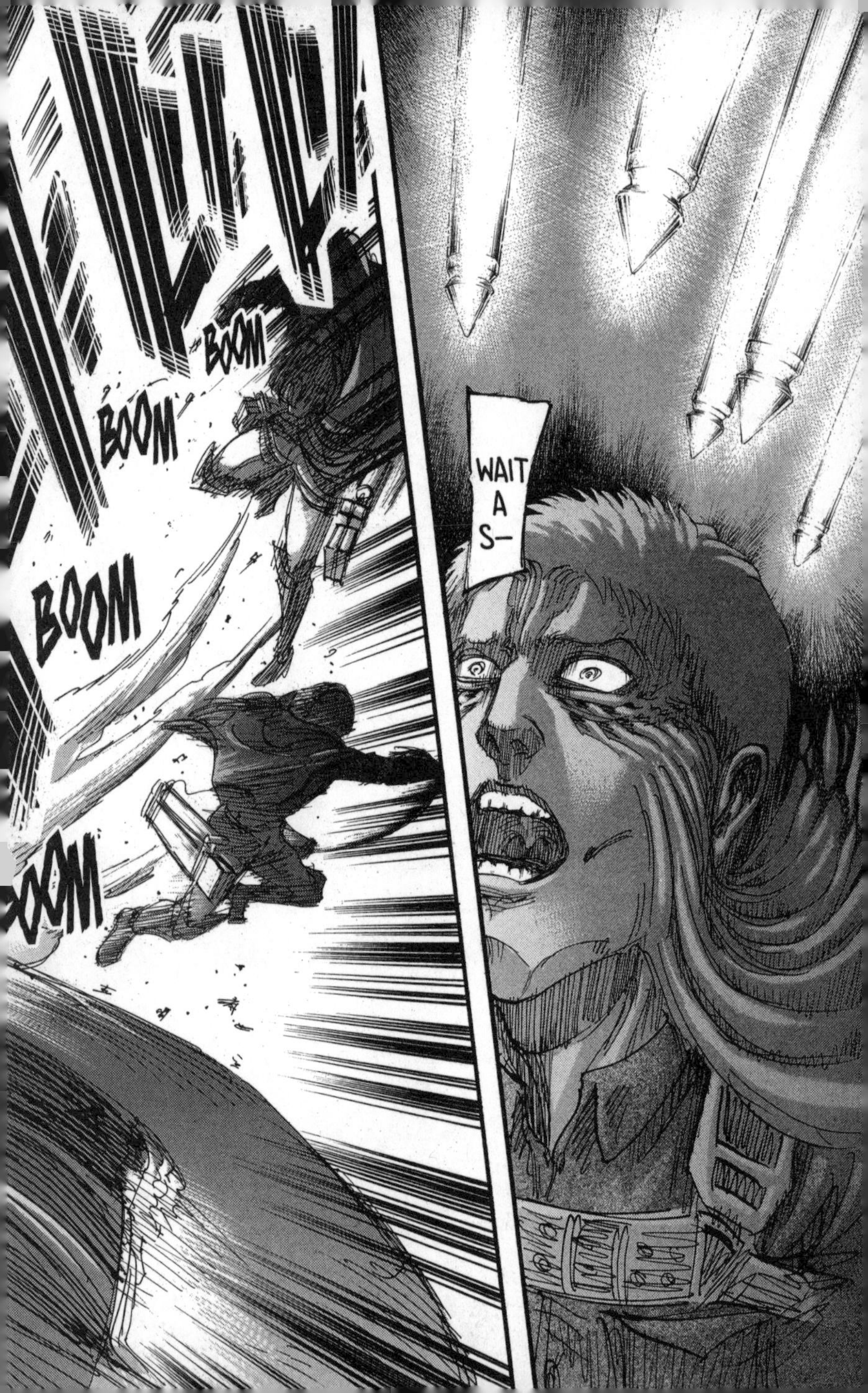
WAIT A S—
BOOM
BOOM
BOOM
BOOM

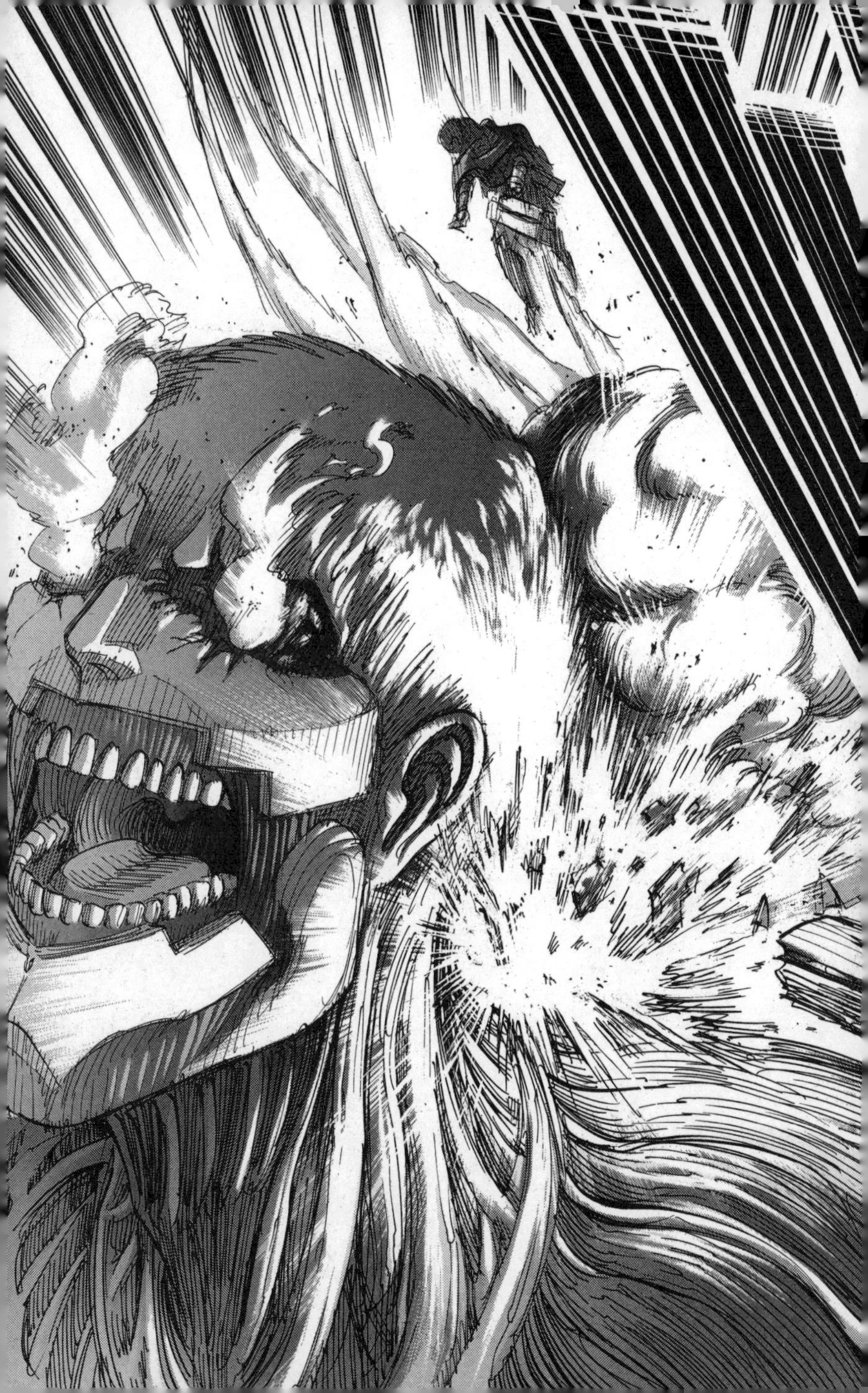

ATTACK on TITAN

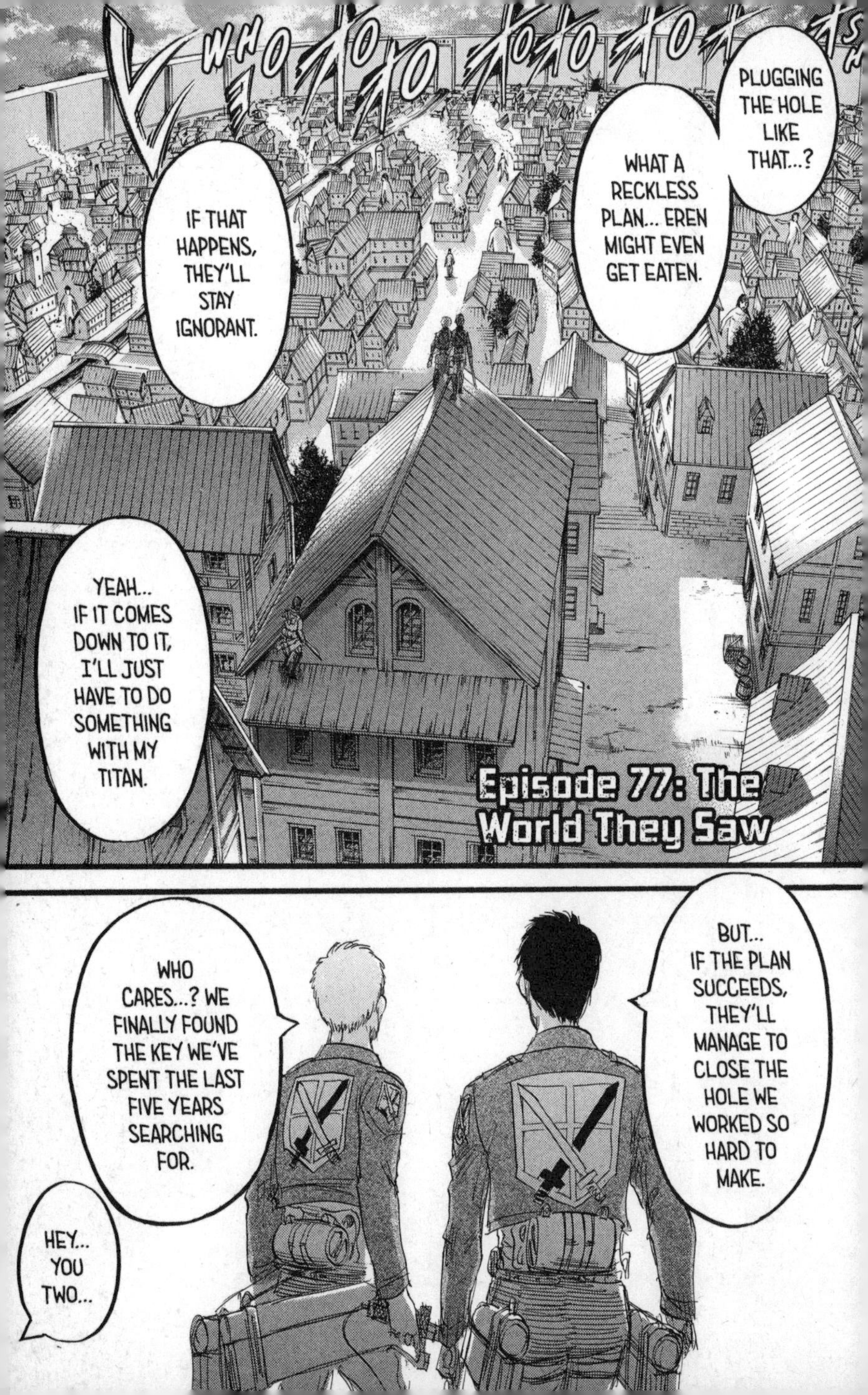
PLUGGING THE HOLE LIKE THAT...?
WHAT A RECKLESS PLAN... EREN MIGHT EVEN GET EATEN.
IF THAT HAPPENS, THEY'LL STAY IGNORANT.
YEAH... IF IT COMES DOWN TO IT, I'LL JUST HAVE TO DO SOMETHING WITH MY TITAN.
Episode 77: The World They Saw
BUT... IF THE PLAN SUCCEEDS, THEY'LL MANAGE TO CLOSE THE HOLE WE WORKED SO HARD TO MAKE.
WHO CARES...? WE FINALLY FOUND THE KEY WE'VE SPENT THE LAST FIVE YEARS SEARCHING FOR.
HEY... YOU TWO...

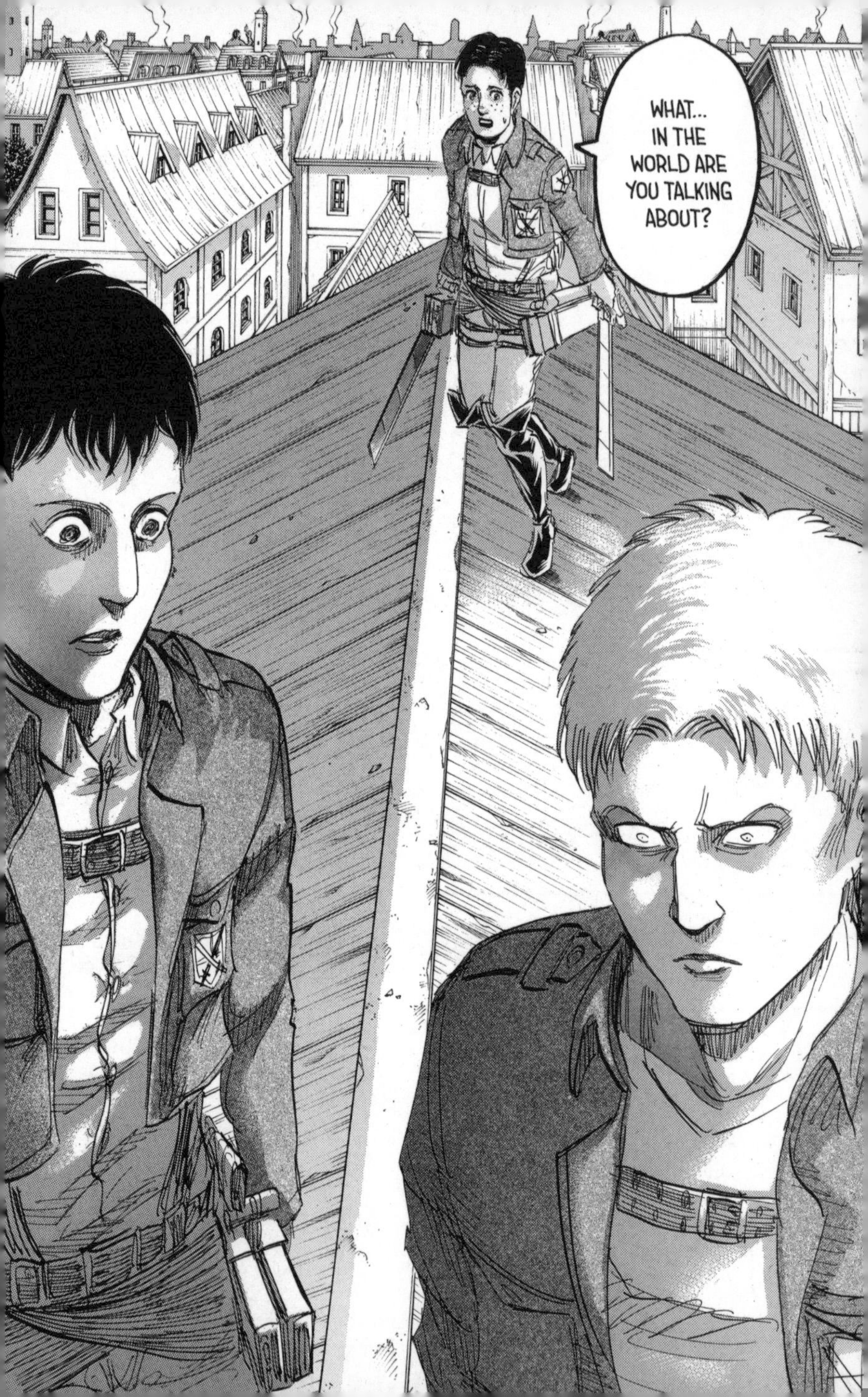
WHAT... IN THE WORLD ARE YOU TALKING ABOUT?

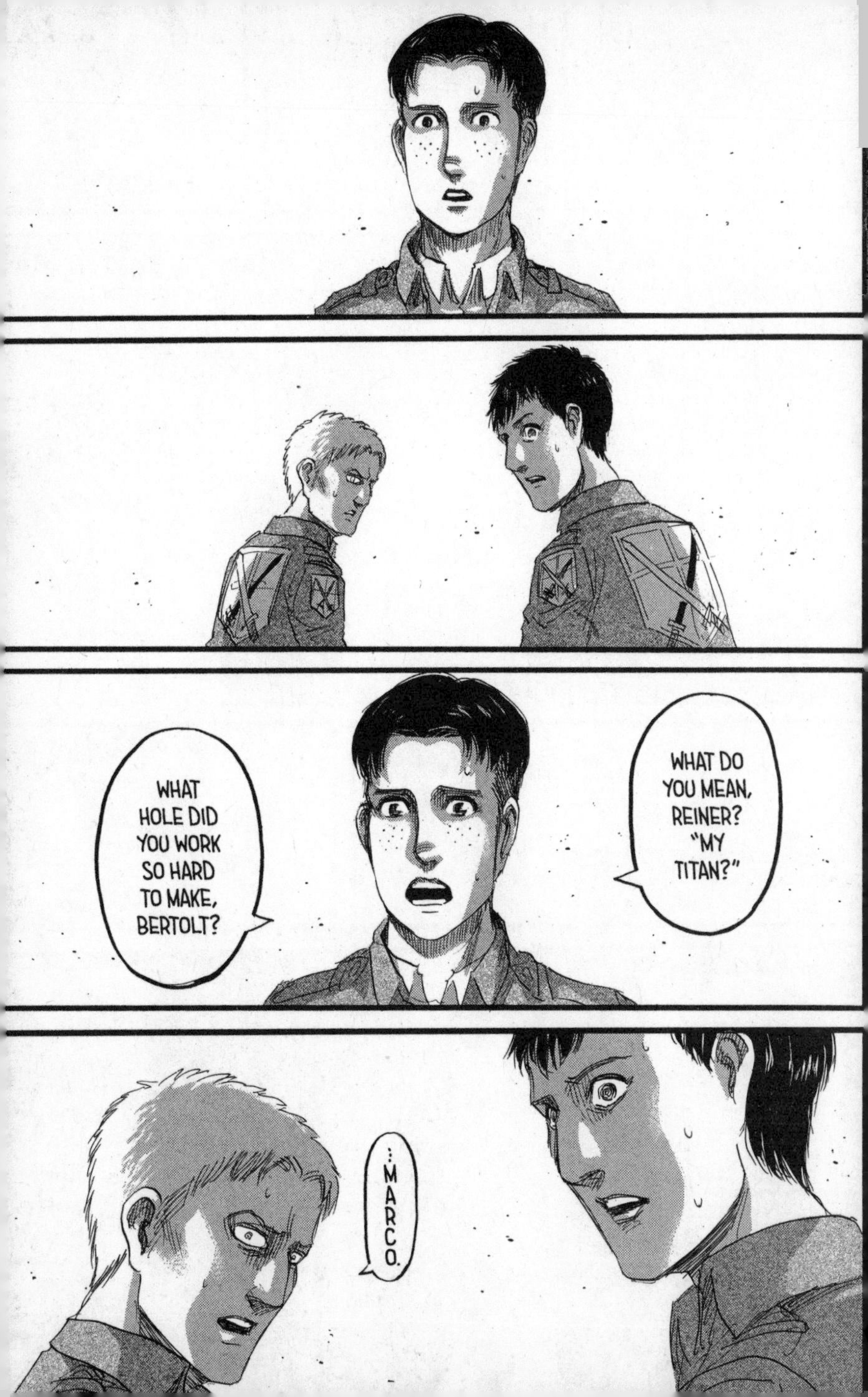
WHAT DO YOU MEAN, REINER? "MY TITAN?"
WHAT HOLE DID YOU WORK SO HARD TO MAKE, BERTOLT?
...MARCO.

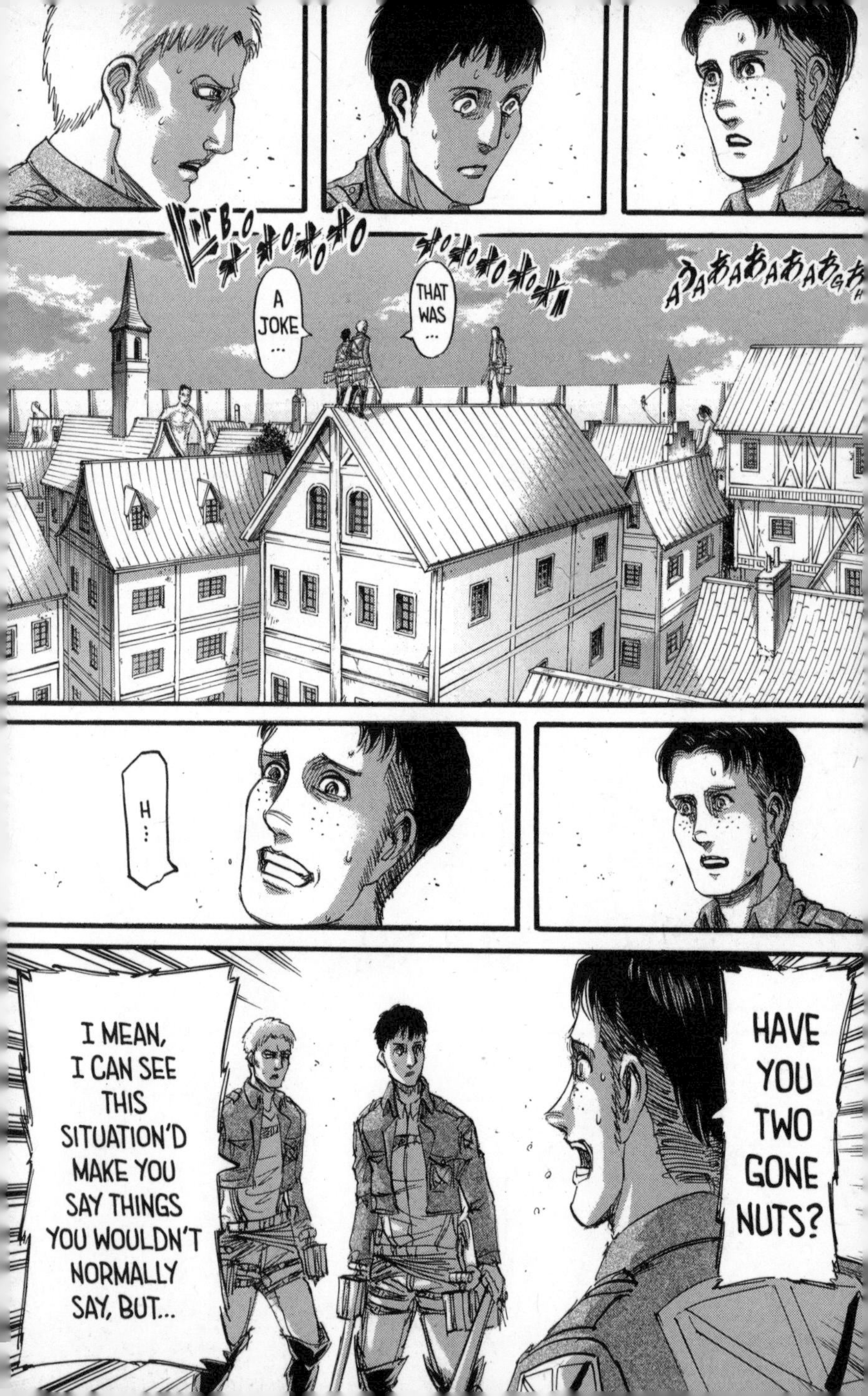
THAT WAS ...
A JOKE ...
H ...
HAVE YOU TWO GONE NUTS?
I MEAN, I CAN SEE THIS SITUATION'D MAKE YOU SAY THINGS YOU WOULDN'T NORMALLY SAY, BUT...

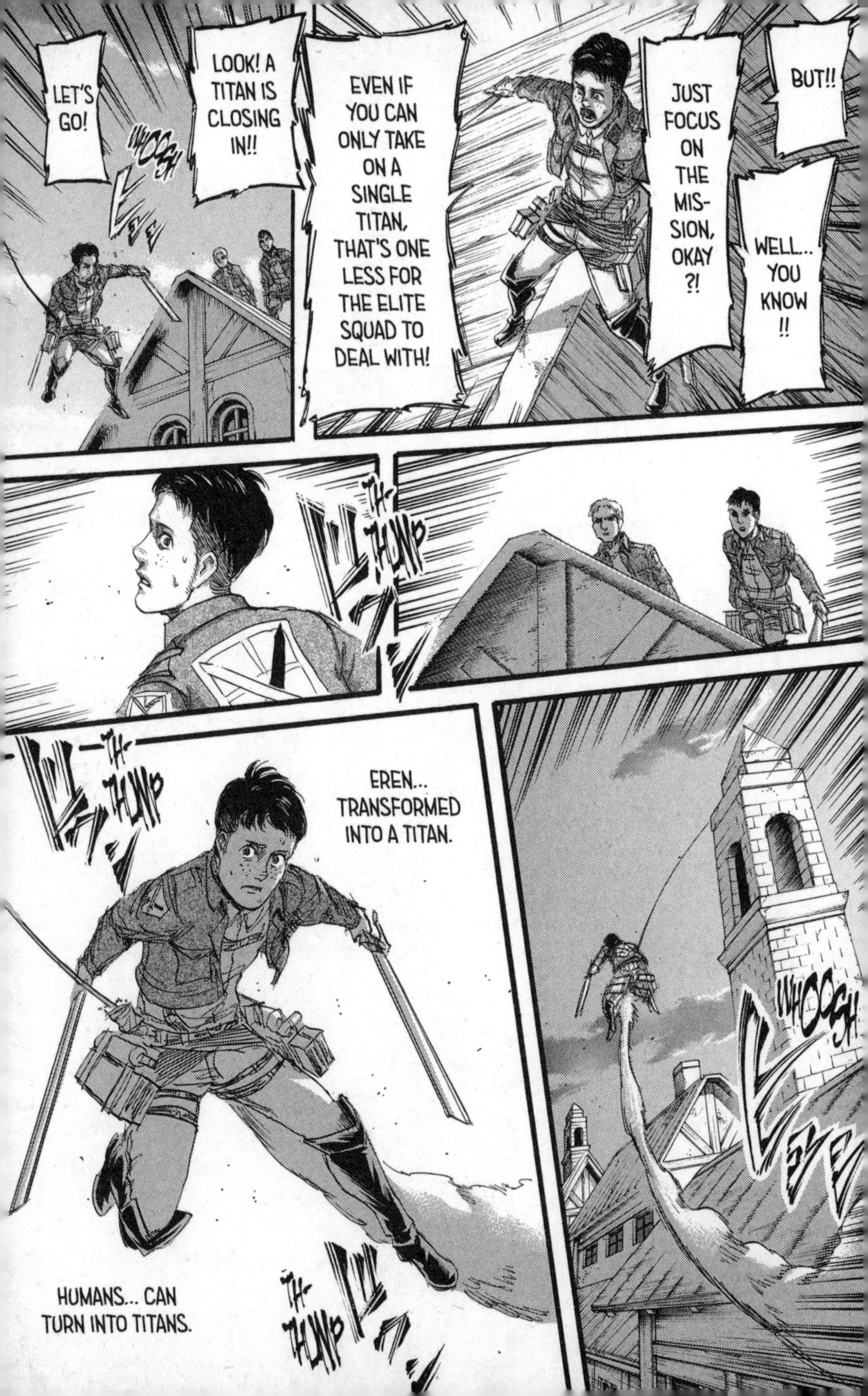
BUT!!
WELL... YOU KNOW!!
JUST FOCUS ON THE MIS-SION, OKAY?!
EVEN IF YOU CAN ONLY TAKE ON A SINGLE TITAN, THAT'S ONE LESS FOR THE ELITE SQUAD TO DEAL WITH!
LOOK! A TITAN IS CLOSING IN!!
LET'S GO!
WHOOSH
TH-THUMP
WHOOSH
TH-THUMP
EREN... TRANSFORMED INTO A TITAN.
HUMANS... CAN TURN INTO TITANS.
TH-THUMP

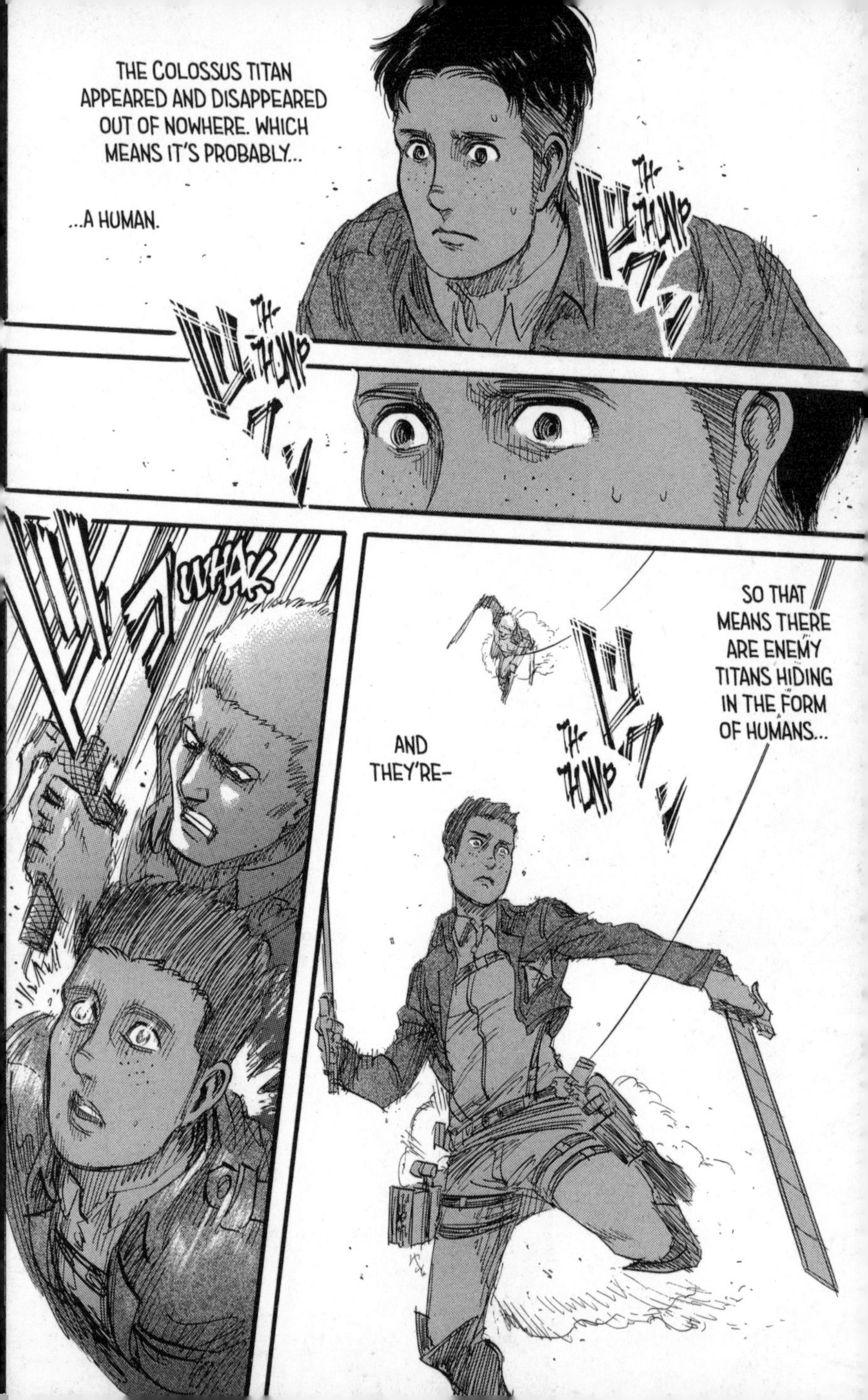
THE COLOSSUS TITAN APPEARED AND DISAPPEARED OUT OF NOWHERE. WHICH MEANS IT'S PROBABLY...
TH-THUMP
...A HUMAN.
TH-THUMP
SO THAT MEANS THERE ARE ENEMY TITANS HIDING IN THE FORM OF HUMANS...
TH-THUMP
AND THEY'RE-
WHAK

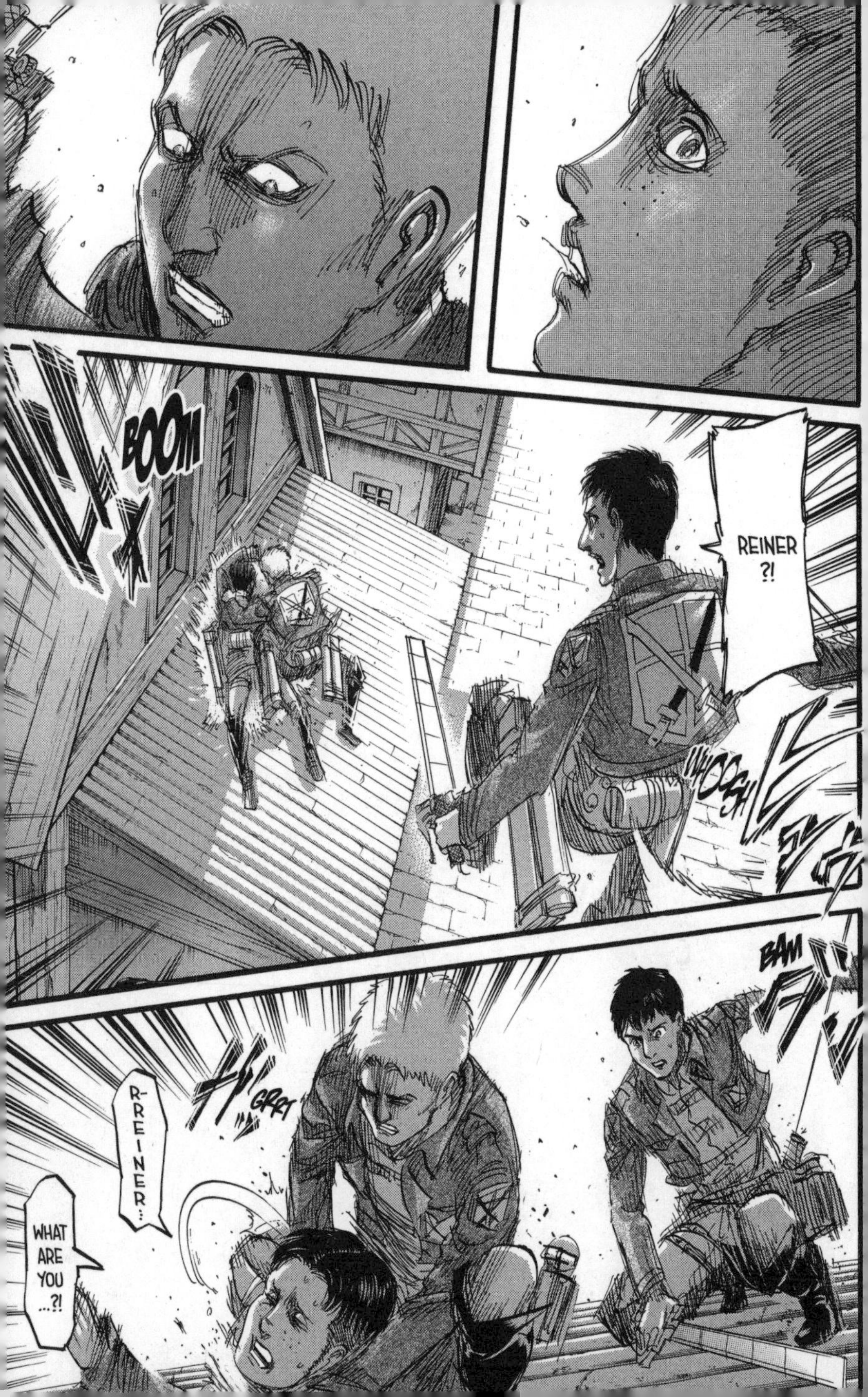
REINER ?!
WHOOSH
BOOM
BAM
R-REINER...
GRRT
WHAT ARE YOU ...?!

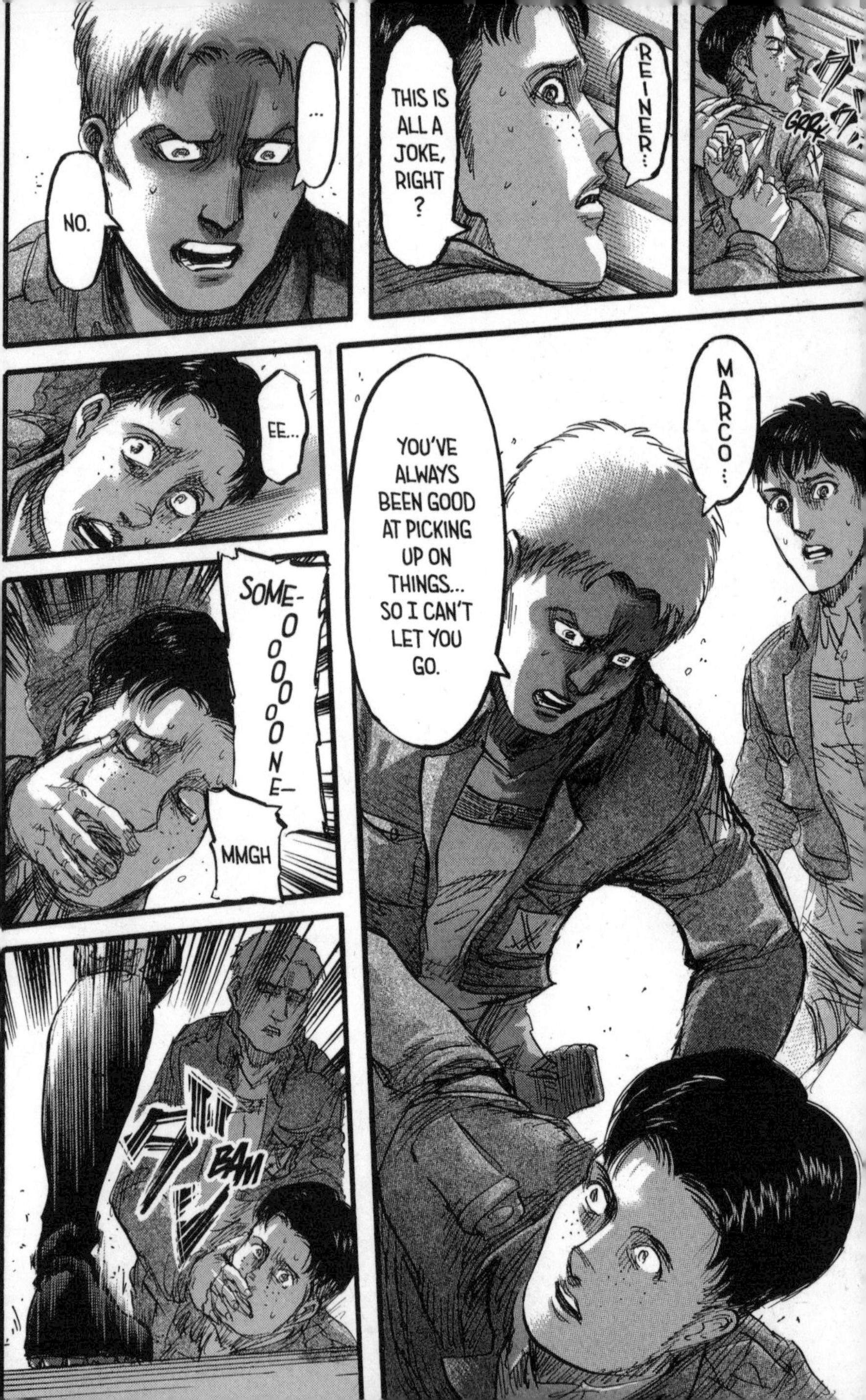
REINER...
THIS IS ALL A JOKE, RIGHT?
...
NO.
MARCO...
YOU'VE ALWAYS BEEN GOOD AT PICKING UP ON THINGS... SO I CAN'T LET YOU GO.
EE...
SOME-OOOOOOOONE—
MMGH
BAM

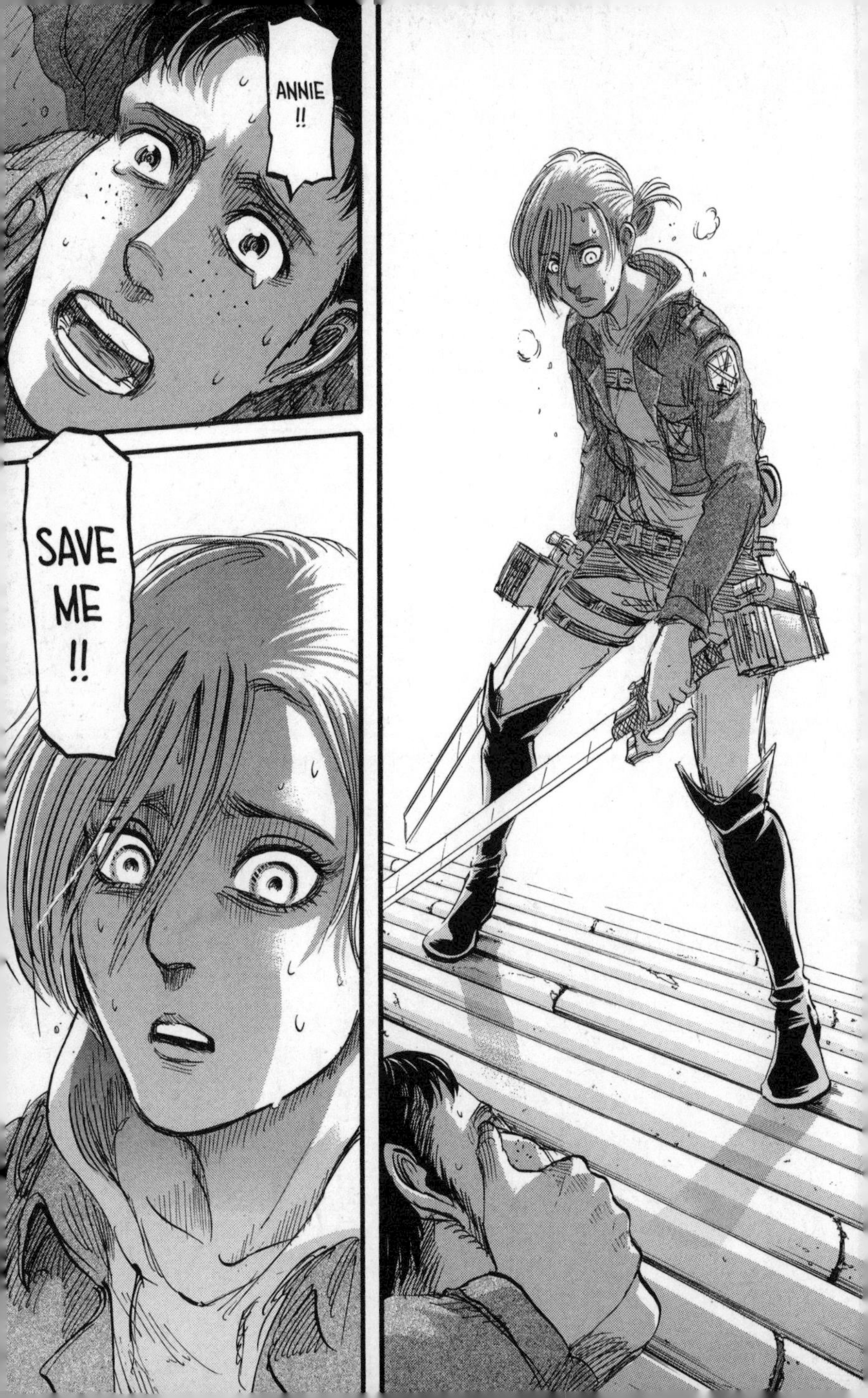
ANNIE !!
SAVE ME !!

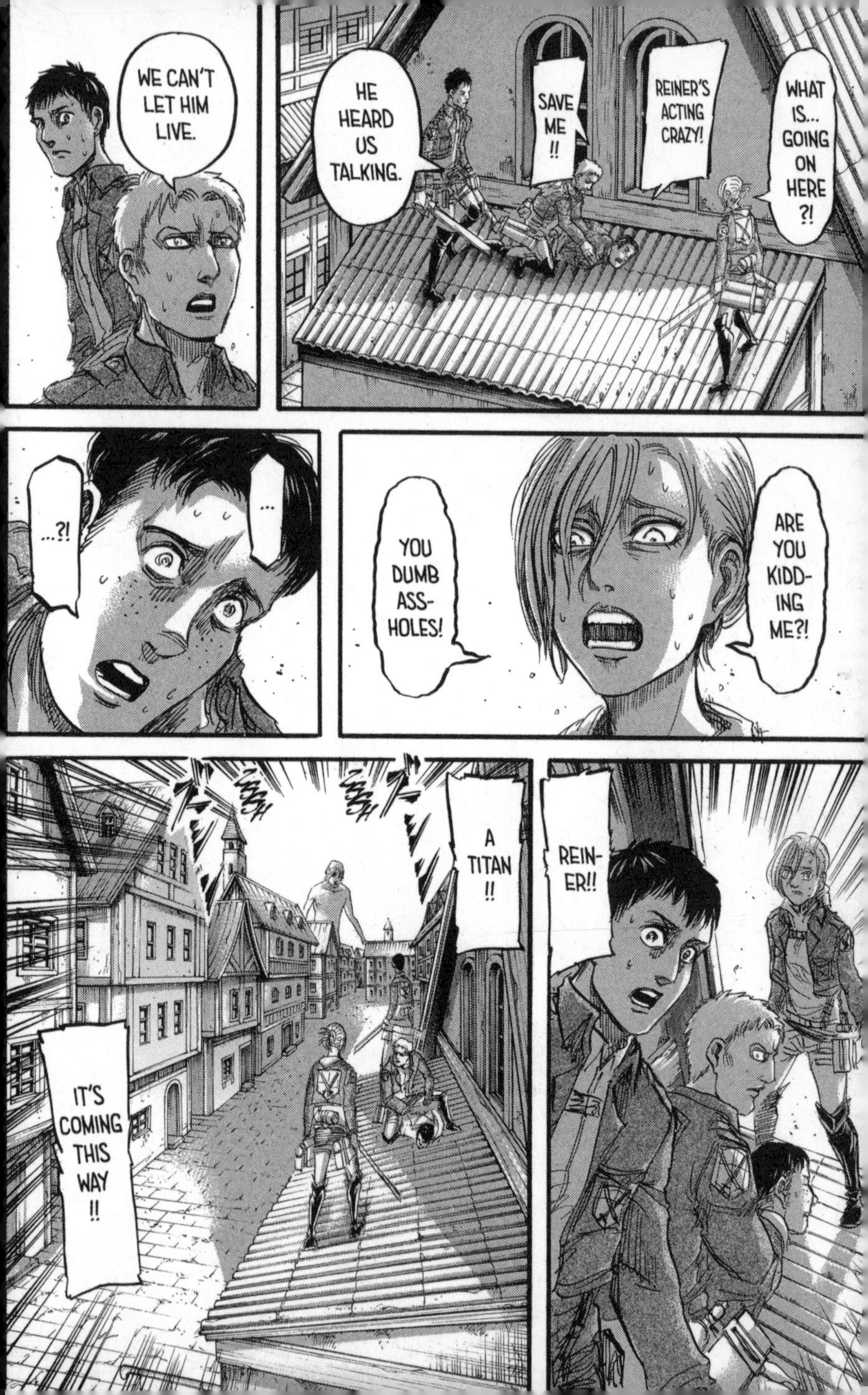
WHAT IS... GOING ON HERE?!
REINER'S ACTING CRAZY!
SAVE ME !!
HE HEARD US TALKING.
WE CAN'T LET HIM LIVE.
ARE YOU KIDD-ING ME?!
YOU DUMB ASS-HOLES!
...
...?!
REIN-ER!!
A TITAN !!
IT'S COMING THIS WAY !!

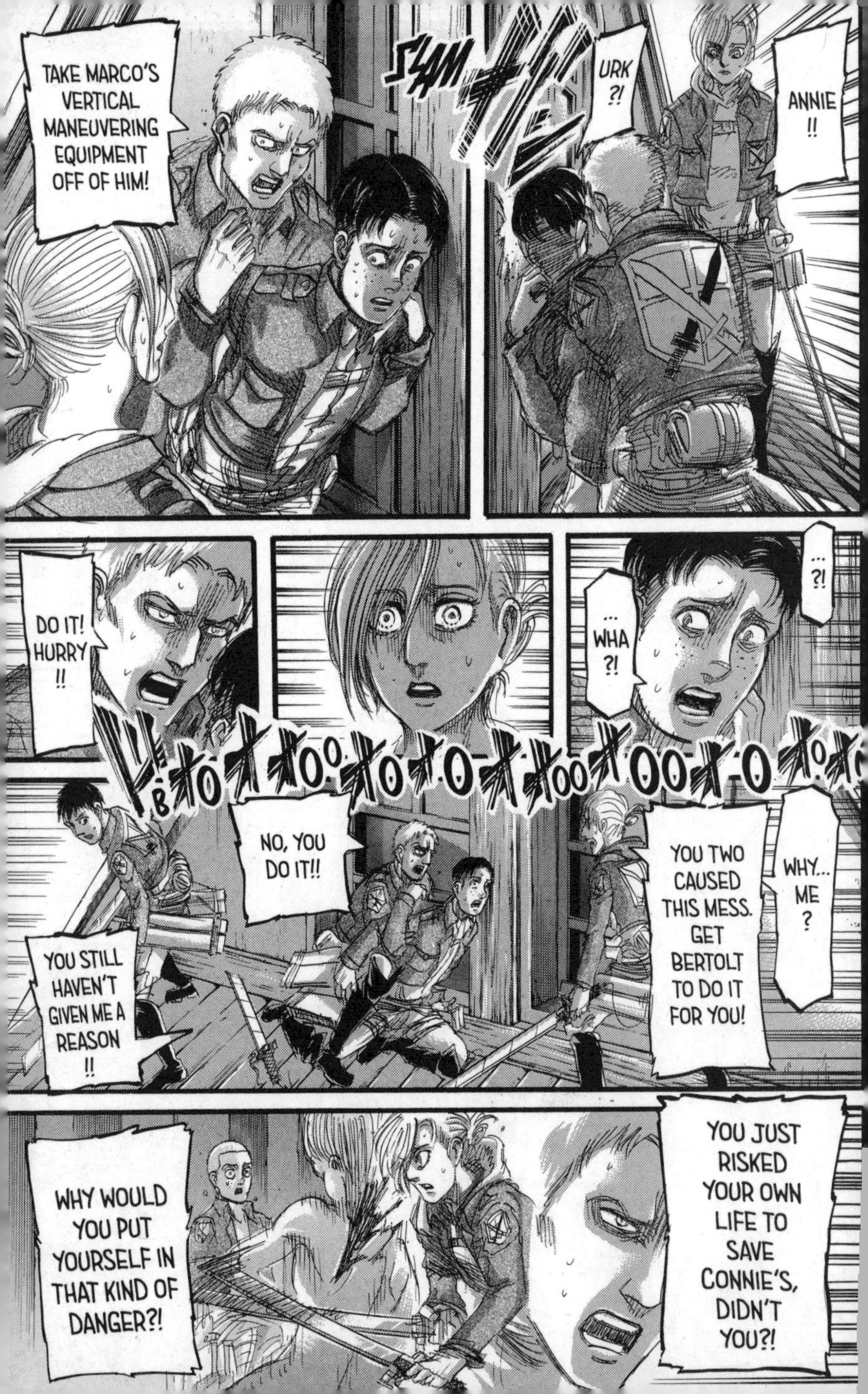
ANNIE !!
URK ?!
TAKE MARCO'S VERTICAL MANEUVERING EQUIPMENT OFF OF HIM!
... ?!
... WHA ?!
DO IT! HURRY !!
WHY... ME ?
YOU TWO CAUSED THIS MESS. GET BERTOLT TO DO IT FOR YOU!
NO, YOU DO IT!!
YOU STILL HAVEN'T GIVEN ME A REASON !!
YOU JUST RISKED YOUR OWN LIFE TO SAVE CONNIE'S, DIDN'T YOU?!
WHY WOULD YOU PUT YOURSELF IN THAT KIND OF DANGER?!

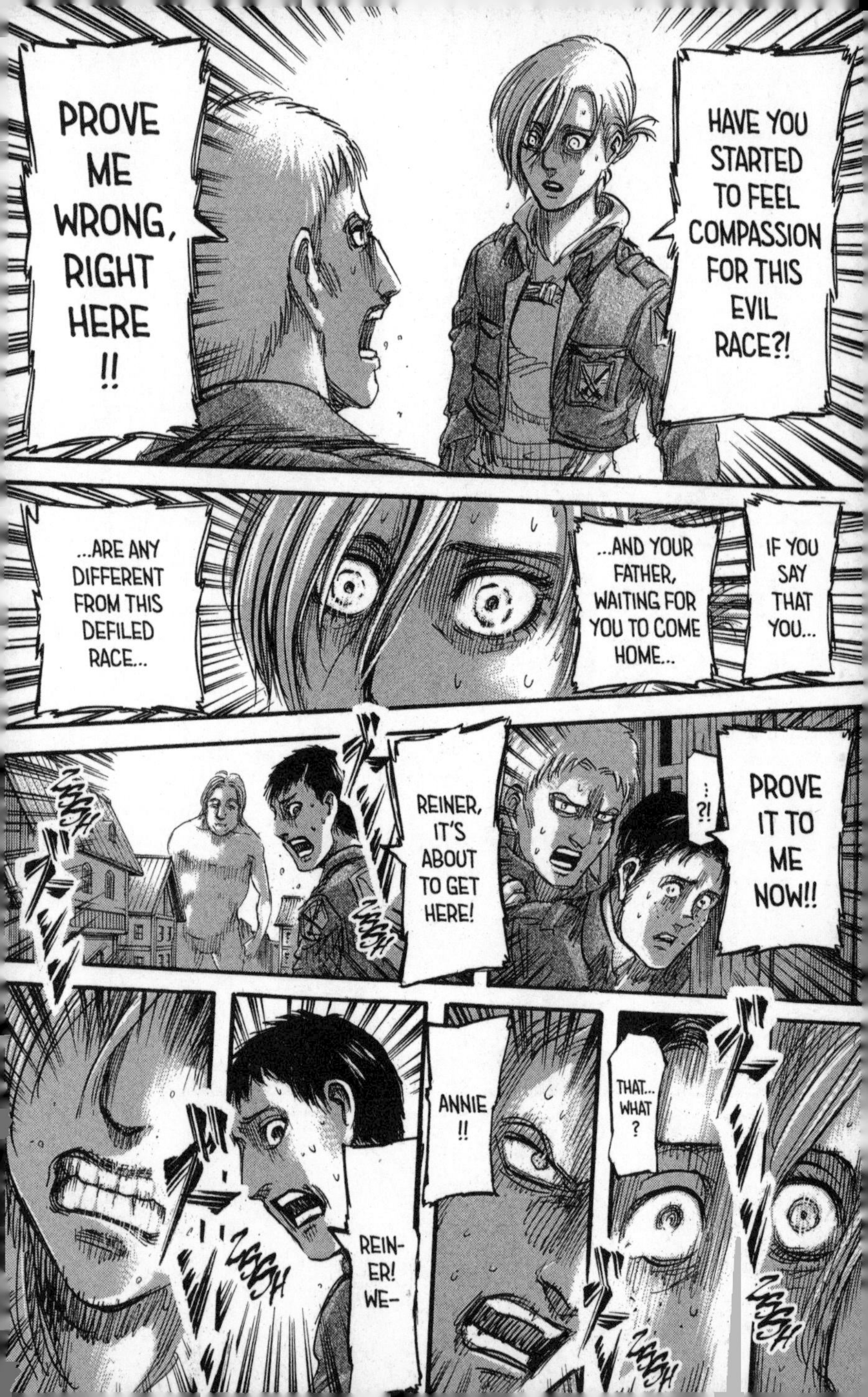
HAVE YOU STARTED TO FEEL COMPASSION FOR THIS EVIL RACE?!
PROVE ME WRONG, RIGHT HERE!!
IF YOU SAY THAT YOU...
...AND YOUR FATHER, WAITING FOR YOU TO COME HOME...
...ARE ANY DIFFERENT FROM THIS DEFILED RACE...
PROVE IT TO ME NOW!!
...?!
REINER, IT'S ABOUT TO GET HERE!
ZSSSH
ZSSSH
ZSSSH
ZSSSH
THAT... WHAT?
ANNIE!!
REIN-ER! WE-
ZSSSH

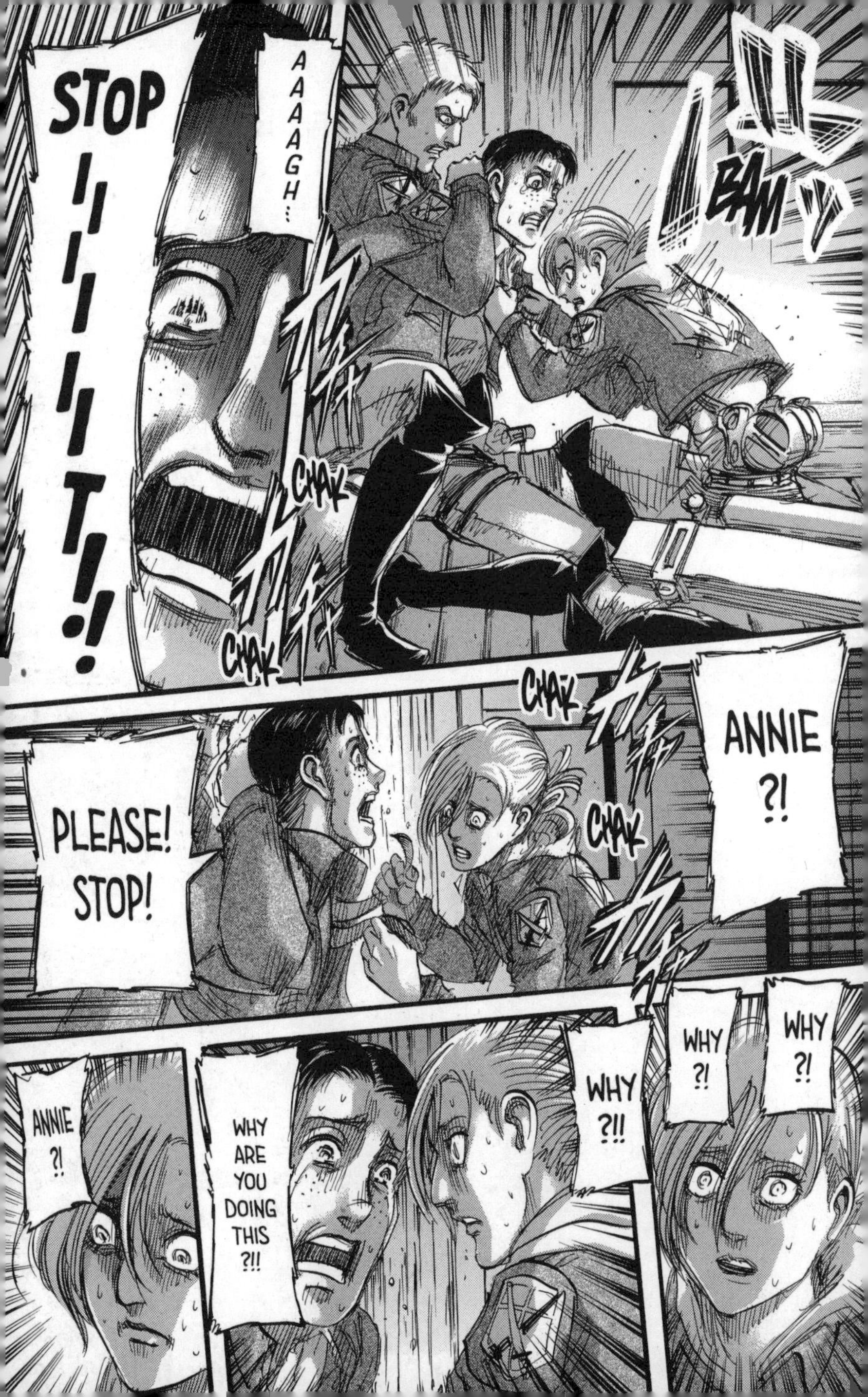
BAM
AAAAGH...
STOP IIIIIT!!
CHAK
CHAK
CHAK
ANNIE ?!
CHAK
PLEASE! STOP!
WHY ?!
WHY ?!
WHY ?!!
WHY ARE YOU DOING THIS ?!!
ANNIE ?!

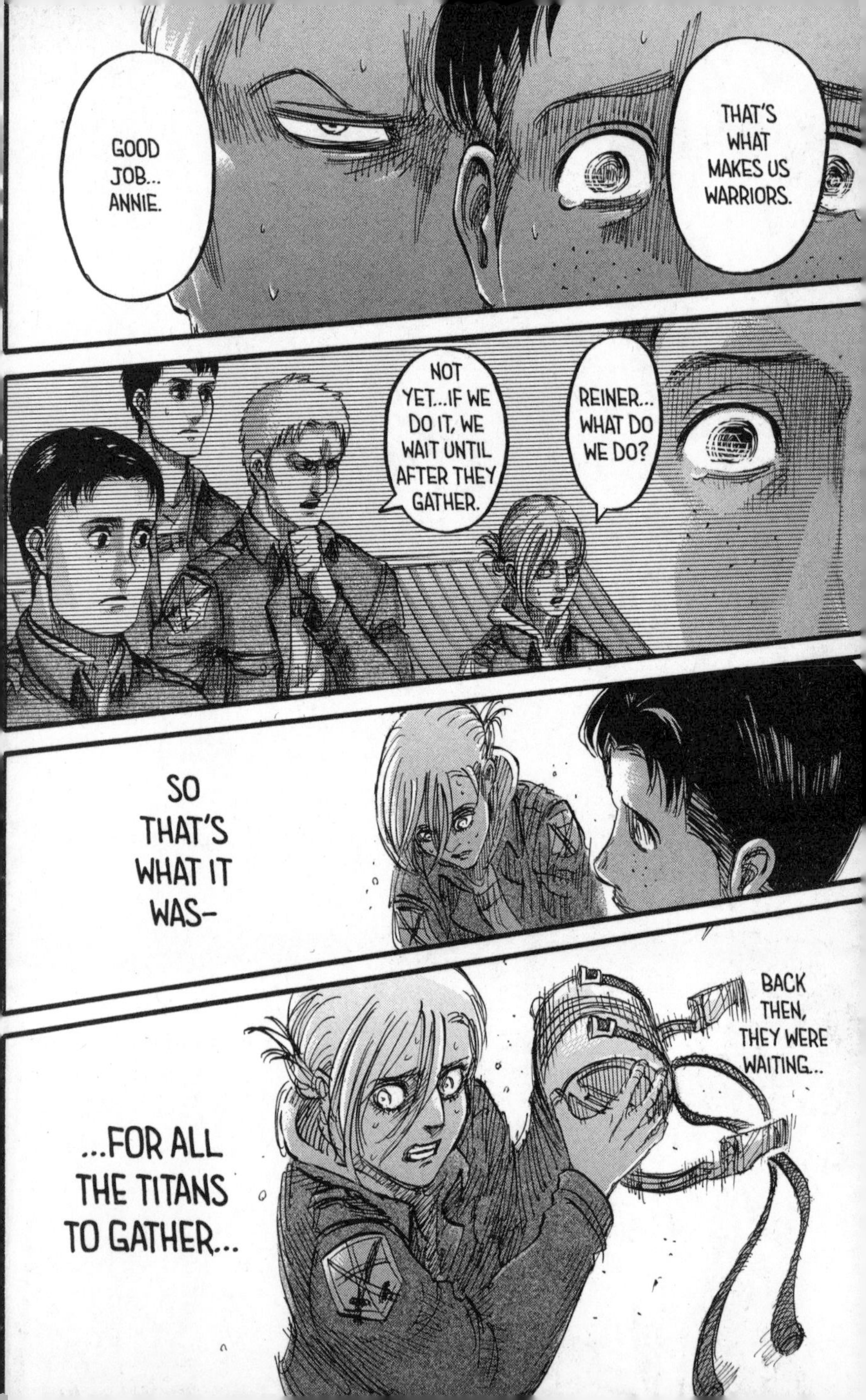
THAT'S WHAT MAKES US WARRIORS.
GOOD JOB... ANNIE.
REINER... WHAT DO WE DO?
NOT YET...IF WE DO IT, WE WAIT UNTIL AFTER THEY GATHER.
SO THAT'S WHAT IT WAS-
BACK THEN, THEY WERE WAITING...
...FOR ALL THE TITANS TO GATHER...

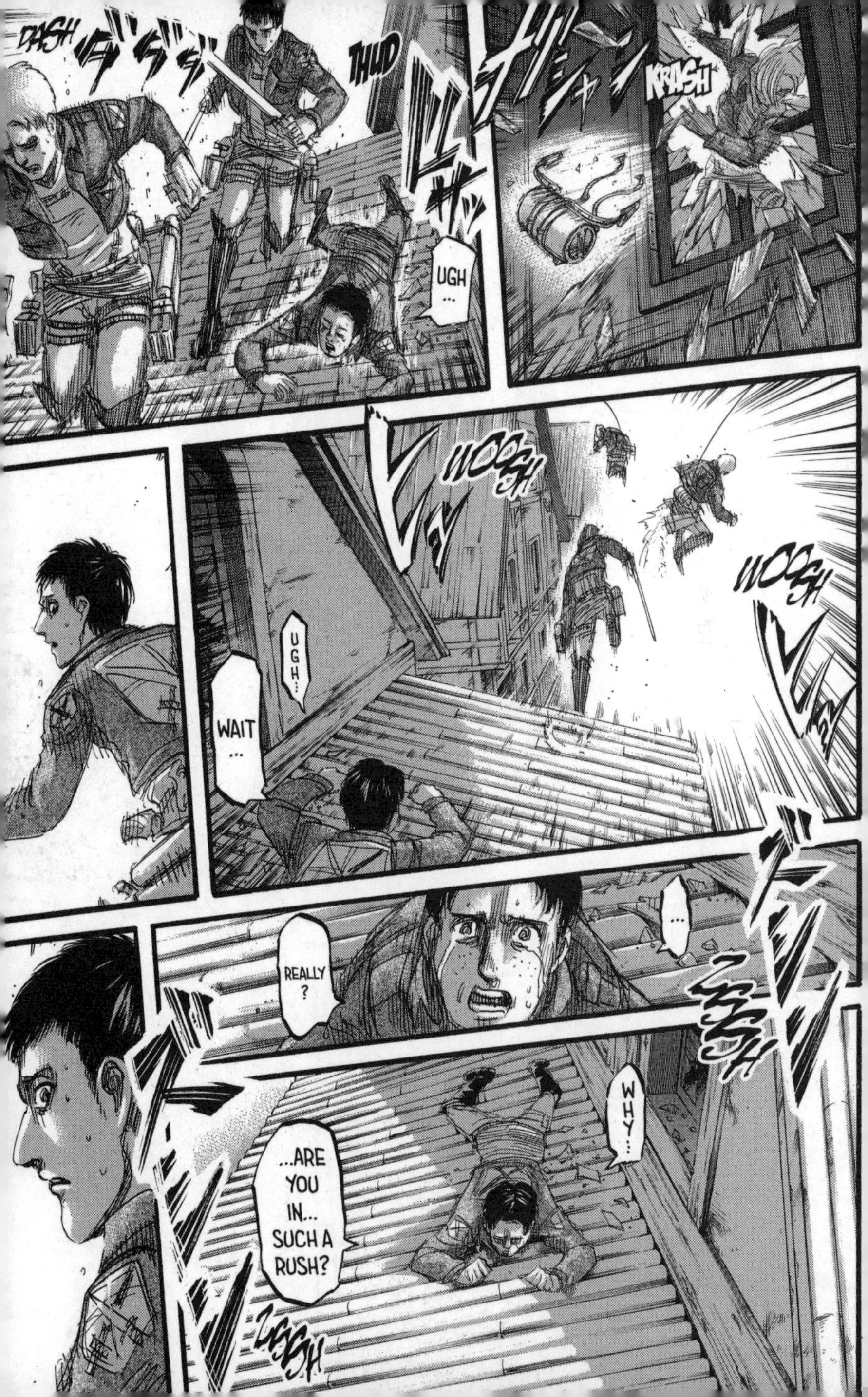
KRASH
THUD
DASH
UGH ...
WOOSH
WOOSH
UGH...
WAIT ...
...
REALLY ?
ZSSSH
WHY...
...ARE YOU IN... SUCH A RUSH?
ZSSSH

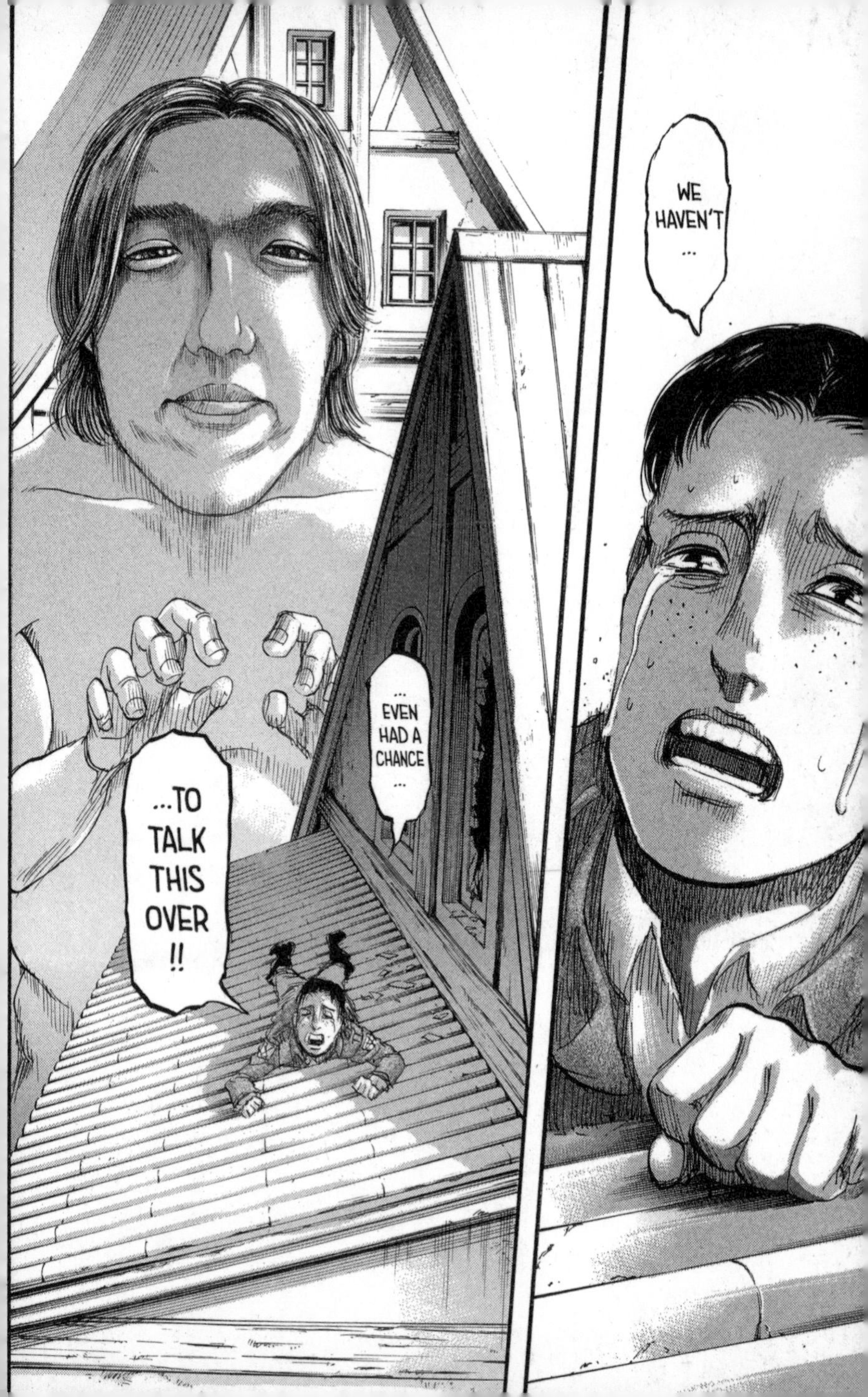
WE HAVEN'T ...
... EVEN HAD A CHANCE ...
...TO TALK THIS OVER !!

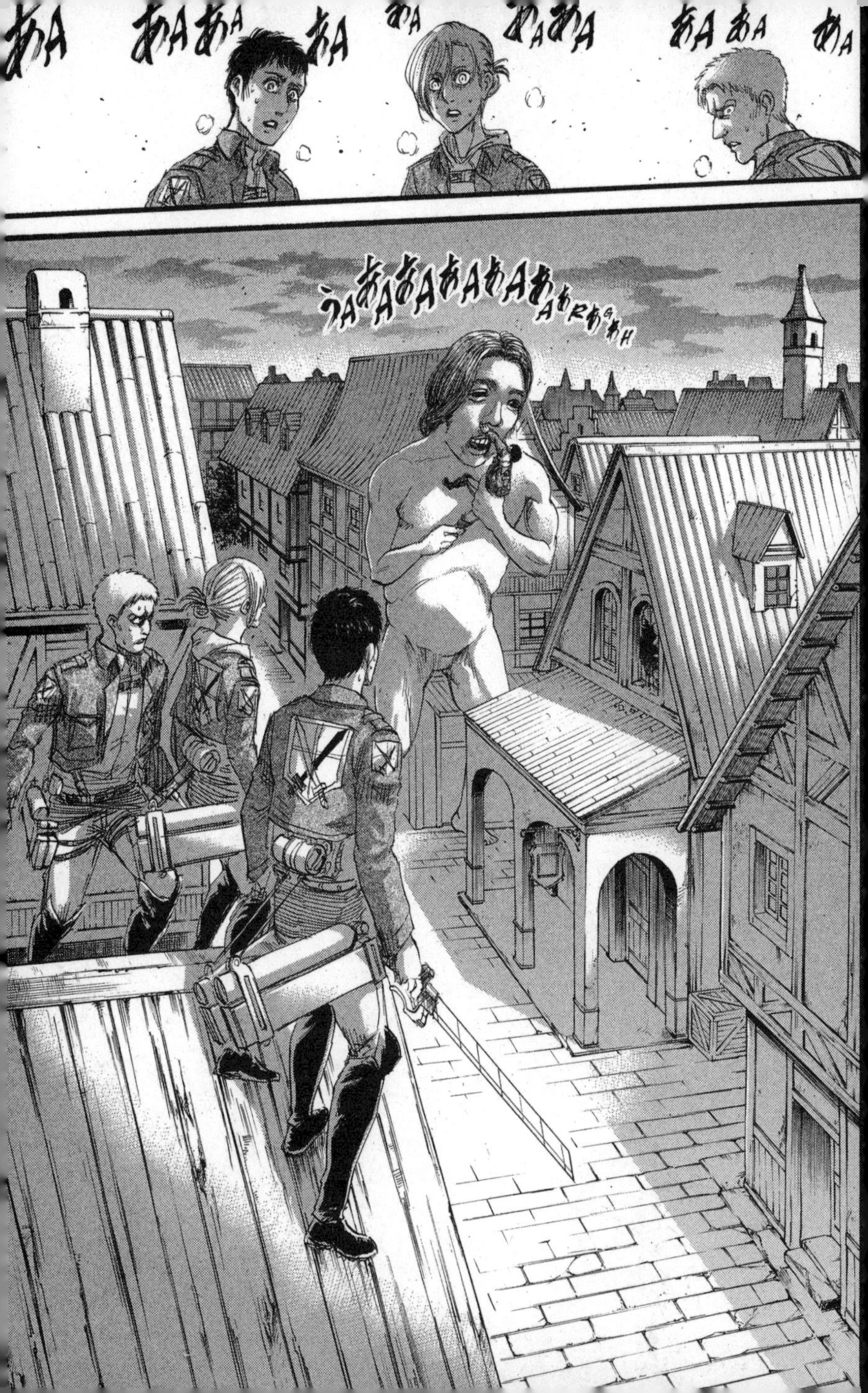
あA
あAあA
あA
あA
あAあA
あAあA
あA
うAあAあAあAあAあAあRあGあH

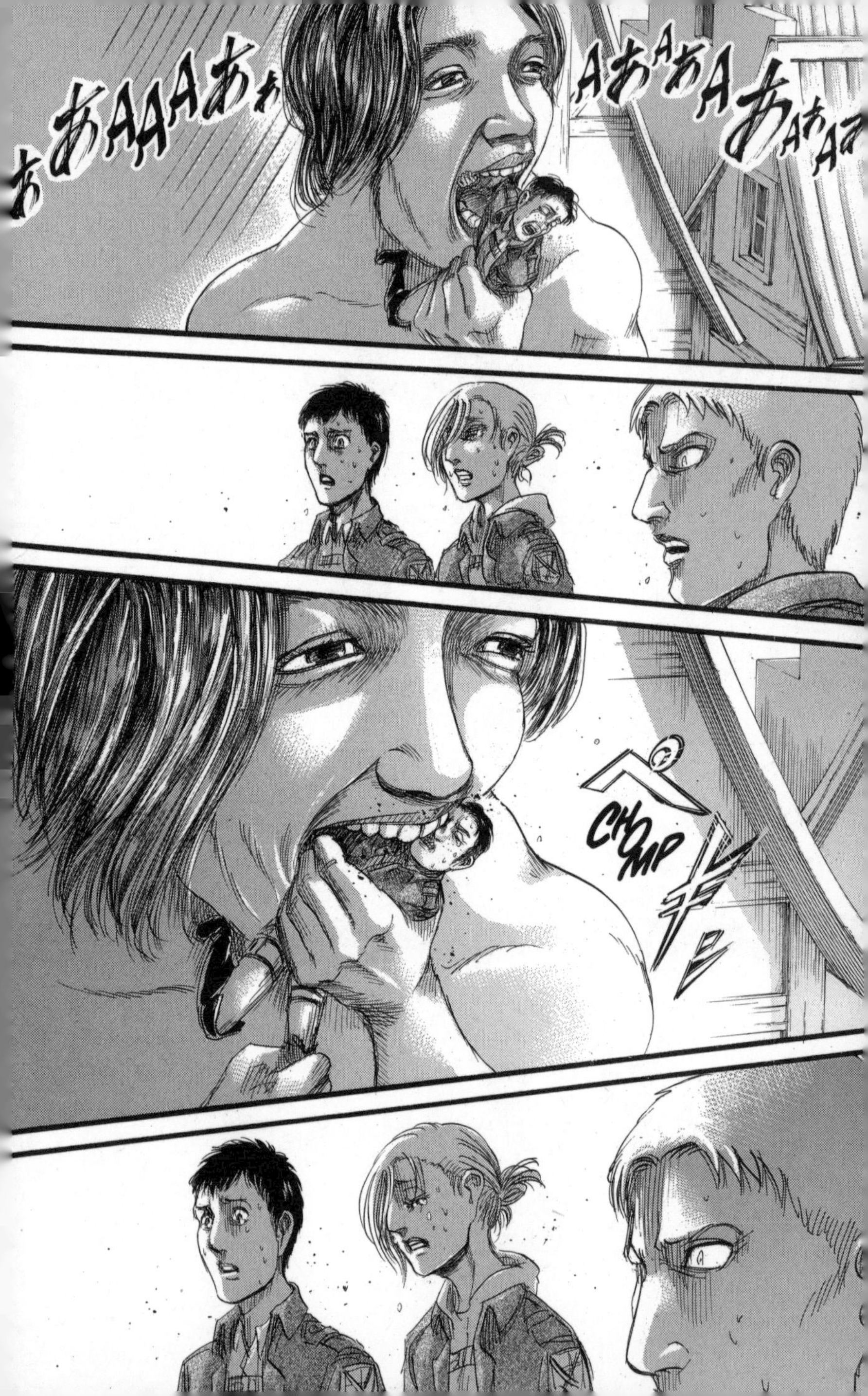

AあAあAあAあA
あああAAAあぁ
CHOMP

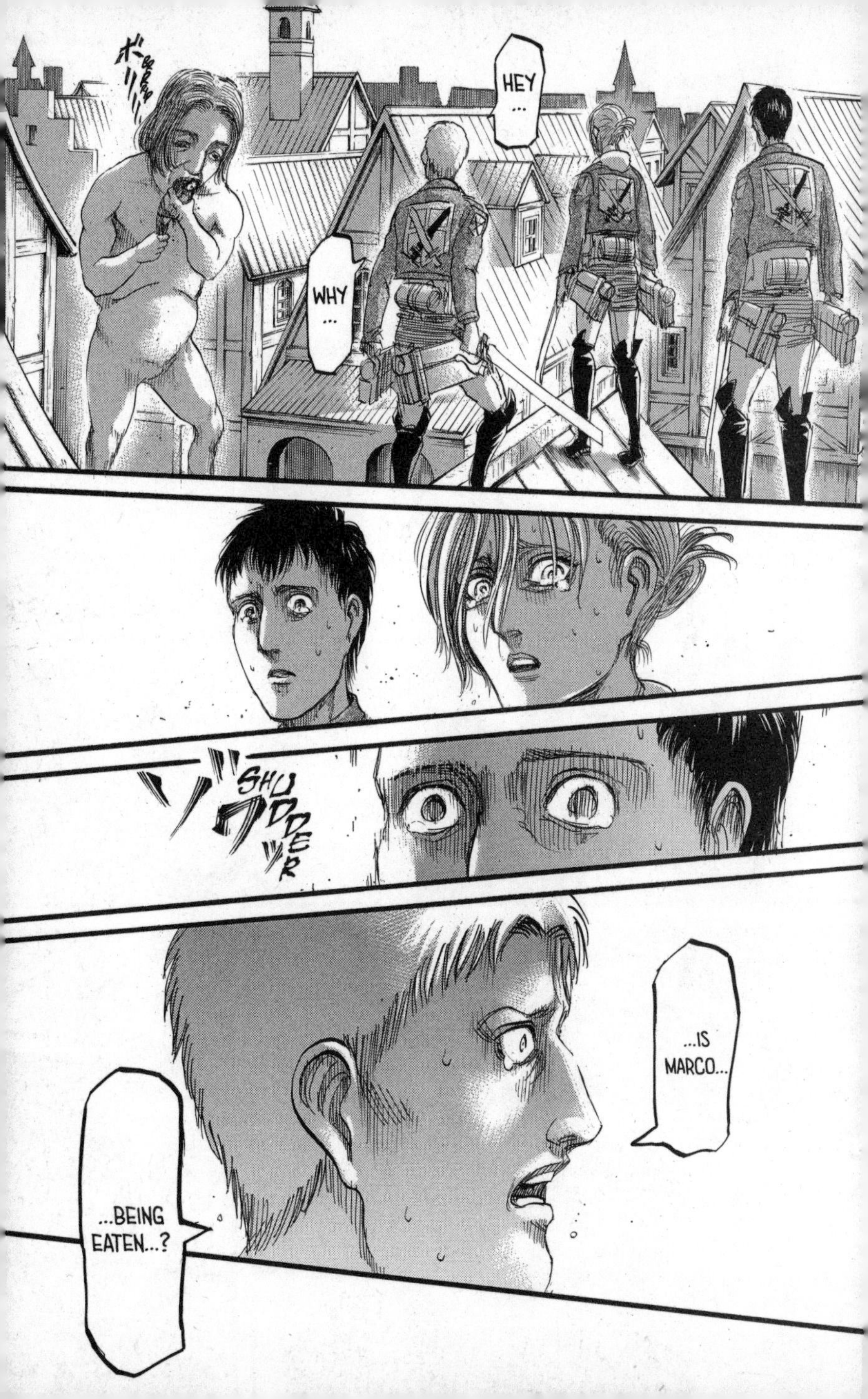
HEY ...
WHY ...
ボーリ
SHUDDER
...IS MARCO...
...BEING EATEN...?

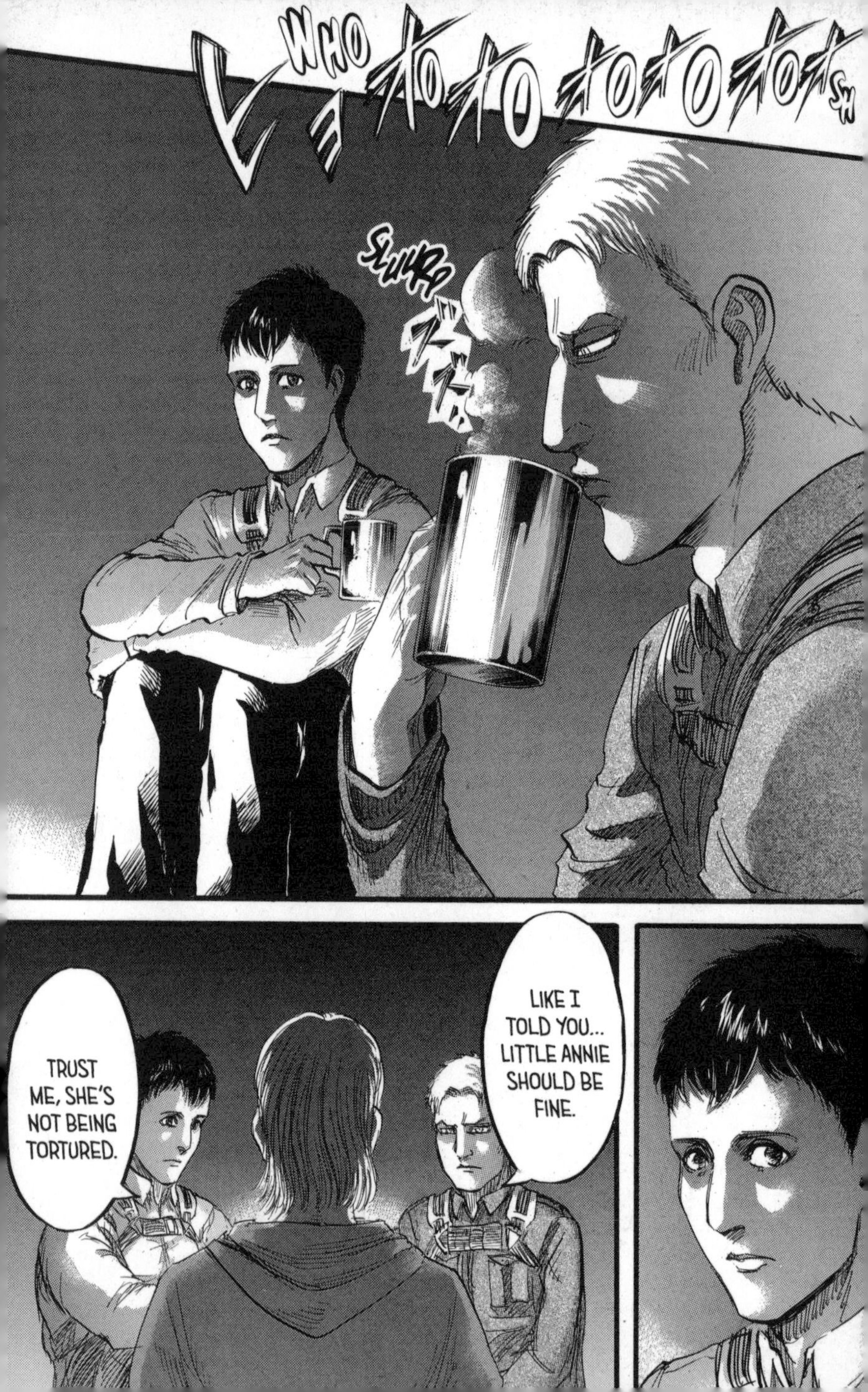
WHO
SH
SLURP
LIKE I TOLD YOU... LITTLE ANNIE SHOULD BE FINE.
TRUST ME, SHE'S NOT BEING TORTURED.

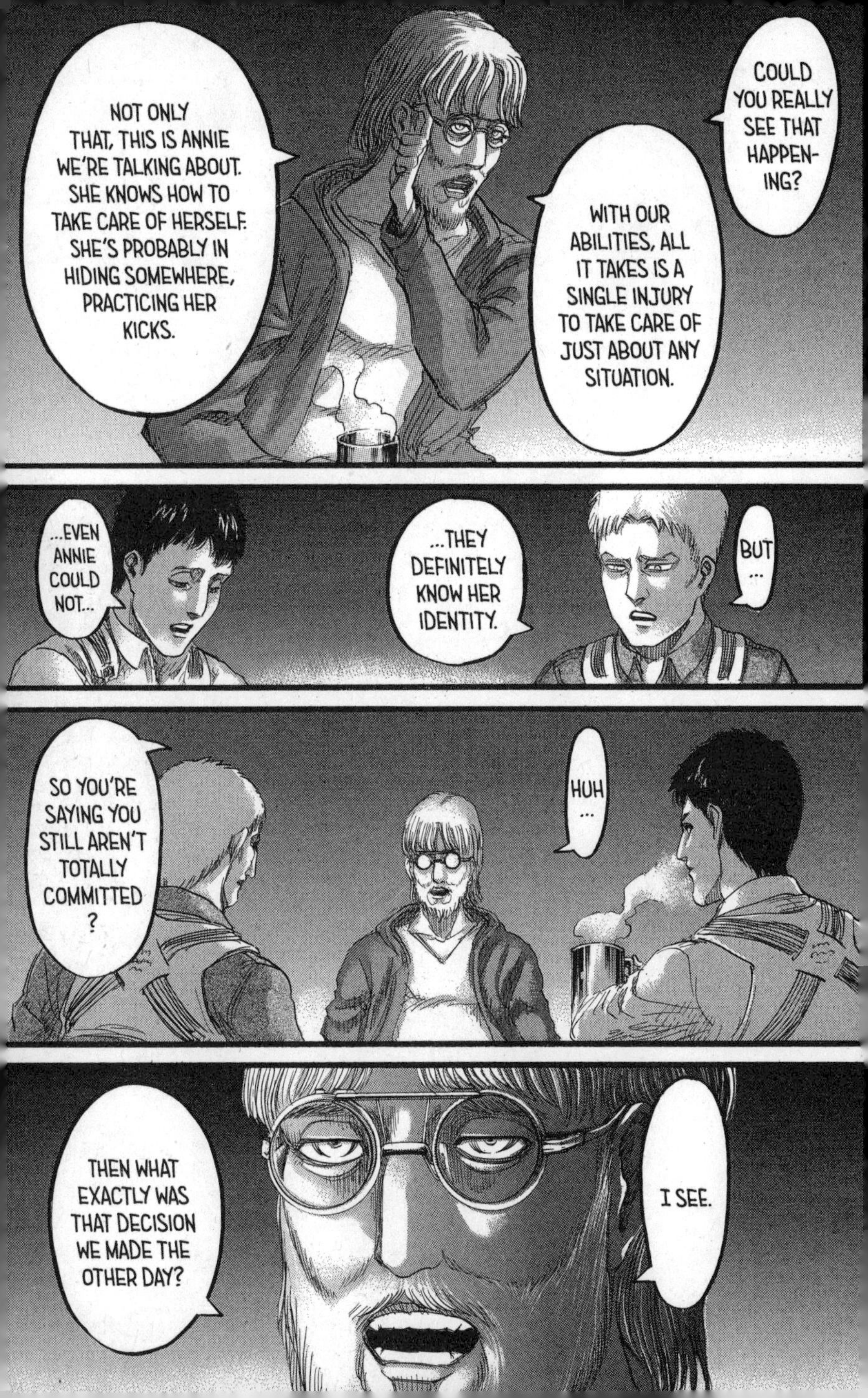
COULD YOU REALLY SEE THAT HAPPEN-ING?
WITH OUR ABILITIES, ALL IT TAKES IS A SINGLE INJURY TO TAKE CARE OF JUST ABOUT ANY SITUATION.
NOT ONLY THAT, THIS IS ANNIE WE'RE TALKING ABOUT. SHE KNOWS HOW TO TAKE CARE OF HERSELF. SHE'S PROBABLY IN HIDING SOMEWHERE, PRACTICING HER KICKS.
BUT ...
...THEY DEFINITELY KNOW HER IDENTITY.
...EVEN ANNIE COULD NOT...
HUH ...
SO YOU'RE SAYING YOU STILL AREN'T TOTALLY COMMITTED ?
I SEE.
THEN WHAT EXACTLY WAS THAT DECISION WE MADE THE OTHER DAY?

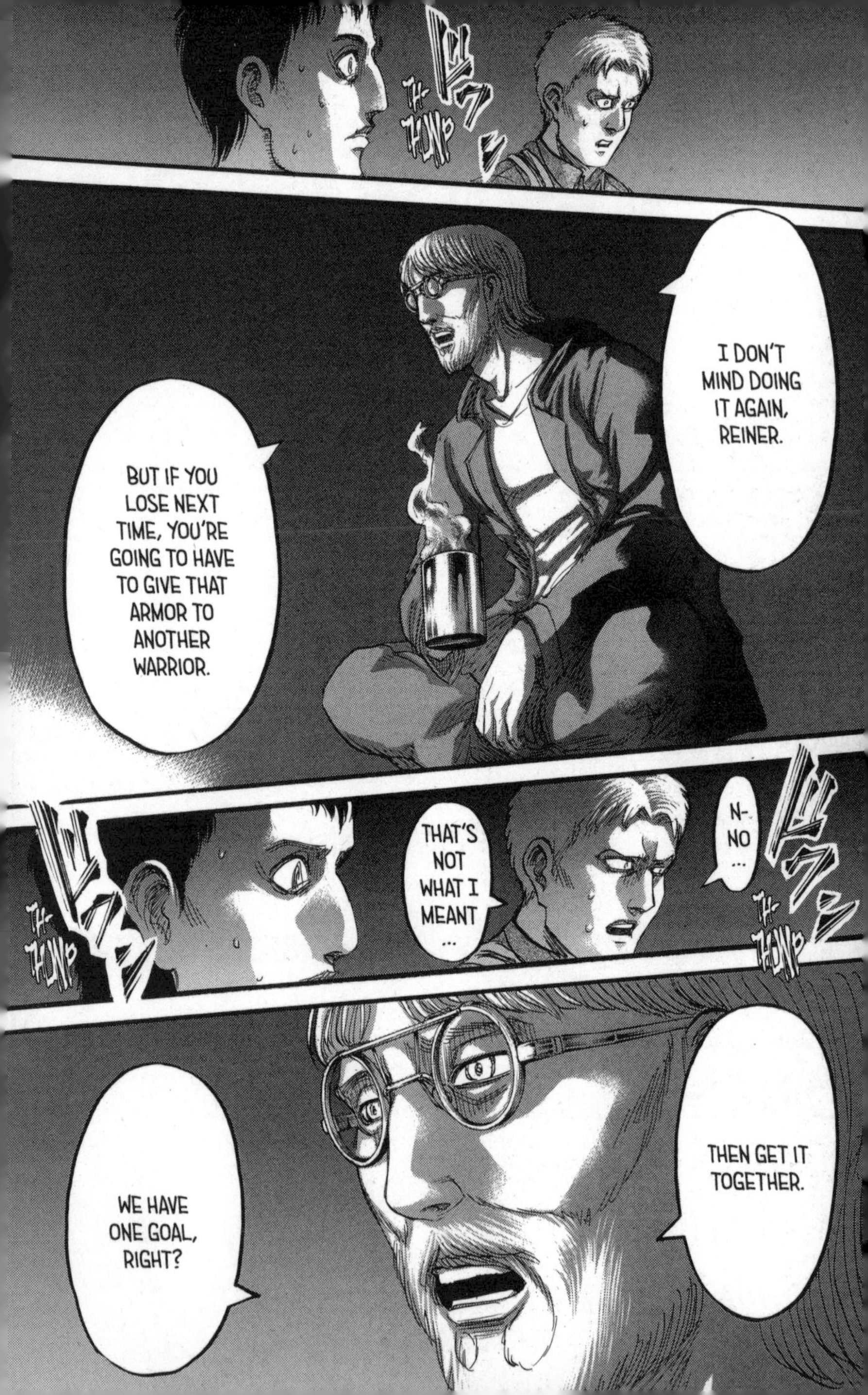
TH-THUMP
I DON'T MIND DOING IT AGAIN, REINER.
BUT IF YOU LOSE NEXT TIME, YOU'RE GOING TO HAVE TO GIVE THAT ARMOR TO ANOTHER WARRIOR.
TH-THUMP
N-NO ...
THAT'S NOT WHAT I MEANT ...
TH-THUMP
THEN GET IT TOGETHER.
WE HAVE ONE GOAL, RIGHT?

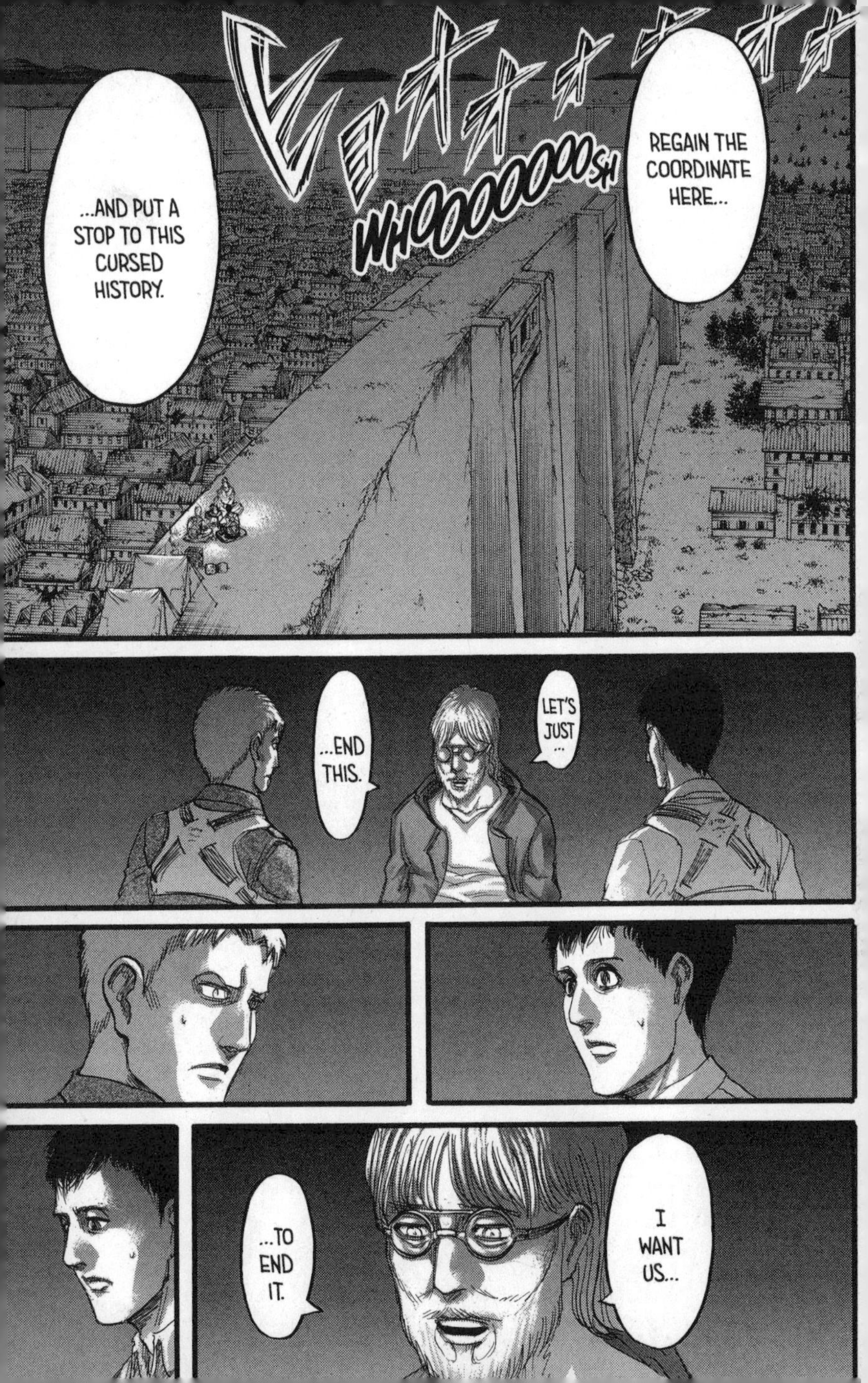
REGAIN THE COORDINATE HERE...
WHOOOOOOOSH
...AND PUT A STOP TO THIS CURSED HISTORY.
LET'S JUST ...
...END THIS.
I WANT US...
...TO END IT.

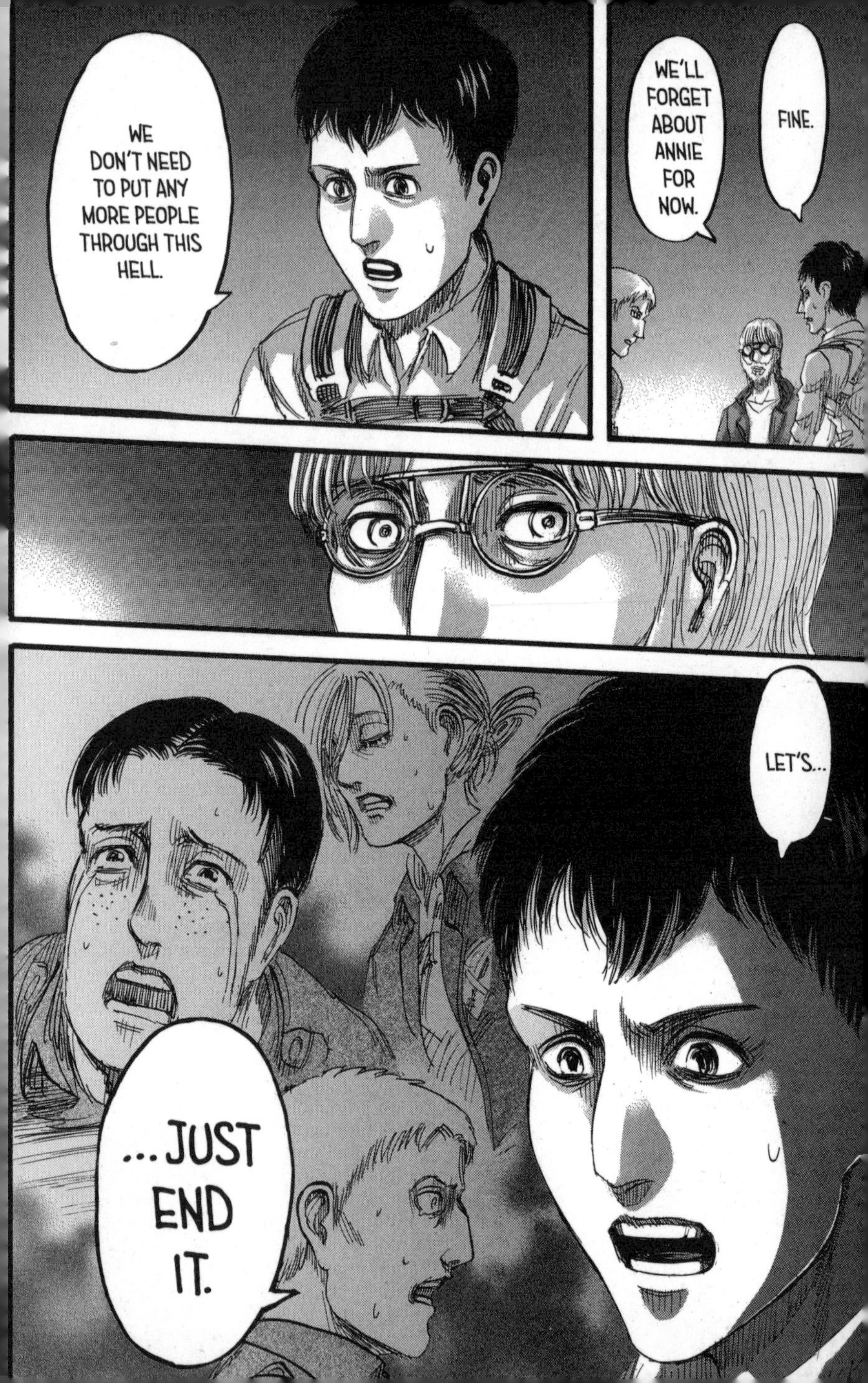
FINE.
WE'LL FORGET ABOUT ANNIE FOR NOW.
WE DON'T NEED TO PUT ANY MORE PEOPLE THROUGH THIS HELL.
LET'S...
...JUST END IT.

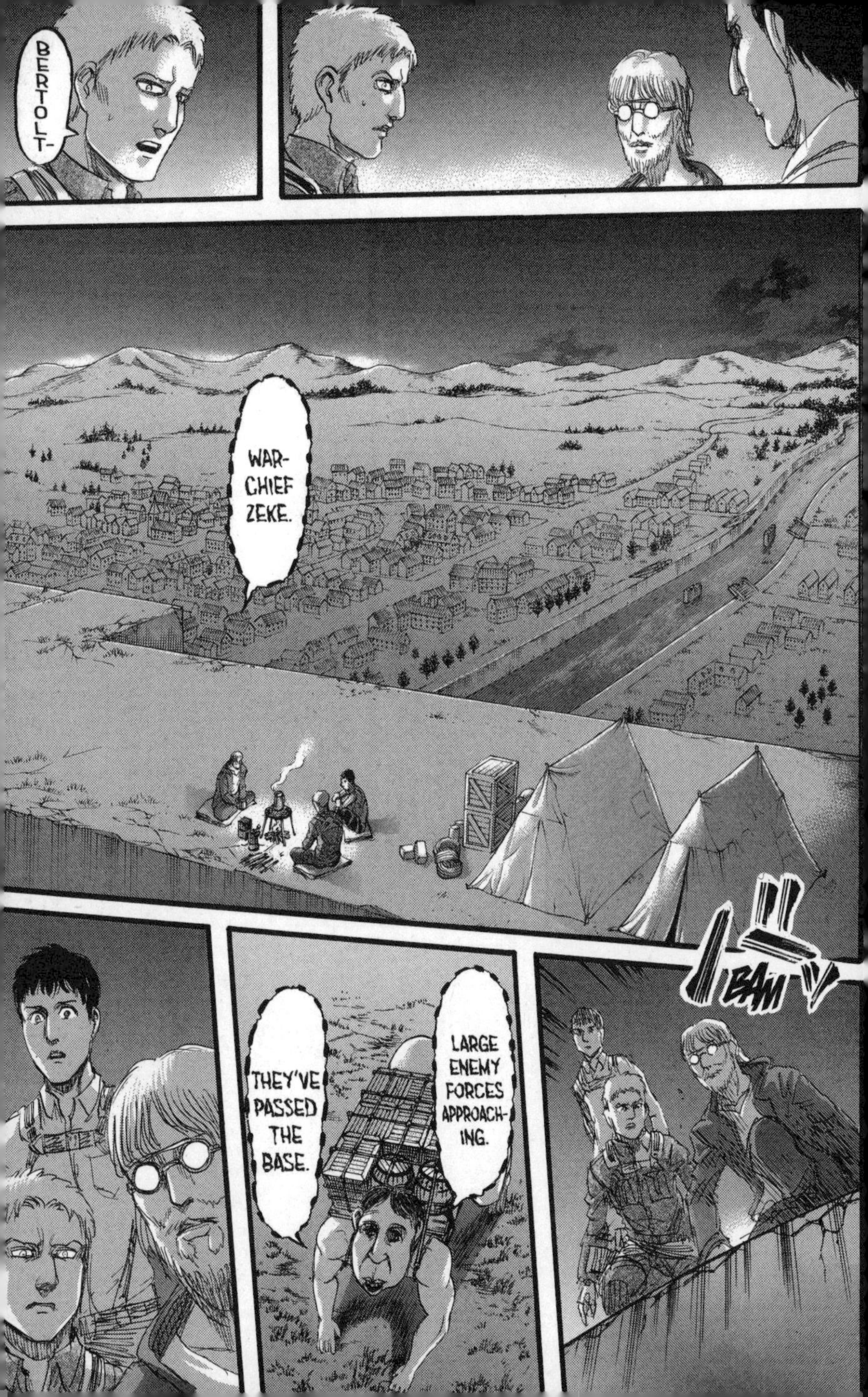
BERTOLT-
WAR-CHIEF ZEKE.
BAM
LARGE ENEMY FORCES APPROACH-ING.
THEY'VE PASSED THE BASE.

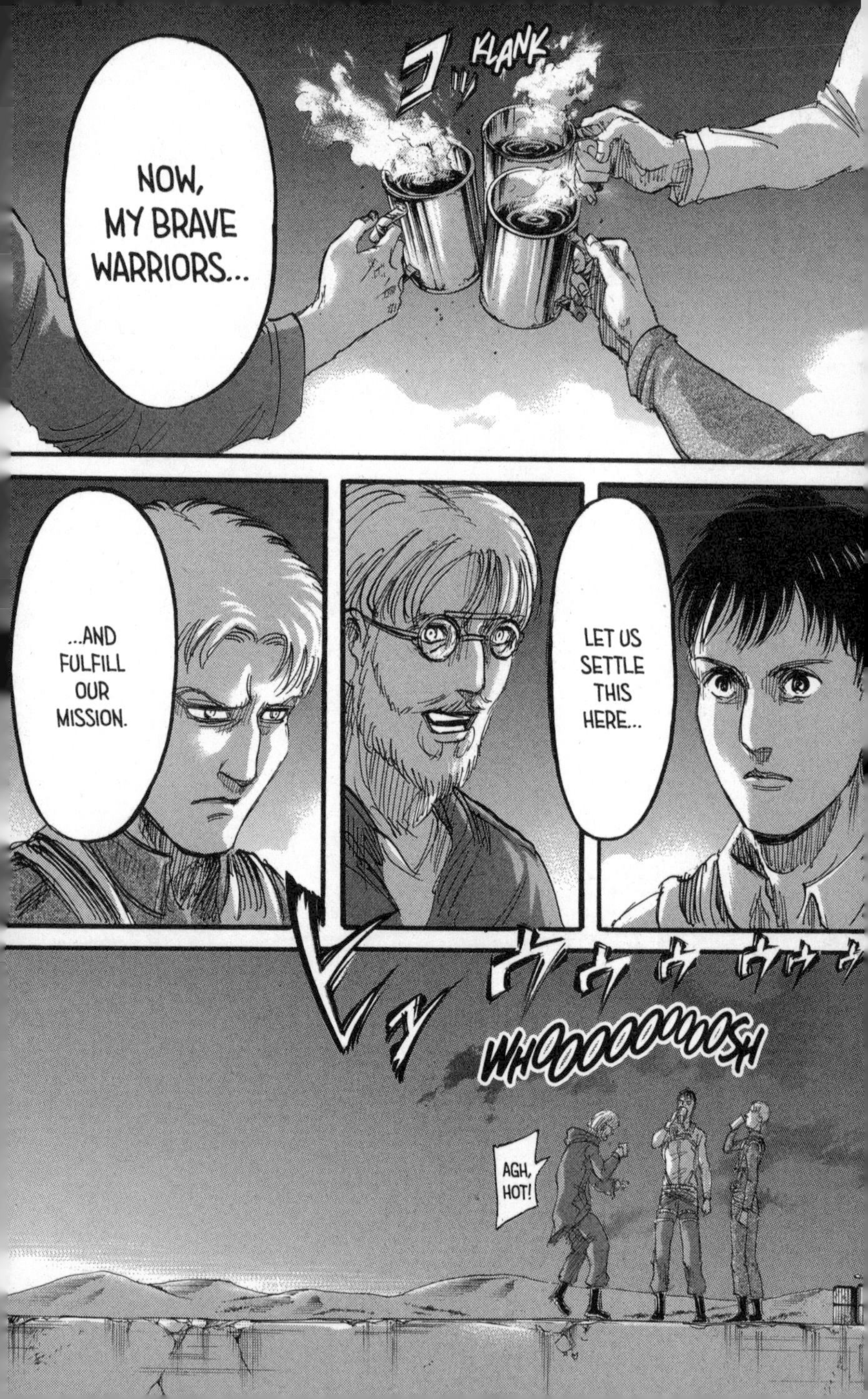
KLANK
NOW, MY BRAVE WARRIORS...
LET US SETTLE THIS HERE...
...AND FULFILL OUR MISSION.
WHOOOOOOOOSH
AGH, HOT!

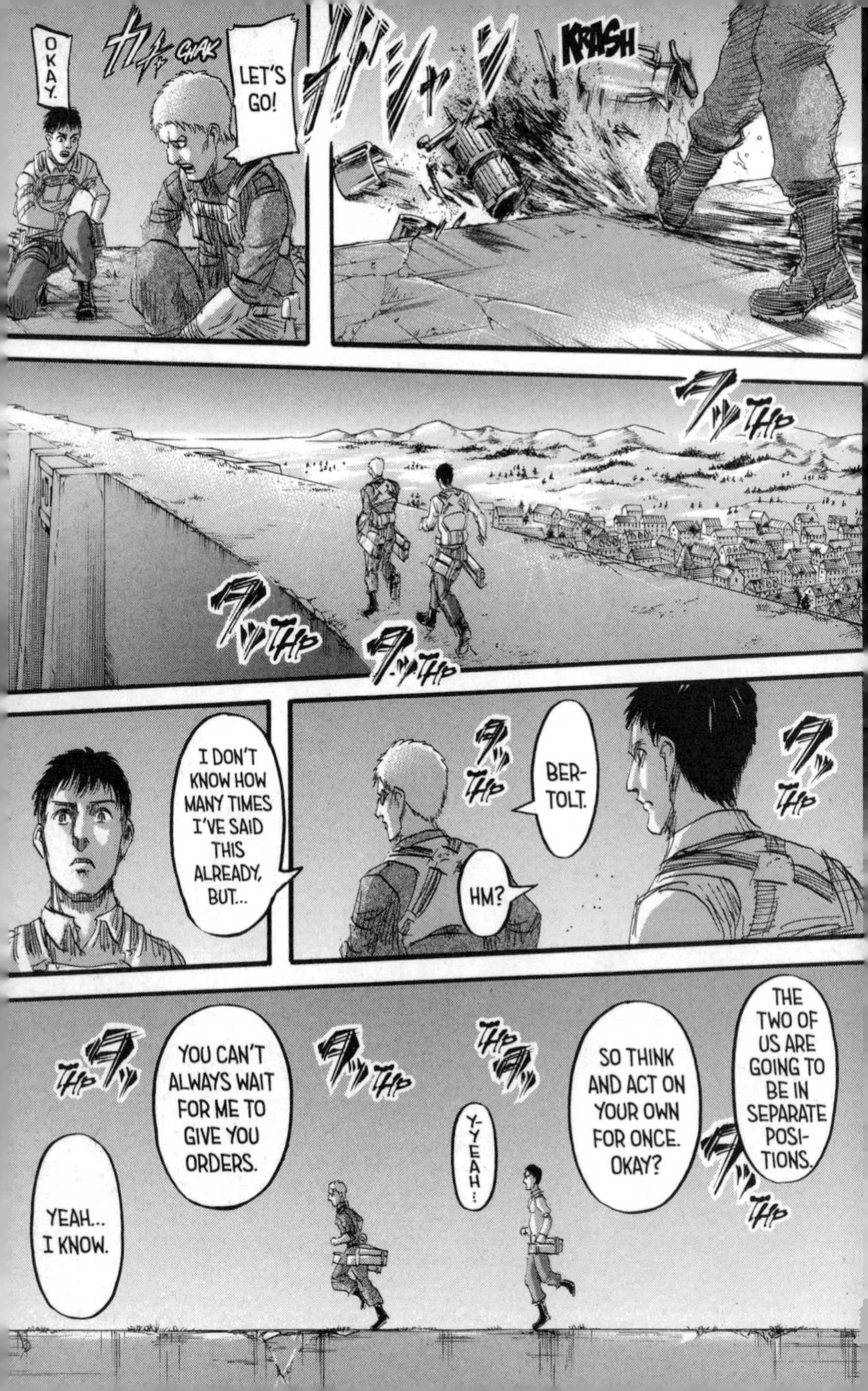
KRASH
LET'S GO!
CHAK
OKAY.
THP
THP
THP
THP
BER-TOLT.
HM?
THP
I DON'T KNOW HOW MANY TIMES I'VE SAID THIS ALREADY, BUT...
THP
THE TWO OF US ARE GOING TO BE IN SEPARATE POSITIONS.
SO THINK AND ACT ON YOUR OWN FOR ONCE. OKAY?
THP
Y-YEAH...
THP
YOU CAN'T ALWAYS WAIT FOR ME TO GIVE YOU ORDERS.
THP
YEAH... I KNOW.

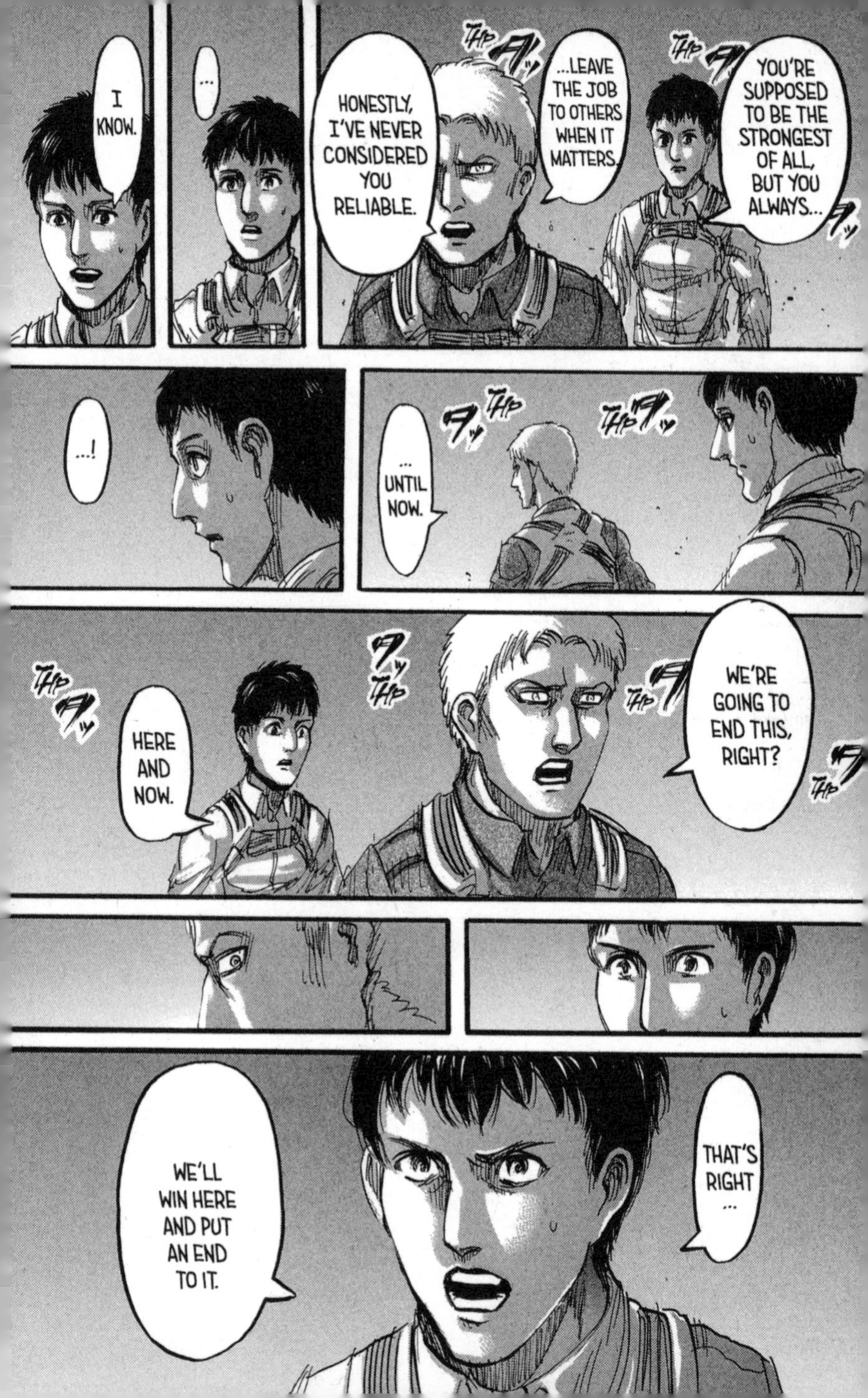
THP
YOU'RE SUPPOSED TO BE THE STRONGEST OF ALL, BUT YOU ALWAYS...
THP
...LEAVE THE JOB TO OTHERS WHEN IT MATTERS.
HONESTLY, I'VE NEVER CONSIDERED YOU RELIABLE.
...
I KNOW.
THP
THP
... UNTIL NOW.
...!
THP
WE'RE GOING TO END THIS, RIGHT?
THP
THP
HERE AND NOW.
THP
THAT'S RIGHT...
WE'LL WIN HERE AND PUT AN END TO IT.

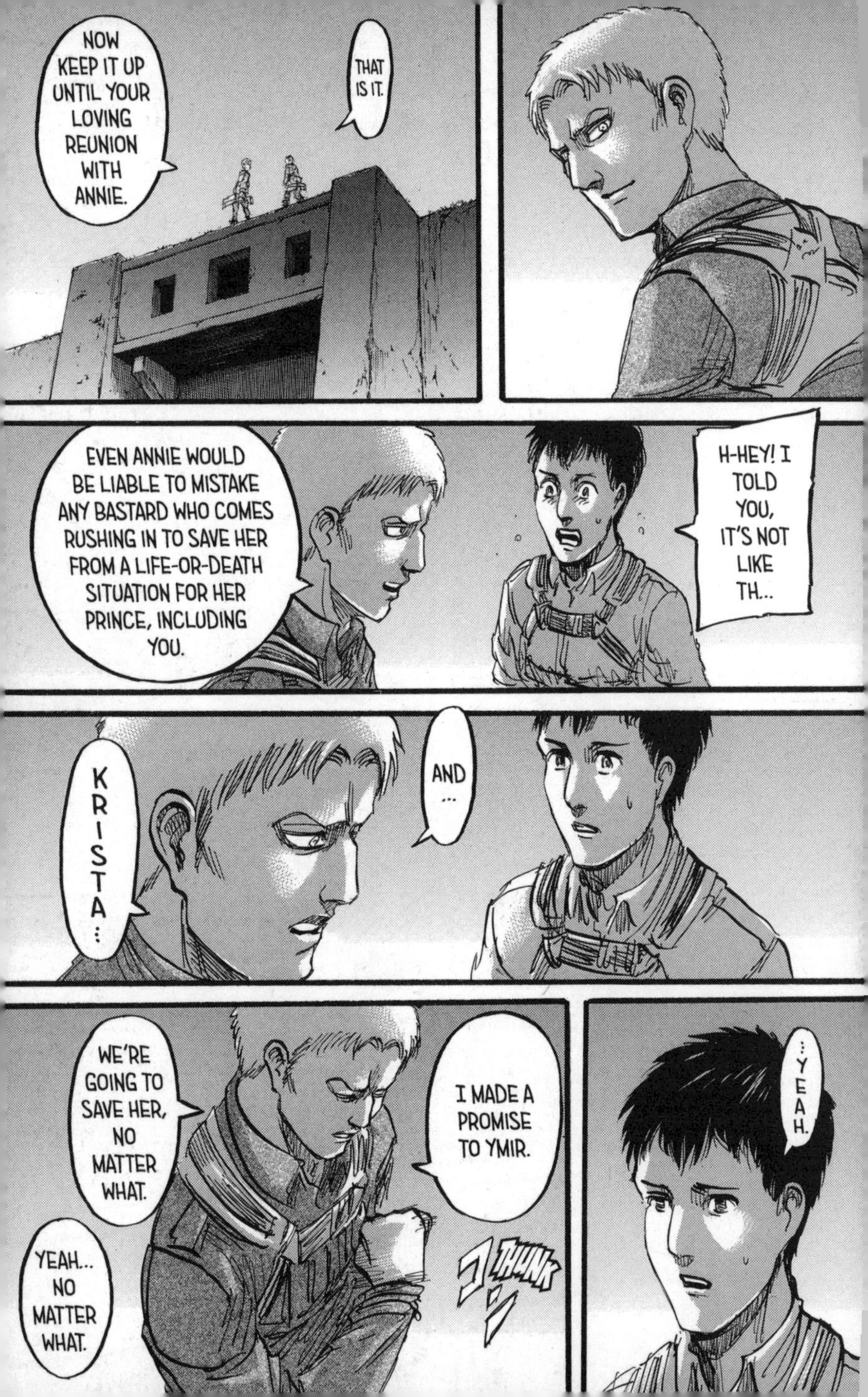
THAT IS IT.
NOW KEEP IT UP UNTIL YOUR LOVING REUNION WITH ANNIE.
H-HEY! I TOLD YOU, IT'S NOT LIKE TH...
EVEN ANNIE WOULD BE LIABLE TO MISTAKE ANY BASTARD WHO COMES RUSHING IN TO SAVE HER FROM A LIFE-OR-DEATH SITUATION FOR HER PRINCE, INCLUDING YOU.
AND ...
KRISTA...
...YEAH.
I MADE A PROMISE TO YMIR.
THUNK
WE'RE GOING TO SAVE HER, NO MATTER WHAT.
YEAH... NO MATTER WHAT.

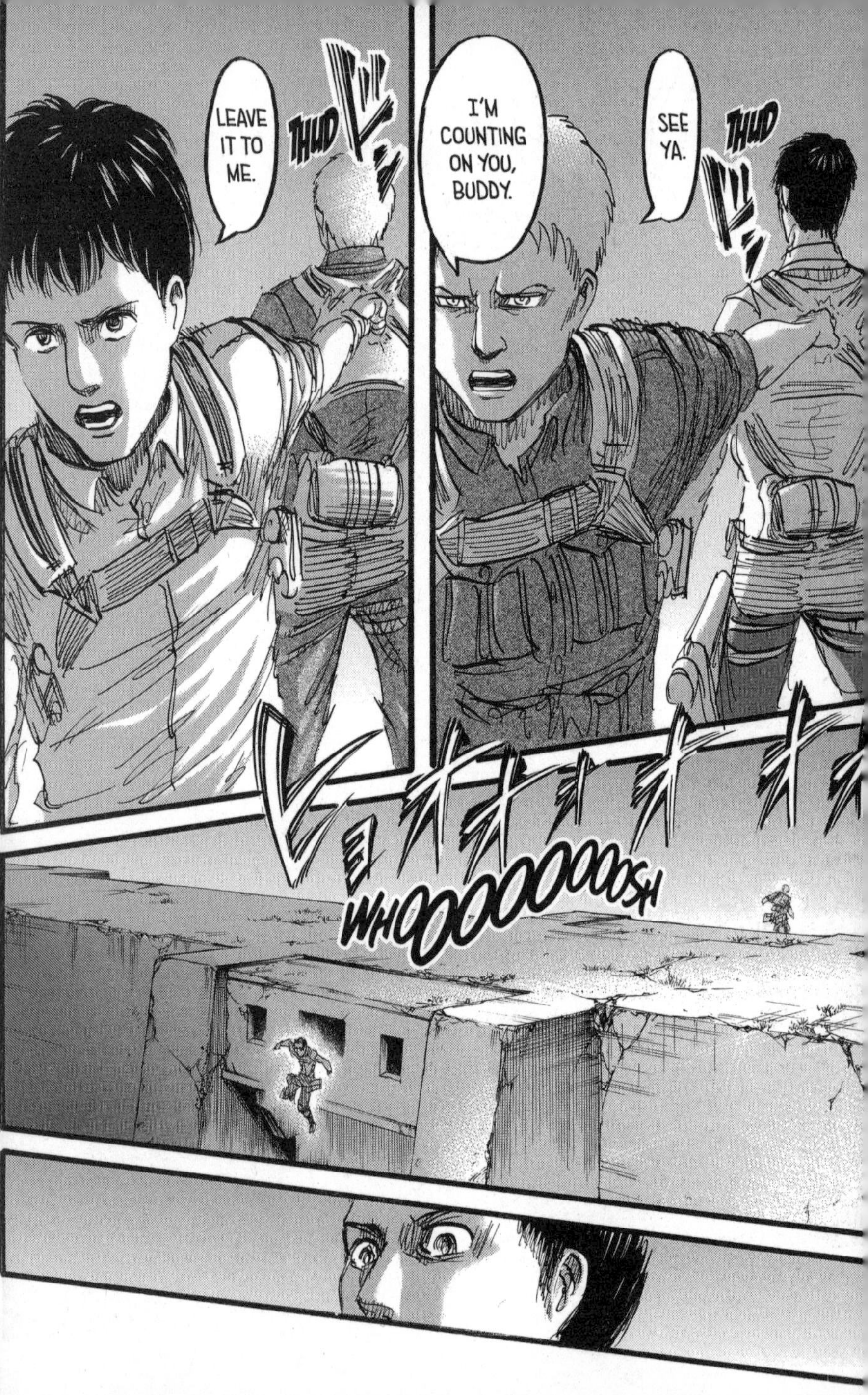
SEE YA.
THUD
I'M COUNTING ON YOU, BUDDY.
THUD
LEAVE IT TO ME.
WHOOOOOOOOSH

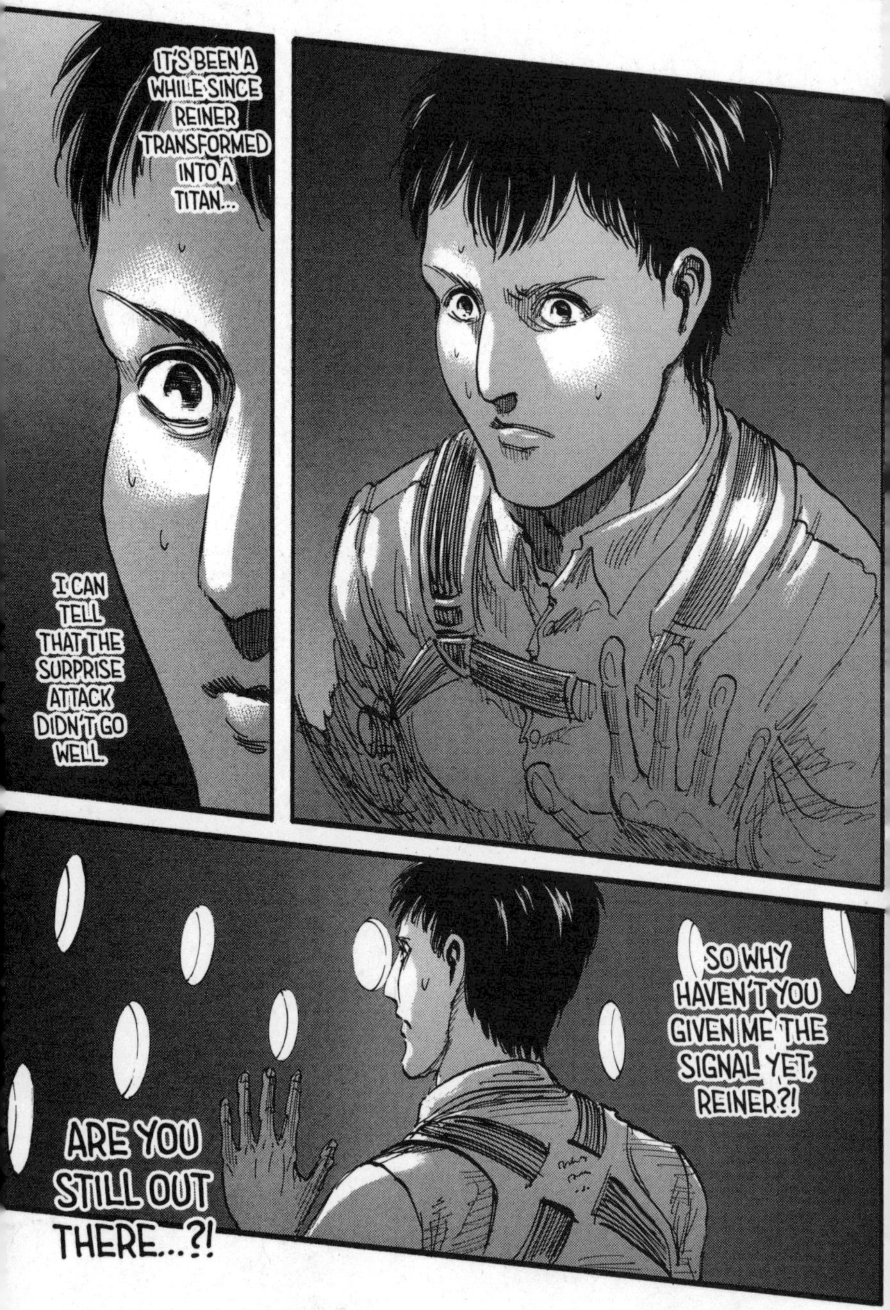
IT'S BEEN A WHILE SINCE REINER TRANSFORMED INTO A TITAN...
I CAN TELL THAT THE SURPRISE ATTACK DIDN'T GO WELL.
SO WHY HAVEN'T YOU GIVEN ME THE SIGNAL YET, REINER?!
ARE YOU STILL OUT THERE...?!

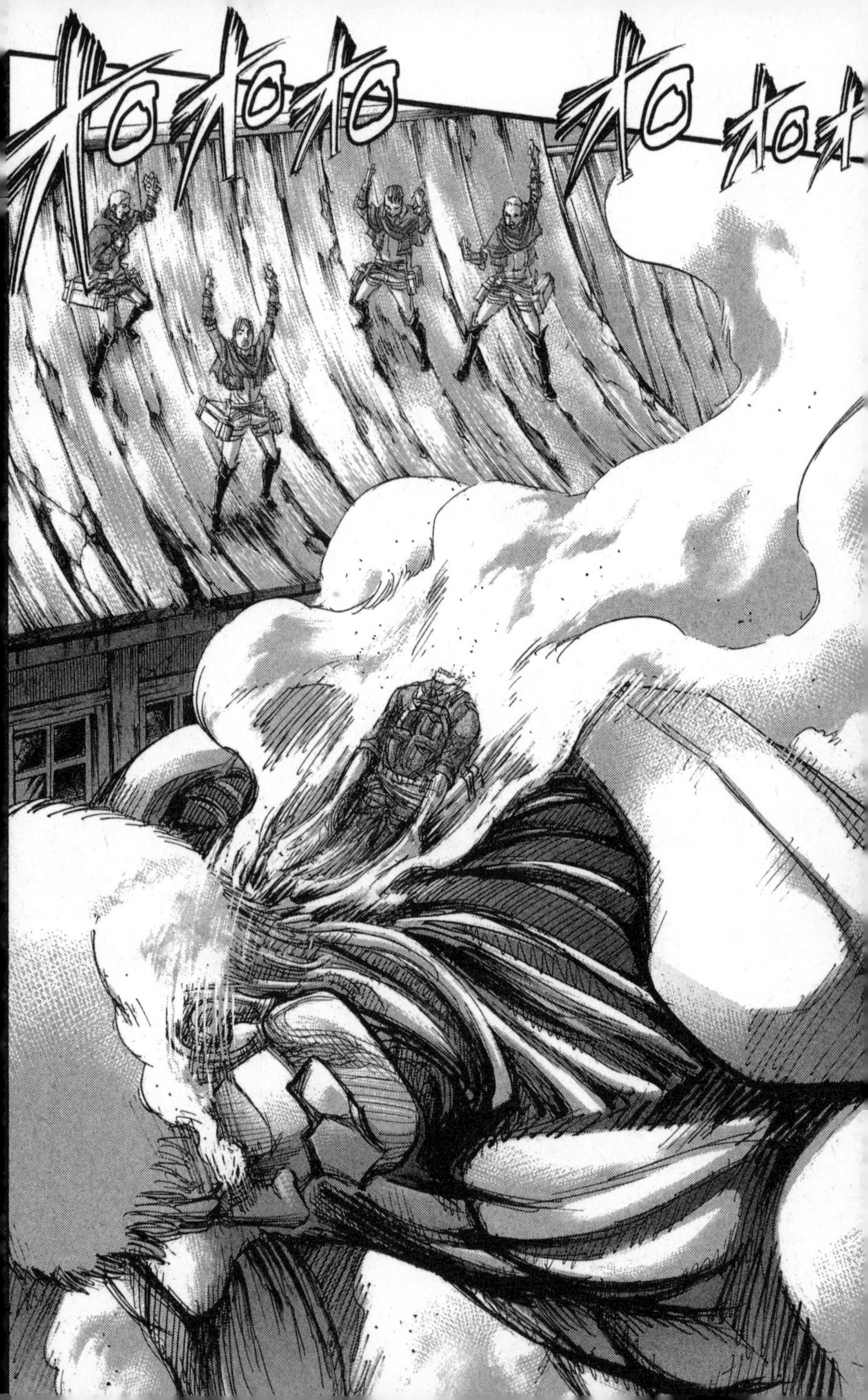

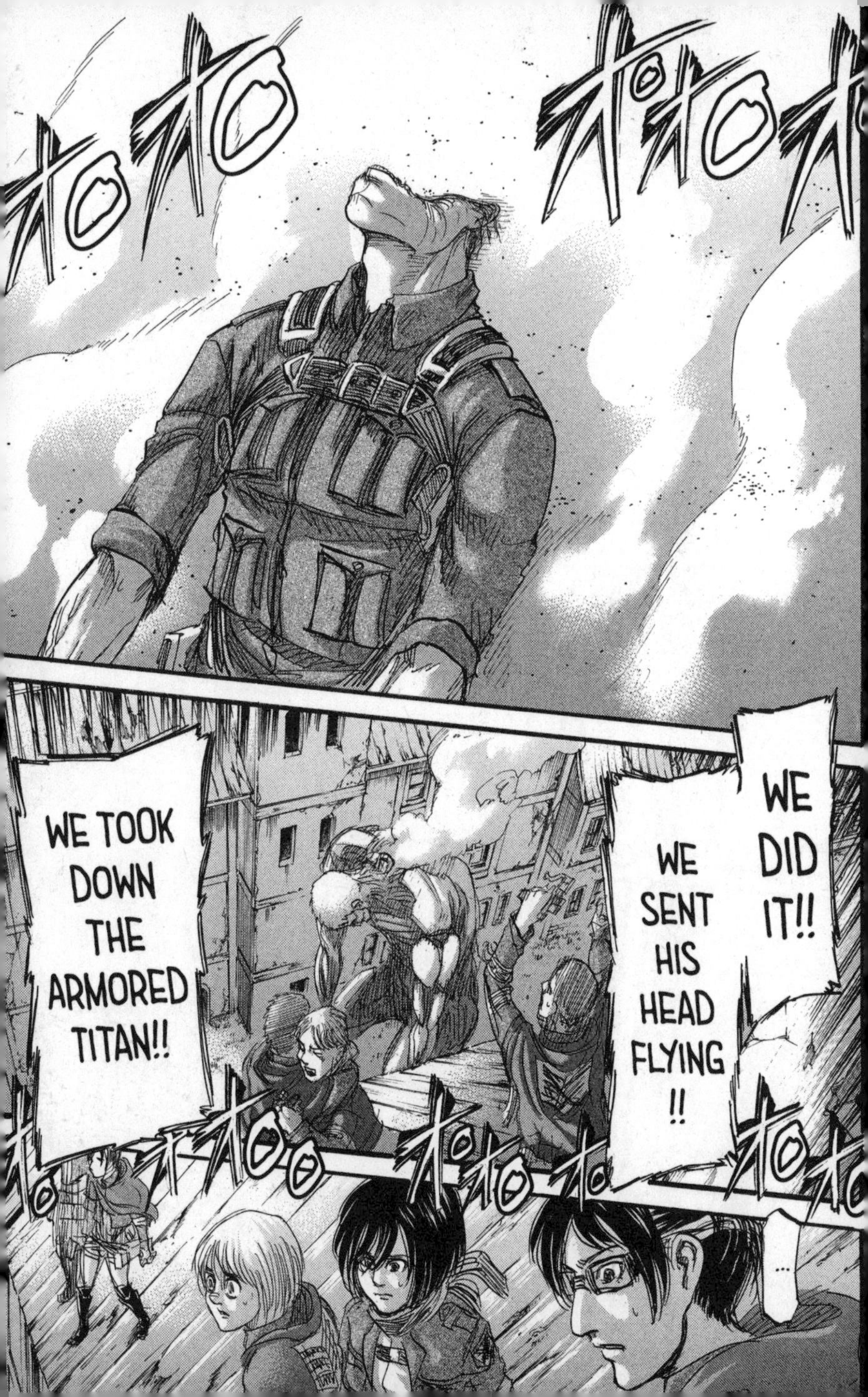
WE DID IT!!
WE SENT HIS HEAD FLYING !!
WE TOOK DOWN THE ARMORED TITAN!!
...

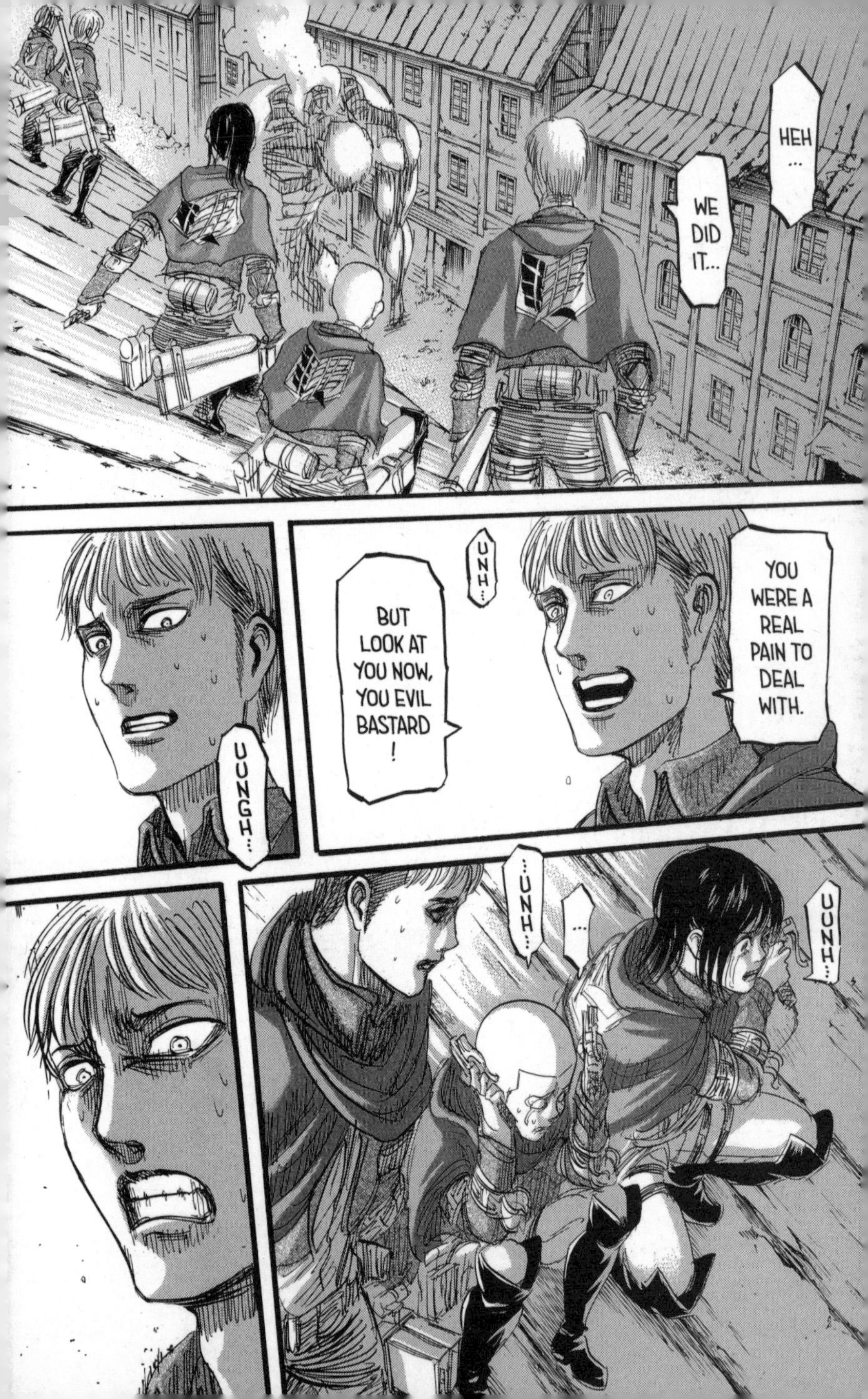
HEH ...
WE DID IT...
YOU WERE A REAL PAIN TO DEAL WITH.
UNH...
BUT LOOK AT YOU NOW, YOU EVIL BASTARD!
UUNGH...
UUNH...
...
...UNH...

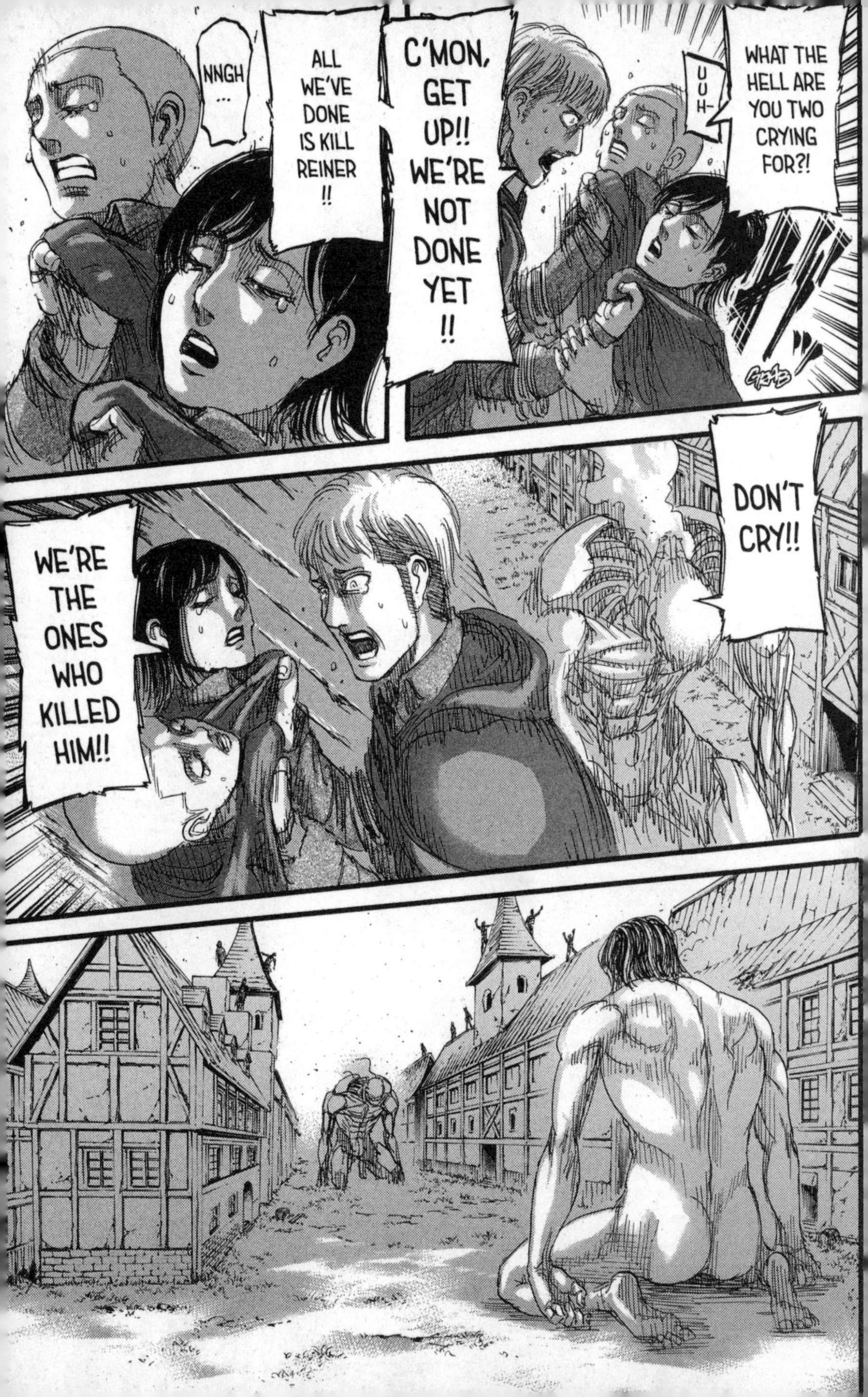
WHAT THE HELL ARE YOU TWO CRYING FOR?!
UUH-
C'MON, GET UP!! WE'RE NOT DONE YET!!
GRAB
ALL WE'VE DONE IS KILL REINER!!
NNGH...
DON'T CRY!!
WE'RE THE ONES WHO KILLED HIM!!

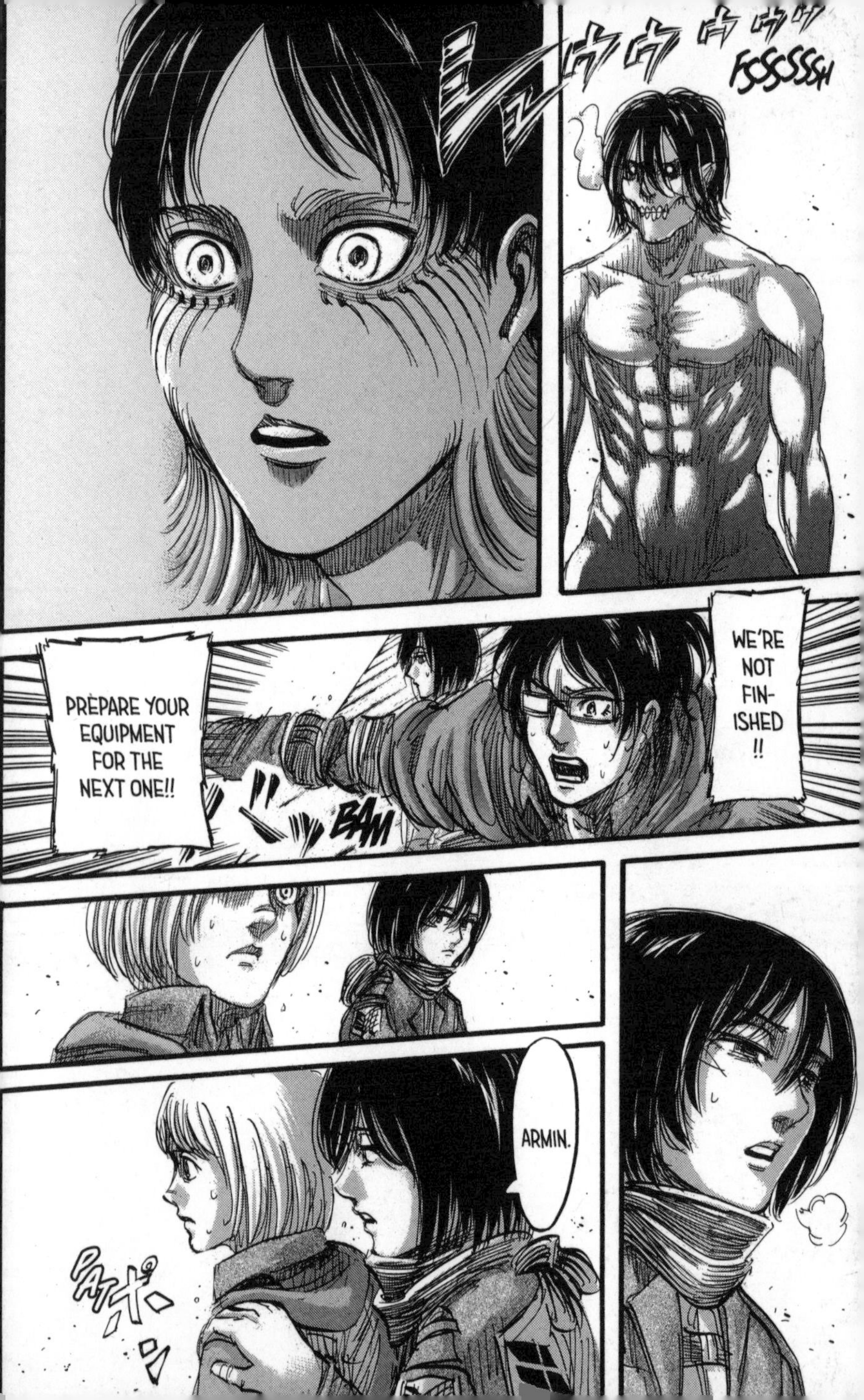
FSSSSSH
WE'RE NOT FIN-ISHED!!
BAM
PREPARE YOUR EQUIPMENT FOR THE NEXT ONE!!
ARMIN.
PAT

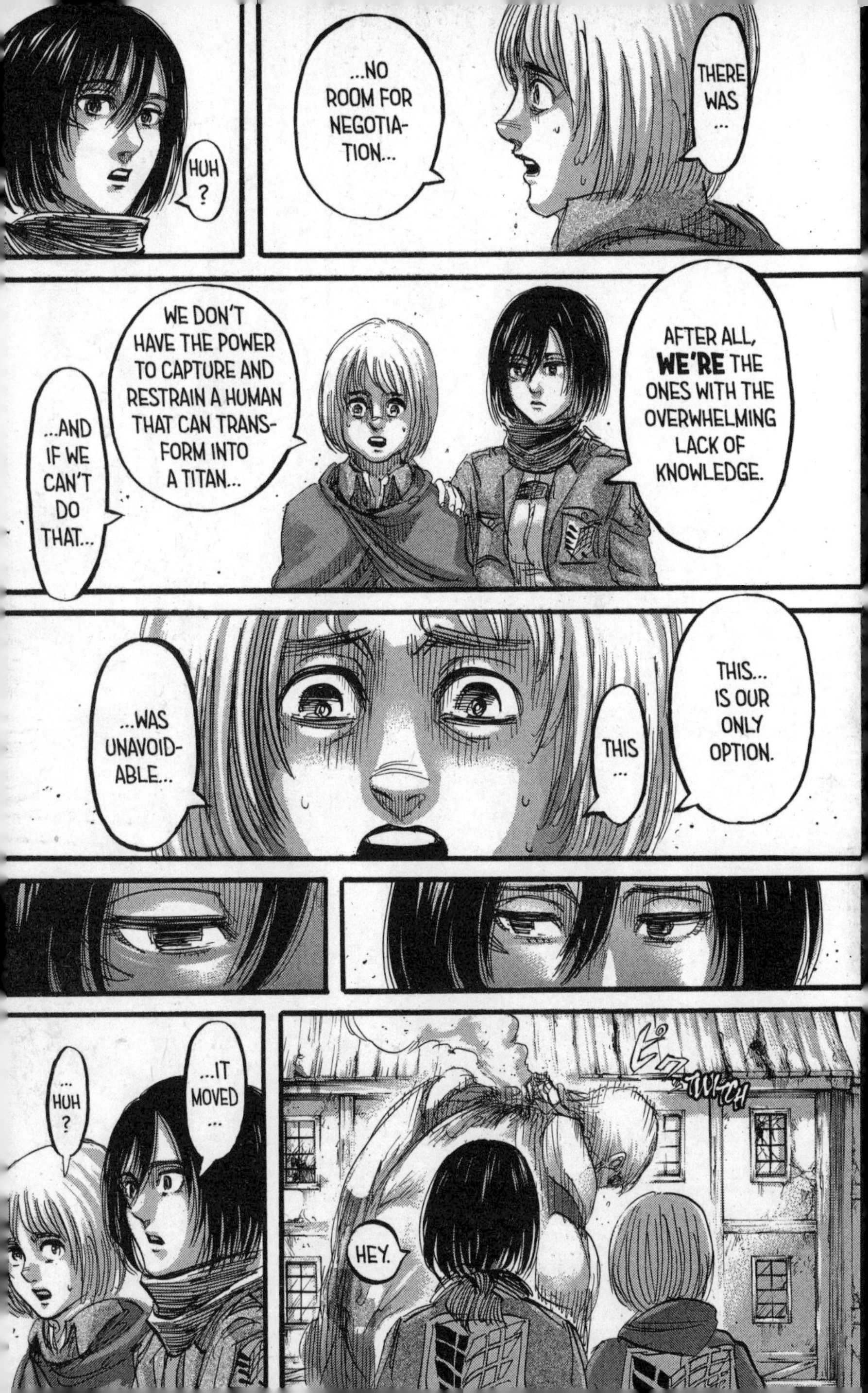
THERE WAS ...
...NO ROOM FOR NEGOTIATION...
HUH ?
AFTER ALL, **WE'RE** THE ONES WITH THE OVERWHELMING LACK OF KNOWLEDGE.
WE DON'T HAVE THE POWER TO CAPTURE AND RESTRAIN A HUMAN THAT CAN TRANSFORM INTO A TITAN...
...AND IF WE CAN'T DO THAT...
THIS... IS OUR ONLY OPTION.
THIS ...
...WAS UNAVOIDABLE...
ピク
TWITCH
HEY.
...IT MOVED ...
... HUH ?

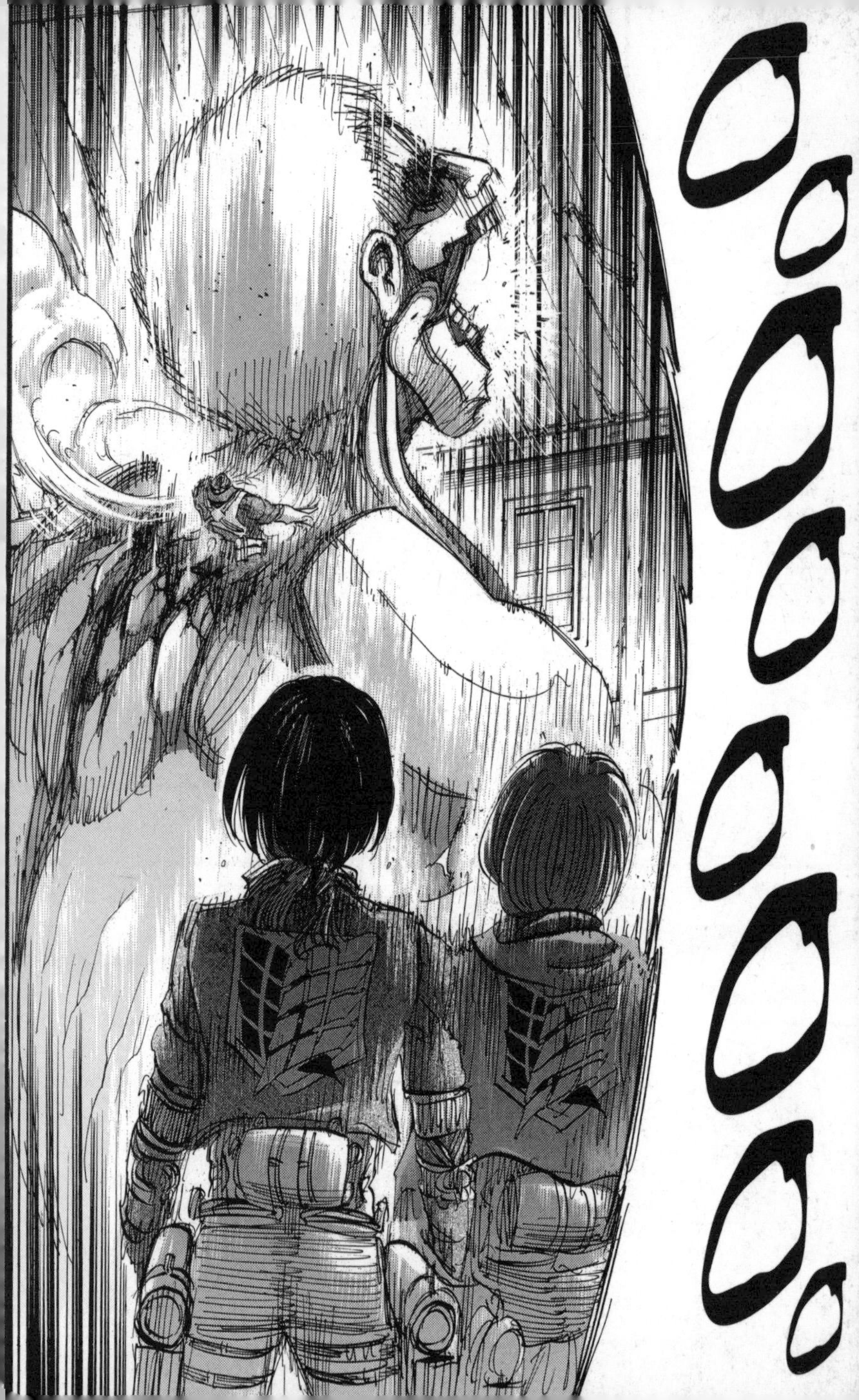

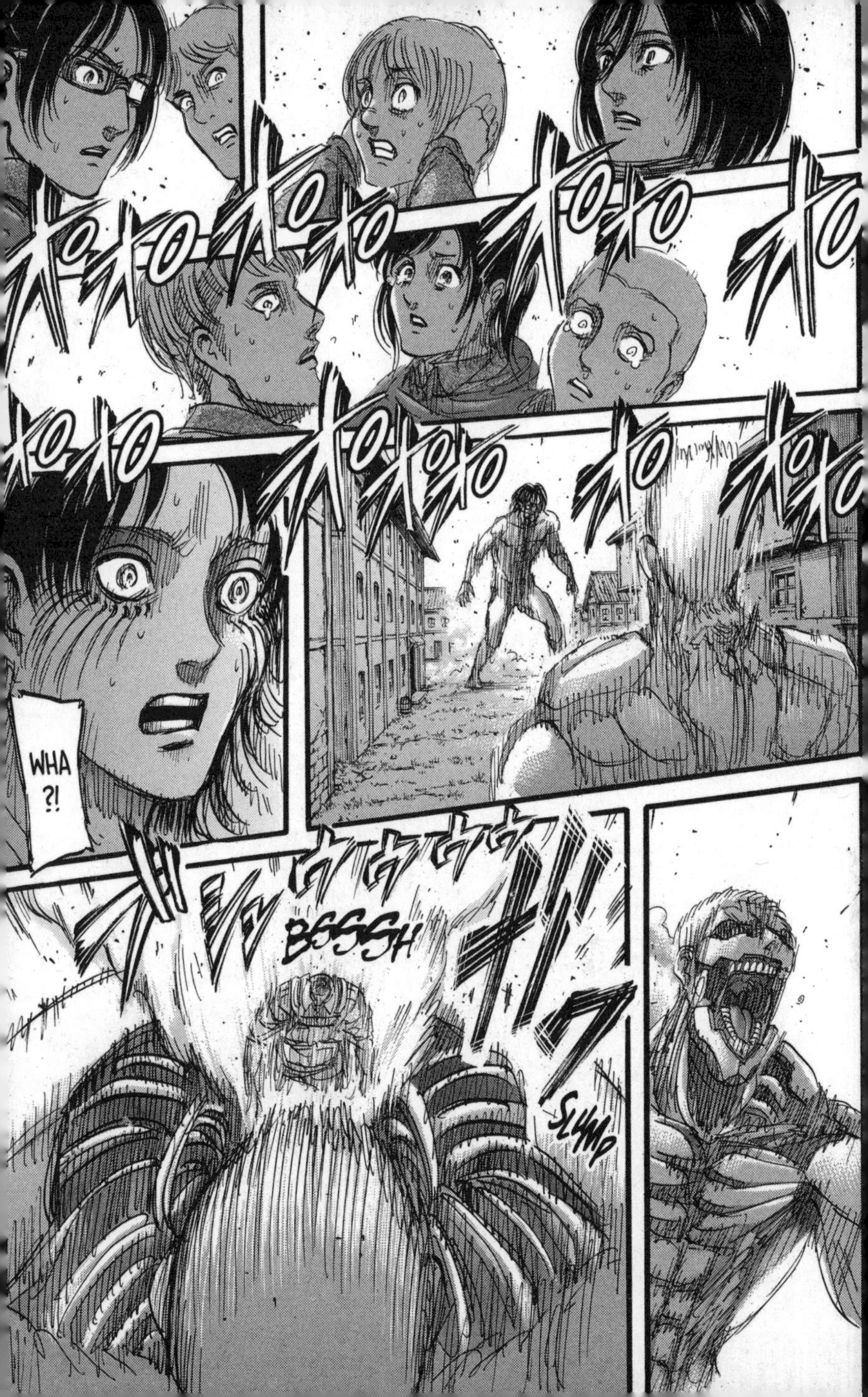
WHA ?!
BSSSH
SLUMP

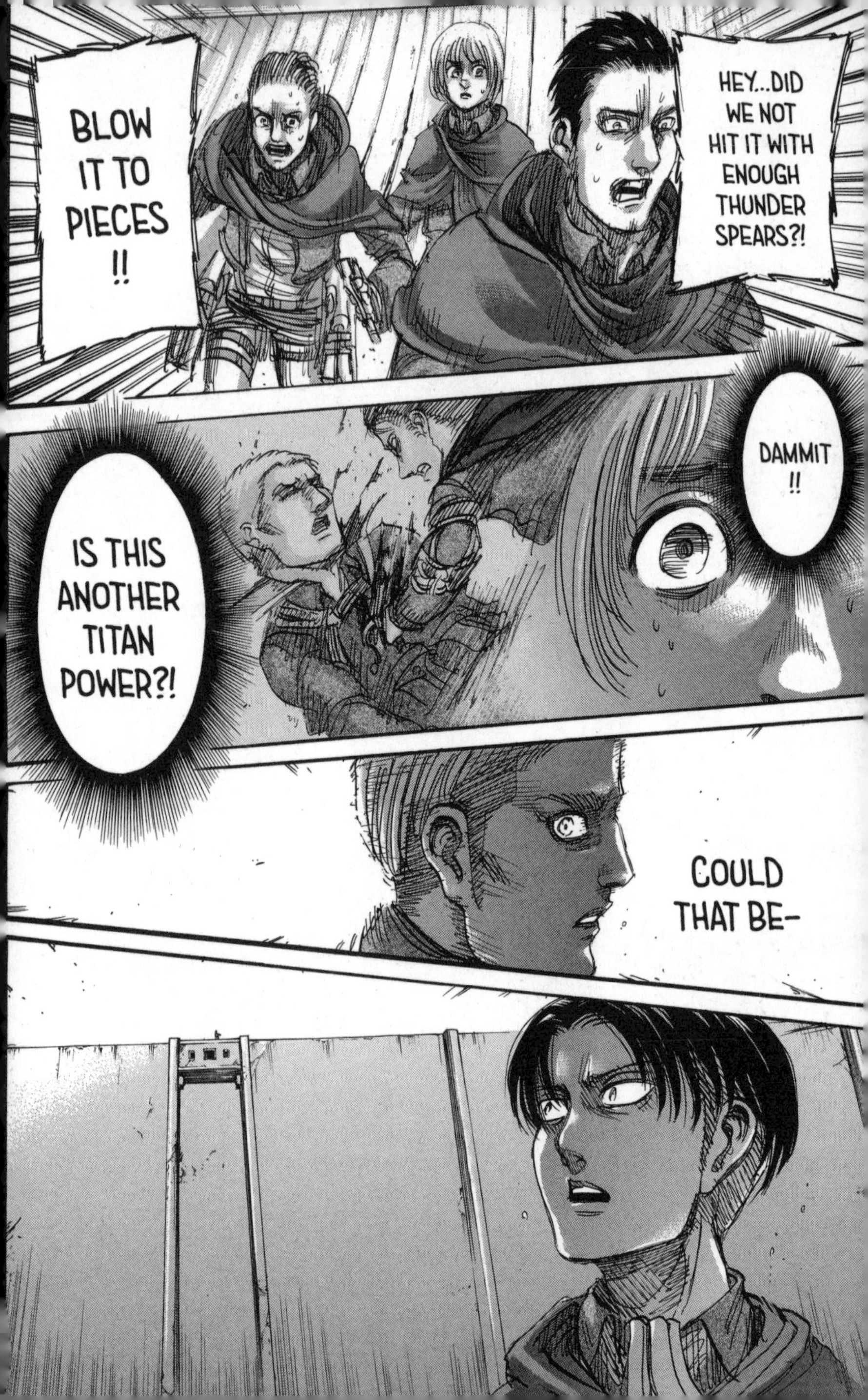
HEY...DID WE NOT HIT IT WITH ENOUGH THUNDER SPEARS?!
BLOW IT TO PIECES!!
DAMMIT!!
IS THIS ANOTHER TITAN POWER?!
COULD THAT BE-

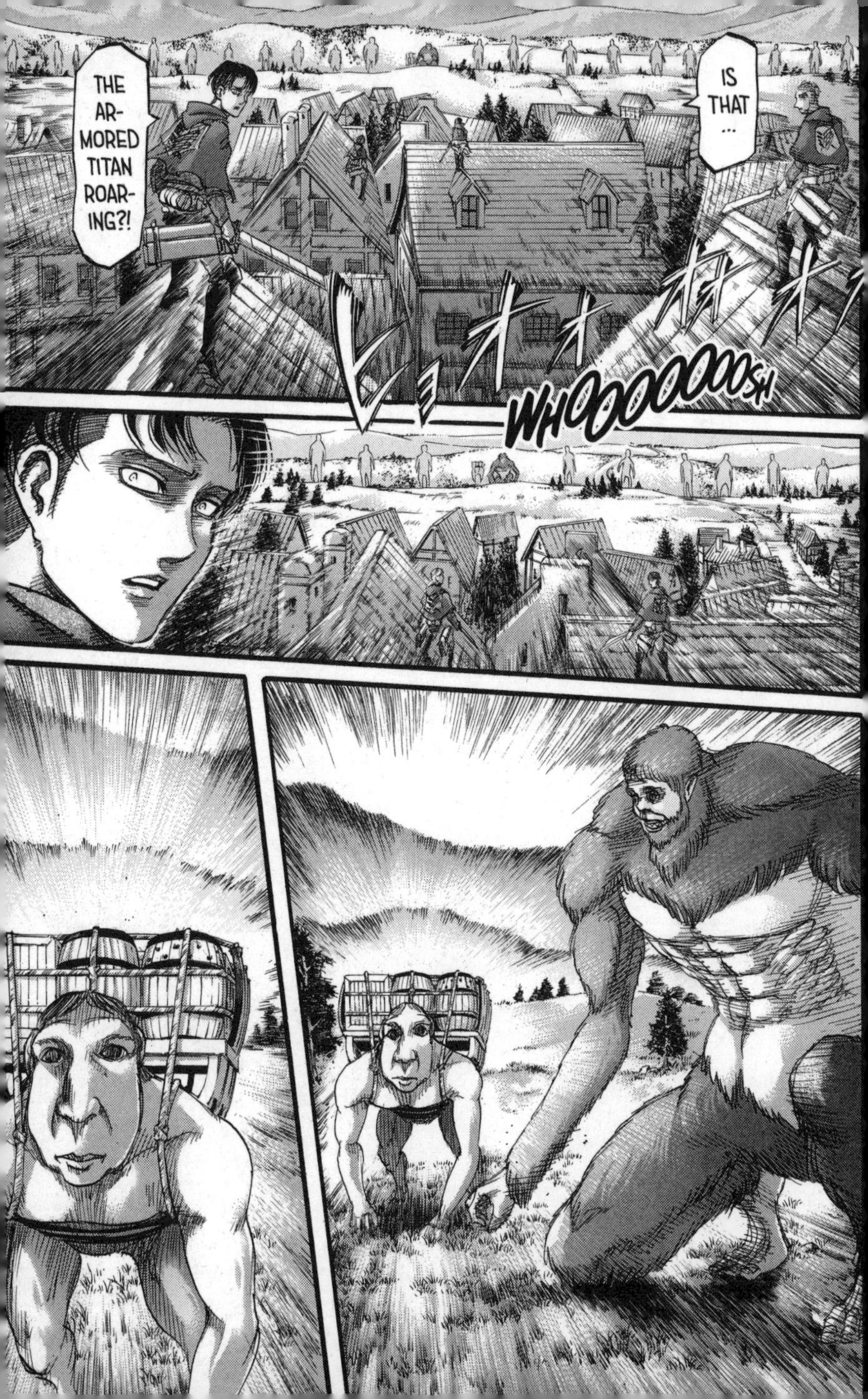
IS THAT ...
THE ARMORED TITAN ROARING?!
WHOOOOOOOSH

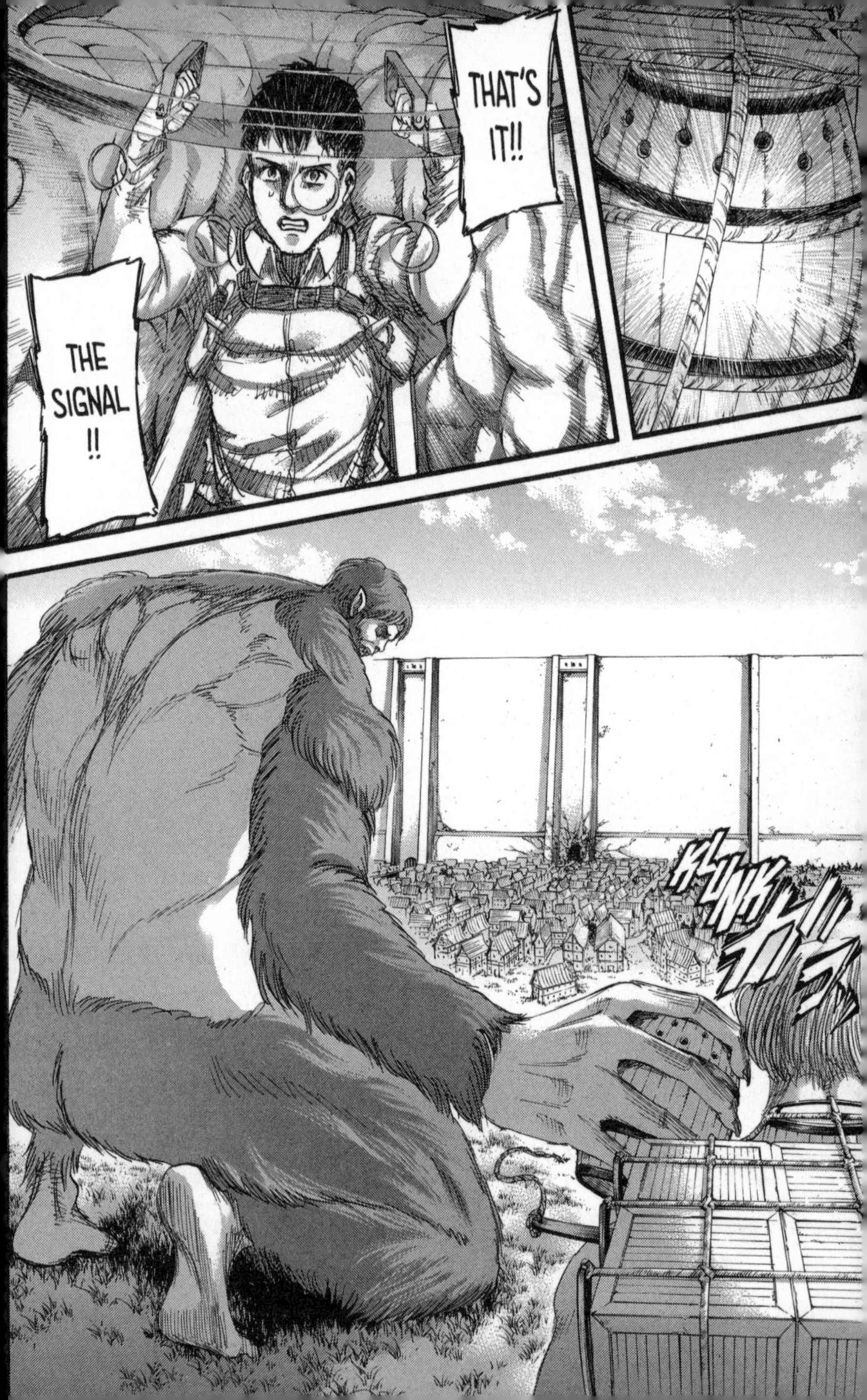
THAT'S IT!!
THE SIGNAL !!
KLUNK

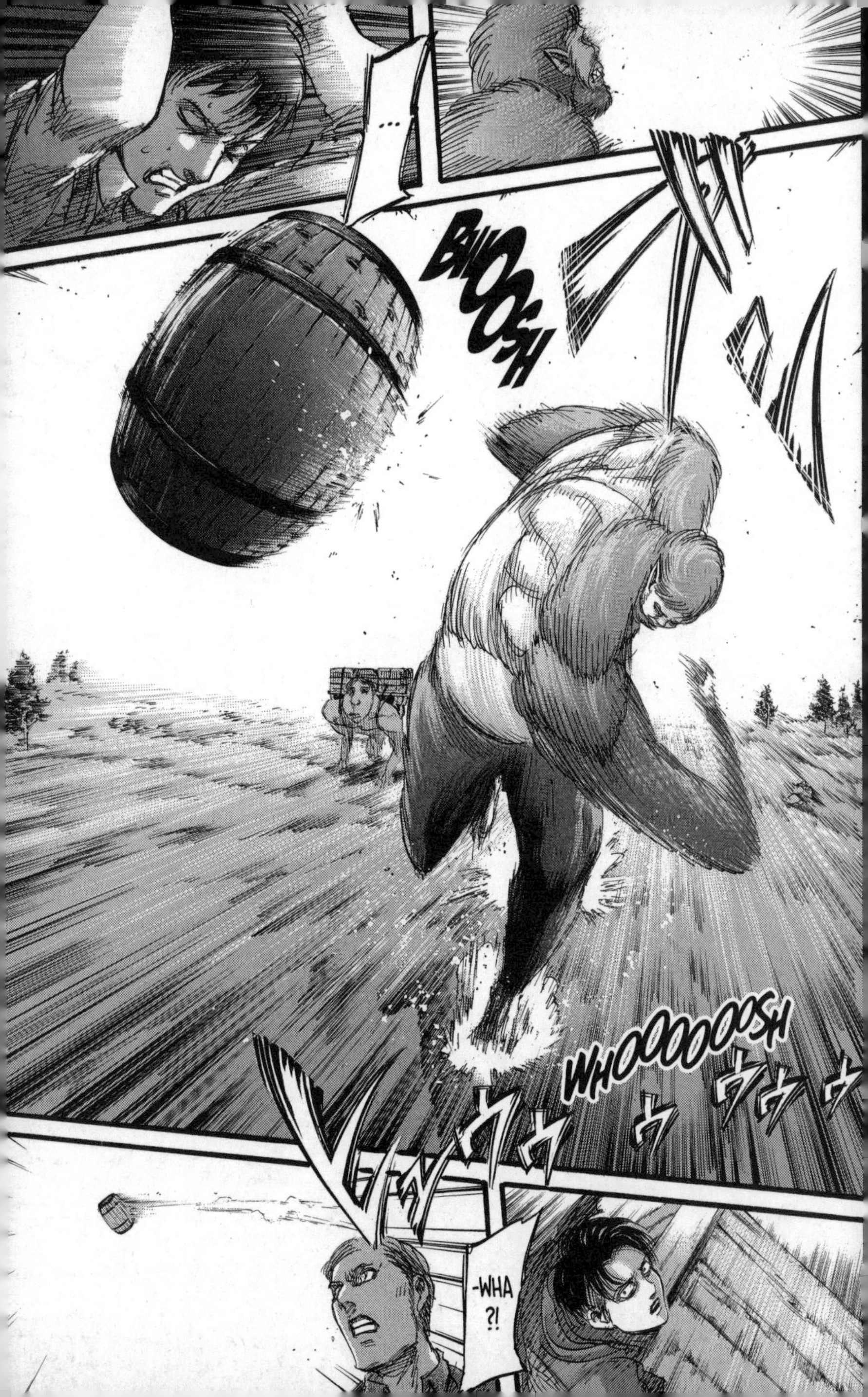
...
BWOOSH
WHOOOOOOSH
-WHA ?!

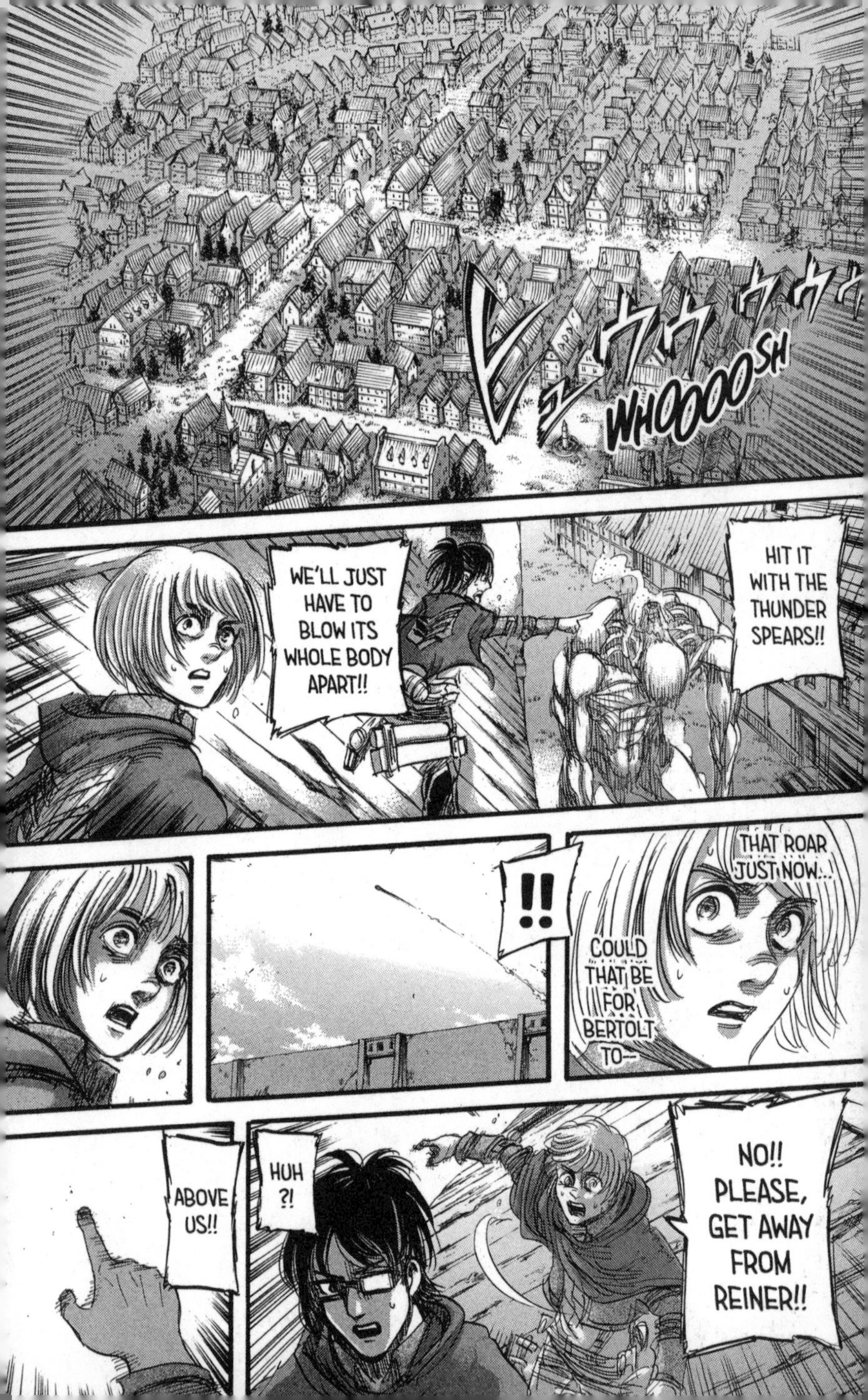
WHOOOOOSH
HIT IT WITH THE THUNDER SPEARS!!
WE'LL JUST HAVE TO BLOW ITS WHOLE BODY APART!!
THAT ROAR JUST NOW...
COULD THAT BE FOR BERTOLT TO—
!!
NO!! PLEASE, GET AWAY FROM REINER!!
HUH ?!
ABOVE US!!

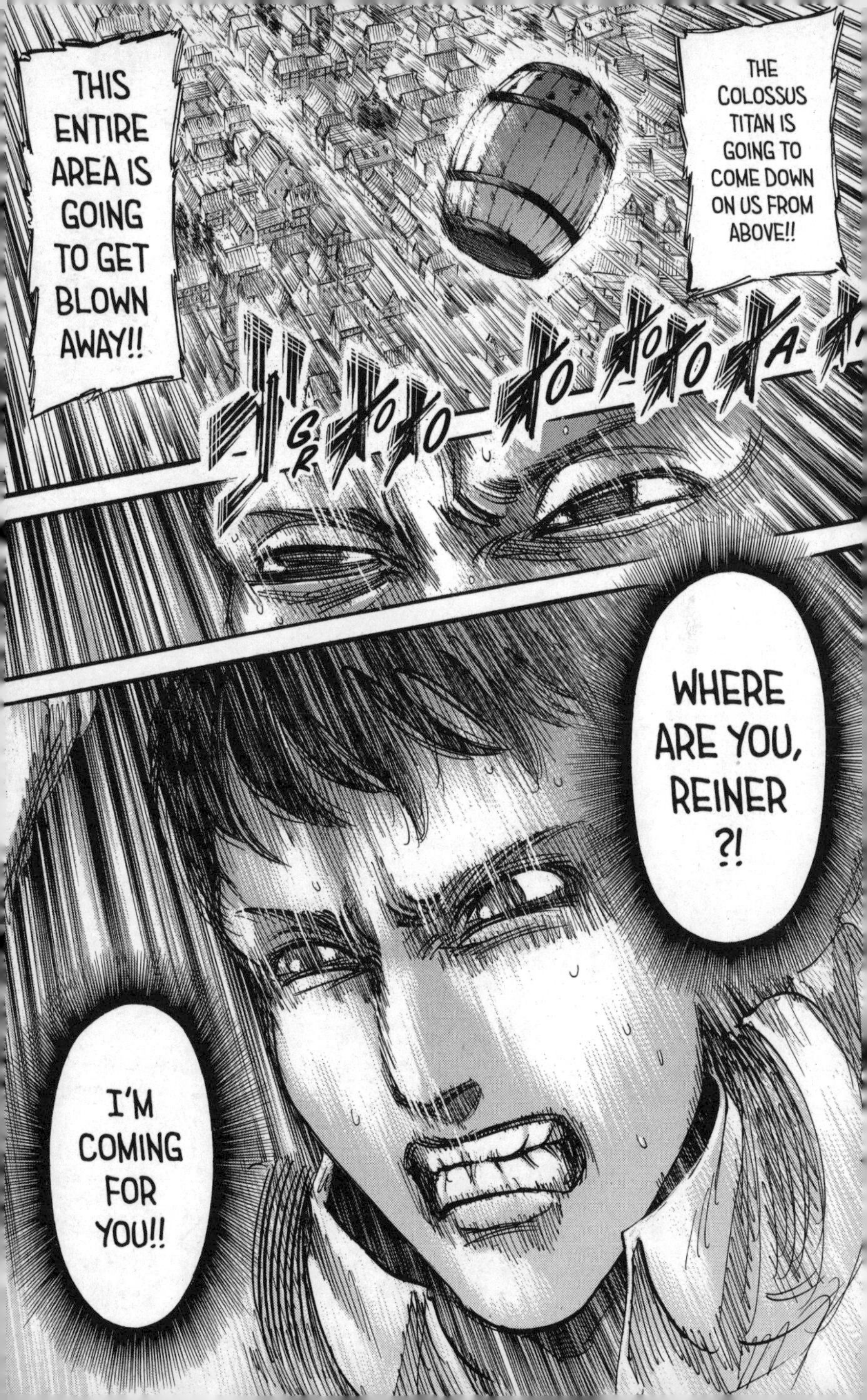
THE COLOSSUS TITAN IS GOING TO COME DOWN ON US FROM ABOVE!!
THIS ENTIRE AREA IS GOING TO GET BLOWN AWAY!!
WHERE ARE YOU, REINER ?!
I'M COMING FOR YOU!!

ATTACK on TITAN

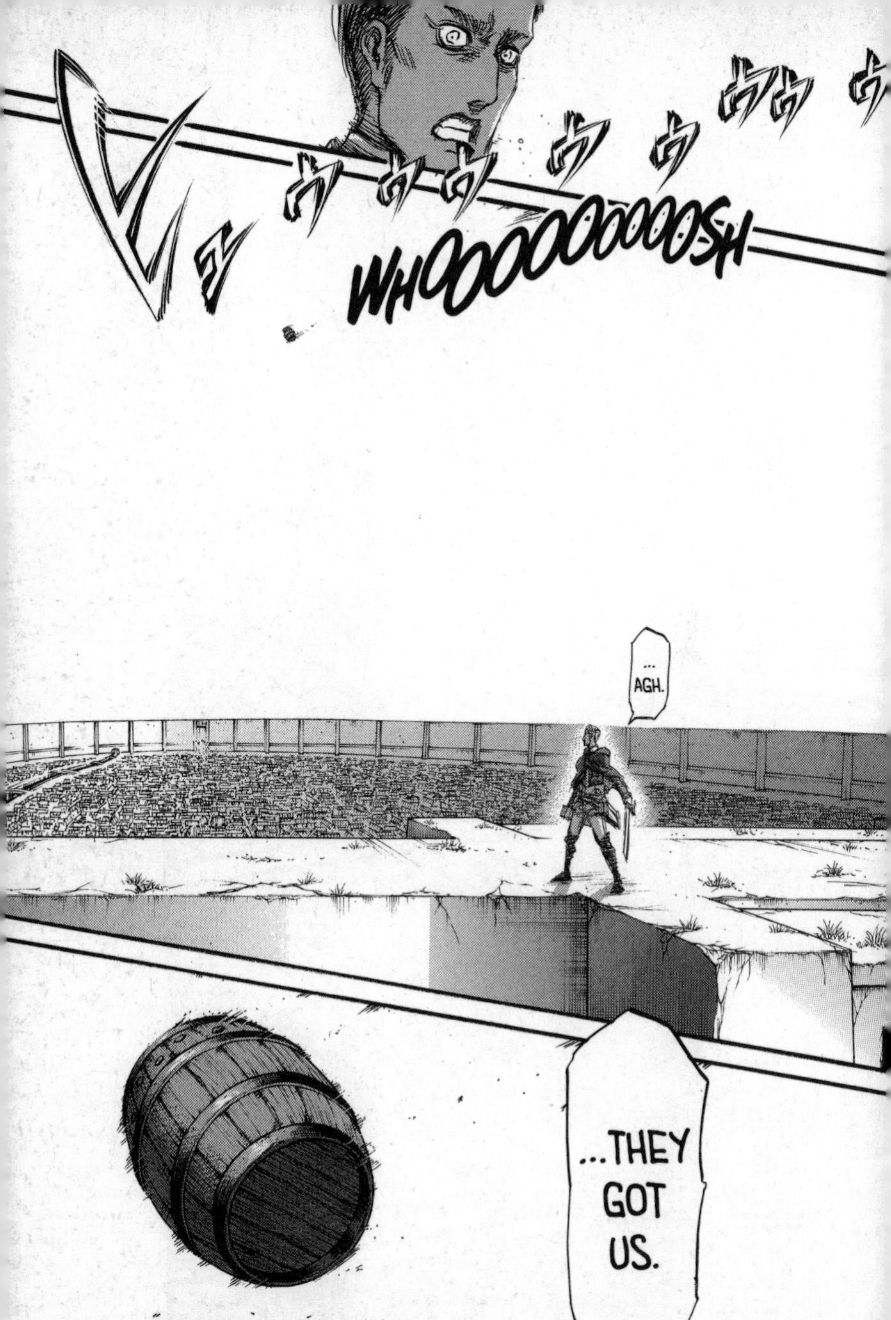
WHOOOOOOOOOSH
... AGH.
...THEY GOT US.

Episode 78: Descent

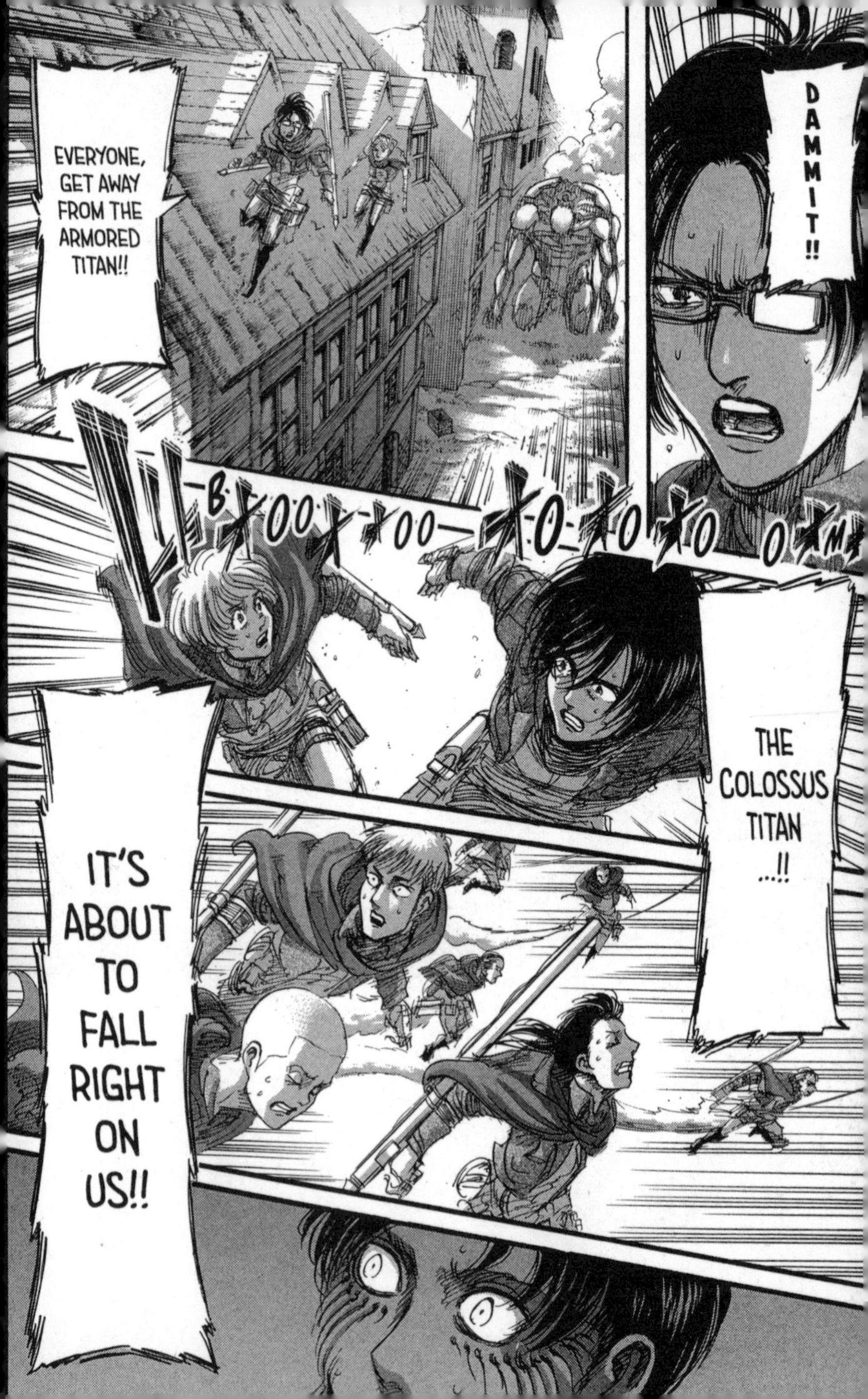
DAMMIT!!
EVERYONE, GET AWAY FROM THE ARMORED TITAN!!
BOOOO—OOOOOM
THE COLOSSUS TITAN ...!!
IT'S ABOUT TO FALL RIGHT ON US!!

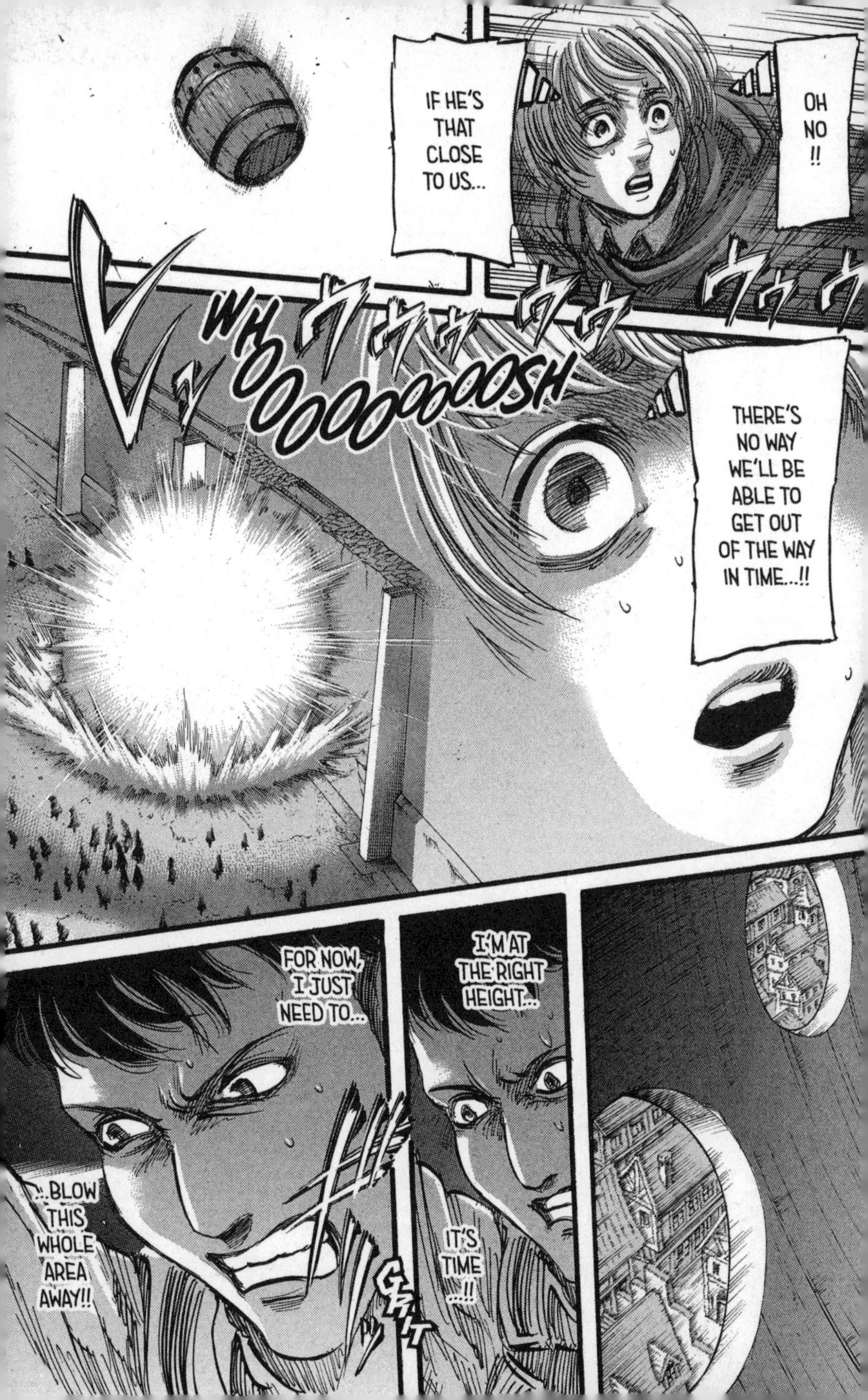
OH NO !!
IF HE'S THAT CLOSE TO US...
THERE'S NO WAY WE'LL BE ABLE TO GET OUT OF THE WAY IN TIME...!!
WHOOOOOOOOOOSH
I'M AT THE RIGHT HEIGHT...
IT'S TIME ...!!
FOR NOW, I JUST NEED TO...
...BLOW THIS WHOLE AREA AWAY!!
GRIT

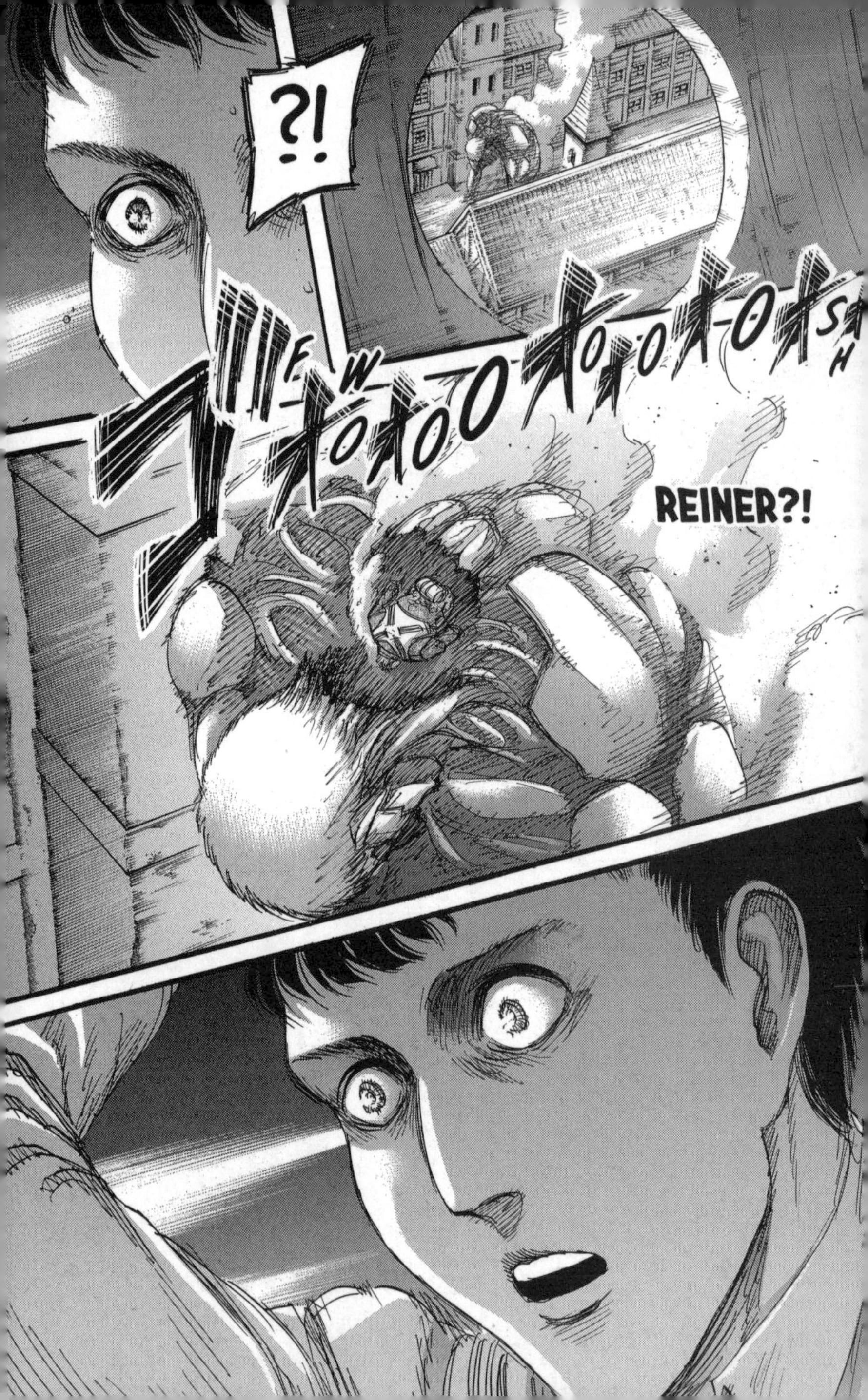
?!
REINER?!

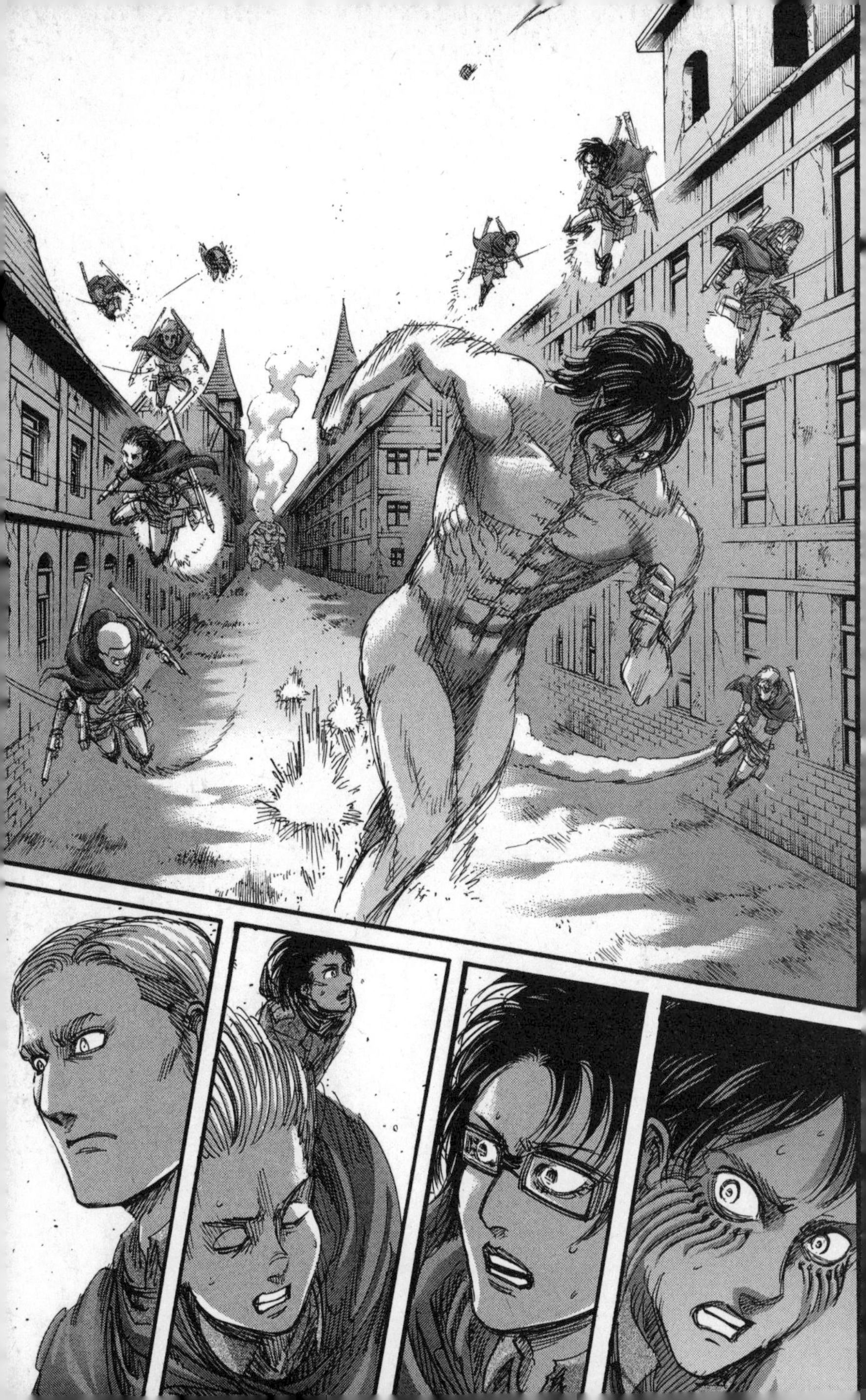

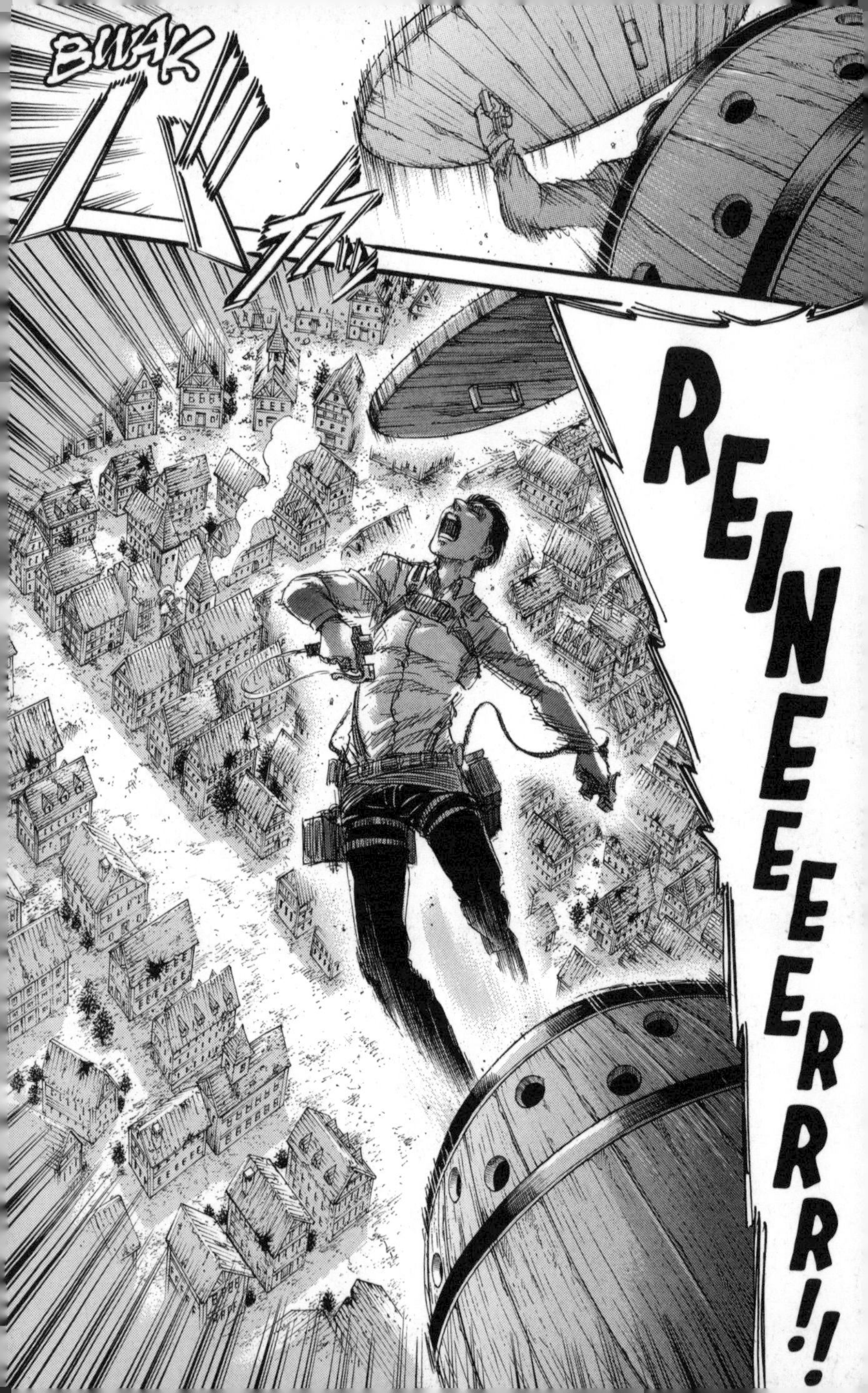
BWAK
REINEEEERRR!!

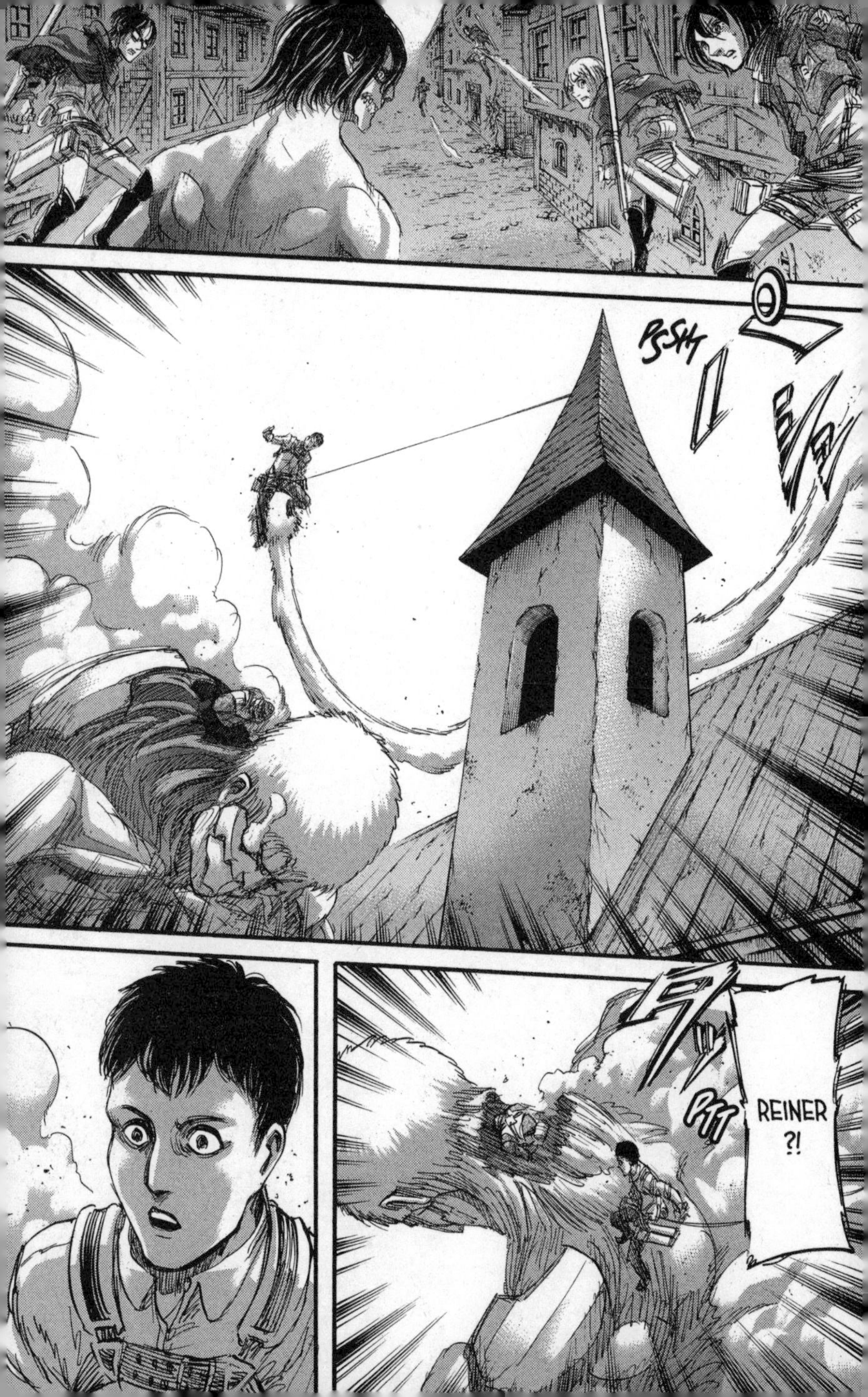
PSSH
REINER ?!

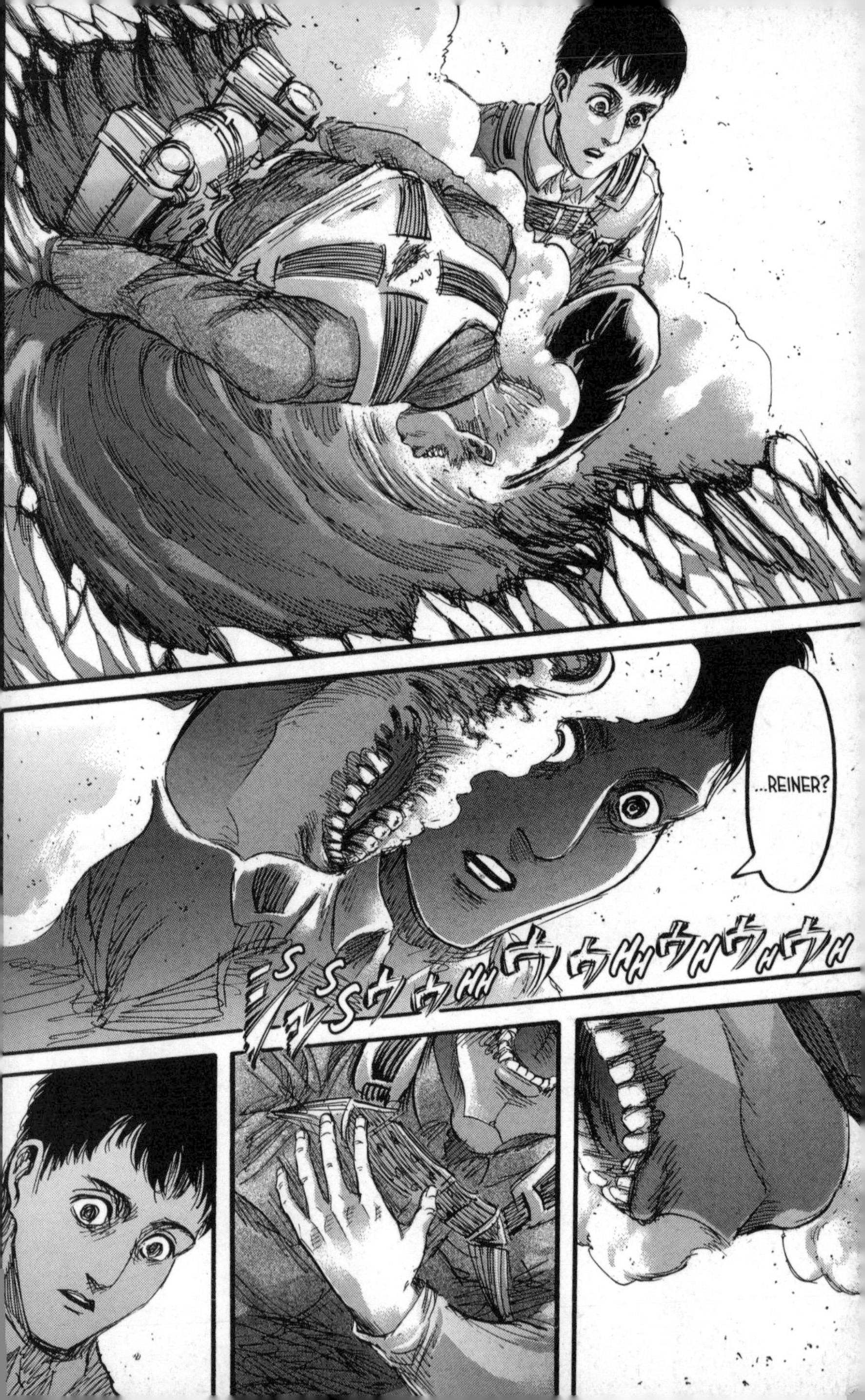
...REINER?

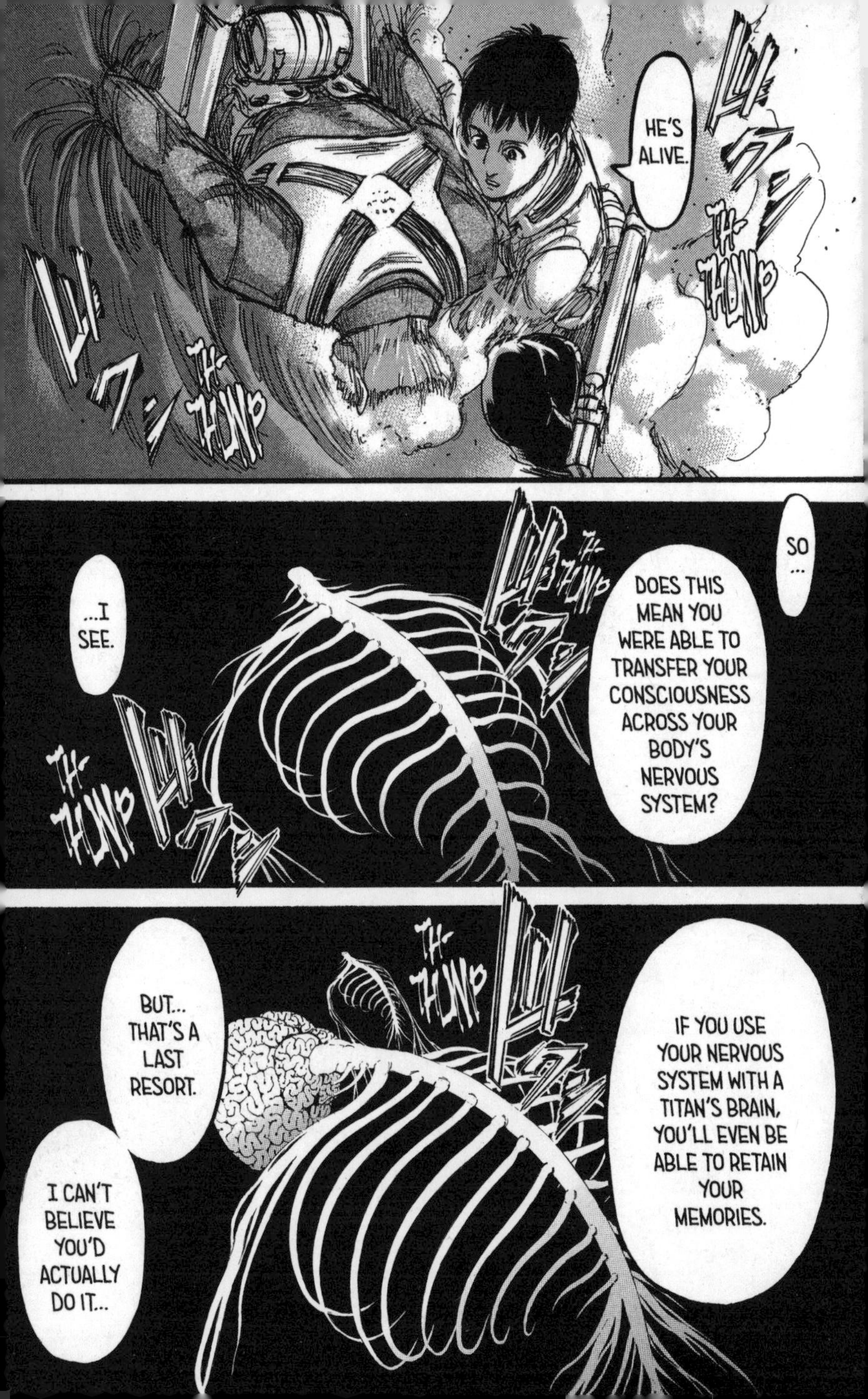
HE'S ALIVE.
TH-THUMP
TH-THUMP
SO ...
DOES THIS MEAN YOU WERE ABLE TO TRANSFER YOUR CONSCIOUSNESS ACROSS YOUR BODY'S NERVOUS SYSTEM?
TH-THUMP
...I SEE.
TH-THUMP
IF YOU USE YOUR NERVOUS SYSTEM WITH A TITAN'S BRAIN, YOU'LL EVEN BE ABLE TO RETAIN YOUR MEMORIES.
TH-THUMP
BUT... THAT'S A LAST RESORT.
I CAN'T BELIEVE YOU'D ACTUALLY DO IT...

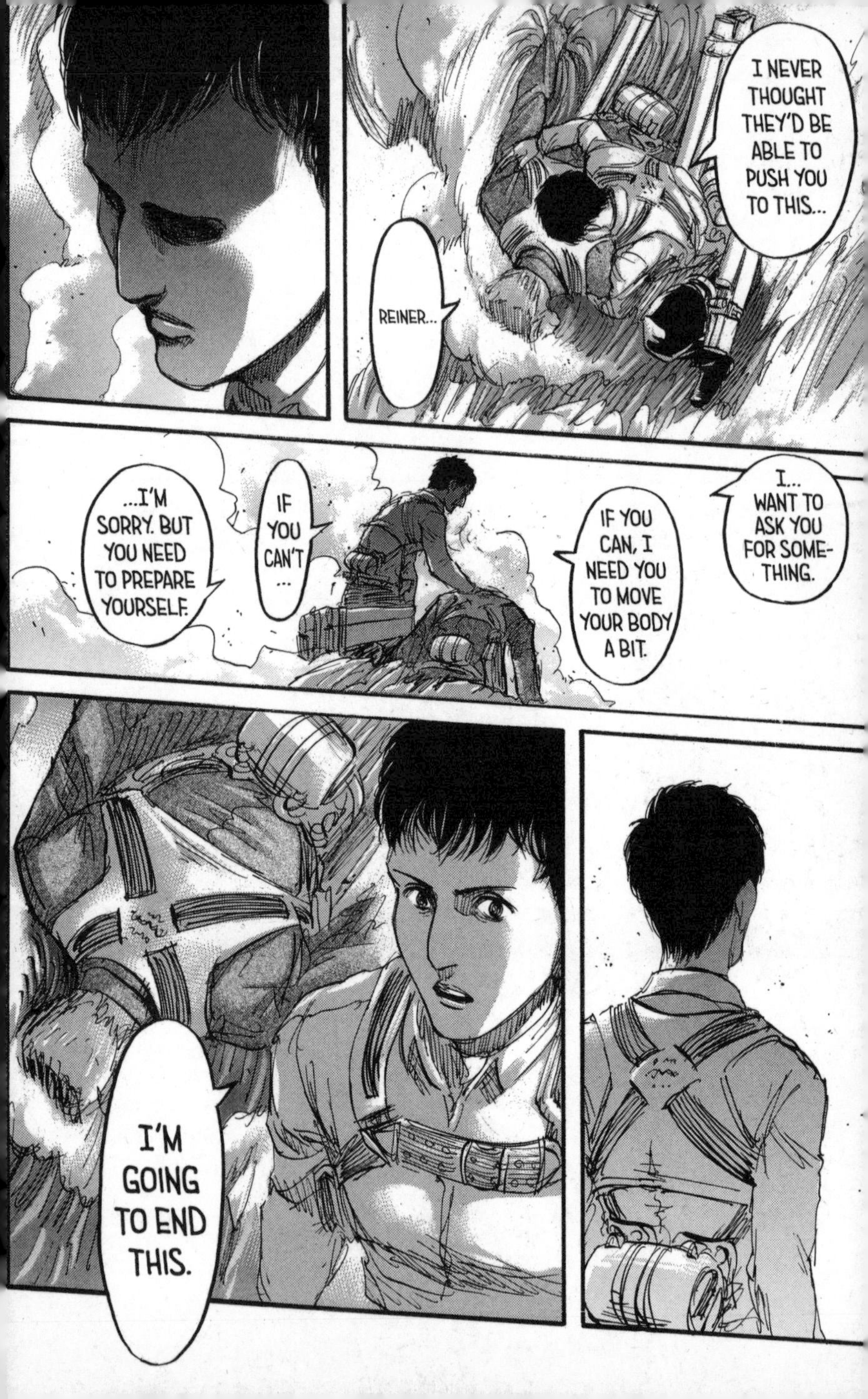
I NEVER THOUGHT THEY'D BE ABLE TO PUSH YOU TO THIS...
REINER...
I... WANT TO ASK YOU FOR SOME-THING.
IF YOU CAN, I NEED YOU TO MOVE YOUR BODY A BIT.
IF YOU CAN'T ...
...I'M SORRY. BUT YOU NEED TO PREPARE YOURSELF.
I'M GOING TO END THIS.

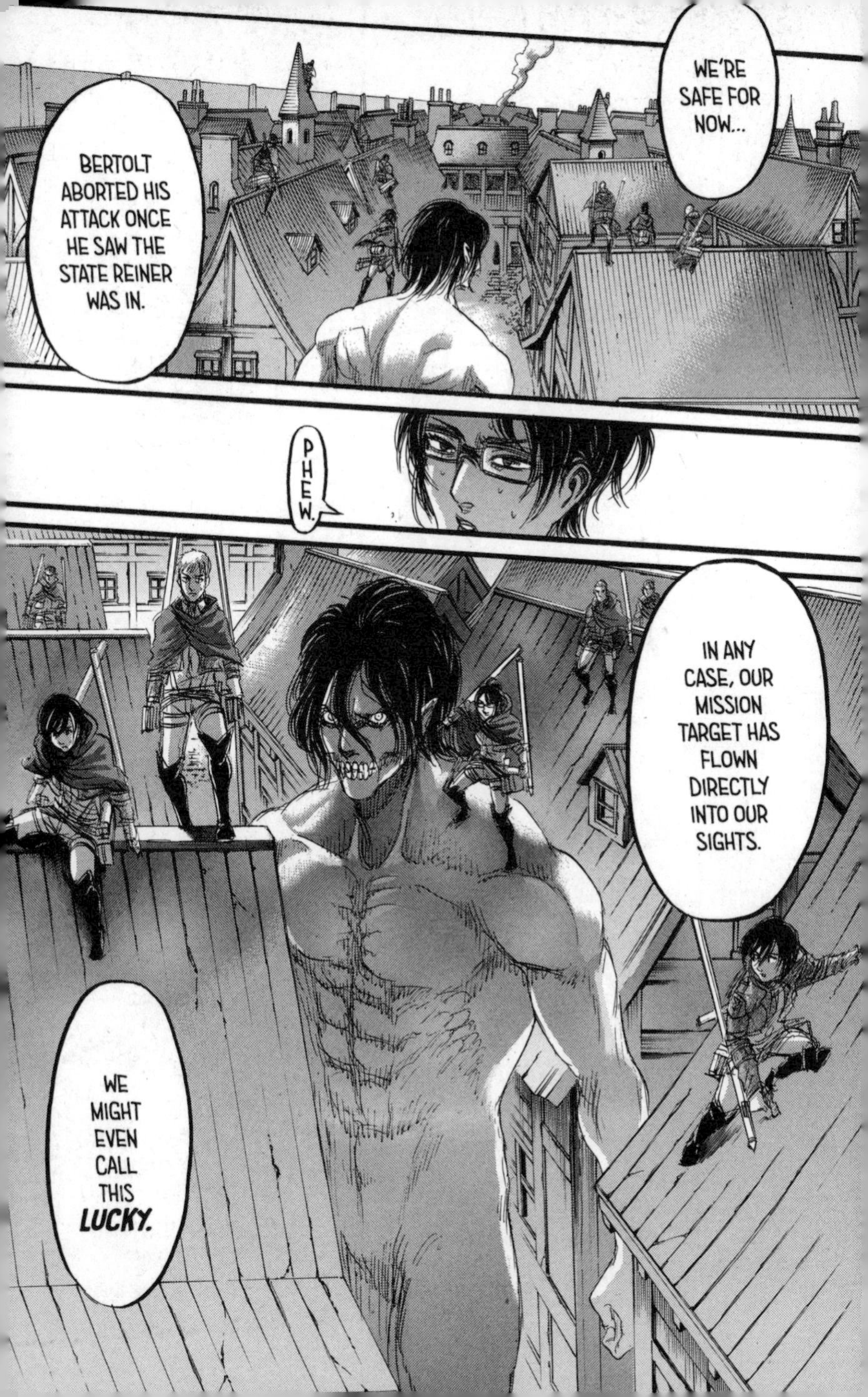
WE'RE SAFE FOR NOW...
BERTOLT ABORTED HIS ATTACK ONCE HE SAW THE STATE REINER WAS IN.
PHEW.
IN ANY CASE, OUR MISSION TARGET HAS FLOWN DIRECTLY INTO OUR SIGHTS.
WE MIGHT EVEN CALL THIS ***LUCKY.***

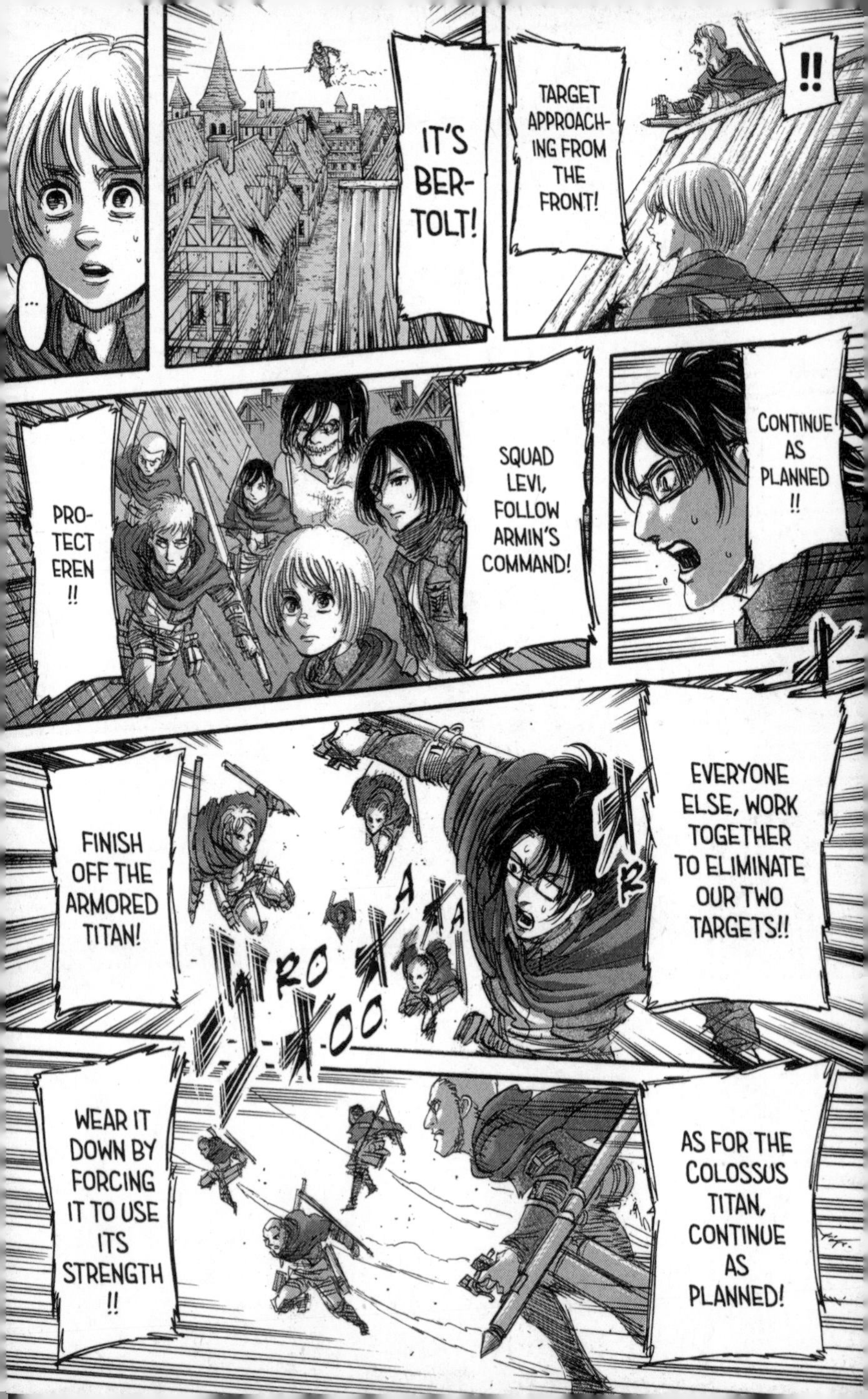
!!
TARGET APPROACHING FROM THE FRONT!
IT'S BERTOLT!
...
CONTINUE AS PLANNED!!
SQUAD LEVI, FOLLOW ARMIN'S COMMAND!
PROTECT EREN!!
EVERYONE ELSE, WORK TOGETHER TO ELIMINATE OUR TWO TARGETS!!
FINISH OFF THE ARMORED TITAN!
AS FOR THE COLOSSUS TITAN, CONTINUE AS PLANNED!
WEAR IT DOWN BY FORCING IT TO USE ITS STRENGTH!!

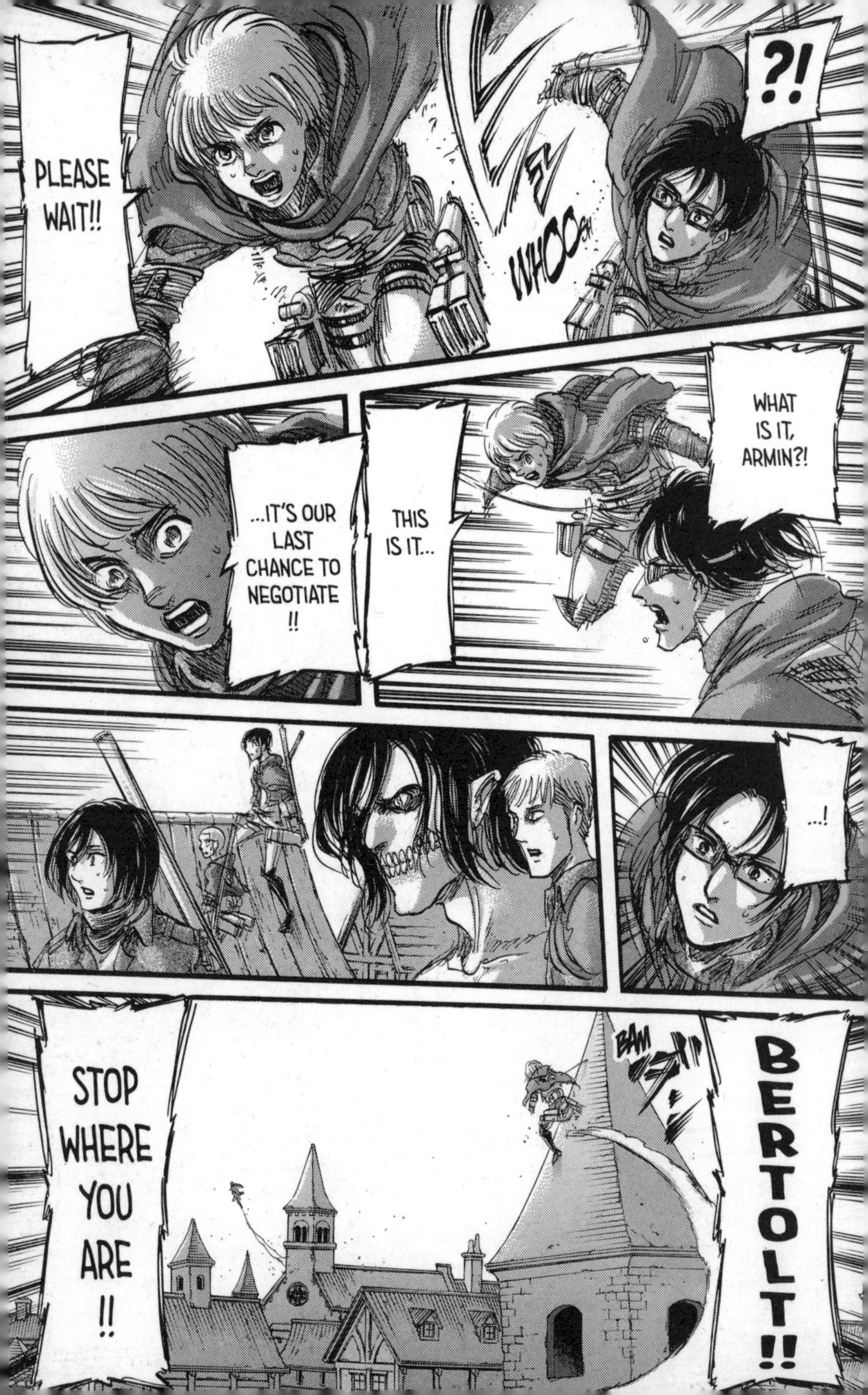
?!
WHOOSH
PLEASE WAIT!!
WHAT IS IT, ARMIN?!
THIS IS IT...
...IT'S OUR LAST CHANCE TO NEGOTIATE!!
...!
BAM
BERTOLT!!
STOP WHERE YOU ARE!!

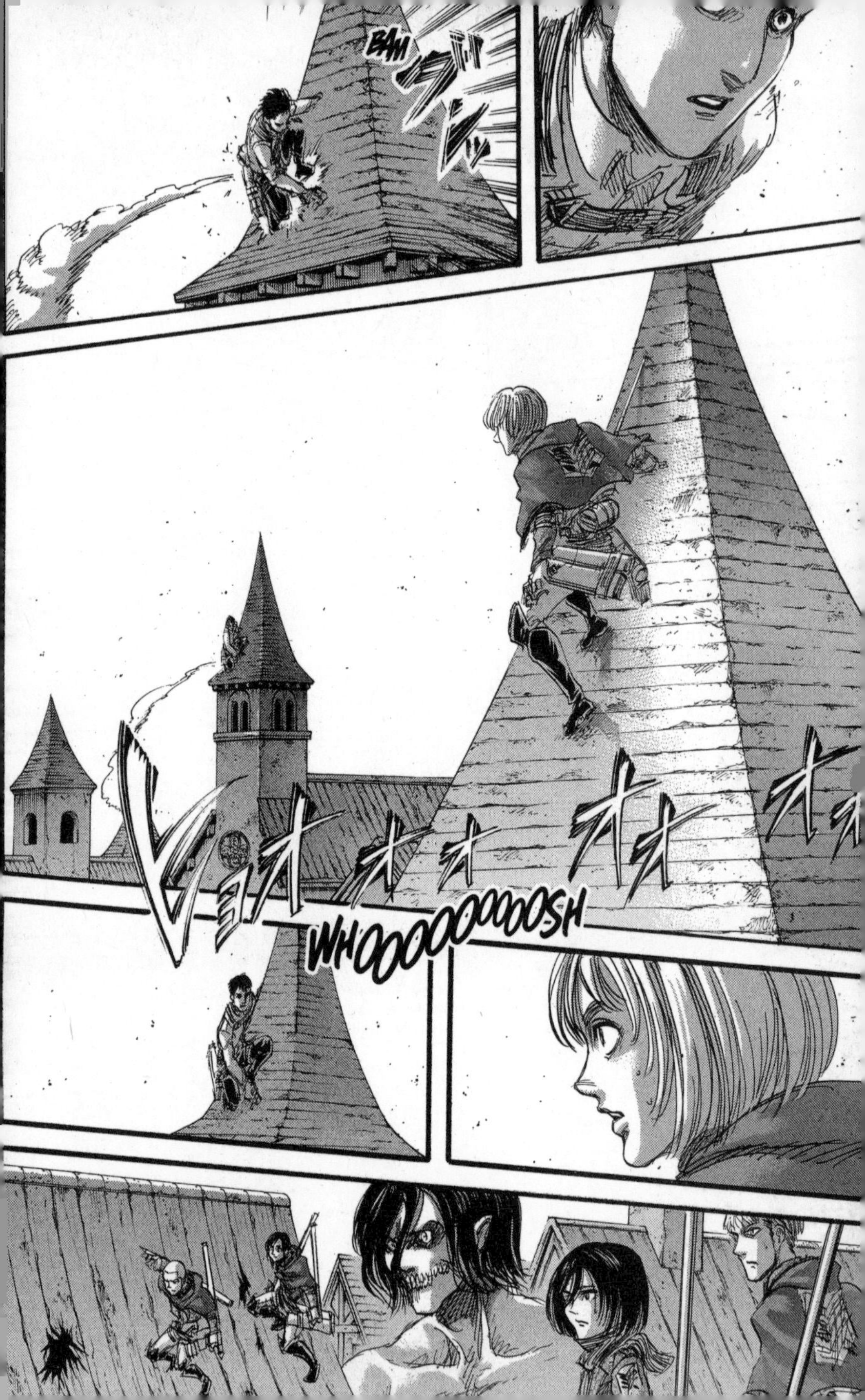
BAM
WHOOOOOOOOOSH

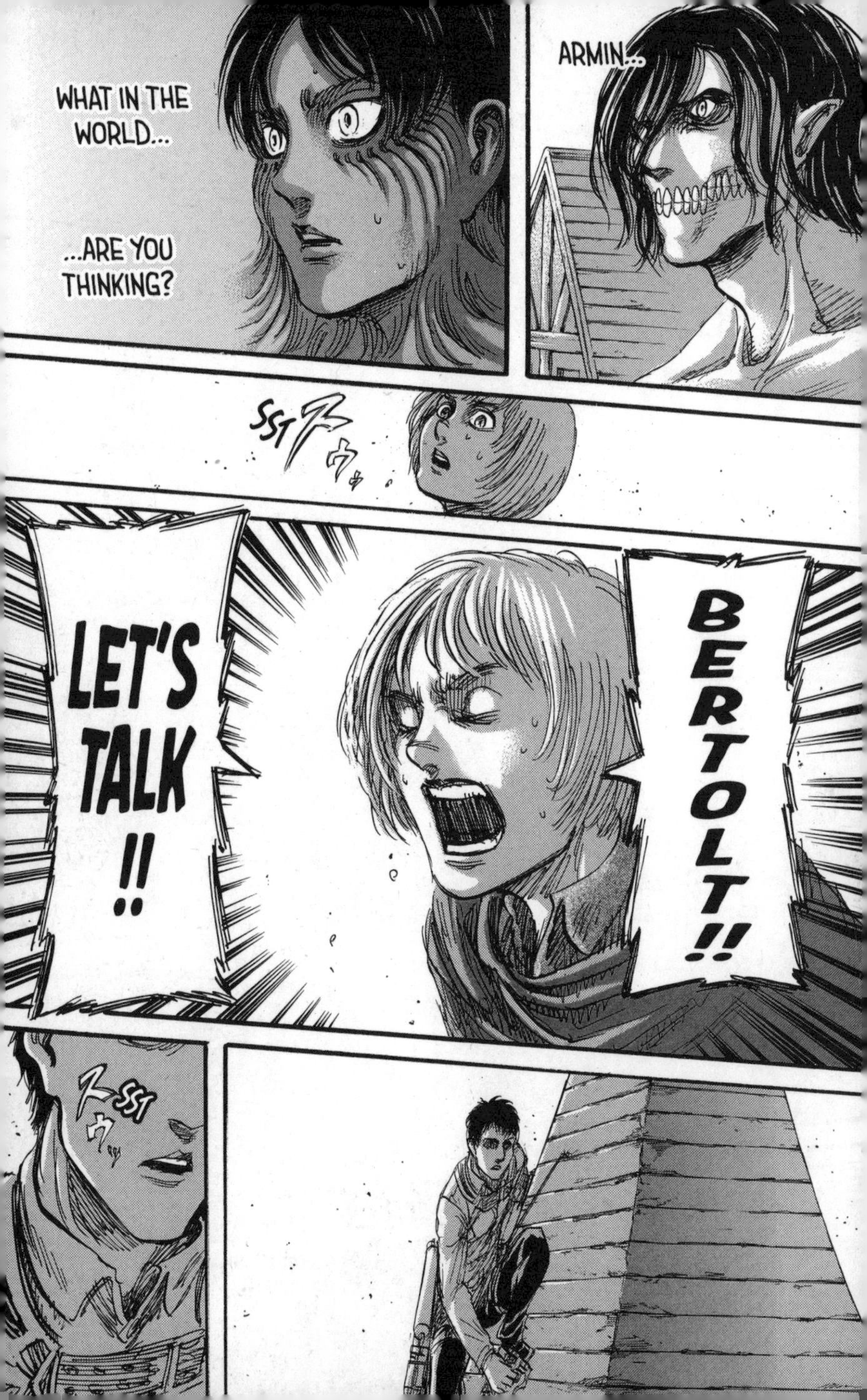
ARMIN...
WHAT IN THE WORLD...
...ARE YOU THINKING?
SSS
BERTOLT!!
LET'S TALK!!
SSS

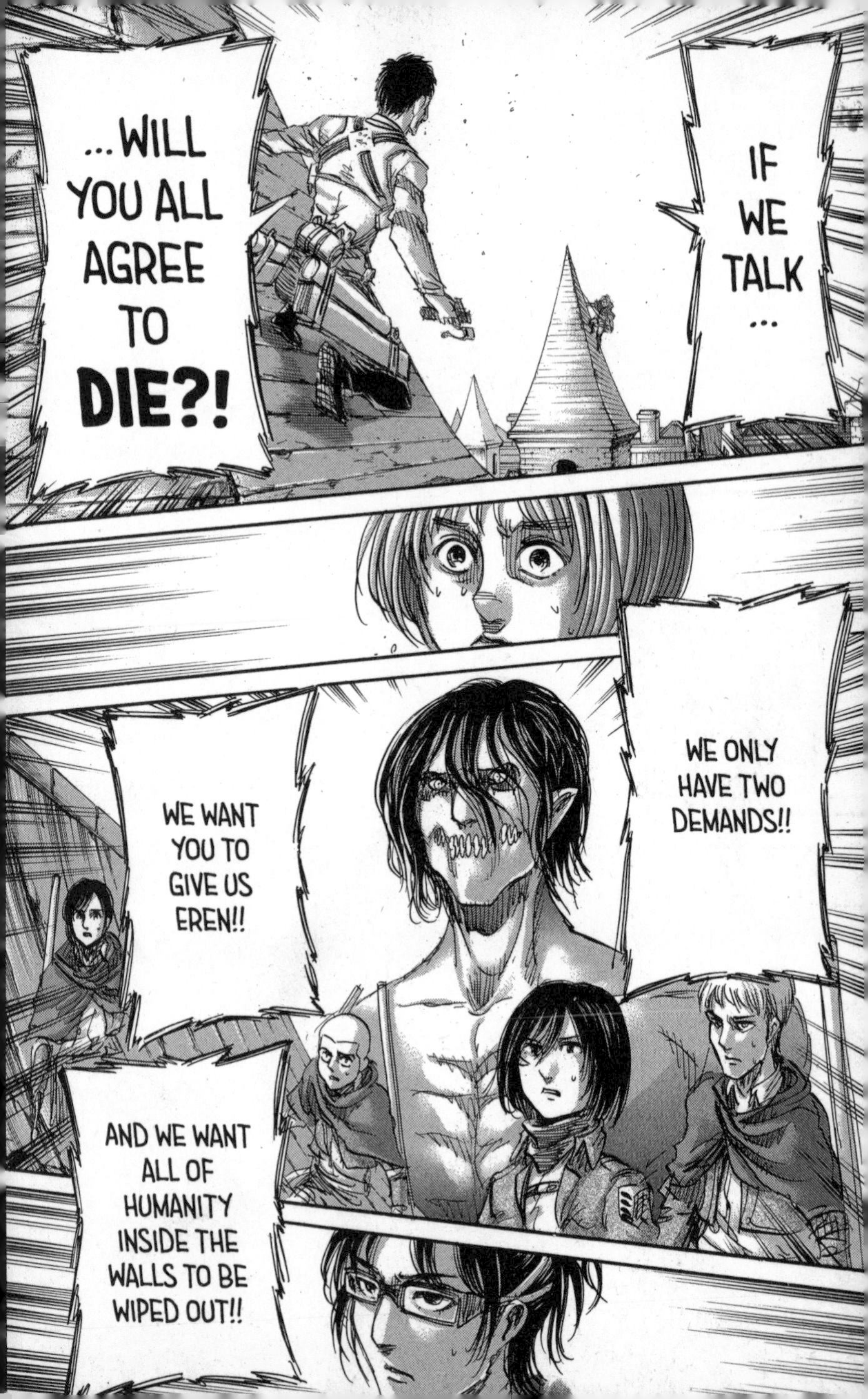
IF WE TALK...
...WILL YOU ALL AGREE TO DIE?!
WE ONLY HAVE TWO DEMANDS!!
WE WANT YOU TO GIVE US EREN!!
AND WE WANT ALL OF HUMANITY INSIDE THE WALLS TO BE WIPED OUT!!

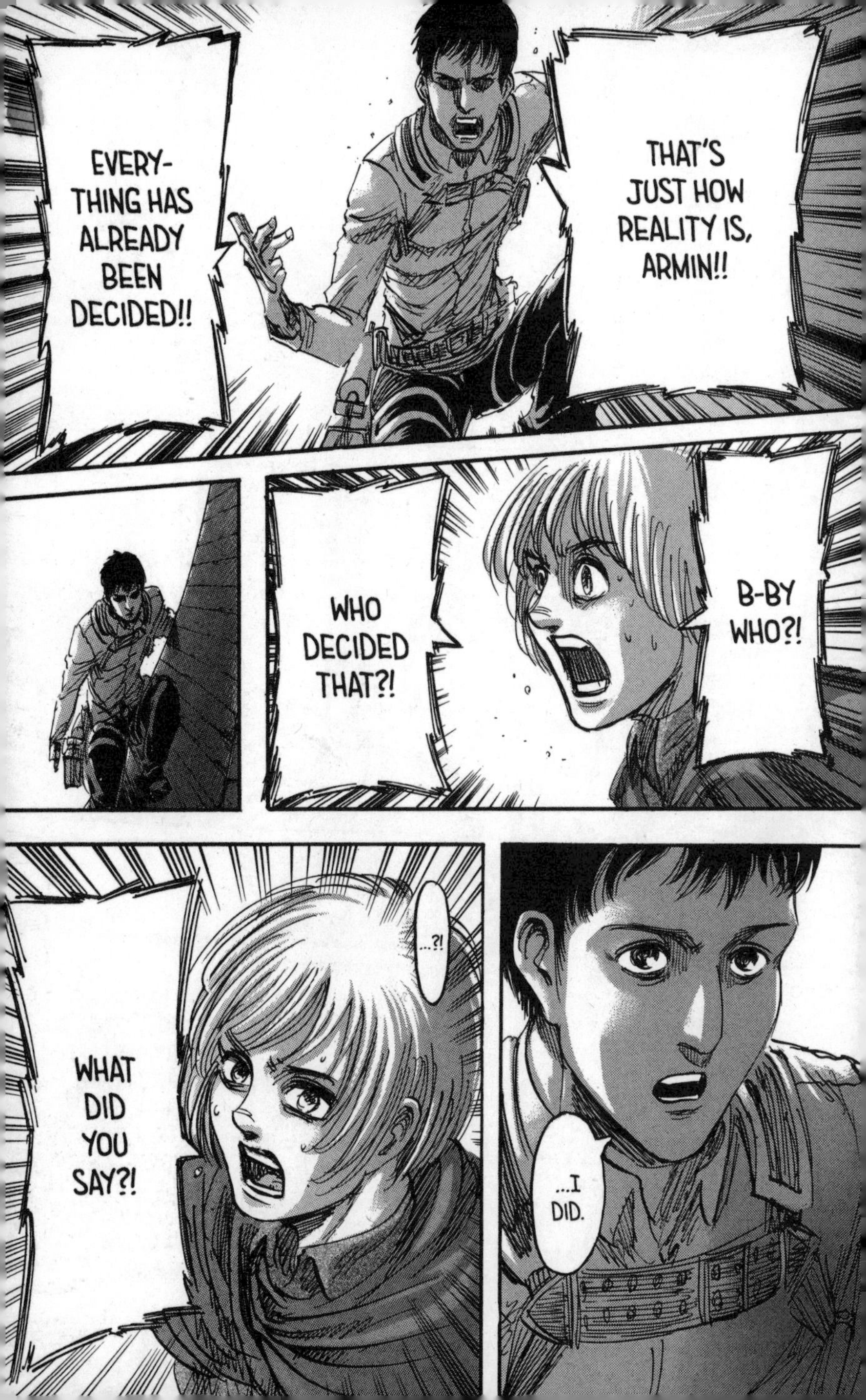
THAT'S JUST HOW REALITY IS, ARMIN!!
EVERY-THING HAS ALREADY BEEN DECIDED!!
B-BY WHO?!
WHO DECIDED THAT?!
...I DID.
...?!
WHAT DID YOU SAY?!

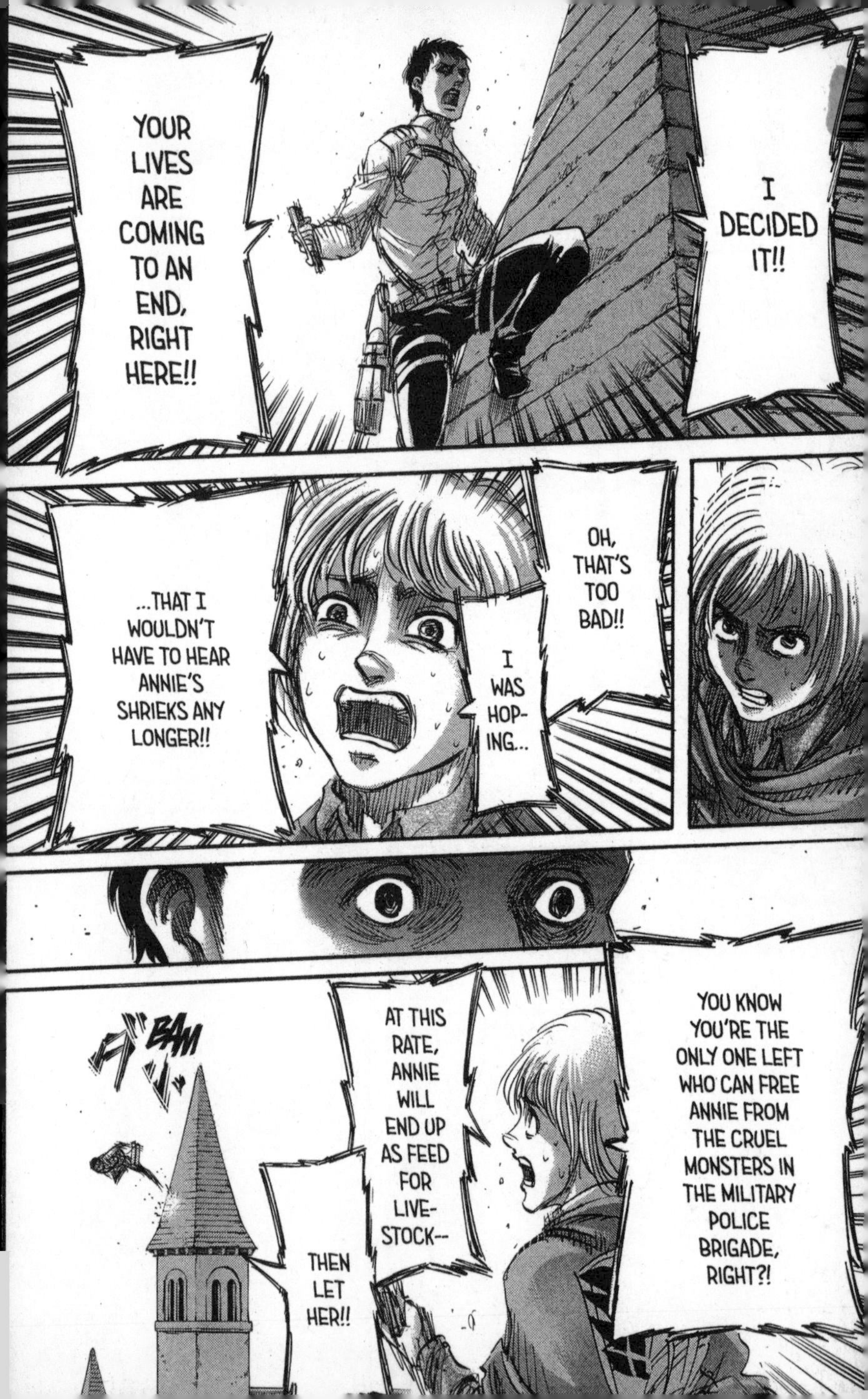
I DECIDED IT!!
YOUR LIVES ARE COMING TO AN END, RIGHT HERE!!
OH, THAT'S TOO BAD!!
I WAS HOP-ING...
...THAT I WOULDN'T HAVE TO HEAR ANNIE'S SHRIEKS ANY LONGER!!
YOU KNOW YOU'RE THE ONLY ONE LEFT WHO CAN FREE ANNIE FROM THE CRUEL MONSTERS IN THE MILITARY POLICE BRIGADE, RIGHT?!
AT THIS RATE, ANNIE WILL END UP AS FEED FOR LIVE-STOCK--
THEN LET HER!!
BAM

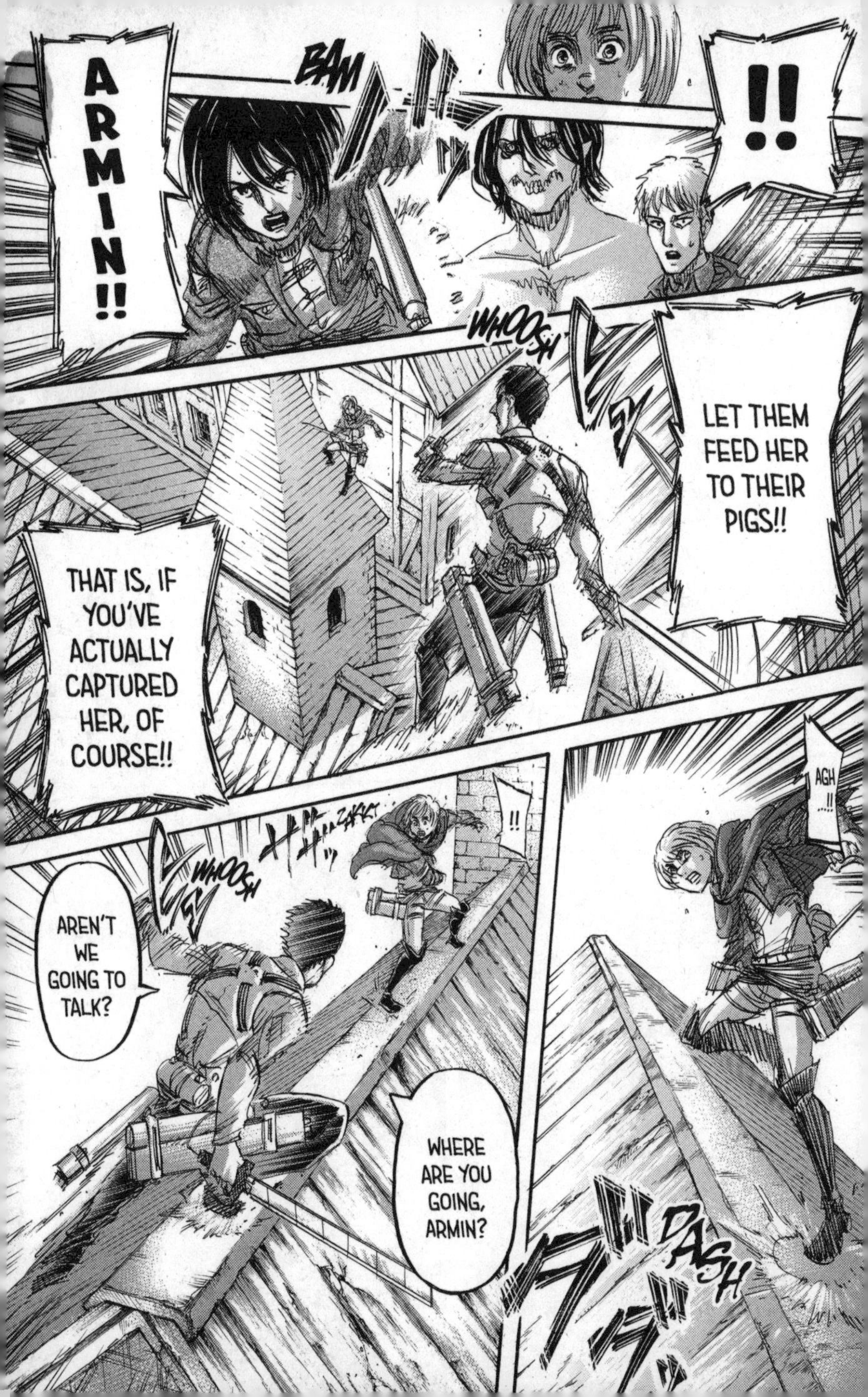
!!
BAM
ARMIN!!
WHOOSH
LET THEM FEED HER TO THEIR PIGS!!
THAT IS, IF YOU'VE ACTUALLY CAPTURED HER, OF COURSE!!
AGH!!
DASH
!!
WHOOSH
AREN'T WE GOING TO TALK?
WHERE ARE YOU GOING, ARMIN?

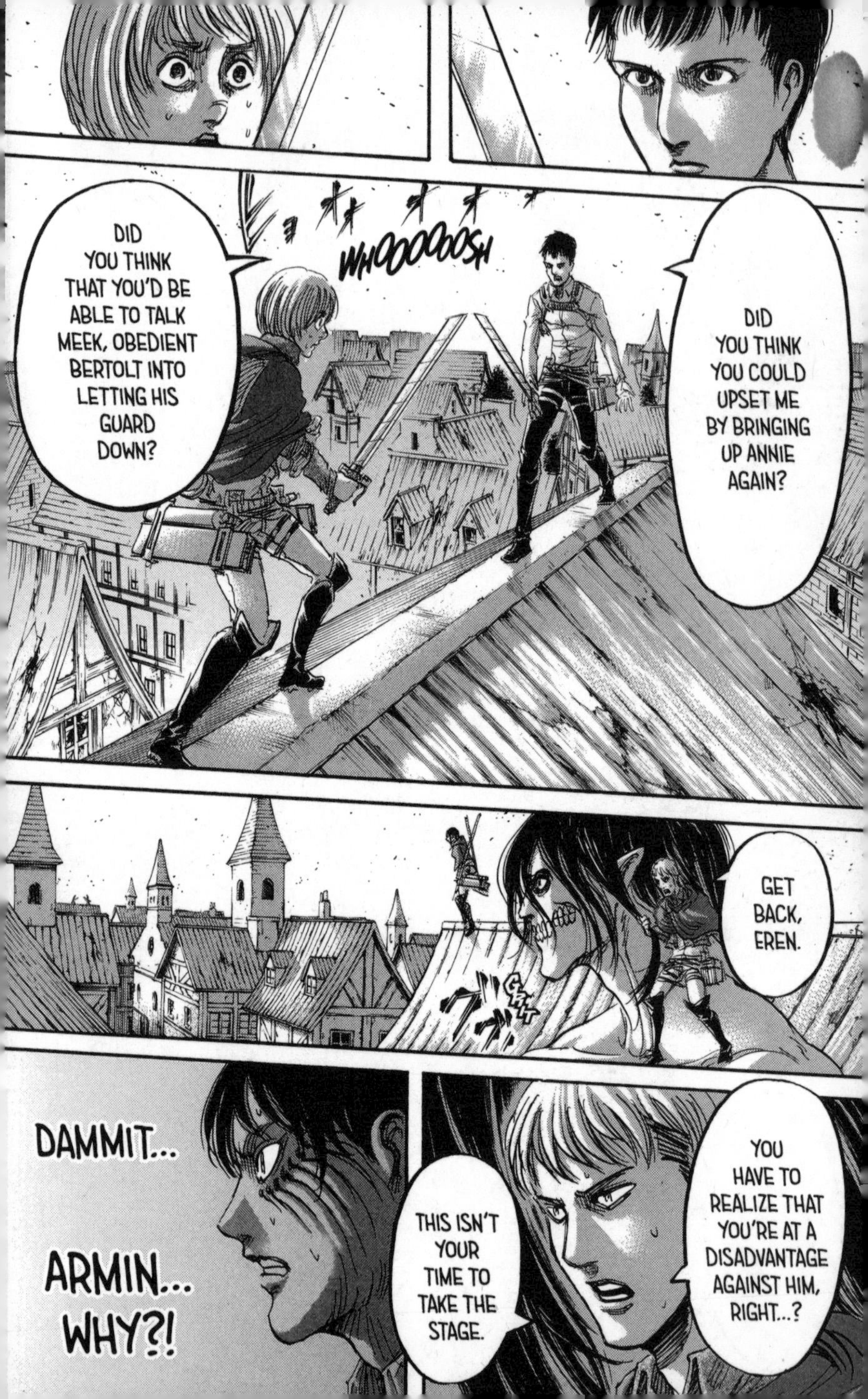

DID YOU THINK YOU COULD UPSET ME BY BRINGING UP ANNIE AGAIN?
WHOOOOOOSH
DID YOU THINK THAT YOU'D BE ABLE TO TALK MEEK, OBEDIENT BERTOLT INTO LETTING HIS GUARD DOWN?
GET BACK, EREN.
GRIT
YOU HAVE TO REALIZE THAT YOU'RE AT A DISADVANTAGE AGAINST HIM, RIGHT...?
THIS ISN'T YOUR TIME TO TAKE THE STAGE.
DAMMIT...
ARMIN... WHY?!

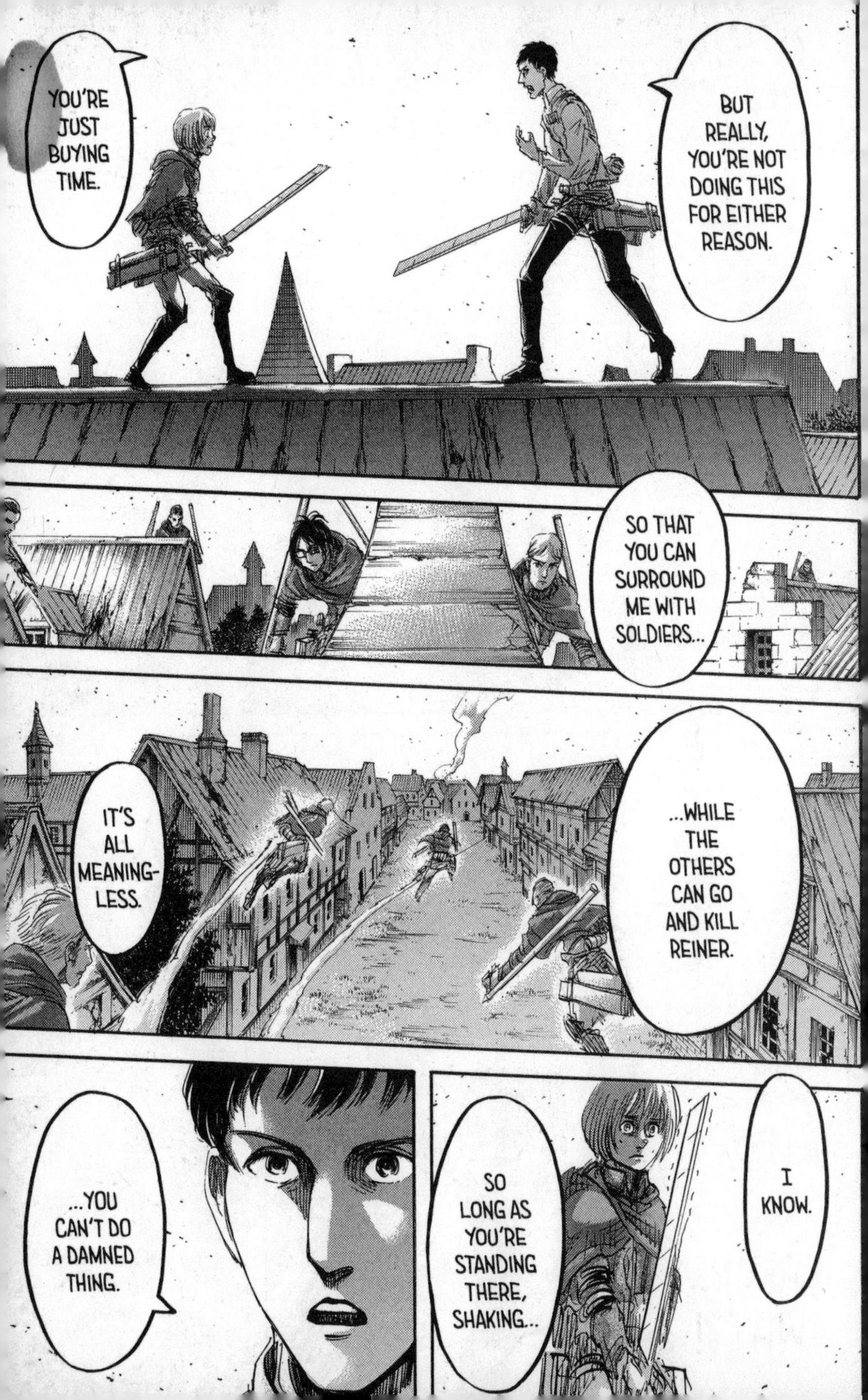
BUT REALLY, YOU'RE NOT DOING THIS FOR EITHER REASON.
YOU'RE JUST BUYING TIME.
SO THAT YOU CAN SURROUND ME WITH SOLDIERS...
...WHILE THE OTHERS CAN GO AND KILL REINER.
IT'S ALL MEANING-LESS.
I KNOW.
SO LONG AS YOU'RE STANDING THERE, SHAKING...
...YOU CAN'T DO A DAMNED THING.

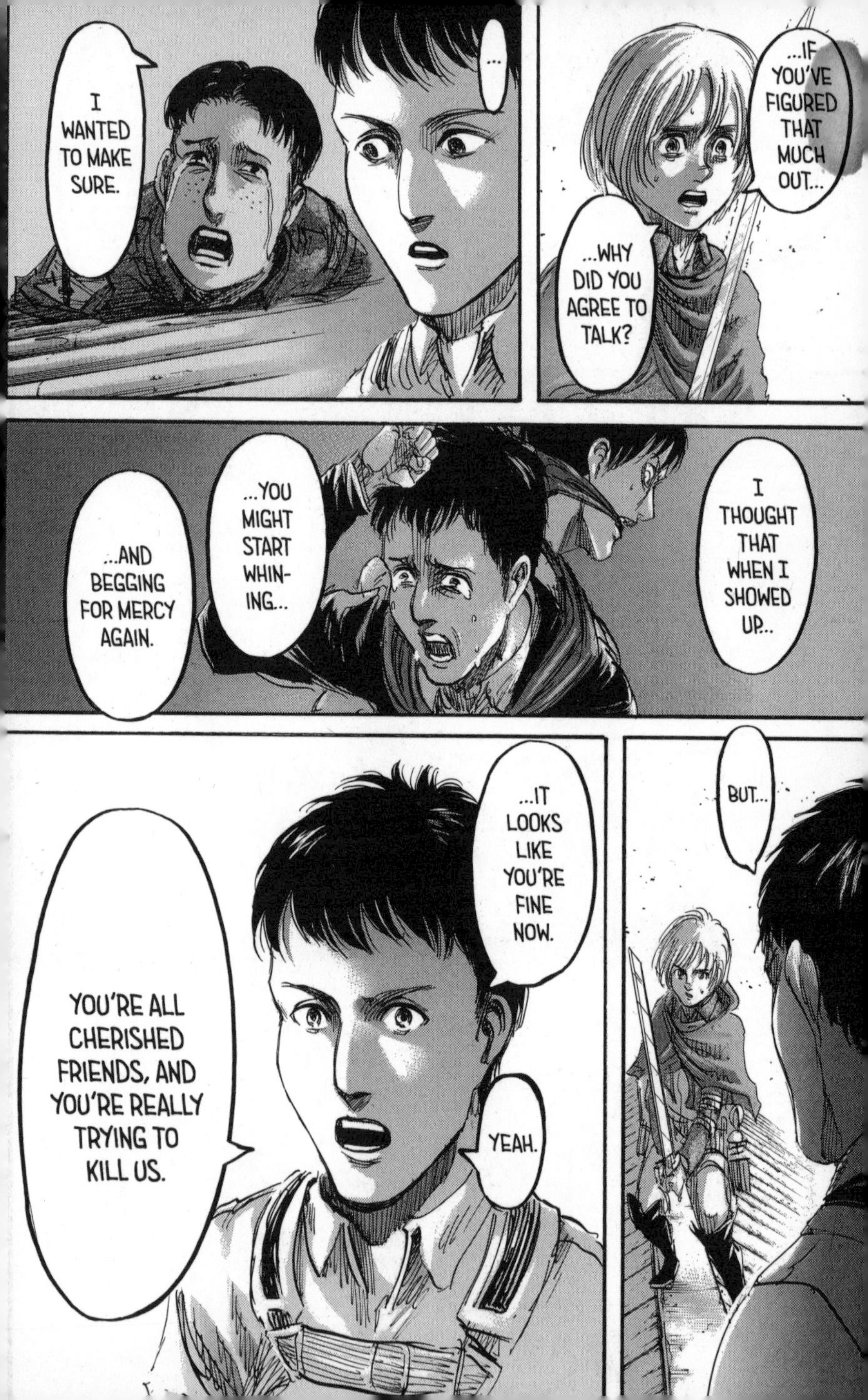
...IF YOU'VE FIGURED THAT MUCH OUT...
...WHY DID YOU AGREE TO TALK?
...
I WANTED TO MAKE SURE.
I THOUGHT THAT WHEN I SHOWED UP...
...YOU MIGHT START WHINING...
...AND BEGGING FOR MERCY AGAIN.
BUT...
...IT LOOKS LIKE YOU'RE FINE NOW.
YEAH.
YOU'RE ALL CHERISHED FRIENDS, AND YOU'RE REALLY TRYING TO KILL US.

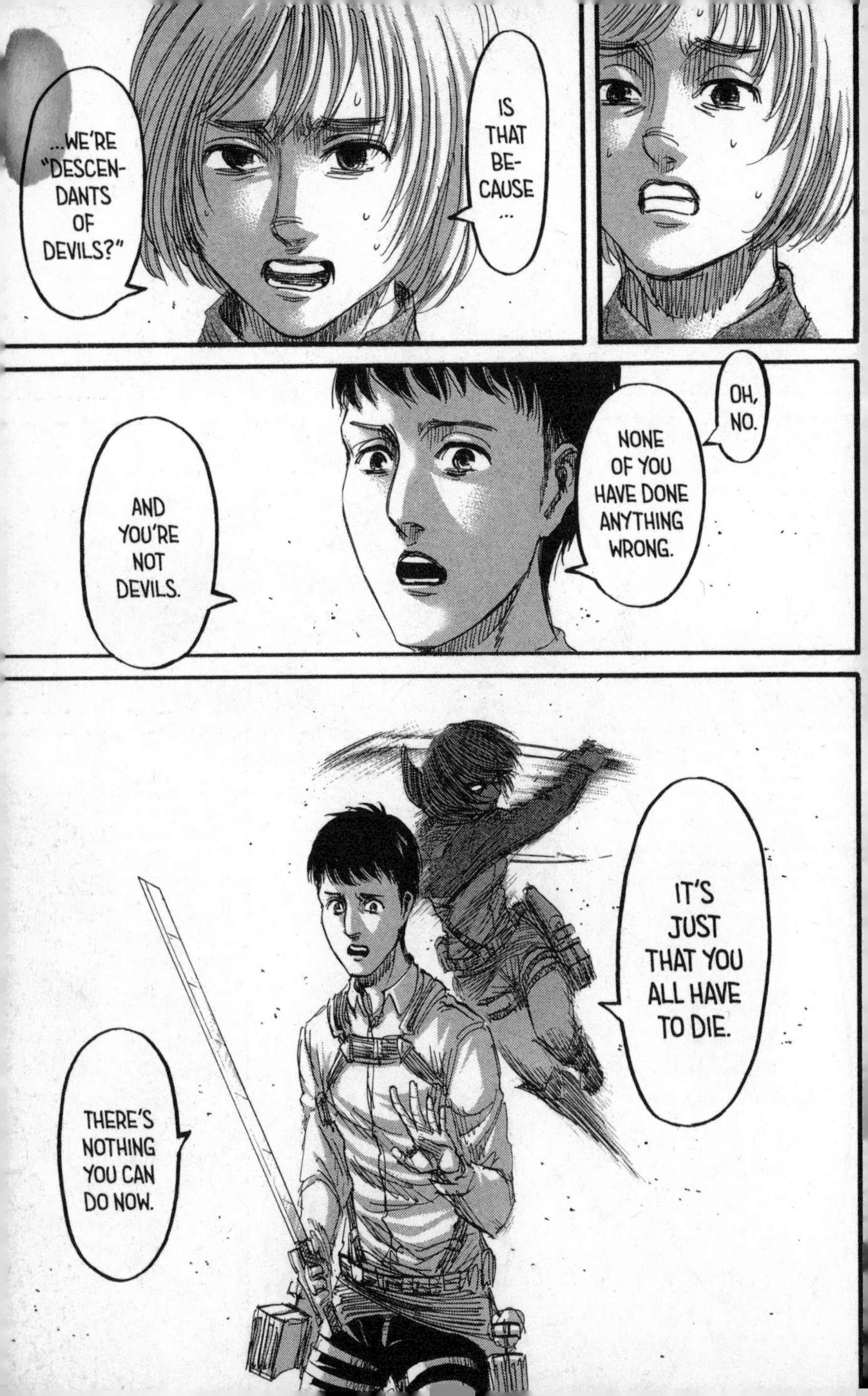
IS THAT BE-CAUSE ...
...WE'RE "DESCEN-DANTS OF DEVILS?"
OH, NO.
NONE OF YOU HAVE DONE ANYTHING WRONG.
AND YOU'RE NOT DEVILS.
IT'S JUST THAT YOU ALL HAVE TO DIE.
THERE'S NOTHING YOU CAN DO NOW.

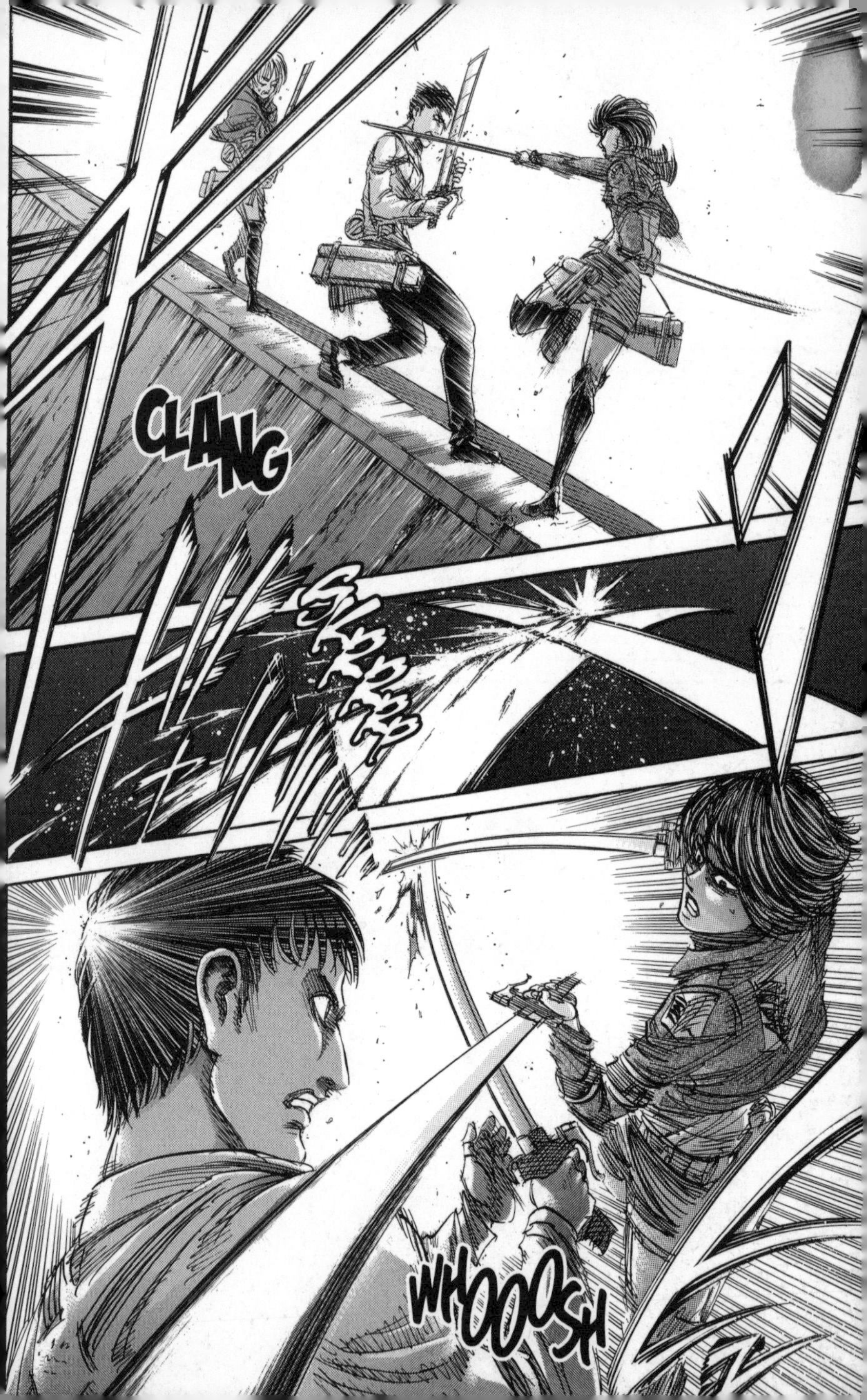
CLANG
WHOOOSH

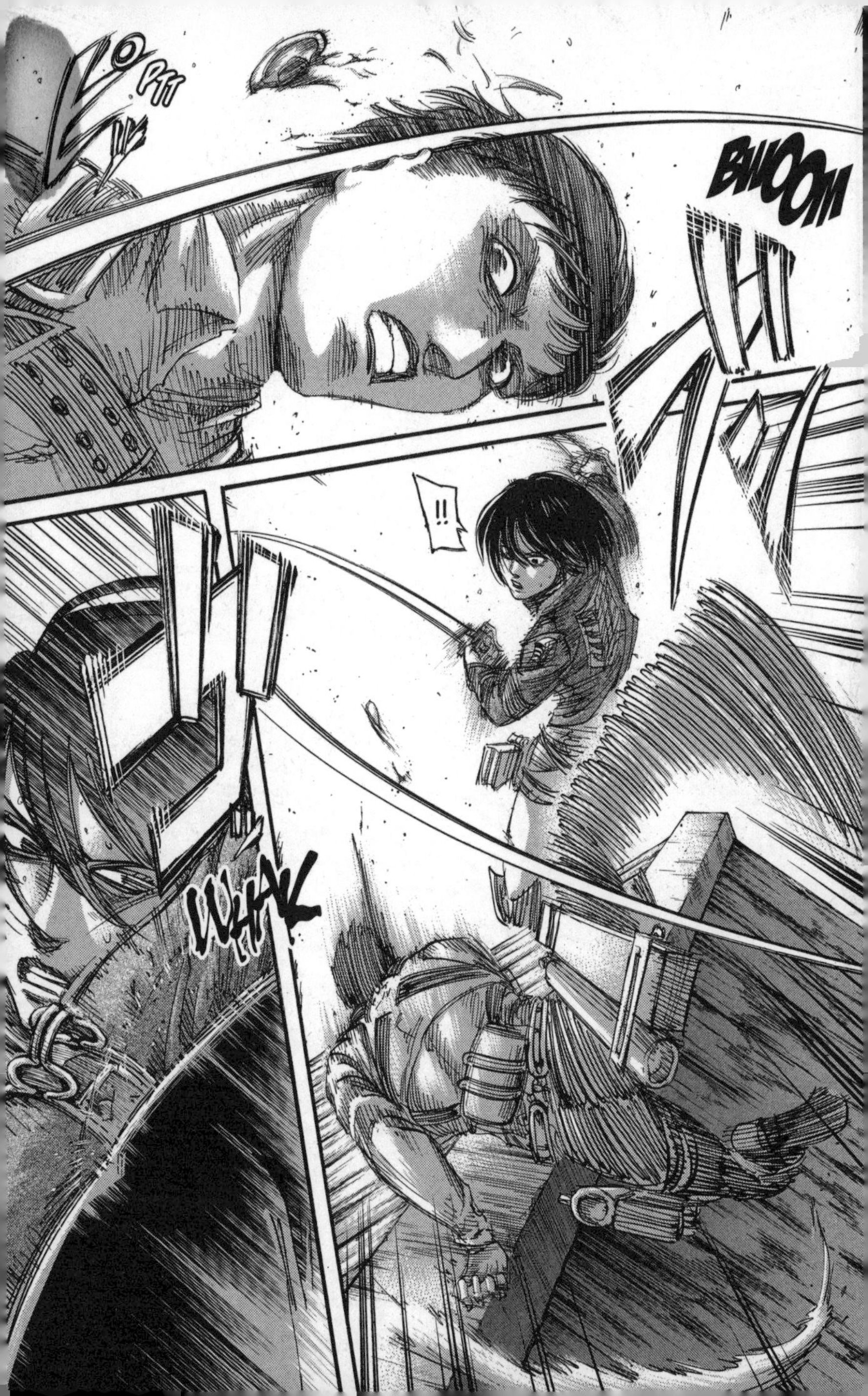
BWOOM
ZOPT
!!
WHAK

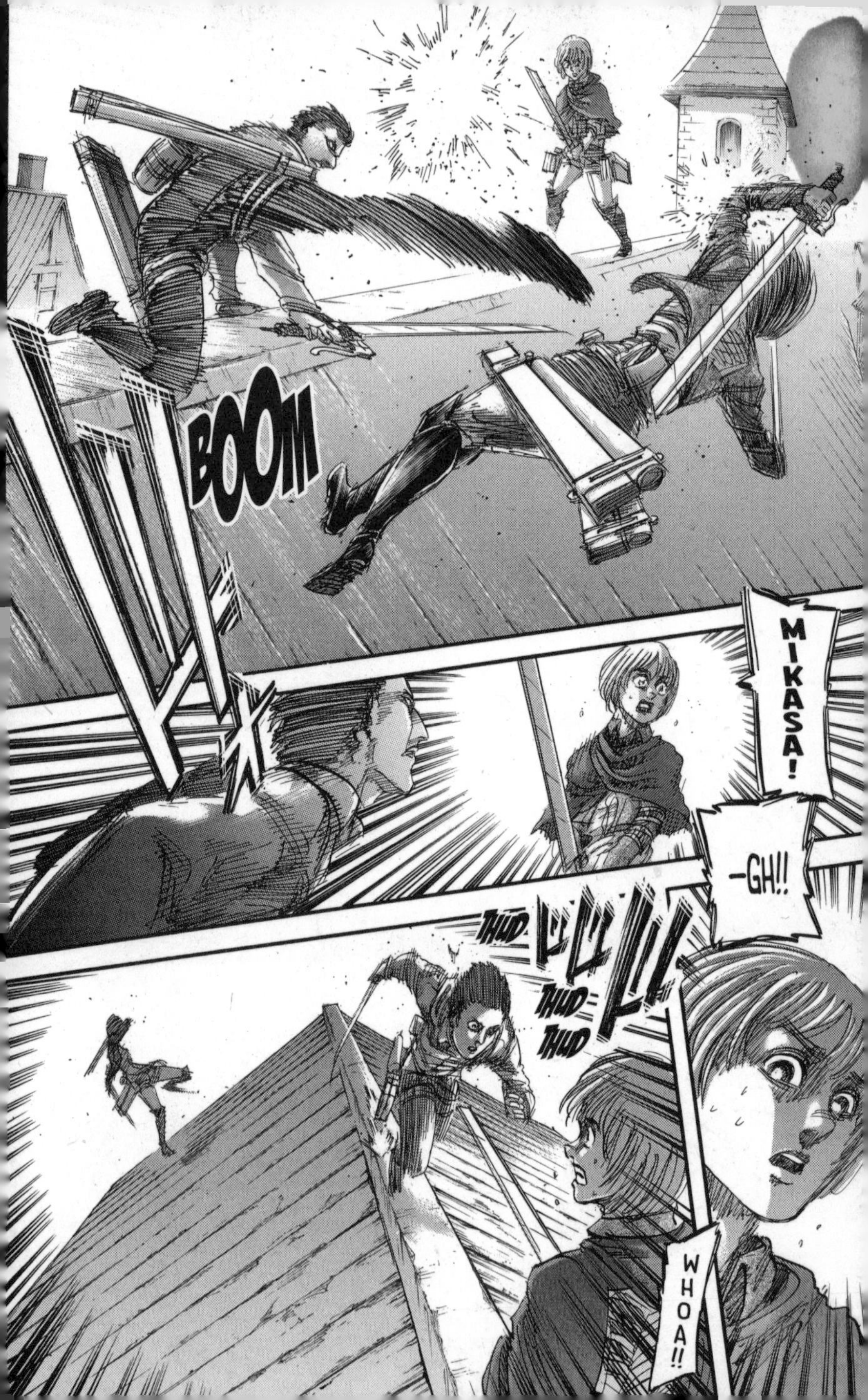
BOOM
MIKASA!
-GH!!
THUD THUD THUD THUD
WHOA!!

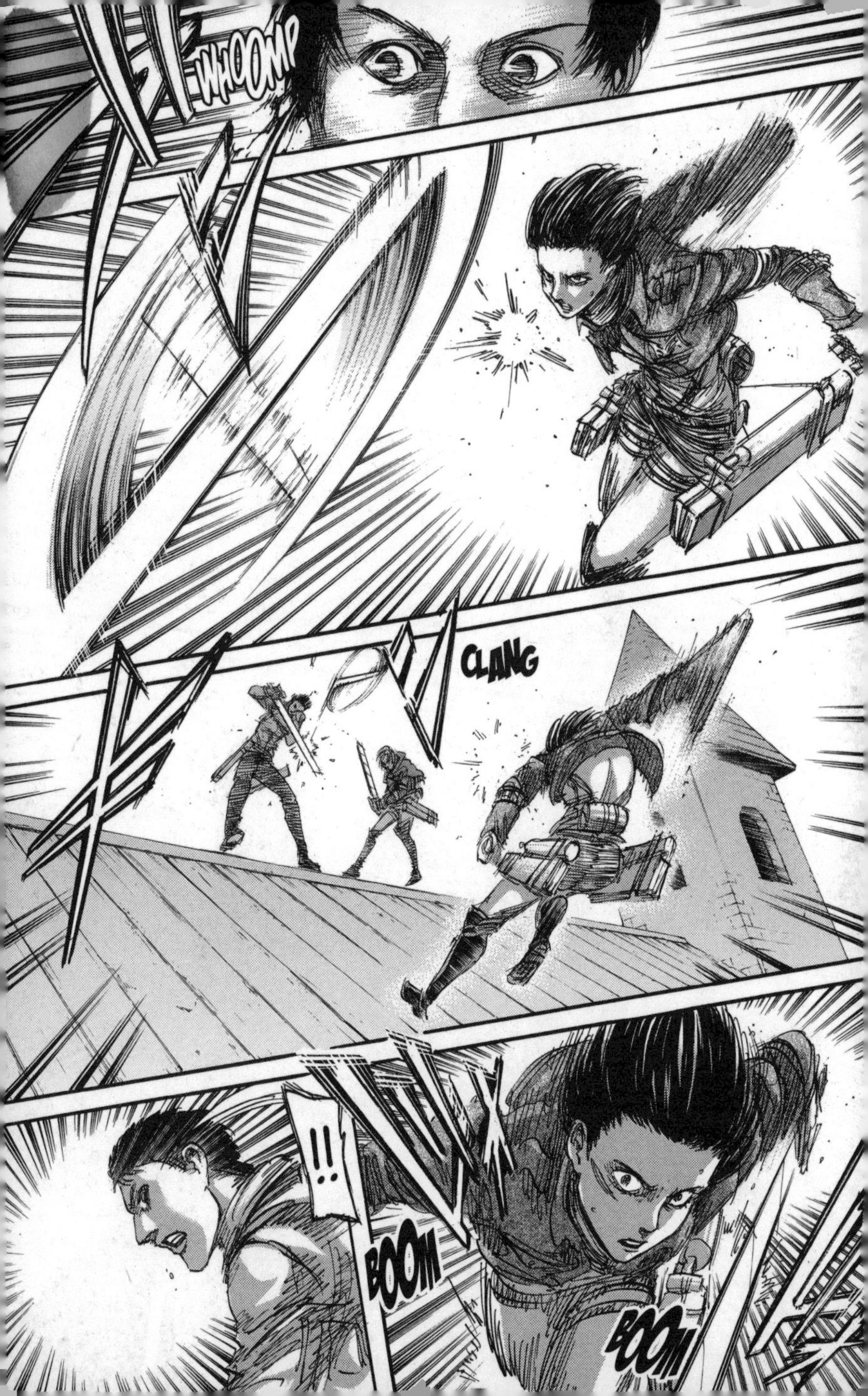
WHOOMP
CLANG
!!
BOOM
BOOM

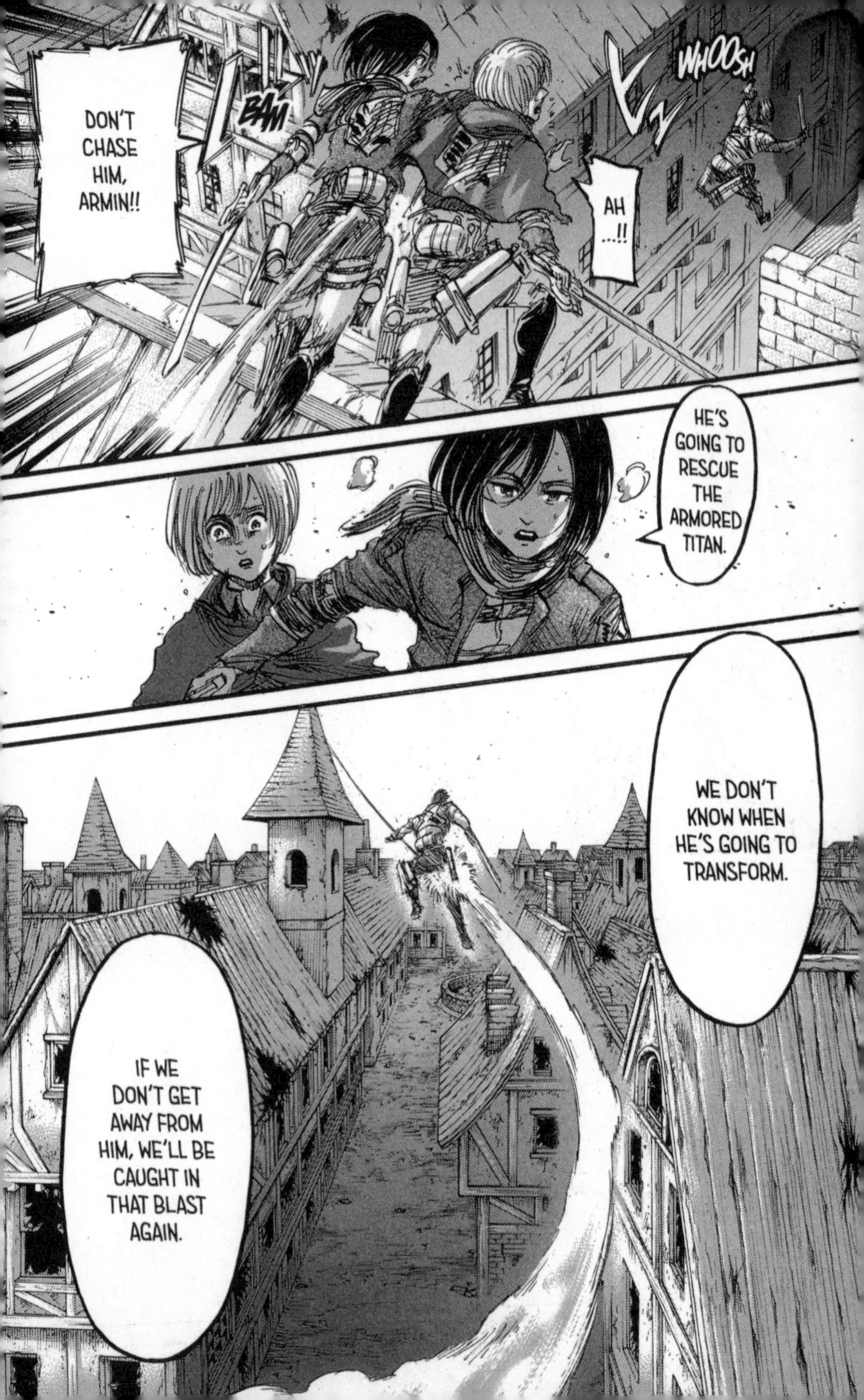
WHOOSH
AH ...!!
BAM
DON'T CHASE HIM, ARMIN!!
HE'S GOING TO RESCUE THE ARMORED TITAN.
WE DON'T KNOW WHEN HE'S GOING TO TRANSFORM.
IF WE DON'T GET AWAY FROM HIM, WE'LL BE CAUGHT IN THAT BLAST AGAIN.

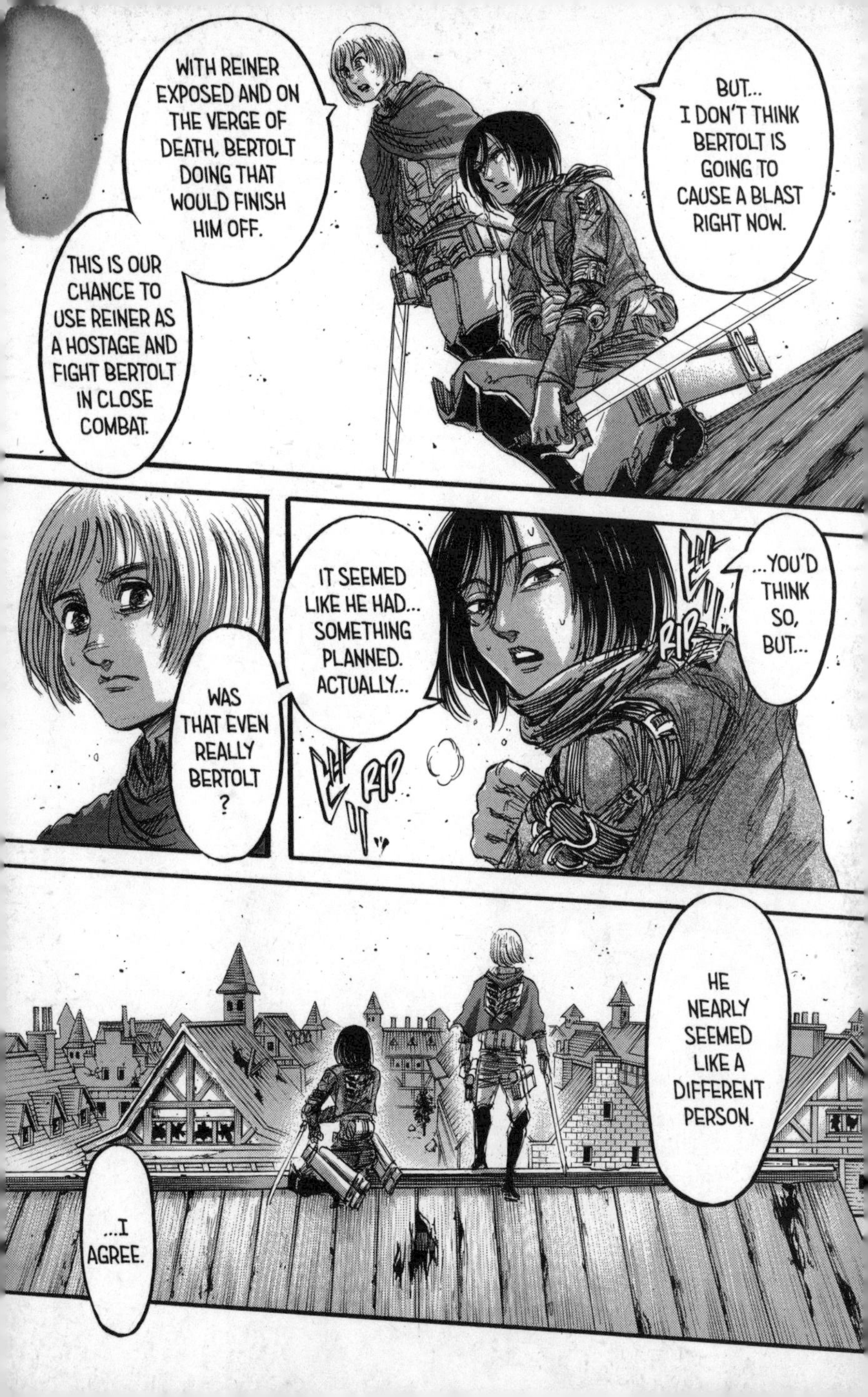
BUT... I DON'T THINK BERTOLT IS GOING TO CAUSE A BLAST RIGHT NOW.
WITH REINER EXPOSED AND ON THE VERGE OF DEATH, BERTOLT DOING THAT WOULD FINISH HIM OFF.
THIS IS OUR CHANCE TO USE REINER AS A HOSTAGE AND FIGHT BERTOLT IN CLOSE COMBAT.
...YOU'D THINK SO, BUT...
RIP
IT SEEMED LIKE HE HAD... SOMETHING PLANNED. ACTUALLY...
RIP
WAS THAT EVEN REALLY BERTOLT?
HE NEARLY SEEMED LIKE A DIFFERENT PERSON.
...I AGREE.

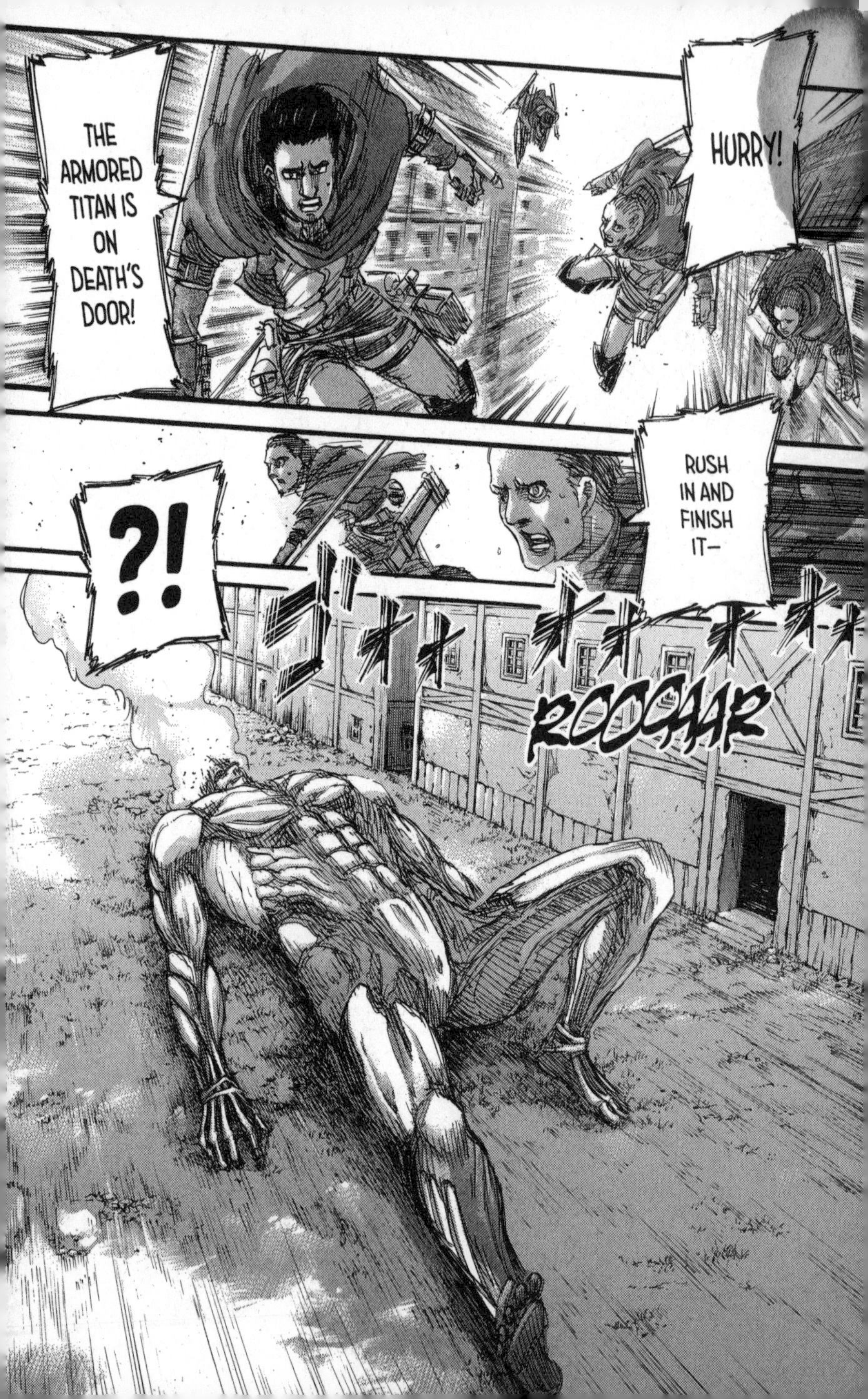
HURRY!
THE ARMORED TITAN IS ON DEATH'S DOOR!
RUSH IN AND FINISH IT—
?!
ROOOAAR

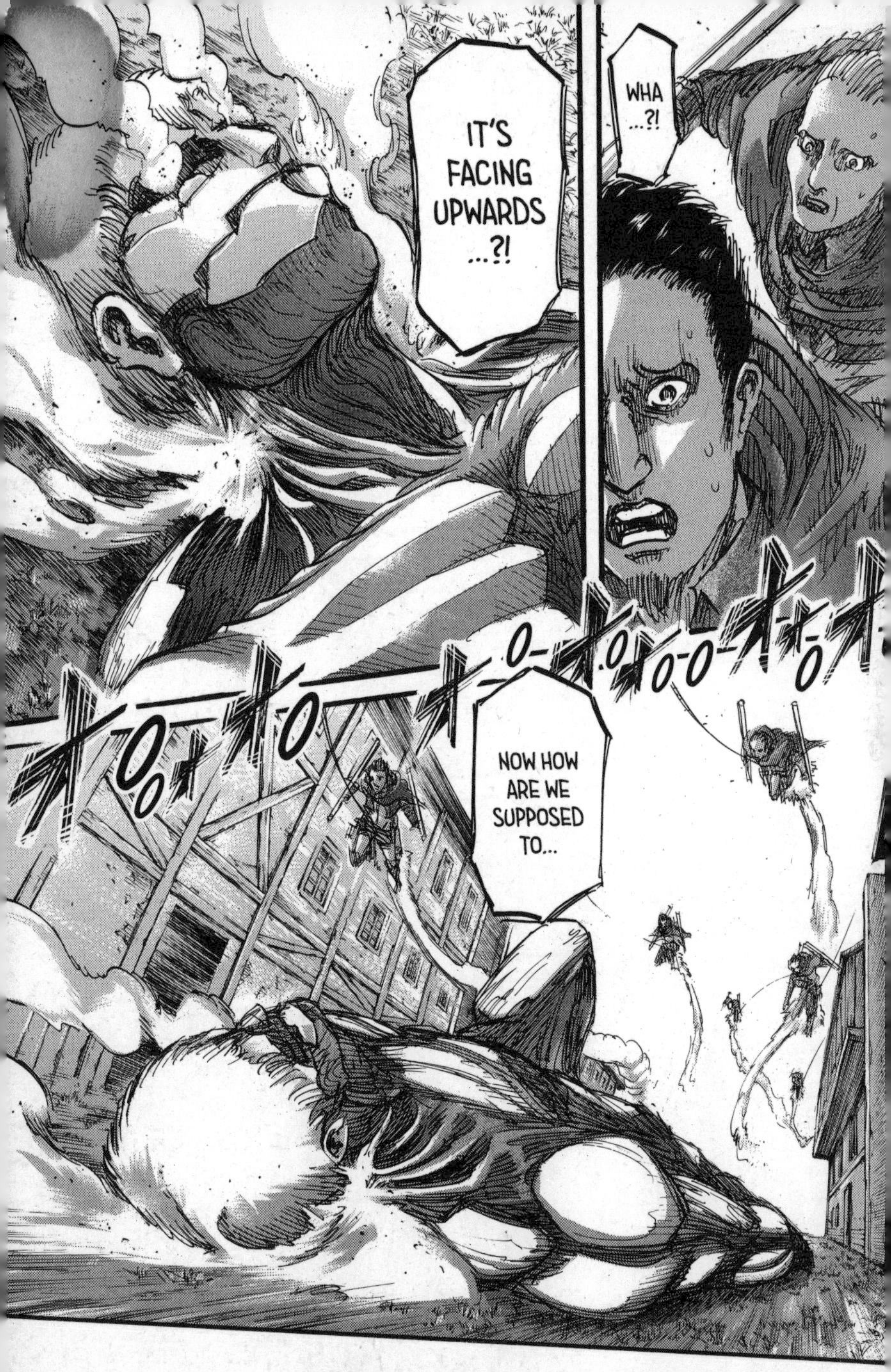
WHA ...?!
IT'S FACING UPWARDS ...?!
NOW HOW ARE WE SUPPOSED TO...

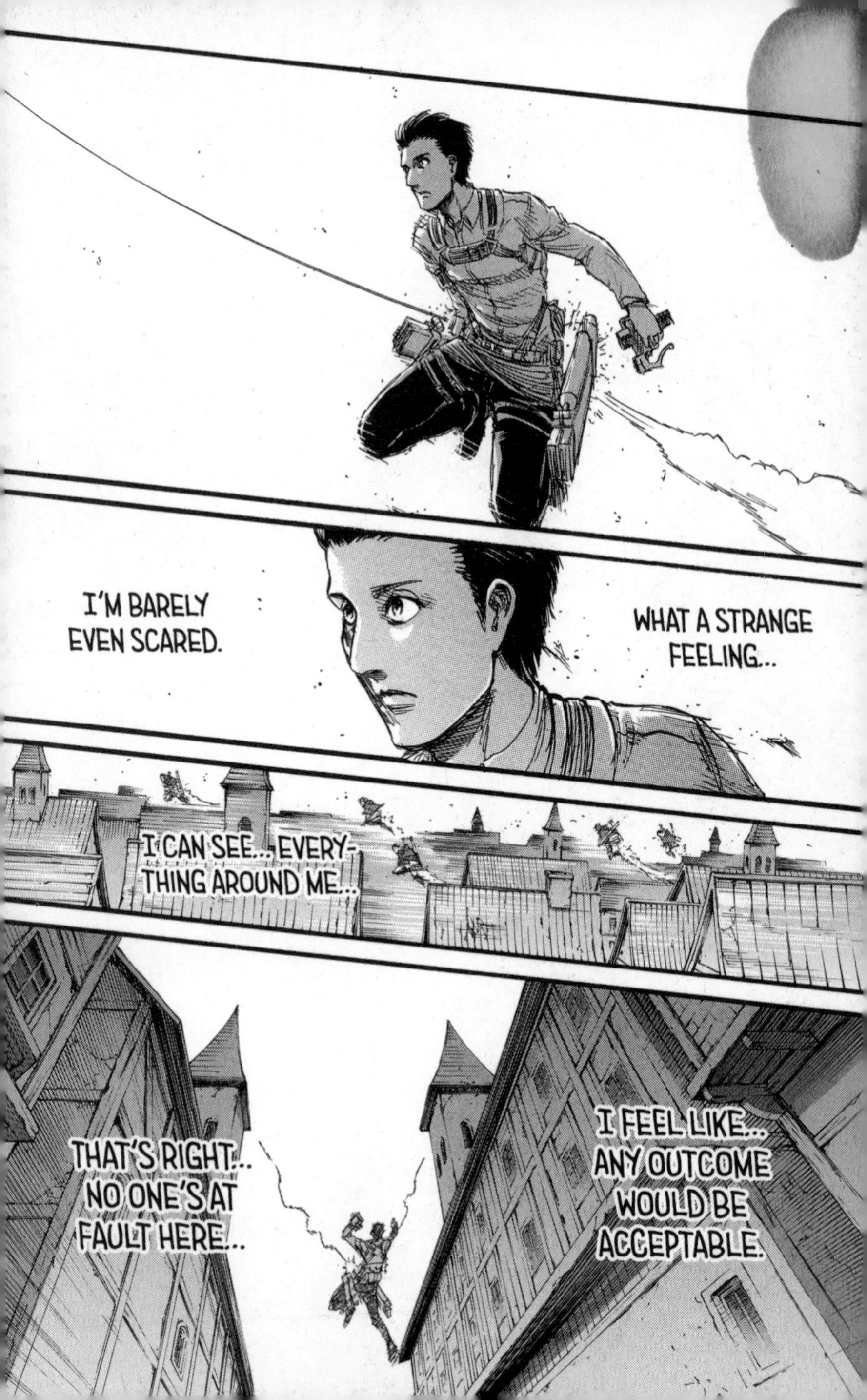
WHAT A STRANGE FEELING...
I'M BARELY EVEN SCARED.
I CAN SEE... EVERY-THING AROUND ME...
I FEEL LIKE... ANY OUTCOME WOULD BE ACCEPTABLE.
THAT'S RIGHT... NO ONE'S AT FAULT HERE...

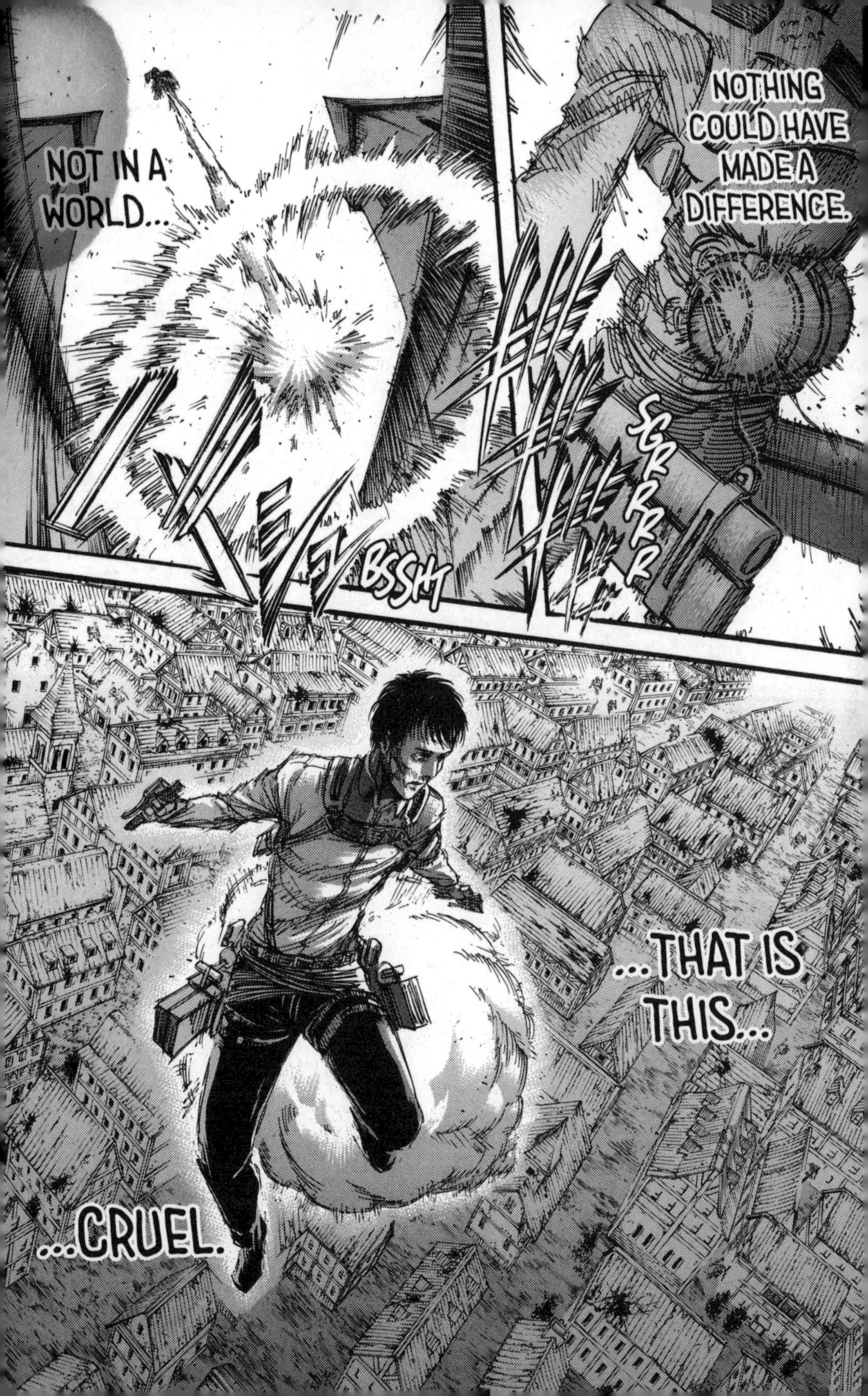
NOTHING COULD HAVE MADE A DIFFERENCE.
NOT IN A WORLD...
SGRRRRR
BSSHT
...THAT IS THIS...
...CRUEL.

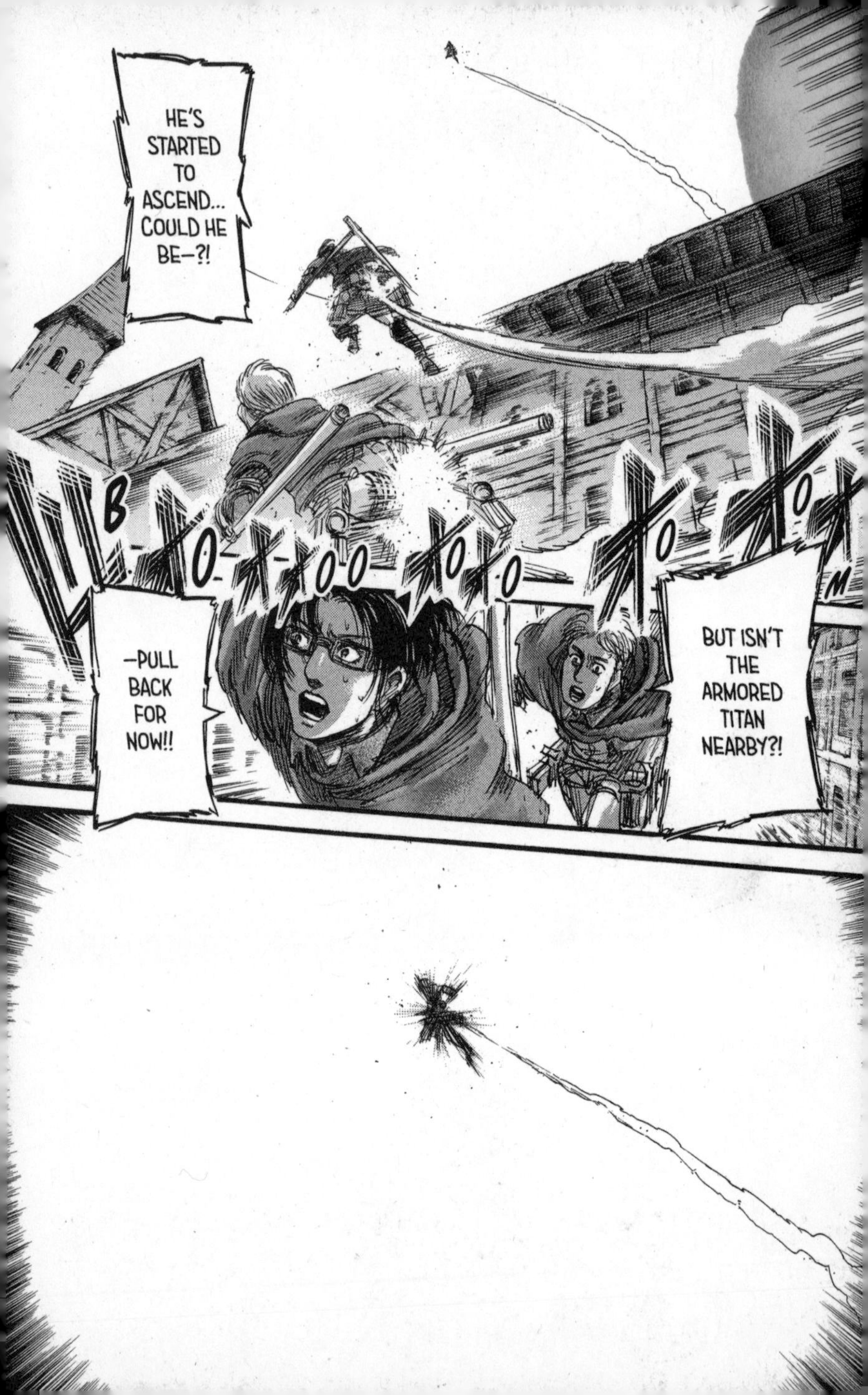
HE'S STARTED TO ASCEND... COULD HE BE–?!
BUT ISN'T THE ARMORED TITAN NEARBY?!
—PULL BACK FOR NOW!!
BOOOOOOOOOOM

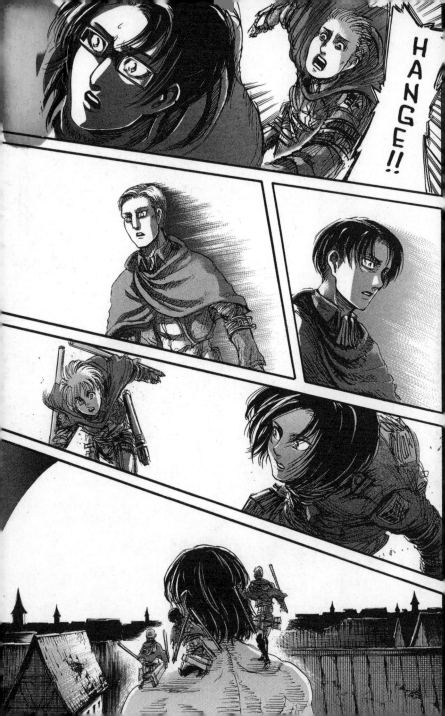

HANGE!!

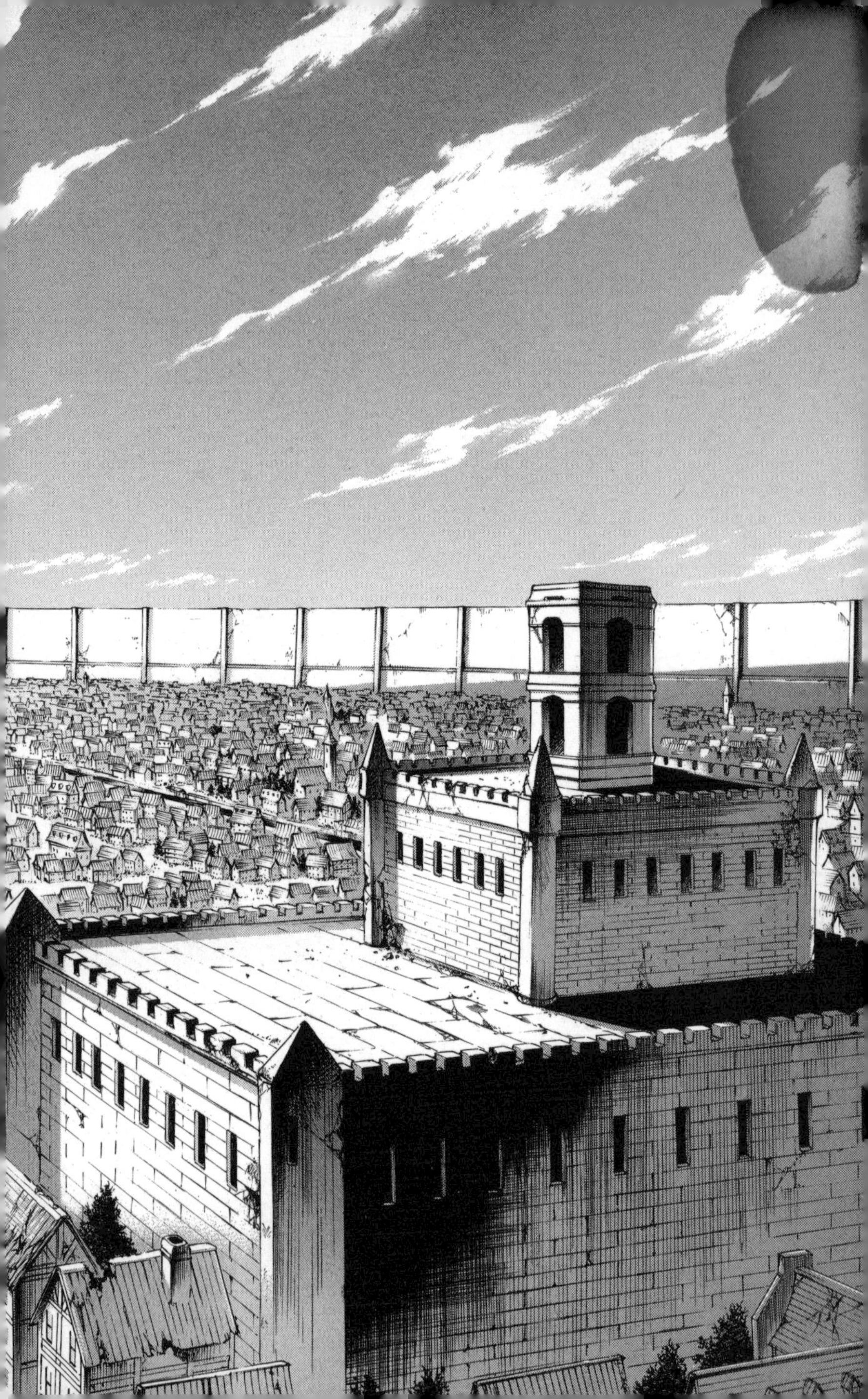

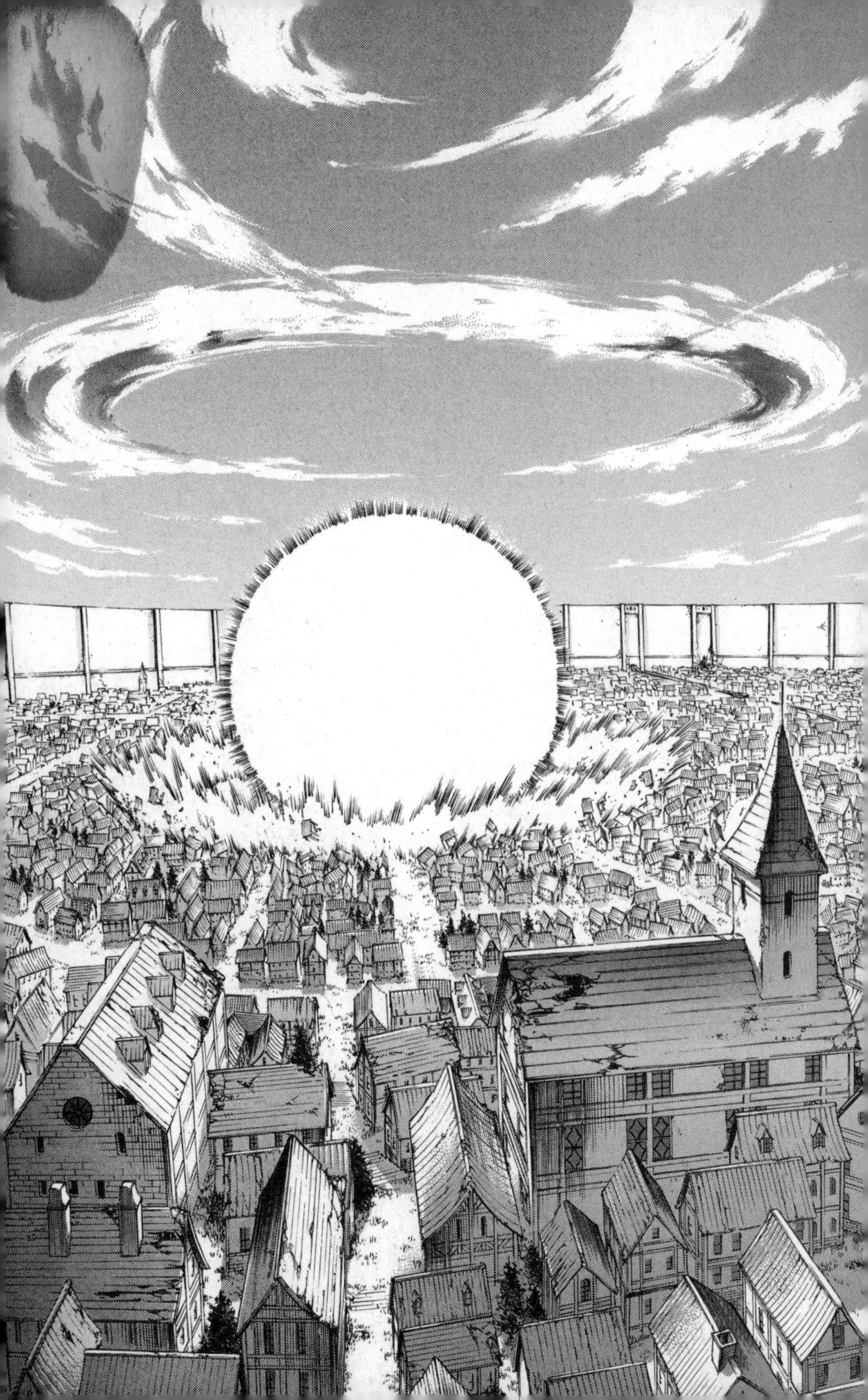

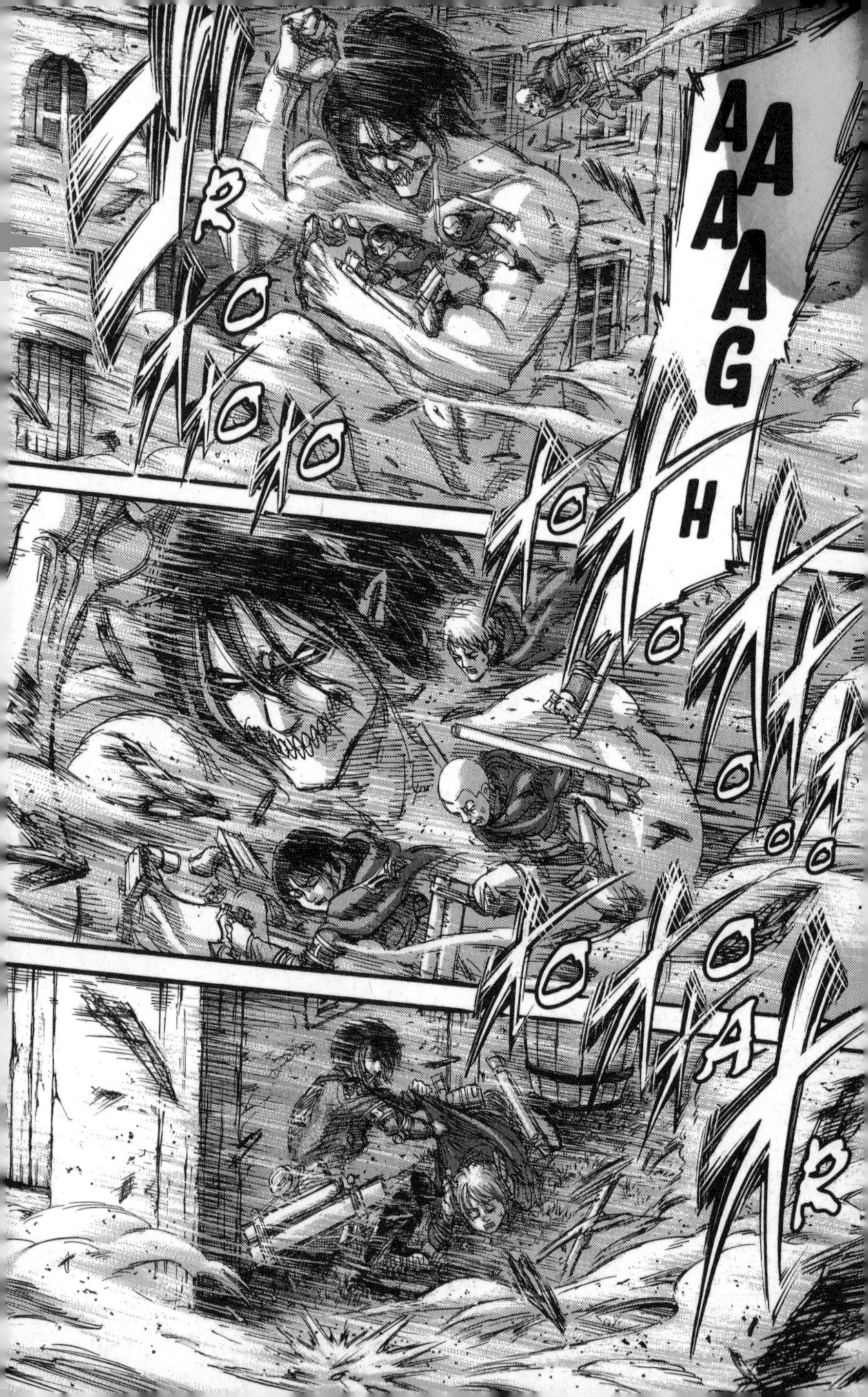
AAAAGH
ROOOO
OOOOOOOO
OOOOAR

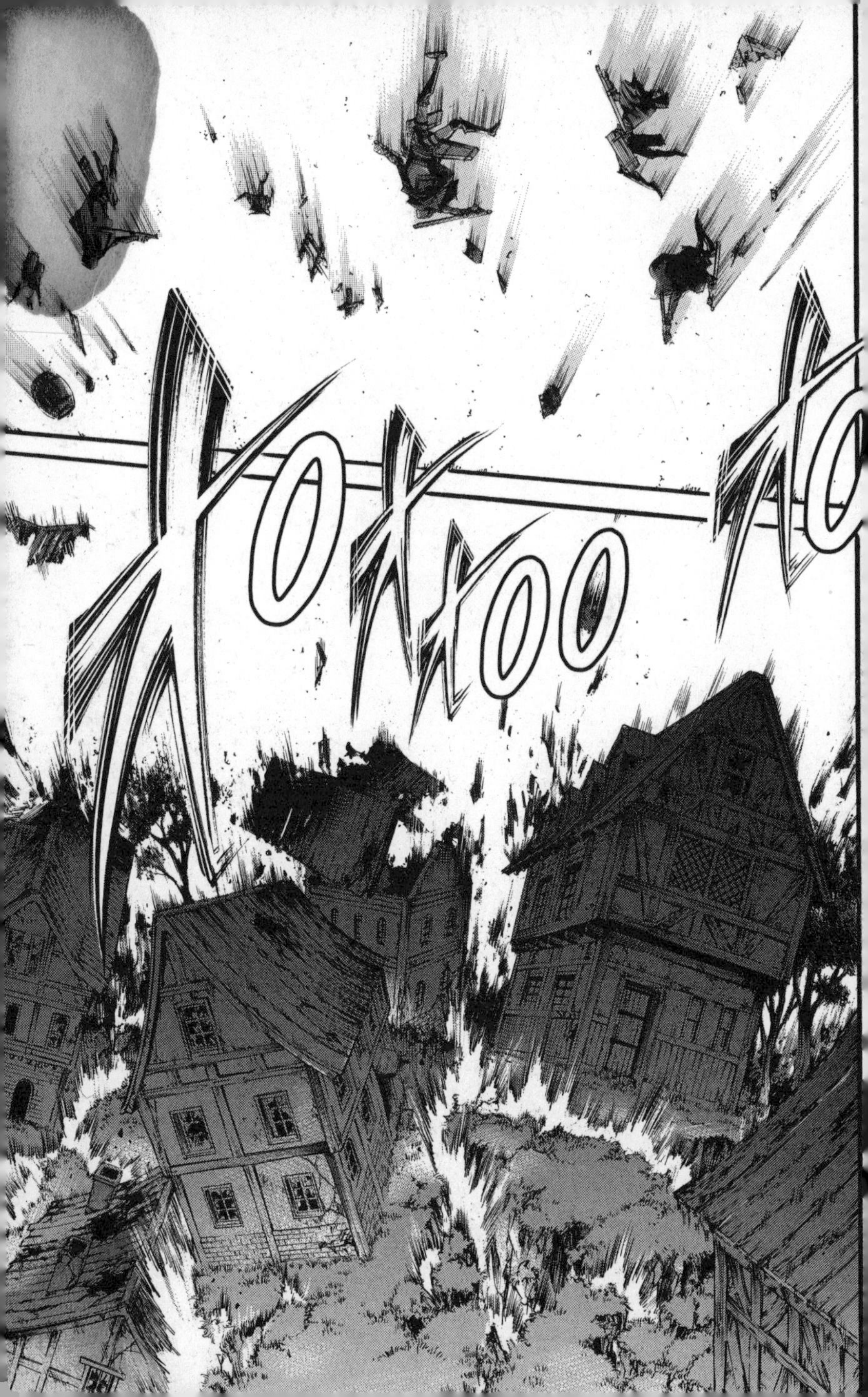

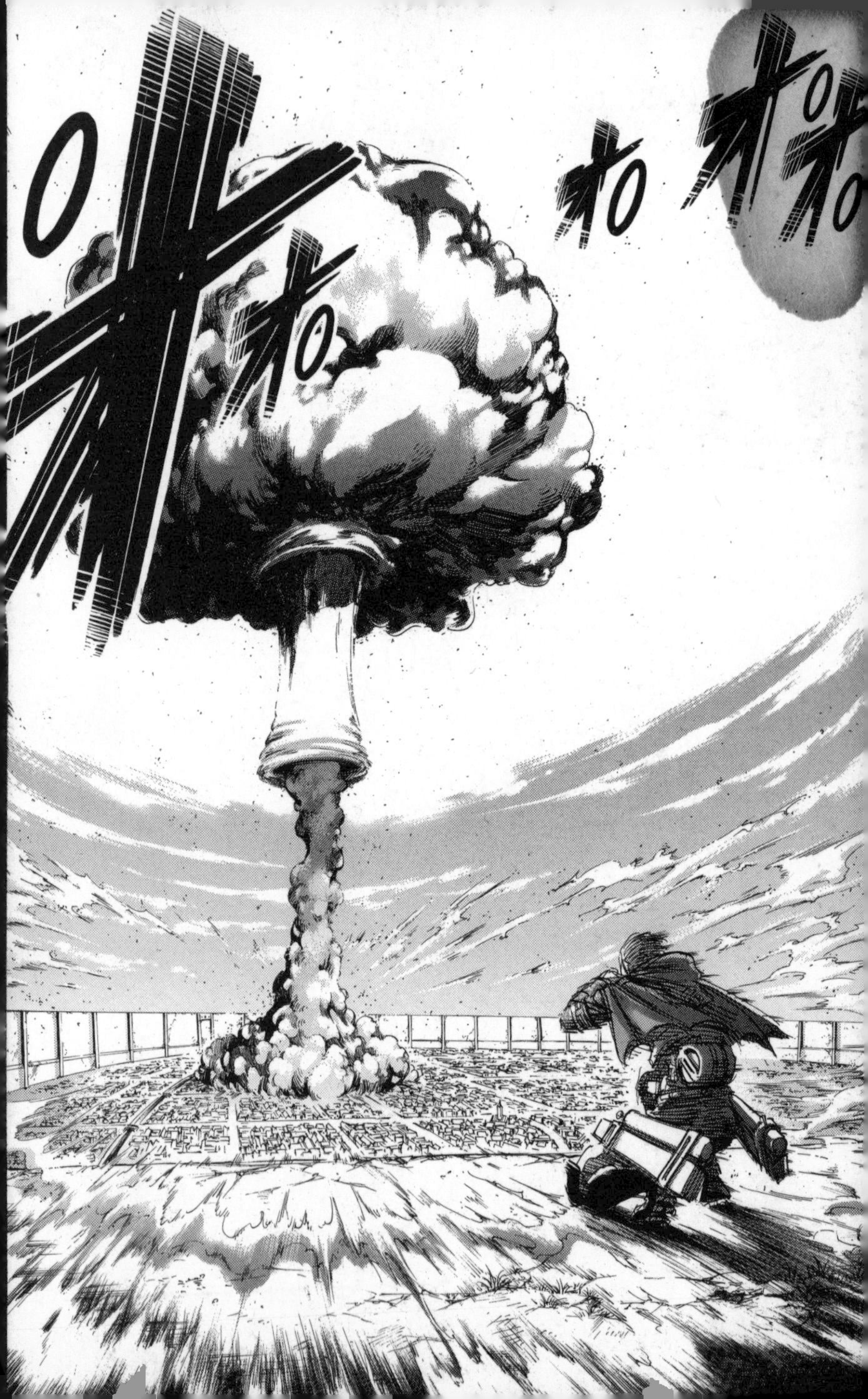

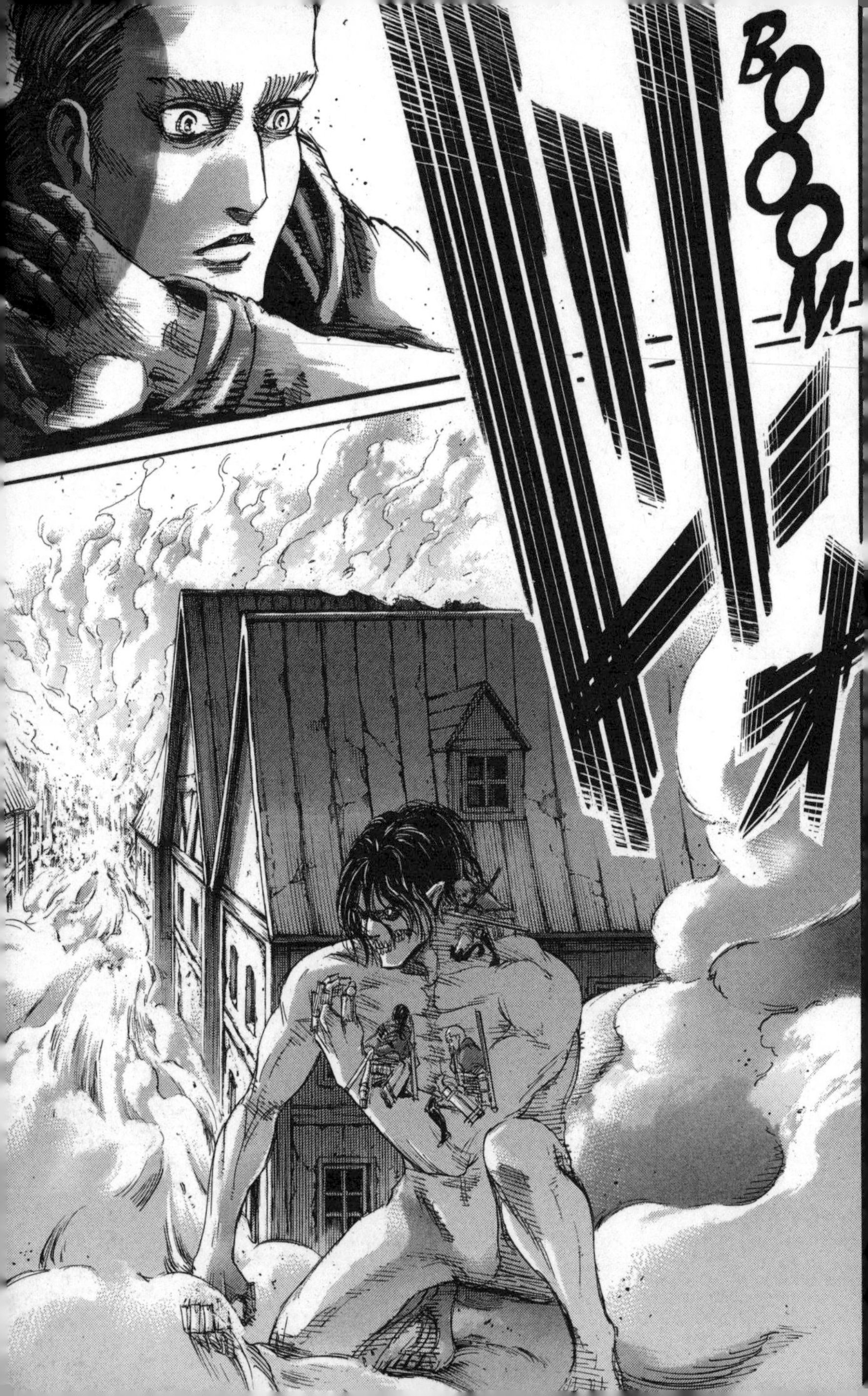
BOOOM

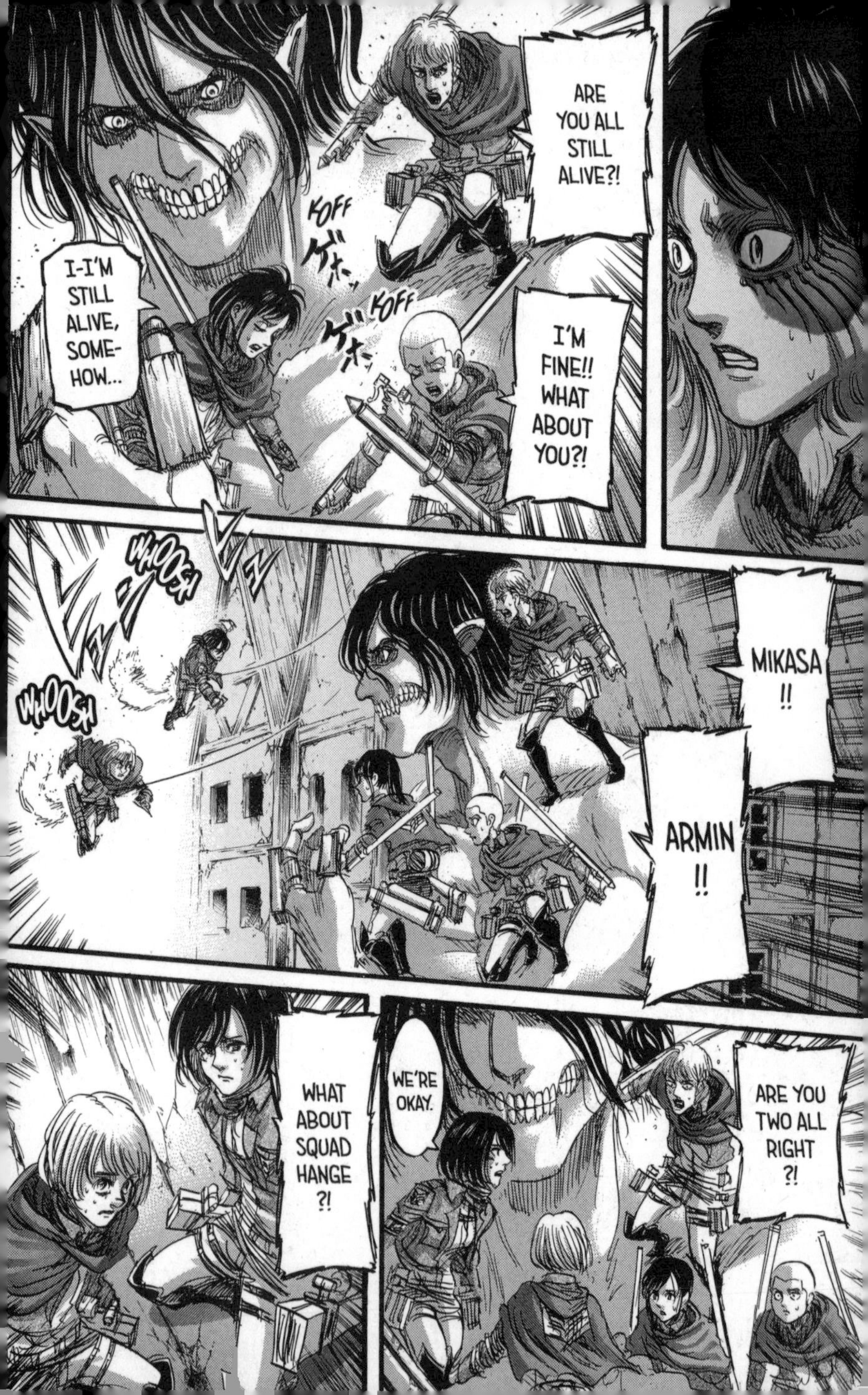
ARE YOU ALL STILL ALIVE?!
KOFF
I'M FINE!! WHAT ABOUT YOU?!
KOFF
I-I'M STILL ALIVE, SOME-HOW...
MIKASA!!
ARMIN!!
WHOOSH
WHOOSH
ARE YOU TWO ALL RIGHT?!
WE'RE OKAY.
WHAT ABOUT SQUAD HANGE?!

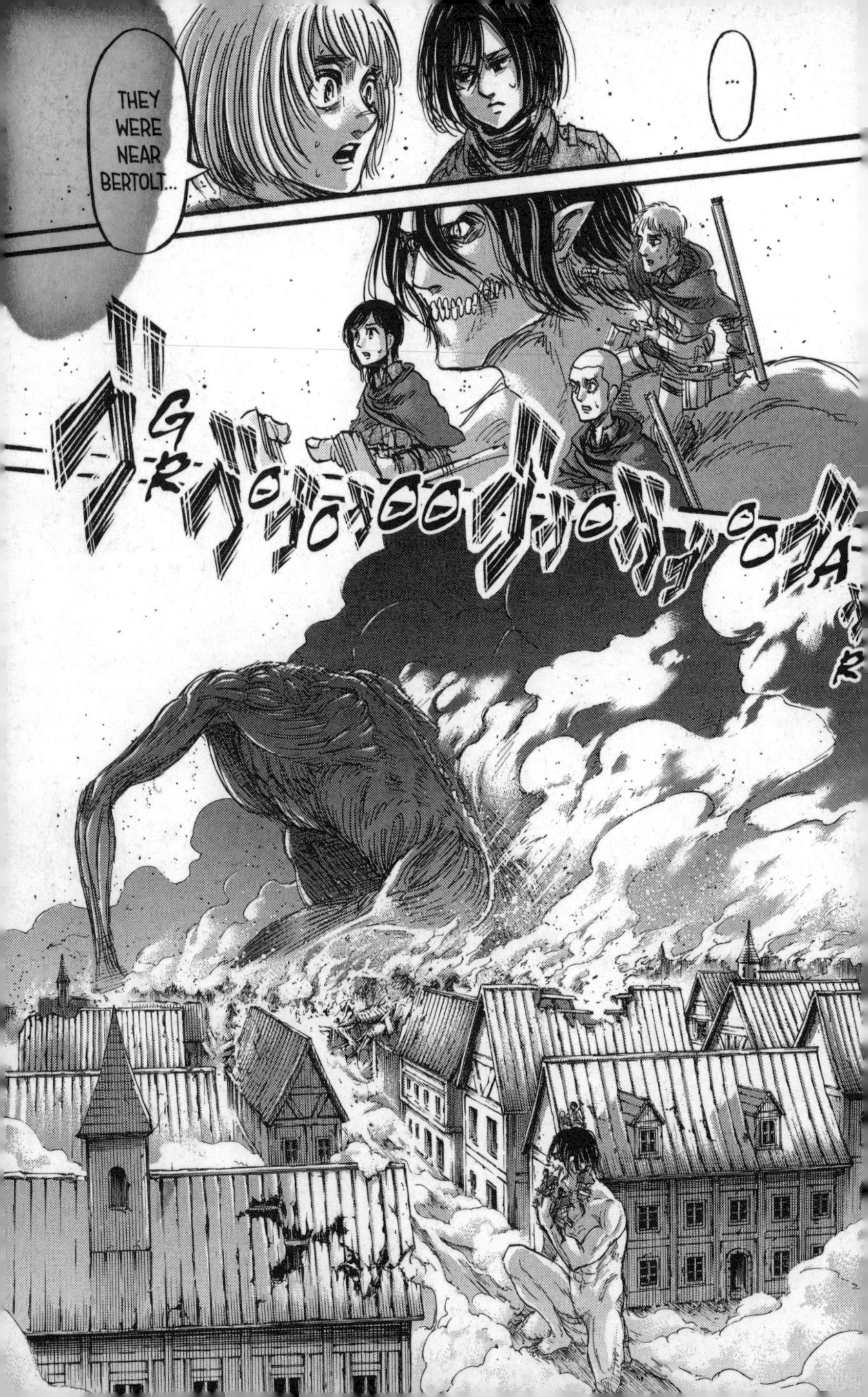
...
THEY WERE NEAR BERTOLT...
GROOOOOOOOOAR

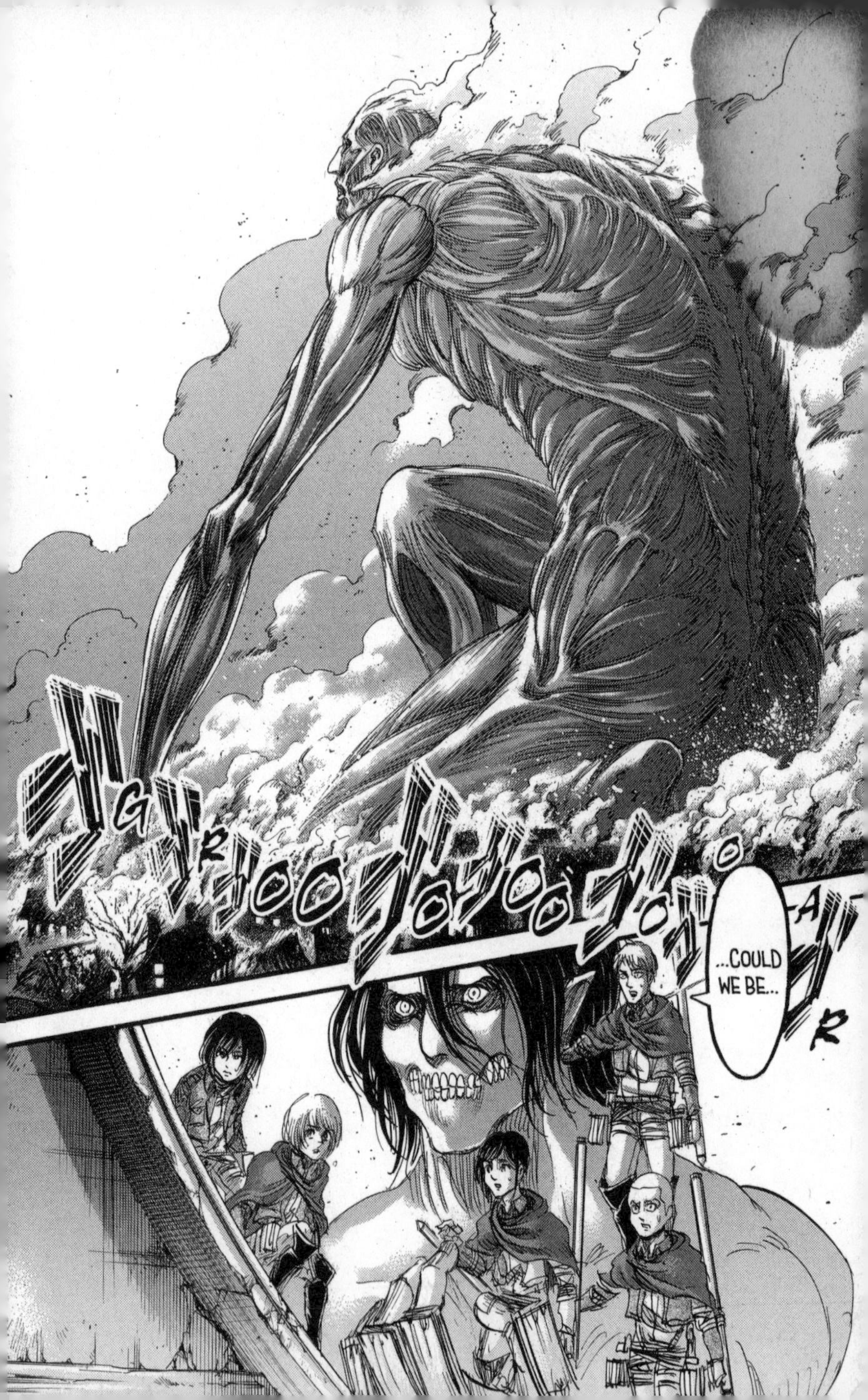
GROOOOOOOOOO
...COULD WE BE...
AR

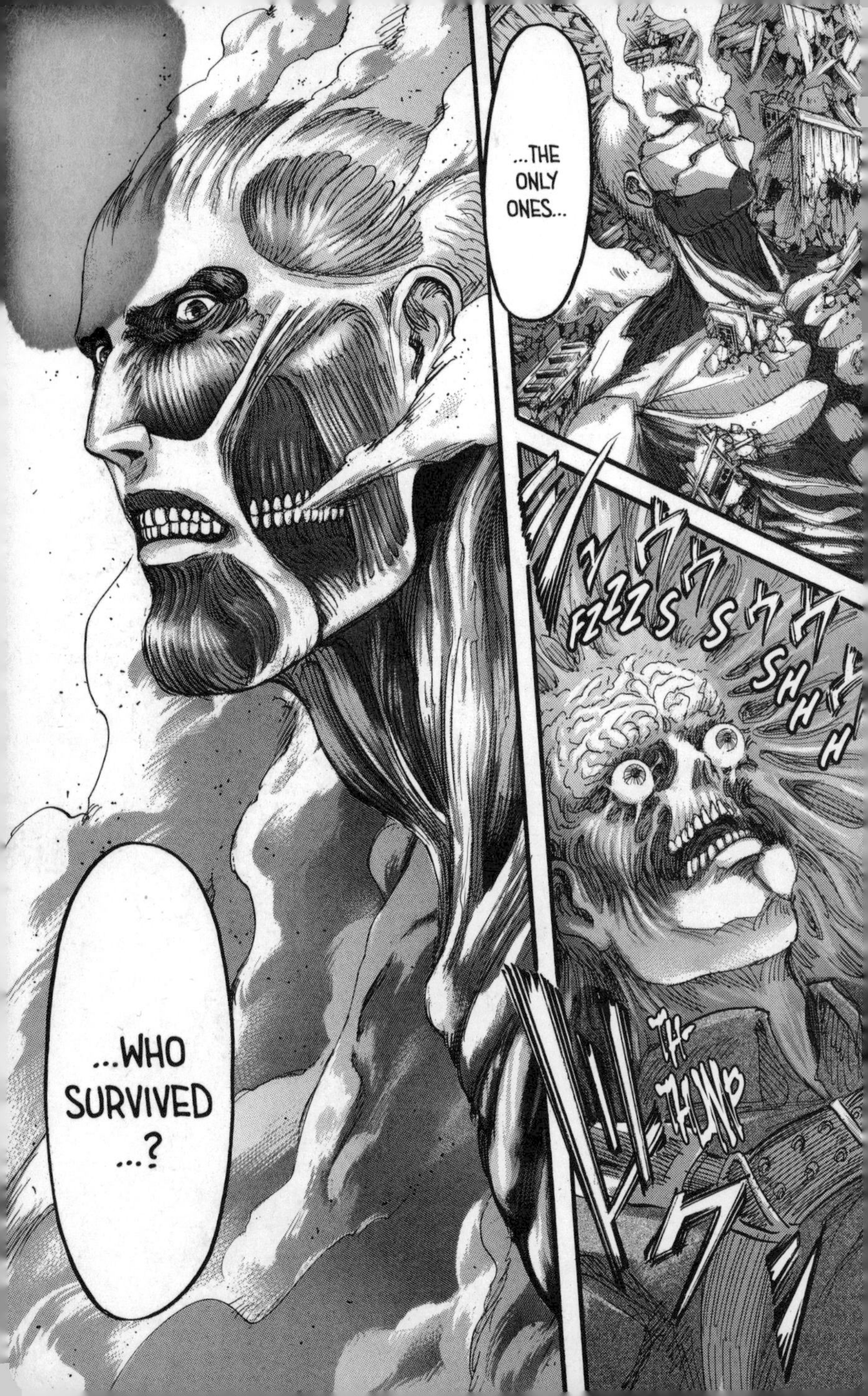
...THE ONLY ONES...
FZZZSSSHHH
TH-THUMP
...WHO SURVIVED ...?

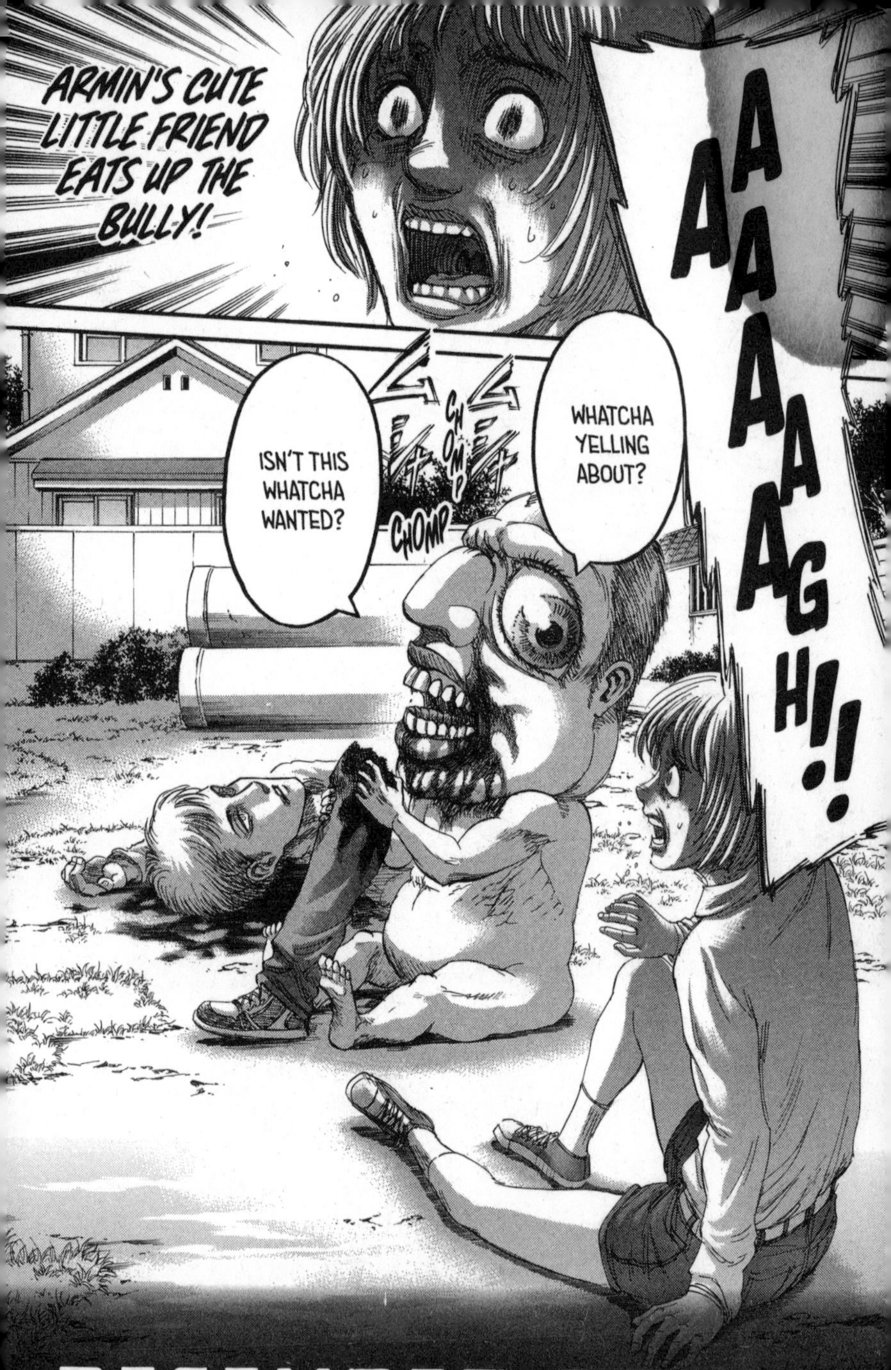

DECEMBER 2016

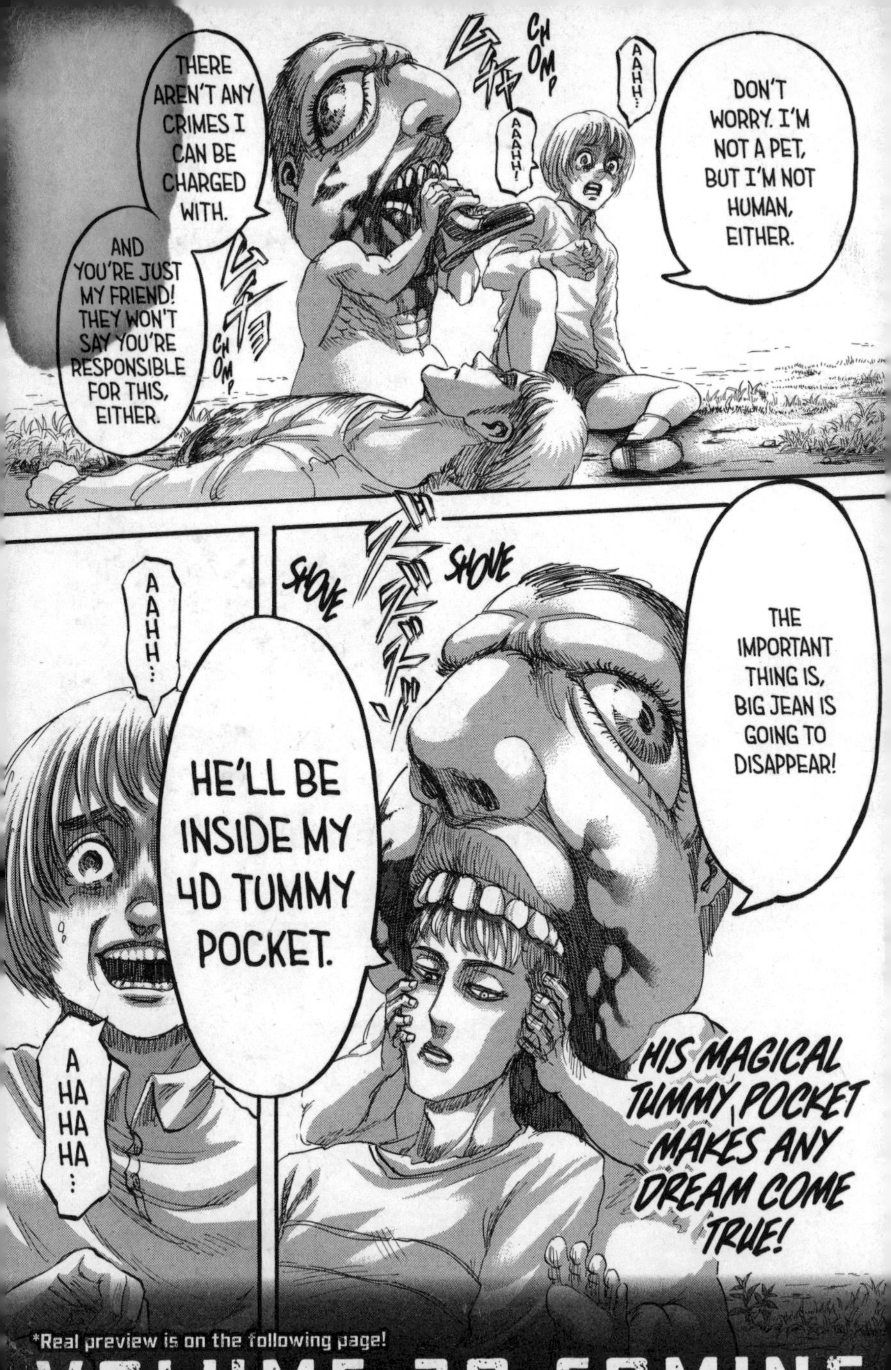
DON'T WORRY. I'M NOT A PET, BUT I'M NOT HUMAN, EITHER.
AAHH...
CHOMP
AAAHH!
THERE AREN'T ANY CRIMES I CAN BE CHARGED WITH.
AND YOU'RE JUST MY FRIEND! THEY WON'T SAY YOU'RE RESPONSIBLE FOR THIS, EITHER.
CHOMP
THE IMPORTANT THING IS, BIG JEAN IS GOING TO DISAPPEAR!
SHOVE
SHOVE
HE'LL BE INSIDE MY 4D TUMMY POCKET.
HIS MAGICAL TUMMY POCKET MAKES ANY DREAM COME TRUE!
AAHH...
A HA HA HA...

*Real preview is on the following page!

VOLUME 20 COMING

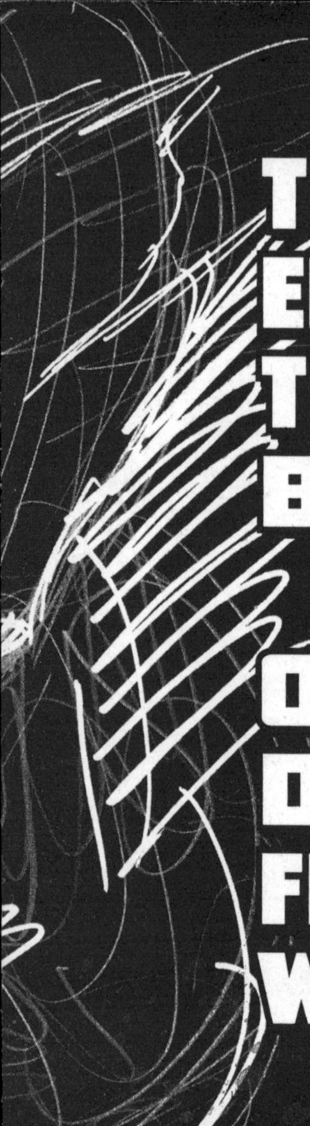

THEIR FIRST ENEMY AND THEIR FINAL BATTLE.

ONE MUST DISAPPEAR FROM THIS WORLD...

VOLUME 20 COMING DEC. 2016!

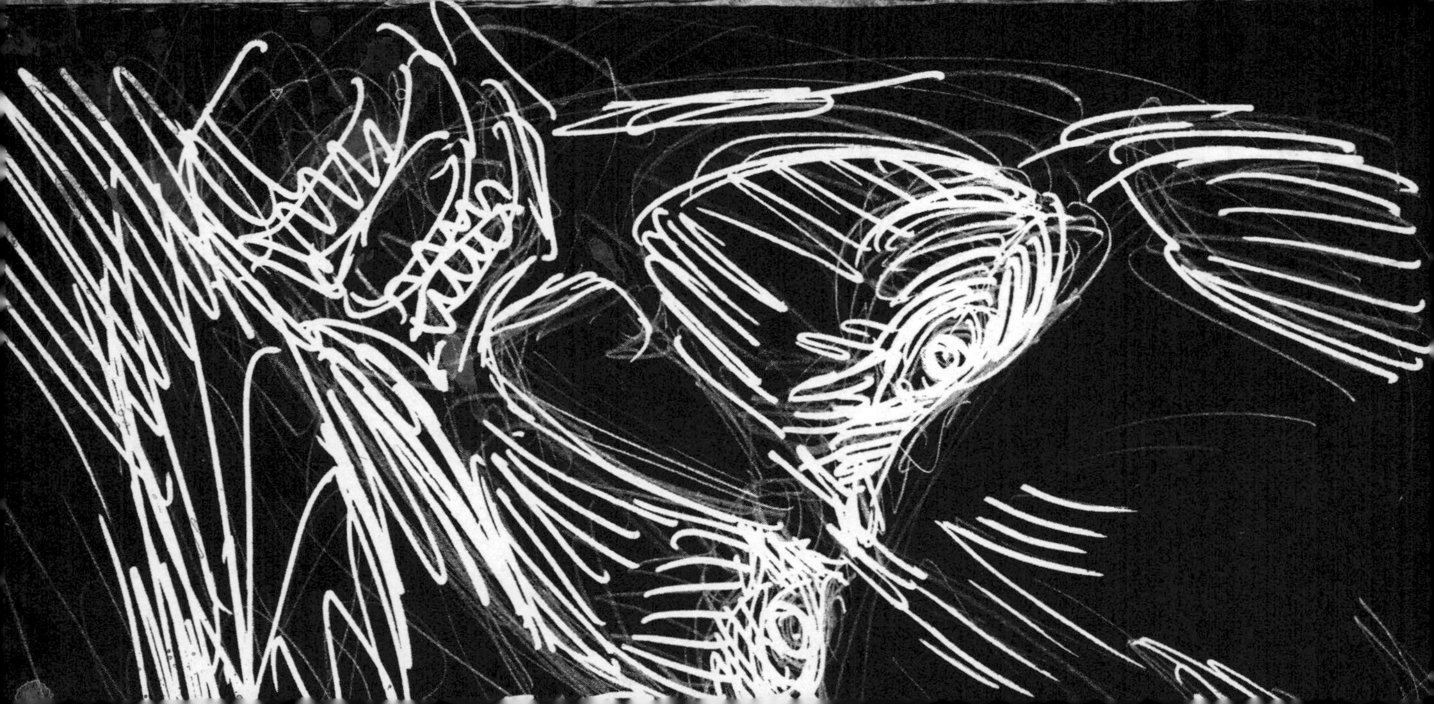

Attack on Titan 19 is a work of fiction. Names, characters, places, and incidents are the products of the author's imagination or are used fictitiously. Any resemblance to actual events, locales, or persons, living or dead, is entirely coincidental.

A Kodansha Comics Trade Paperback Original

Published in the United States by Kodansha Comics, an imprint of Kodansha USA Publishing, LLC, New York.

Publication rights for this English edition arranged through Kodansha Ltd, Tokyo.

First published in Japan in 2016 by Kodansha Ltd., Tokyo as *Shingeki no Kyojin*, volume 19.

ISBN 978-1-63236-259-9

Original cover design by Takashi Shimoyama (Red Rooster)

Printed in the United States of America.

www.kodanshacomics.com

9 8 7 6 5 4 3 2 1
Translation: Ko Ransom
Lettering: Steve Wands
Editing: Ben Applegate
Kodansha Comics edition cover design by Phil Balsman